Ruth Sidney Charney

TEACHING CHILDREN TO CARE

Classroom Management for Ethical and Academic Growth, K–8

Preface by Nel Noddings

REVISED EDITION

All net proceeds from the sale of *Teaching Children to Care* support the work of Northeast Foundation for Children, a non-profit educational organization whose mission is to foster safe, challenging, and joyful classrooms and schools, K–8.

© 1991, 2002 by Northeast Foundation for Children

ISBN 1-892989-08-5

Library of Congress catalog card number 2002101113

Cover and interior photographs: Peter Wrenn

Additional photographs: Marlynn K. Clayton, Jan Doyle, Apple Lord, Elizabeth Willis

Cover and book design: Woodward Design

NORTHEAST FOUNDATION FOR CHILDREN
85 Avenue A, Suite 204
PO Box 718
Turners Falls, MA 01376-0718
800-360-6332

www.responsiveclassroom.org

08 07 06 05 04   9 8 7 6 5 4

To my best teachers:

My parents, Hattie and George
My husband, Jay
My children, Daniel, Emma, Apple, Hannah, and Lisa
My grandchildren, Natasha and Karina
And my dear friend Jane Lazarre

Table of Contents

Preface   1

Foreword   3

SECTION I: Building a Learning Community   7

1. Intentions   17
2. I See You, I See Everything   27
3. Making the Rules with Children   69
4. Teaching the Rules   107
5. The Critical Contract: A Student's Individual Goals for the Year   123

SECTION II: Making the Community Work   139

6. Using Logical Consequences When Rules Are Broken   143
7. Time-Out: Establishing Boundaries and Promoting Self-Control   165
8. The Five Percent   191
9. Working Together to Support the Rules   211

SECTION III: The Voices of Teaching   227

10. Empowering Language: Say What You Mean and Mean What You Say   233
11. Stress the Deed, Not the Doer   247
12. The Voices of Authority   265

SECTION IV: Further Strategies for Difficult Classroom Behaviors   273

13. Problem-Solving Class Meetings   277
14. Teachers as Mirrors: Using Social Conferences   305
15. Individual Contracts   339

SECTION V: Clear Positives   361

16. Teaching by Clear Positives: Revisiting Ideals   369
17. Clear Positives in Action   383

CONCLUSION: Authentic Teaching   403

Appendix A   409
Appendix B   413
Appendix C   419
Appendix D   425
Appendix E   427

Recommended Resources   433

Preface

TEACHING HAS ALWAYS BEEN a demanding job, but today it is especially difficult. Unparalleled interest on the part of government and the public is evident and, in some ways, welcome. But the focus of that interest is far too narrow. Wise parents and teachers want more from our educational efforts than higher test scores.

Ruth Charney gives teachers help on things that really matter. She wants children to learn how to care for themselves, their fellow students, their environment, and their work. Her book is loaded with practical wisdom.

To give readers a sense of how important Charney's themes are, I'll say a bit about just two of them. Charney reminds us that our words make a difference, and she urges us to separate the deed from the doer: "I like you. I don't like this behavior." Not only should teachers convey this message when a child misbehaves, but children should also learn to cast their complaints against others in this positive way. In everything that is said, we should try to confirm the best in each child and to preserve relations of care and trust.

Positive language is important in guiding academic progress as well as acceptable classroom behavior. I was reminded of my own early years as a high school math teacher. Intending to be helpful, I would often say "It's easy! Just watch," and then I'd show how easy it was for me. But it wasn't easy for many of my students, and my having pronounced it easy made them feel stupid. Later I learned that it is better to say "This may be hard, but you'll get it. I'll help." When a child responds with "That wasn't so hard!" both the teacher and student feel great.

Charney's approach to homework is wise and courageous. She lets children know that "getting homework" is a sign that a teacher thinks they are ready to do independent work, and she offers techniques for getting them ready. She also asks educators to think critically on issues involving homework: Is homework really helpful for all elementary children? Are there some who would do better without it? Are there other ways to help children learn how "to plan, organize, and think through" their work? Homework should serve significant educational purposes and, if children are unable or unwilling to do homework at a given stage, we must find other ways to pursue those purposes. Homework is not an end in itself.

Using Charney's positive approach to classroom management, the whole school day will probably go better. The time spent on learning to care is not wasted; it is not time taken away from academic instruction. Kids who are friendly, happy, and cooperative tackle their academic work with more confidence, and both teachers and students enjoy greater success. They are not adversaries but partners in caring and learning. Charney deserves our thanks for showing how it can be done.

—NEL NODDINGS

Professor Emeritus
Stanford University

Foreword

I WROTE THE FIRST EDITION of *Teaching Children to Care* in 1991, when I had been teaching for twenty years. The book was one teacher's attempt to extract and organize lessons out of experience—my own teaching experiences as well as the many classroom stories I heard from other educators.

Respected education professor Nel Noddings has said that schools should be "places in which teachers and children live together, talk to each other, reason together, take delight in each other's company." A philosopher, mother, and former math teacher, she continues, "Like good parents, teachers should be concerned first and foremost with the kind of people their charges are becoming." My intention in writing *Teaching Children to Care* was to share what I had learned about how to help students become the kind of people we want them to be.

The revision of *Teaching Children to Care*, ten years later, has been a project of addition. The book's essential points remain the same, but its scope has broadened—a necessary result of my venturing into new teaching territory since the first writing. The text remains largely anecdotal and personal in voice, but it is enriched with new juicy stories as well as additional insights and exciting innovations gathered from recent work with teachers in diverse communities.

In the last ten years, I have honed and challenged my skills as a teacher of seventh and eighth graders. This book, therefore, now integrates more examples related to middle school classrooms. There are descriptions of activities suitable for this age group around building community, generating rules at the start of the year, cooperative learning, and "road-tested" problem-solving techniques.

There are also ideas for promoting the habit of meaningful conversation between teachers and middle-school-age students. This is especially important at a time when tragic incidents of school violence have led us to ask hard questions.

We ask what schools are doing wrong, as well as what could have gone so terribly wrong within the individual students who committed the violence. There are no simple answers, but my work with middle schools convinces me that student-teacher conversation is a bedrock element that must be structured and scheduled into the day-to-day business of school. When we talk with our students, we allow them to feel known, and they must feel known to feel valued and have a sense of belonging. Meaningful conversations are not a guarantee against violence, but cultivating meaningful conversations is one thing that schools can do better.

The new material in this edition of *Teaching Children to Care* also reflects a widespread trend, noted by psychologist Daniel Goleman, that children come to school less able to pay attention and less able to motivate themselves. Children today are "more lonely and depressed, more angry and unruly, more nervous and prone to worry, more impulsive and aggressive," Goleman writes. Recently I observed a first grader pop in and out of circle time, sometimes withdrawing to his own drumbeat, sometimes leaving on command for some act of aggression. Far from a simple distraction, his behavior required constant monitoring. Despite adult interventions, however skillfully and calmly executed, one child like this (and some classes have more than one) can drain the teacher and upset the fragile harmony of the classroom. Teachers are all too familiar with such situations, and so one chapter of this book now focuses on new approaches and strategies to help our "five percent," as these most difficult and burdened children are sometimes called.

Finally, this new edition is informed by the ongoing work of Northeast Foundation for Children in promoting the use of the *Responsive Classroom*® approach in K–8 classrooms. The original edition was written just as the six components of this approach to teaching and learning were finding clear articulation. Outreach was just beginning. In the years since, thousands of classroom teachers and hundreds of schools and school districts in Maine, Texas, California, Florida, Ohio, Minnesota, and other states have used the approach. In the process of taking our message and methods to others, we have grown. While holding on to the central intent of managing classrooms in a way that allows children to gain self-control and invest in their learning, the Foundation continues to observe and reinvent, to modify and expand, to make sure our approach is adaptable to different environments and, at the same time, has universal efficacy. (See the end of the book to learn more about the *Responsive Classroom* approach.)

The past ten years have not all been about change, however. Those years have also reinforced for me what is most basic and striking about teaching: the fact that teachers, working alone or in concert, are able to construct and shape learning communities. I have seen teachers transform dull or even hostile environments to make space for laughter and tears, for eager successes and successful failures, for bold hope and hopeful daring. And the fact that our capacity to nurture students' social and intellectual growth is connected to how we manage our classrooms— I learned that over and over again.

Recently, I attended a conference devoted to the topic of safe schools. The audience, made up of elementary through high school teachers and administrators, was asked the following question: "If you could give children one idea—just one— knowing they would carry that idea with them throughout their lives, what would it be?" Animated conversations followed as we avidly chatted with a nearby partner. Our answers, reported back to the assembly, included the notions of respect, kindness, civility, dignity, the Golden Rule. "Where is algebra?" the keynote speaker asked. Algebra does matter, of course, but it is apt to matter for more children when we reinforce the belief that how they interact with one another matters every bit as much. The need to integrate our social and academic visions for our students is just as urgent as it ever was.

Another thing that has not changed is the nature of doubt and uncertainty in teaching. In 1991, I wrote that teaching is by definition uncertainty. Ten years later, and after thirty years in classrooms, it is still a truthful claim. As I prepared a demonstration lesson for a group of seventh graders, I felt my stomach coil into knots. My seasoned wrinkles and gray hair, trophies (or scars) of longevity, were no insurance against the unpredictable, our children. There is no insurance. There is only the measured poise, the rehearsed face to maintain should a disaster occur, and the faith that what may break may also be fixed.

A colleague, one of the new passionate young teachers with whom I work, recently told me, "Teaching is the most exhausting thing I've ever done. I'm exhausted all the time. I've never been so exhausted." I looked at him at first in disbelief, taking in his youth, his athletically fit frame and Outward Bound leadership adventures, and then, with a nod, acknowledged our common ground. We all leave our classrooms with the tapes running, wondering who or what we forgot. Our shoulder bags are heavy with the past and future—papers to correct, plans to make for the next day, supplies to scrounge. Our heads are stuffed with children, crammed full of problems to resolve and next steps to identify. Our bodies are pumped with the success of the day or pressed down with the failure of a single moment.

The teacher's day doesn't end at three o'clock. I know teachers and principals who drive children to the eye doctor to make sure those glasses are repaired; teachers who keep special stashes of peanut butter and crackers for the students without breakfast or lunch; principals who keep stocks of warm jackets and extra boots, or go door-to-door to raise the extra dollars needed to fund critical programs. I know so many teachers who provide the special outings to museums or camps to extend horizons in more than one way. A friend recalled the need to periodically bunk children in her own house when their parents went on overnight drinking binges.

And even with the most loving care and the best teachers, children fail. They mess up; they defy parents or teacher and go their own, sometimes self-destructive, way. Despite our tireless efforts and sometimes exceptional talents, we have only partial control over the results that are our children. Teaching is, by definition, uncertainty.

I attempt with this book to reconcile these uncertainties through the ordering of experiences, an ordering which, by necessity, places the integrity of theory against the immediacy of the classroom. The theories concern what is known about how children learn and how they develop.

I hope with this ordering also to reveal an approach that allows educators to gain confidence in their own agency, to find purpose and sustained strength in spite of uncertainty. I hope to offer a way of teaching and learning that frees teachers, despite sure obstacles, to pass on an affection for moral and ethical behavior in order to create schools in which "teachers and students live together, talk to each other, reason together, take delight in each other's company."

—RUTH SIDNEY CHARNEY

SECTION I
Building a Learning Community

Introduction

"Good morning"

The children drift into school in the morning and make their way into the classroom. The teacher stands by the entrance and welcomes them. A message is on the chart next to her.

"Good morning, Leah... Hi, Andy... Morning, William... Morning, Renee. I like your new scarf."

Leah mumbles a response. Andy nods and scurries off. William waves, sort of. Renee continues, head down, into the room. The teacher, feeling like a piece of furniture, realizes that she is now getting cranky.

At Morning Meeting time, she informs the group, gathered in a wide circle, that she looks forward to seeing them and that she likes to show this with a "Good morning." What is she to think, she asks in a somewhat joking way, when she says "hello" and someone says back, "mmf" or "grrr," or pulls back—she imitates a turtle receding into a shell. Giggles. The children enjoy the pantomime. How nice it feels, she tells them in a more serious vein, to hear a hearty round of "Hello" or "Good morning" or "Nice day." Perhaps we just need some warm-ups, she suggests.

"Good morning, Eddie." Eddie smiles and looks around. "What might Eddie say now?" the teacher asks.

"'Good morning, Ms. Charney'?" a student ventures.

"Yes. I'd like that. Eddie?"

"Good morning," Eddie manages in a quiet voice.

"Good morning, Justin."

Justin replies with spirit, "Good morning, Ms. Charney."

"I like that nice strong voice, Justin. I also like hearing my name."

Then Justin is asked to greet someone else in the circle, until there is a full round of "Good mornings" and every single person in the class has been named. Every student has been greeted and has named and greeted another. In this "game," each child is spoken to, is named in a friendly manner, and is responsible for continuing in that manner. The mood of the circle is now awake and even gay. "Yes," the communication implies, "we are glad to be here. Yes, we are glad to see each other."

The "Good Morning Game" initiates each Morning Meeting until there is a spontaneous flow. Weeks later, the teacher bends over the very quiet Eva. "Good morning, Eva."

Eva, with a shy, crooked grin, looks up, and with her face almost touching her teacher's face, says, "Good morning." In a sudden gleeful gesture, the two rub noses and then go off to work. ❖

The water table

The group at the water table has been instructed that water stays in the water table. Water may go in buckets, in funnels, in vials, but not on each other. That is the rule.

The class has practiced good ways to keep the water in the table. They have demonstrated ways to pour. They have also practiced using a mop. They have been eager to try out this new area in the room for a "choice" activity.

Ricky is quick to garner vials, buckets, and hose-like extensions for his work. He deftly hooks up a pump to a hose and, with proper pressure, releases a stream of water through the hose into a bucket. Ricky casts a furtive eye about the room. Next there is a high-rising spout, then a minor geyser, and finally a predictable eruption cascading out of the bounds of the table, drenching the floor and his neighbor's feet.

"Ricky, you wet me!" cries the offended child.

"I didn't mean to. It was an accident," he retorts, with an equally indignant stare, looking for the whereabouts of the teacher. I observe that Ricky, with his furtive glance, is not merely exploring the force of his instruments, the thrill of seeing water travel a distance. He is also testing the limits of his force and the distance between him and the teacher.

"Ricky. I noticed that you were doing some interesting experiments.

I also noticed that you weren't using the rules. You need to leave the water table now. Perhaps tomorrow you will choose to remember to use our rules." ❖

Sherill

The fifth grade class is writing. Sherill has been looking about, putting occasional marks on her paper, erasing, crossing out, staring out the window. For a while she appears to study her friend, who is busy writing and writing. "Did you see Jesse's haircut?" she whispers, trying to start a conversation.

Rachel looks up from her writing and nods, but she quickly loses interest in Sherill's comments and returns to her own story. Sherill gets up and flounces across the room in the direction of a pencil sharpener, weaving in and out of the tables, her arms swinging recklessly. The inevitable happens: A folder goes flying off a desktop, its pages scattering across the floor.

"Can't you watch out!" cries Beth, as she gets up to collect her sheets of writing.

"I'll get you!" Sherill hurls back and stomps over to her seat.

"Sherill," the teacher says softly. "You seem to be having a hard morning. Perhaps you'd like to tell me about it...or maybe even write about it. Sometimes when I'm in a lousy mood or having a bad day, it helps me to write a letter to a friend, even if I don't send it. And some people like to write in their journal or make up a scene for a story. What do you think would work for you now?"

Sherill shrugs. "I don't have a friend to write to."

"You could write to me."

"Maybe."

"See what happens. I'll check back in a few minutes."

Sherill laboriously smoothes a fresh piece of paper, selects pencils, and, head close to the page, begins to write. Gradually, the tension in her face and her fingers relaxes. She writes continuously until the period is over, then carefully folds her paper and slips it into her desk. As she gets up to go to her next group, she calls over to Beth, "Wanna have lunch?" ❖

THIS BOOK IS ABOUT MANAGING A CLASSROOM so that it is nurturing, respectful, and full of learning. It is about teaching children to care. It draws on my many years as a teacher in inner-city schools and, more recently, in an independent school that was founded in order to apply a developmental point of view. The most important thing I have learned is that discipline is a subject to be taught, just as reading or arithmetic is taught. It is taught, year after year, without apology. It is taught with the conviction and affirmation of the teacher.

I started out knowing so little. I was ill prepared to succeed in the classroom, but I learned. What I have learned will always need to be refined and revised, but it has given me focus and courage. I hope that readers will gather strength and renewed vigor from this book so they can face the endless lists of challenges: unruly Jerome, "Make me" Annie, Sean of the Spitball Hall of Fame...the fights before and after school, the lunchroom frenzies, the boots that Lee denies he put in the toilet...the pencil that belongs to Chris that Jenny insists she found in her desk...the notes, the secrets, the cliques...the ragged transitions, the minimal effort on assignments, the no-effort excuses...the tattling, the teasing, the sneaking....Teachers face enormous pressures. It is a struggle just to survive as a proud teacher of today's children in schools that may lack even the basics. It is a challenge to help children grow up to be decent and kind, and to retain faith in ourselves, our children, and our expectations. To meet these challenges, we need to know how to manage a classroom and how to teach our children to behave.

TEACHING CHILDREN TO CARE

We need to know how to pass on an affection for moral and ethical behavior in a difficult world.

Thirty-five years ago, I was applying for my license as a New York City public school teacher. There was an oral exam. I recall my innocence uneasily and the scene vividly. I entered a dimly lit classroom. In the rear of the room sat three crouching figures. In my mind, they were all in black cloaks! One of the figures was making a rasping sound as she filed her nails. The filing stopped only as the question was read in an absurdly slow and nasal voice:

"Imagine that you are teaching a lesson. From the back of the room, one of the students tosses a paper airplane. You ask him to stop. He does it again. What will you do?"

I answered the question with all the cockiness and confidence of one who had never taught. It was actually so simple. In my mind, there were two choices.

The first choice would be to take the "Tough Authority" approach and invoke a chain of command that would end in a punishment for the misbehaving student:

"Either you stop or I will take away your paper and book."

The student is on a roll. Quietly, he extracts page 37 from his geometry book and folds it neatly into a 747 design, which swoops and crashes only moments after I have made my decree.

"That's IT! Jane, go get the principal."

The principal calls the boy's mother. The mother calls the father, and then the boy gets in trouble, which assures his future cooperative behavior in my class.

The second choice, I thought, would be to assume that the student was simply not interested in the geography lesson that was underway. If properly motivated, no child would misbehave. Thus the answer would be to refocus the lesson. I would pick up the airplane and begin a brilliant lesson on aerodynamics:

"What is it that makes planes fly?"

"I dunno."

I hold up the paper model. "What is it that makes this plane fly?"

"I threw it."

I am not to be put off with such wit. I take out a flat sheet and ask, "If I threw this paper, would it fly?"

"Nah."

Soon the recalcitrant student and others in the class are enthralled and productively exploring the mysteries of flight. They are comparing model planes. They are observing and calculating the flight patterns of different wing designs. Robby is making a graph. Christine is measuring distances to the quarter inch. Our previously disruptive student leaves on a mission to the library to look for books on airplanes.

I used the second approach for my answer. When I finished, the examiners thanked me. I left feeling confident and righteous. The rasping had stopped, and I had passed the exam. I went on, with license in hand, to teach my first class. (Later, I discovered that I was not being graded on the content of my response. I was not graded on my educational expertise. My examiners were attending not to teaching skills, but to my syntax. Because I spoke in English sentences, I passed.)

I also later realized that my answer was a daydream, a fine fantasy. It wouldn't happen like that. It could happen that such a wonderful exercise would infuse the classroom, but not without what I had yet to learn: classroom management.

I went into my first classroom knowing about curriculum, interesting new ways to teach math and reading, and how to get terrific materials. I had spent a lively summer in a workshop, building, planning, and collecting. I set up my first grade room in centers with tri-wall dividers I had constructed myself. I had an easel in the art corner. I had a salt-water aquarium in the science center. I had over twenty new books in the library and all different shapes and colors of pasta in the math center. On the first day of school, I surveyed an inviting and rich learning environment. I was proud of it all.

I will never forget what Grady and Jerome and Michelle did to that room in the first week. The paint from the easel went straight onto Jerome, who then went straight to the principal's office. Pockets were heavy with pastas, which were eaten raw, thrown, and stepped on, but not sorted or classified. The salt-water aquarium soon resembled the Meadowlands Swamp, a repository for just about everything. Books were torn in an effort to speed-read, and rather than the eager and busy sighs of intent learners, there were whines and whimpers:

"Teacher, LOOK."

"Teacher, he broke my pencil."

"Teacher, what do we do now? Is it time to go home?"

It was a disaster. I felt personally wronged. I blamed the children. I blamed the school. I blamed everyone and anyone. I cried and was ready to quit. I knew that I had to quit or I had to learn to run a classroom. In that crisis, I decided to learn. I cleaned up the mess. I junked the dividers. I observed other teachers—experienced teachers who still smiled. I began again. From that awful beginning came the greatest insight of my teaching life: A teacher can teach children to behave.

With time, patience, and determination, I could get Jerome's paint on the easel. After two years, Grady stopped puncturing materials and people. The books were being read. The pastas were sorted. The children made choices. It became a learning room. I understood that children didn't need to come to school knowing positive behavior. But they had to have a chance to learn it deliberately, slowly, and with encouragement. I realized that I can teach it—that we can teach it. I can look at my next smart aleck or menace and think confidently, "I'll get you. You'll learn!"

In my living room, there is a painting. It shows a world of red and green and yellow. Circling the world are children holding hands. Carefully etched in and out of the circle is a bright blue sky and a radiant sun. It was painted in June by Jerome, my most careless painter the previous fall. It was a present to his teacher.

In this book, I share techniques that I used with Jerome and others. I describe approaches and tools I use to set up rules, expectations, and significant consequences. These ideas are based on my own experiences and the insights and work of many, many teachers. The book is strongly influenced by my work for the past twenty years with Greenfield Center School, a unique collaboration of teachers working toward a functional, caring community for both children and adults.

These teaching approaches also represent what I have learned from the work of educational and developmental theorists. Their writings are liberally quoted throughout the text, and their ideas are etched into, and between, the lines of the book. (Their works are included in the list of recommended resources at the end of this book.) I did not invent this material, but I patiently collected and collated what I understood from observations and readings until it felt like my own. I hope teachers will treat this book the same way. It is meant to be a living and livable guide. If some of these approaches don't work for you, I hope you will find yet another way.

The aim of every chapter and every technique is the creation of self-control and community, which I define as the capacity to care for oneself, for others, and for the world. A single, basic goal is to teach children in such a way that they gain affection for ethical behavior.

"I'll try myself"

"Jessica called me a bad name."

"Did you talk to Jessica?"

"Yes. I tried to, but she wouldn't listen."

"What do you want to say to Jessica?"

"Not to call me names."

"Show me. How will you tell Jessica that you don't like names?"

"Jessica, I don't like when you say I'm stupid."

"I wonder if you did something to make Jessica mad? What do you think?"

"Well… 'cause I didn't want her to take the markers 'cause she keeps them too long."

"Oh. So maybe you should have shared the markers. Do you want to try to talk to Jessica again by yourself, or do you need my help?"

"I'll try myself." ❖

IN THIS SECTION, I introduce and describe the basics of building a learning community in the early weeks of the year. This work serves as a foundation and reference point throughout the year and sets the tone and expectations necessary for a productive, exciting, and safe classroom community:

- Chapter 1 defines the goals of self-control and community.

- Chapter 2 describes the techniques of the first six weeks and their extension through the rest of the year.

- Chapter 3 offers some ways to create workable classroom rules with children.

- Chapter 4 explains the importance of teaching the rules so that they are understood and practiced in the real life of the classroom.

- Chapter 5 describes the creation of a "Critical Contract," a technique for involving parents, students, and teachers in setting a student's individual goals for the year.

CHAPTER 1
Intentions

*The development of a child's potential depends on
the ability of the teacher to perceive the child's possibilities,
to stimulate the child to learn, and thereby to make
the child's latent potentiality a reality.*

RUDOLF DREIKURS
Maintaining Sanity in the Classroom

WE NEED TO APPROACH THE ISSUES of classroom management and discipline as much more than what to do when children break rules and misbehave. Rather than simply reacting to problems, we need to establish an ongoing curriculum in self-control, social participation, and human development. We need to accept the potential of children to learn these things and the potential of teachers to teach them.

The best methods, the most carefully planned programs, the most intriguing classroom centers, and the most exciting and delicious materials are useless without discipline and management. The children can hurl the Legos and crash the blocks, or they can build fine bridges. They can ingeniously combine rubber bands and paper clips to bombard classmates, or they can construct mobiles and invent robots. The critical difference is the approach to discipline and management. It is not enough (and not possible) to motivate students continually with dazzling demonstrations of paper-plane aeronautics or new adventures. We spend too much time looking for gimmicks and catchy topics to teach when we should be looking for something else. Children don't learn by being entertained. They learn by doing, and by finding success in the doing.

We go into teaching prepared to teach reading, math, writing, and social studies. We prepare for subjects. When I have to stop a lesson to remind Cindy not to interrupt, to address the sarcastic remarks David made to Patty (who gave a wrong answer), or to quiet the voices of students not part of my group, I clench my teeth and mutter about "wasting time." Incorrectly, I start to feel that discipline is a time-waster, a symptom of problem students and poor teaching. If only I had the good class!

I do love to teach reading, writing, and math. I love to help children decode new words, to share discussions about evil fictional characters, and to help them compose a thoughtful essay. But I've also come to love being a "disciplinarian."

I have grown to appreciate the task of helping children learn to take better care of themselves, of each other, and of their classrooms. It's not a waste. It's probably the most enduring thing that I teach. In a world filled with global violence and threats of environmental devastation, where drugs and guns are easily available, learning to be more decent and to build caring communities is hardly a waste of time.

TAKING THE TIME

TIME IS GOLDEN. How we use our precious classroom time defines our priorities. Our schedules often become a battleground for conflicting interests.

In a public school in Connecticut, a number of third through sixth grade classrooms in the school began conducting Morning Meetings as a half-hour ritual each day. The class gathers, gives greetings, shares important news, and enjoys a game or interesting group activity. Teachers, students, and parents overwhelmingly agreed that it contributed to a friendlier, more relaxed atmosphere. "You get to know other people better and find out things about them," wrote one student.

Both teachers and students looked forward to their Morning Meetings to hear each other's news, play together, and get set for the day. But two years later, the school's fall writing mastery test scores were low. There was a school-wide mandate for more writing instruction. Teachers began to ask, "Is it OK if I do my meeting for just twenty minutes?"

The meeting time, which helps children and teachers look forward to school, was put in competition with instructional objectives. Could these teachers squeeze more writing into an already heavily scheduled day? To squeeze in more, they had to squeeze something out—or burst!

In this battle for time, we need to remember that academics and social behavior are profoundly intertwined. In this case, the opportunities to talk and listen in Morning Meeting provided some of the conversation and confidence critical to the writing process. A responsive audience of teacher and peers offers a powerful incentive to share through writing and to care about school. The more children care about school (because of friendly feelings, the chance to be heard, or things they want to find out), the more likely they are to grow academically as well as socially (Gresham and Elliott 1990).

A curriculum which permits us to teach self-control and social participation takes time. Time to stop lessons when the tone of the room is awful. Time to discuss what went wrong out at recess. Time to tell others about the baseball game, the new baby sister, the death of a pet. Without time in our day to talk to children and to allow them to talk to each other, there will be no discipline, only disciplining.

DISCIPLINE AS LEARNING

THE WORD *DISCIPLINE* is derived from the Latin root *disciplina,* meaning learning. It needs to be associated positively with acts and feats of learning rather than negatively with punishing. Teaching discipline requires two fundamental elements: empathy and structure. Empathy helps us "know" the child, to perceive his/her needs, to hear what s/he is trying to say. Structure allows us to set guidelines and provide necessary limits. Effective, caring discipline requires both empathy and structure.

There are two basic goals in teaching discipline:

+ Creation of self-control

+ Creation of community

Creation of self-control

WE NEED TO STRIVE for the creation of self-control in children. It is the first purpose of classroom management. This purpose is summed up by a quote from John Dewey in his pamphlet *Experience and Education,* first published in 1938. Dewey writes, "The ideal aim of education is creation of power of self-control" (Dewey 1963, 64).

The key word for me in this quote is "power." Power, says Dewey, is the ability to "frame purposes, to judge wisely..." (Dewey 1963, 64). The power of self-control is the power to assert oneself in a positive way. It involves the capacities to regulate oneself, to anticipate consequences, and to give up an immediate gratification to realize a long-term goal. It includes the ability to make and carry out a plan, to solve a problem, to think of a good idea and act on it, to sift alternatives, to make decisions. For children, it is the ability to enter a new group and say hello, to make new friends, to choose activities, and to hold fast to inner thoughts and beliefs. It isn't an innate power, says Dewey, but one that is "created."

I see children, given time and attention, demonstrate the power of self-control daily. I observe five-year-olds during their first week of school trying to sit still in a circle, a clutch of wiggles, wagging hands, and babbling voices. Six weeks later, there is a real semblance of order. They are working on "being the boss" of their own bodies, staying "parked" in their spot, keeping their hands only on themselves, listening. Maggie's hand starts to go up while Mikey is telling a story about his bike. When she sees a slight shake of her teacher's head, she remembers, and her hand goes down. She will wait until Mikey is done talking to tell about her bike, "'cause the same thing happened" to her on her bike. Self-control allows listening and waiting.

Aviva and Jason are young adolescents. They bring to their sixth grade classroom a summer's worth of growth in "attitude." They have learned to roll their eyes, to pout and scowl when anything "babyish" is suggested—and just about everything that's suggested is! They are understudies in the drama of "cool," which can mean refusing to participate or play class games and following rules only with a grudging shuffle.

TEACHING CHILDREN TO CARE

At first, Aviva and Jason feel "picked on" when their teacher lets them know they must work on "controlling their faces" and refraining from other gestures of disdain. Later, as they search for a balance between the requisites of "cool" and a satisfying, controlled involvement in learning with others, they are able to say that they really didn't intend to offend anyone.

Merely removing external controls, Dewey stated, is not "a guarantee for the production of self-controls." Instead, it often leaves children "at the mercy of impulses" (Dewey 1963, 65). I have witnessed tense and troubling scenes when teachers abdicate their authority, leaving children without the protective guidelines of clear limits, boundaries, or strategies.

"How will you decide who goes first?" Left on their own, children may decide on the basis of who is biggest and most threatening, who has the loudest voice, or who wears the most expensive clothes. But proposing and modeling some alternatives (odd number of fingers, pick-a-number, cut the deck, "eenie-meenie-minee-mo") imposes the reins of justice where tyranny or anarchy might have governed.

"You have five minutes to see if you can figure out a way to work together and get along; otherwise, you'll have to work by yourself. I'll be back to see what you decided." Teachers provide choices, even time limits, as a natural constraint so that children don't keep spinning their wheels, and to assure children that the teacher will help them out of the rut, if necessary. But children need opportunities to make the ruts.

If self-control is established at one point along the continuum of growth, it doesn't mean that problems, conflicts, and stunning bursts of impulse and disobedience will be erased. Getting older is not a promise of getting better, especially if "better" is to be even-tempered and of predictable mind. Getting older means encountering difficult, and often painful, issues of growing up, separation, and identity. The cheerful five and spirited six may evolve, at seven, into a child troubled by change, clinging to routines, fearful of risks, and worried about criticism. A headache attends every new math lesson. Tears follow the loss of a game of tag. Then the fretful seven becomes the gregarious, easy-going eight, who bounds into school until she decides to join the boys' kickball game at recess and gets banned from the girls' clique and jump-rope games.

Our best management techniques will not eliminate these issues from our classrooms. They will only help us deal with them in ways that promote children's self-control and ethical conduct. I emphasize three main points in this assertion that the first purpose of classroom management is the creation of self-control:

✦ We need to teach self-control in the same way we teach our academics, as a recognized and valued part of our school curriculum.

- Creating self-control involves teachers and children in ongoing interactions which draw on the experiences and context of day-to-day life in school.

- The acquisition of self-control leads to a more fully engaged and purposeful school life. It fosters positive self-assertion and allows children to plan, make decisions, and carry out purposeful activities. It allows children to become more productive and successful in school.

Creation of community

What good is academic learning if young people
don't learn to become contributing members of society?

JANE NELSEN
Positive Discipline

IN TODAY'S WORLD, it is particularly urgent that we extend beyond the domain of self and the lessons of self-control. We need to find connections to others and to feel ourselves members of many groups—intimate groups, community groups, and a world group. These connections and responsibilities need to be taught as well. We need to teach children to give care as well as to receive care. We must help them learn to contribute, to want to contribute.

Belonging to a group means being needed as well as to need, and believing that you have something vital to contribute. Every child can contribute care for others in many ways—by listening with attention and responding with relevance, by showing concern for the feelings and viewpoints of others, by developing a capacity for empathy.

We all have an inherent need to be useful and helpful to others. But because it is inherent doesn't mean that it automatically flourishes or is tapped. In our society, there are people who suffer from a lack of meaningful work. Children, too, can suffer from a partnership of neglect and indulgence that results in a lack of meaningful responsibilities. These children are not expected to demonstrate care, not accustomed to taking care of others. Creating community means giving children the power to care.

My thesaurus shows that the word care has some interesting and varied connotations. It can mean "to take care"—to trouble oneself, to give thought, forethought, painstaking attentions. Or it may mean "to care for"—to provide for, to look after, to show regard. It can also refer to worry, as in "having cares" or "cares and woes."

Thus, caring is a burden, a commitment, hard work. When we teach children to care, we ask them to accept this burden, to commit themselves to the hard work of caring.

Teaching children to care often means helping them find ways to express their care. When confronted with a classmate's loss and sadness, what can they say? What can they do? "You can say 'sorry,'" we tell them. "You can make a card or keep the person company."

I see children struggle to make a place in their group for newcomers. How can they reach out? I know that the new students are lonely, miss their old friends, and need new ones. I see that the other children are unaware, comfortable in their old groupings and familiar routines. They are only eight, I remind myself, still awkward in social behaviors. Yet, they can learn to take notice and respond. With help, they may offer "Want to join our jump-rope game?" or "Want to have lunch at my table?"

"You have a gift to give," I sometimes inform children, as I seek their help in including someone new, or someone it's easier to avoid. There is a clear sense of self-worth, well-being, and pride when children show the ethic of caring. Even though it's seldom spontaneous, it improves the world, and "I," at six or ten or forty, did that improving.

To create community and to teach caring is an ongoing challenge. My group of fourth and fifth graders were planning a party day for the successful completion of their school store. It was a day earned from the proceeds of their work. To start and maintain the store, they had shopped each week, ordered merchandise from catalogues, kept account books, computed prices, and learned to be kindly shop-keepers. They had given over recess times and stayed after school. They had cleaned up. Some had complained of overwork and some had gotten headaches, but they had kept it going for a year, and now they could celebrate.

At first it wasn't clear how to celebrate and how much of the profit from the store might be used for a party. After several discussions, there was a proposal to divide the assets into three chunks. One chunk would be reinvested in the store, but what about the other two? As I listened, I was sorely tempted to manipulate the outcomes. I was queasy during their discussions when the percentages for the "good cause" and "their cause" were tilted in favor of the latter.

The end results were not the most generous. Still, the students were stretching. They were giving some of their earnings to others in the community: the homeless, whom they read and heard about but didn't really see, and the "battered," who were also a faceless presence in their lives. These problems and others were largely abstractions—and these children were still concrete learners. Without direct, personal experience with these problems, the children's intellectual grasp of these issues had a fragile foothold.

To themselves, the students gave a party: video, pizza, soda, and soccer game. They accepted, with grumbles, the teacher's ruling of no R-rated movies. They accepted, with resignation, that not all would get their first choice, but that no complaints were allowed. They enjoyed their morning movie, their midday pizza lunch, and their afternoon soccer game. Then there was a request for ice cream.

"We still have some money left."

"No. No ice cream," I replied.

"You're mean," said a whiny voice.

"No fair," said another.

"It's our money," joined yet one more.

This went on for a few minutes until I lost patience and felt that a sermon was inevitable and irresistible.

"What a privileged day," I began. "You have enjoyed so much. When you continue to ask for more and use those whiny voices, you sound ungrateful. When you try to manipulate and complain, you sound greedy. I don't like it. It's time to appreciate what you had and stop asking for more."

It was time for an adult to reset the boundaries, to provide limits and expectations. It's still hard at age ten or eleven to locate those end points. Sometimes a teacher simply has to yell "Enough, already!"

There were certainly other stretch marks to this experience. Even with its last-second deterioration, the celebration capped a positive learning experience for the group. They had made group decisions and abided by them. They shared in the enjoyment of their party. They kept to the limits of their spending and honored their pledge to give away one-third of their earnings to help others. I recall one student saying persuasively in class discussion, "Our parents will support the store more if we give money away to a good cause." If that is not the crux of virtue, it still indicates that generosity is expected. It is part of a caring community.

Some years ago, my daughter shared a dream with me. In the dream, she was invisible. No one could see or hear her. She alone could see and hear everyone else. What she could see were people trying frantically to escape as bombs dropped into her school, and what she could hear were cries for help. "Let this be a nightmare!" she screamed. "Let me wake up."

I didn't know how to comfort and reassure my daughter, how to erase her nightmare. I didn't know how to assuage her fears. Should I have lied to her, promised her that the world is safe? That children are not in danger, that violence is not real?

Or should I tell her the truth, that her nightmares aren't much different from many adults', because our world is often circumscribed by violence?

Yet I don't dare be discouraged. I am invigorated by the dedication of so many colleagues and students to making the world a safer place. Part of our mission is to create communities with fewer nightmares, where self-control and care for others minimizes the possibility of violence.

....

FIGURE 1.1

Building Community

We build community each day when we expect children to:

✦ **Know names**—know and use each other's names, get to know each other's interests and feelings

✦ **Take turns**—without arguing, pouting, or quitting

✦ **Share**—attention from the class, private time with the teacher, space at the sandbox, space at the computer, snacks, crayons, markers, etc.

✦ **Make room in the circle**—for latecomers and for children who aren't "best friends"

✦ **Join activities and small groups**—in a constructive way

✦ **Invite others to join**

✦ **Be friendly**—greet and include others (not only friends) in conversation and activities

✦ **Cooperate**—work on projects, solve problems, and play games with input from everyone

✦ **Solve conflicts**—by talking about problems, sharing points of view, reaching mutually acceptable decisions without name-calling or hurtful behavior

These community expectations are balanced by respect for individual needs—there are times during the day when you don't have to share, you get to pick your favorite, you get what you really need.

....

Allison

A group of three children in the second grade class were seated around a table, busily shaping and molding chunks of clay. Their chatter kept pace with their hand work. The teacher, moving about the room, stopped to observe the threesome.

Allison turned to Bobby and said, "After school, I'm gonna get you...and then I'm gonna punch your head in."

Bobby ignored her and turned to Juan. "Look at mine. It's a flying gorilla."

"Blood will come out of your nose...," continued Allison.

The teacher approached Allison, knelt next to her, and cupped one hand over her clay and the other around her shoulder. "Stop your work for a moment and listen to me."

Allison reached for her clay, but turned back to her teacher. "What?"

"I just heard something that I really don't want to hear in our classroom. I heard some threats. Threats talk about ways to hurt people. You have a much more important job here. Do you know what that job is?"

"No...doing your work?"

"Yes. Doing your work of taking care of each other. That's a very important job that you have here. Not to threaten each other...but to take care of each other. I know that you can do that."

"She won't," announced Bobby suddenly.

The teacher nodded firmly, "She will!" ❖

Works Cited

Dewey, John. 1963. *Experience & Education.* First Collier Books Edition. London: Collier Books.

Dreikurs, Rudolf, Floy C. Pepper, and Bernice Bronia Grunwald. 1982. *Maintaining Sanity in the Classroom: Classroom Management Techniques.* Second edition. Philadelphia, PA: Taylor & Francis, Inc.

Gresham, Frank, and Stephen N. Elliott. 1990. *Social Skills Rating System.* Circle Pines, MN: American Guidance Service.

Nelsen, Jane, EdD. 1996. *Positive Discipline.* Revised edition. New York: Ballantine Books.

CHAPTER 2
I See You,
I See Everything

I SPEND THE FIRST SIX WEEKS OF SCHOOL teaching children how to behave. It rarely takes less time; sometimes it takes more. It takes six weeks even when many of the students were in the same class last year and have been in the same school for several years. I cannot presume that what was so clear last year is remembered and accepted this year. I start again.

I do not apologize for this use of time. It is not a waste, not a way station along a more important course of educational mastery. It is the critical foundation of learning. It is the first curriculum. I call it "classroom management." The emphasis is not on the three *Rs* of *readin'*, *'ritin'*, and *'rithmetic*, but instead on *reinforcin'*, *remindin'*, and *redirectin'*. This approach requires teaching proactively. Proactive teaching involves presenting and helping children practice appropriate attitudes and behaviors rather than constantly reacting to inappropriate ones. We need to focus systematic attention on our expectations of children and our methods of teaching those expectations.

In the Introduction to this section, I described my initial teaching disasters. From my colossal mistakes grew important insights. The first and perhaps most important understanding was that to feel safe, children must feel seen.

A first classroom

I had participated in a stimulating summer workshop for teachers. In the workshop, I had learned to tie-dye, make musical instruments, play logic games, and build simple structures with tri-wall carpentry. I proudly and enthusiastically fashioned my classroom in Harlem, New York City, from all I had learned that summer. I organized my room in centers, each wonderfully partitioned (with MY dividers!) for definition and privacy. I littered the areas with "goodies" I had made or salvaged.

I soon discovered, however, that when I was watching the group in the art area, I couldn't see the math corner. When I concentrated on the library, I couldn't see the easel or the science corner. And when I was working at the blackboard, I couldn't see anything at all!

Frequently, as I skirted the room, or disappeared into one of my centers, the children couldn't see me, either. I quickly turned into a whirlwind. The students tested the durability and scaling potential of my tri-walls and chased after me with a constant bleat:

"Look at me, Teacher."

"Look at my drawing, Teacher."

"Teacher, look what Jerome did to my book."

"TEACHER! LOOK!"

It was worthy of one of the classic primers: "Run, Teacher, Run. See Teacher Run. Run. Run. Run." I became weary and suffered serious headaches.

I was not a quick learner. After several weeks of wiping up spills, re-gluing bindings on books, making excuses to the principal for the disorder in the halls, blaming everything and everyone—from "these children" to "this system"—I had had enough. I swept the room clear of partitions. I removed three-fourths of the materials. I plunked my chair

down in the middle of the room and me down with it. In a fine, firm, clear (maybe even loud) voice ripe with conviction, I announced, "I see you. I see everything." ❖

I REALIZED THAT CHILDREN NEED TO BE SEEN. It was a simple matter of safety and a more complex matter of recognition and trust. Developmental studies tell us that five-year-olds need to be seen so that they can be free to venture off, leaving the enclosure of the teacher for new experiences with play and work. Six-year-olds need to be seen so they will not climb walls. But I have also found that seven-, ten-, and thirteen-year-olds need to be seen, just as they also need their private nooks and crannies. They need the encouragement and validation that comes from our best attention to their efforts. They need the safety that comes from the belief that their teacher sees them, knows them. Mutual trust grows from this security. When all children feel seen, they are released to work.

"I see you" is not a threat, but rather a message of caring and regard. When we say "I see you," the "seeing" is not always literal. We may see our children and trust them, at times, to be on their own. But not during the first six weeks. The first six weeks is a time when we focus on getting to know our students.

Michelle

I was watching Michelle at the easel, anxious that she not get distracted and wander the room with paint brush extended. She painted a house, added windows, put in curtains, and even added what looked to be figures in one of the windows. Then she took her brush and painted long, abrupt slashes of red, covering and mixing with the browns of the house. The red got thicker, the strokes more intense. After the red, there came wide swathes of black, until the other colors only peeked from the edges, the building and figures entirely obliterated.

It was the first I knew about the fire that had destroyed her home. It was the first glimpse I had of what might be prompting her sometimes dreamy and distracted behaviors. Because I took the time to observe, I could talk about the story behind the painting and help her classmates understand that the picture was not really "a scribble-scrabble," as Jeremy was quick to label it.

If we see our children in the process of doing, we may be able to glean what is under the layers of a now-puddly painting, or what is behind confusing or distracting behaviors. ❖

"I SEE YOU":
Noticing What Children Do Right

MY CHAIR, TABLE, OR DESK is where I can see the entire classroom. When I work with a small group, my chair is turned so that I see the room. I often gather the whole group in a circle so that everyone sees everyone else. I walk in the back—not the front—of the line. I want to see everyone. And students know that I see because I let them know with my comments, over and over. I continue to believe that the ways we see our children and the ways that they know they are seen by their teachers contribute significantly to the tone of the classroom.

I see Devon struggle with his writing, puncturing holes in the paper in frustration. I see Lisa avoid the expected routines in her scramble to make contact with her friends in the morning. I see Beth test limits. I see Molly waver in her new role as a friend of boys as well as girls. I see Chris "forget" his have-to's so he can play games. I see my students enter our room, heads down, neglecting common courtesies.

But primarily I see the efforts, persistence, and desire of the children to please. They *want* to meet the expectations of their teachers, follow the rules correctly, execute each new skill, and succeed in their new class. To sustain that hope, I must focus on their positive energy and accomplishments:

- ✦ "You are remembering how to keep your bodies still."

- ✦ "I see that you are remembering to raise your hands."

- ✦ "I notice the way many of you look at Jamie when he speaks."

- ✦ "Thanks, Jessica and Tim, for wiping off the paint jars and getting the lids nice and tight."

- ✦ "Monica, I see you worked hard to make your butterfly sketch so realistic."

- ✦ "Thank you for fixing the pencil sharpener."

- ✦ "I notice that you are waiting so patiently for your turn to drink, Angie."

- ✦ "You are ready so quickly today for math group."

- ✦ "I like the way you included new people in your project."

- ✦ "I see that you are really trying to make those letters even. It looks hard."

- ✦ "Andy, you've helped Laura a lot. You can do your own work now."

30

+ "I notice that a lot of people in this group are interested in the news."

+ "I see... "

Commenting on what you see

... for children, hope is as important as breathing.

SARA RUDDICK
Maternal Thinking

EACH TIME YOU COMMENT, your tone and language are extremely important. For example, when a child runs down the stairs, you might say, "Jimmy, don't run down the stairs" or "No running, Jimmy. That's the rule." But rather than catching and correcting Jimmy, you could remind and redirect him instead. "I see too many steps, Jimmy. Show me again how you walk down the stairs." The result is a positive accomplishment rather than negative "discipline." Appropriate comments are:

+ Encouraging—They support children's efforts.

+ Specific—They name a behavior or accomplishment and avoid general labels of "good" and "bad."

+ Positive—"Show me what you will do..." rather than "Don't do that."

Some examples of positive attitudes and language are provided in Figure 2.1. I concentrate on reminding, reinforcing, and redirecting. Remember that the focus of this entire approach is noticing what children do *right*.

FORMULATING EXPECTATIONS

OF COURSE, BEFORE WE CAN EXPECT CHILDREN TO DO RIGHT, we must teach them what we mean by "right." As we get to know our children, we must also establish and communicate our expectations. Expectations are an essential step between intention and achievement. We must first know what our expectations are and then communicate them clearly to the children. Then we can translate our expectations into daily classroom life with the children. We teach our expectations in many ways.

We build expectations into the routines, rituals, and special situations and events of the classroom. Routines and rituals offer children opportunity for instruction and

FIGURE 2.1

Commenting on What You See

Here are some examples of commenting on what you see.

Reinforcing group and individual efforts

✦ "You remembered to carry the scissors point down."

✦ "I notice that you remember where to put your work so I can find it."

✦ "You are really scrubbing the brushes."

✦ "Many of you like to share your drawings. The nice comments I hear really help people want to share."

✦ "I notice lots of different ideas and ways to draw trees. It's neat that people have different ways to do things."

✦ "I notice that most of you are taking time to read the directions and are now figuring out things for yourself."

✦ "Nick and Judy, you worked hard to solve that problem on your own this afternoon."

Reminding (review and practice)

✦ "Before we go to our next period, remind me, what are the three things you will need to do?"

✦ "Who remembers what you will need to get for writing? Show me."

✦ "Remind me, what do you do if you can't think of how to spell a word?"

✦ "Who remembers where to find a dictionary in our room? Show us."

✦ "If someone asks you to play a game, what are friendly ways you might respond? Remind me."

✦ "Remind us of what happens in our class if someone makes a mistake."

✦ "Jackie, I see you walking around the room. Remind me, what's your job right now?"

- "Denise, remind me of what happens if someone needs to use the markers you are using. What can you say?"

Redirecting

- "Pencils are for writing, Stephen... [Teacher takes the pencil away]. When you are ready to use the pencil appropriately, tell me and I'll give it back."

- "I hear a lot of talking. This is your time to get your folders—silently, now."

- "Crystal, I see you floating around the room. You seem to be having a hard time making a choice today. You may either do a math puzzle or do your science observation. I'll be back in a minute to see what you have decided."

- "We agreed to throw the ball underhand and not whip it for this game. I'll take the ball now. Maybe we can try again tomorrow."

- "I see a lot of silly-looking stuff at this table. I'll hold your papers for now. Tell me when you're ready to begin work."

....

daily practice. We make our expectations explicit through the ways we structure independence, self-regulation, and cooperation. For example, classroom materials can be carefully labeled and organized and explored through Guided Discovery lessons (see discussion later in this chapter). Afterwards, they are accessible to children and are under the children's care and responsibility. We are translating our expectations about independence, responsibility, and sharing into explicit behavioral expectations. In another example, when children face each other around a circle or a table, the implicit concept of a participatory community is made explicit.

We provide choices and create experiences that allow children practice, practice, and more practice in intellectual and social skills. Children need to practice making responsible academic choices. They also need to practice saying hello, raising their hand, and keeping their hand in their lap when someone else is talking. They need to practice getting help from peers and drawing on "classmate expertise"—finding the one who knows how to put the yarn on the needle or multiply fractions. When they make social mistakes, they must practice repairing them through consequences that hold them accountable but that don't belittle or defeat them. We also teach social expectations through the authenticity of our relationships with children and our affection for them—our knowing of the children and what they care about. We teach rigor by coming to our classes with careful lesson plans. We teach respect when we are willing to listen and build understanding. We teach kindness through moments of personal attention and compassion. As Marilyn Watson says, children are more apt to develop core values when they feel connected to those who model and teach such values (Watson 1998). Figure 2.2 summarizes some of the expectations that need to be taught to build a learning community.

....

FIGURE 2.2

Teaching Expectations
During the First Weeks of School

General expectations

For students to take care of themselves, each other, and their classroom, they must:

✦ Listen to the teacher and to each other

✦ Know and use all classmates' names

✦ Greet someone, each day, by name

✦ Participate in setting personal goals and articulating "hopes and dreams" for the year (see Chapter 3 for a discussion of "hopes and dreams")

✦ Move with purpose and safety around the room

✦ Use and maintain appropriate noise and activity levels

✦ Resolve conflicts with fairness and without the use of force

✦ Be honest about mistakes and learn to make reparations without loss of face

✦ Play games in ways that are fun and safe for all

✦ Share respectful and interested questions, comments, experiences, and opinions in the group

✦ Be inclusive and friendly to all, not just to best friends

- Establish solid work habits and the ability to draft, revise, critique, and appreciate their own best efforts
- Work independently and cooperatively in small and large groups
- Assert personal needs with teachers and peers
- Contribute to the community

Some specific expectations

For a classroom to function well as a learning community, students must:

- Know and get excited about the different areas and materials in the room
- Learn the routines of the bathroom, the lunchroom, and recess
- Recognize and respond appropriately to signals
- Learn how to invite people to join a game
- Learn what to say if someone wants to join their game
- Learn how to choose good books from the class library
- Learn how to share a box of crayons or three pairs of scissors among eight children
- Learn how to toss a ball in a safe way
- Learn how to do homework, put a heading on a paper, and turn work in to the proper slot
- Learn how to fill out an assignment book
- Learn where to put lunch boxes, backpacks, and treasures from home

....

STAGES

CLASSROOM MANAGEMENT IS, in part, a process of instilling expectations, routines, and skills which allow children to work with competence on their own, in a group, or with a partner. To accomplish these tasks, we first must establish that we see children take care of the classroom. It doesn't work to try to rush or condense the process. Rules and skills need to be explained, modeled, practiced, then tried in real situations. I need to be able to say "I know you know how to do... how to take care of... how to manage yourself during... And I know that because I've *seen* you do it."

But how can I do all this seeing?

How do I begin to teach a group to understand place value and how to trade seventeen ones for one ten and seven ones, and still keep track of that bunch in the library corner? How do I see if Jeffrey bluffs or reads? How do I have a conference with Kate about her story if I stop every two minutes to remind the group working on their spelling to spell rather than chatter? How do I notice who is remembering to put caps on the markers, put crayons carefully back in the box, replace the lid of the glue pot, and return the glue pot to the shelf? How do I notice all that when I am instructing my group to blend consonant sounds with a short "a" vowel?

I DON'T! When I am immersed in teaching a group new skills, I need to give them undivided attention. So, I do *not* begin the year teaching complex new concepts or the intricacies of a new subject. When algebra class meets, the focus is on establishing the routines of keeping assignment books, organizing a notebook—setting up and practicing good work habits. The "real meat" will wait a few days or even a number of weeks. Small-group reading instruction will wait as well. Lessons still need to be engaging and appropriate—and challenging—but the teacher's focus must be on establishing basic expectations and skills rather than on helping children master new material.

I spend six weeks helping children generate hopes and dreams for the school year, goals to reach for, and rules for the classroom; six weeks building community with read-aloud stories and room-beautifying class projects. I spend six weeks taking students through a draft-by-draft sequence for completing a project, until everyone has a beautiful piece of finished work to post on our bulletin boards. I spend six weeks teaching children how to choose books and art materials, sometimes even how to turn the pages of a book or put the caps back on the markers. I teach them to make a heading on their writing assignments, monitor their own voice levels, make efficient transitions, ask for help from classmates, work cooperatively, and many more how-to's. This instruction takes patience, determination, and confidence that it is important work.

I "open" the classroom gradually. Only some of the areas will be used the first week. Only some of the materials are out on the shelves. New materials are introduced slowly. New expectations and responsibilities are also introduced gradually, in three stages. Each stage has its own tasks, objectives, and criteria for moving to the next stage.

Stages one and two take place largely during the first six weeks of school but are reinforced the rest of the year. Stage three begins toward the end of the first six weeks and continues through the rest of the year.

- ✦ Stage one focuses on the class, as a whole, learning expectations for behavior.

- ✦ Stage two introduces the responsibilities for working in small groups, and for working independently while the teacher concentrates on a small group.

- ✦ Stage three initiates the skill and content instruction planned for the year, such as instruction through math and reading groups.

These are broad, overlapping categories, but they do outline a progression that I take every one of my classes through. How quickly we move through the three stages, however, will vary with the unique character and rhythm of each class. Some of my classes, for example, need more time to establish whole-group routines and coherence, while others "gel" as a group but take more time to build independence and inter-reliance in small-group situations. The pace is adjusted by the teacher's assessment of the learning rather than enforced by any strict time guidelines.

STAGE ONE:
Whole-Class Learning

THE BASIC GOALS FOR THIS INITIAL STAGE are listed below. In general, children are developing the work habits and behaviors which create competence and promote respect. They are learning to:

- ✦ Listen

- ✦ Use kind language

- ✦ Ask questions

- ✦ Share solutions to problems

- ✦ Put things away

- ✦ Have fun and enjoy jokes (that don't rely on teasing)

- ✦ Get ready in a timely way

- ✦ Know everyone's name

- Generate and follow the rules of the classroom
- Carry out orderly transitions

Stage one is devoted to whole-class activity. It is a time to set a tone and set expectations, a time to create a positive group ethic. Teaching some basic routines that we often take for granted and holding group meetings help accomplish these goals.

Establishing some basic routines

A safety signal

Inside the classroom, a bell rings. It's the class signal that means "freeze." "When you hear that signal, you stop—you stop everything. You face the person who gave the signal. You are ready to listen."

The bell rings. Children freeze… somewhat. Matt is still finishing his drawing. Cathy continues to drink from the fountain. Angie moves over to get next to her friend. A clutch in the library area continues to read.

"I see that many of you know just what to do when the bell rings in our class. I see Jonathan has stopped and is looking right at me. I see that Jessie has put down his pencil and is looking at me. I see that the group working at the math table is still and ready to listen. I don't yet see EVERYONE. Go back to work. I will ring the bell again. I hope this time I see everyone freeze."

The quick response to the bell improves, but when the teacher begins her message, talking and distractions resume. It will take more than one practice and more than one day to work on *staying* frozen until the "melt" signal is given. The bell is an essential safety system. The teacher must be able to get the attention and hold the attention of the entire class, even when groups are deeply involved and scattered about the room. Or, in the rare case of an emergency, the teacher needs to silence the room, make an announcement, and begin the transition. Later, even students may ask to use the signal. A student might ring the bell and say to the class, "I can't find my book. Did anyone see it?" or "It's kinda noisy here. Would people please be quieter?"

A few years ago, a school in Washington, DC, had adopted a raised hand as the school-wide quiet signal. It was late fall, and Barbara Freeman's second grade class was highly proficient with this signal. But now the students were on a field trip, far from the confines of classroom routine. In addition, Ms. Freeman found herself momentarily in charge of two additional classes while waiting for some hold-up to be cleared. The groups were becoming impatient. Ms. Freeman raised her hand and, to her happy surprise, sixty children stopped, looked, and listened quietly while she explained the wait, gave new directions, and let out a deep and relaxed breath.

Circling up

We are about to go outside to play a group game. Week one—day one. I give the class two directions: "I want you to hold hands and make a circle when you get out on the field. I will count and see how quickly you can do that." Curiously, I have found that the older the children, the harder this will be. I am prepared to be patient.

I walk at the back of the line. The children are ahead of me. As they reach the field, they form a loose huddle. Some take hands. Many race about looking for just the "right" hand. I am counting "1… 2… 3… " Jed won't hold a girl's hand. Marty is trying to find her best friend's hand. "18… 19… " Sam is exploring the limits of arm spans until bodies jerk and tumble. "35… 36… 49… 50… " And there is a collected mass that is holding hands, an approximation of a circle. I am still counting. Their faces show puzzlement. Why am I counting if everyone is holding hands?

"Does this look like your idea of a circle?" I ask. "How will you make it a circle?" Some move out, some move further in. Back to counting. After almost five minutes, they are standing still, holding hands in a circle. They have carried out the simple directions.

"Well," I say, "you did it. It took to the count of 250, a long time. I expect you to do this to the count of 20. Last year's class record was 10. I noticed that some of you quickly took a hand. Some of you stood still and waited patiently. Some of you helped create a circle. Let's see everyone help this time. I will say 'scatter.' At the

signal 'Allee-allee-in-free,' I will expect you to circle up and hold hands. Twenty seconds! Scatter!"

This technique conveys a tone. Does the teacher mean what she says? Does she care *how* something is done, not just *that* it gets done? Are there expectations about care and treatment of others, such as refusing to hold the hand of someone of the opposite sex or only holding hands of your "friends"? When all children are expected to hold all hands, the message is that we are all friendly to each other in this class. Period.

The process also reinforces the belief that behaviors need to be taught and learned, and that learning them is not a waste of time. The smooth transition, the "good circle," the quiet line-up, or the responsive class meeting won't happen the first time, but they will get better the next time. They will be even better the third time.

The bathroom routine

Establishing a routine for students to go to the bathroom on their own is a basic and fundamental piece of management. It reinforces a sense of autonomy and self-regulation. Few classrooms have their own bathrooms, so unless children go on schedule with a teacher, they must take care of themselves on their bathroom trip. If a child doesn't follow the rules, you might say, "You'll have to wait until a teacher is able to go with you. It's *your* choice." Children can quickly assume this responsibility, but we shouldn't take the bathroom routine for granted. Deliberately teaching it increases the potential for self-control—even when the teacher isn't watching.

Of course, there are lapses. Six-year-old boys may attempt a mad dash into the girls' bathroom. Six-year-old girls come back giggling or in a snit to expose this outrage. Eight-year-olds need reminders that bathrooming is not a social event—"You do not need to go every time a friend needs to go." Many ten-year-olds also love to congregate for social purposes, to tell secrets or gossip out of sight of the teacher (they hope). Restless students make numerous forays, especially when the classroom subject matter befuddles them. Graffiti and petty vandalism are common bathroom misdemeanors.

I recall when Maurice's mother came to school to find out why I never let Maurice "go." Maurice, it turned out, never went to the bathroom because he was afraid to go by himself. A small, reticent child, he was picked on and teased. "Baldy-bean" they called him, and snatched his protective cap off his head. It was Jerome and Grady who proposed confidently, during class meeting, that they escort Maurice to the bathroom "so he don't need to be scared of nothin'." Jerome and Grady were usually the class bullies, apt to exploit classmates cheerfully. For a nickel, they would ensure a safe passage from school to home—safe mostly from them. In this instance, however, the escorting accomplished several important changes in our classroom. It helped Maurice go to the bathroom. It also helped Maurice feel he had friends in school. And it helped Jerome and Grady be friends instead of bullies.

It may seem easier, though terribly time-consuming, to take children to the bathroom. Many schools still require this. It avoids hassles and problems. Or does it? It is my strong contention that the routines of our classrooms must be used as opportunities to teach decent behavior, not to constrict it.

So with our fives we practice going to the bathroom, walking down the halls, first together and then in pairs. We teach our sevens to put up a name card on a "Bathroom Out" hook and to remember to remove the card when they return. We are prepared to reinforce and remind, because if students "forget" the rules or choose not to follow them, they may lose the privilege of going to the bathroom on their own—at least until they are ready to show they remember and choose to follow the class rules. There are consequences, but not consequences which release children from their job—safe and proper bathroom conduct.

Some activities for the early weeks

Journal writing

It is journal writing period in Ms. Nophlin's second grade classroom early in the third week of school. Part of the language arts program, journal writing integrates a sequenced syllabus of phonetics, sight words, and grammar with the children's personal experiences. This class is eager to do their best, but their focus lasts only for short spurts before restless energy erupts.

They have been making slow and steady progress since the first day, when they had unwrapped their notebooks to great fanfare and explored the properties of the classic mottled black-and-white composition books. (See "Guided Discovery" later in this chapter.)

"When I open this notebook, what will I find?" Ms. Nophlin had quizzed that first day.

"Nothing!"

"Why do I give you nothing?" she had teased them.

"So we can write," had come the response.

More questions and conversation in the following days had helped construct the concept of a journal—a written record of a person's words, ideas, and stories.

In small, incremental steps over the past two weeks, Ms. Nophlin has been teaching students to use their notebooks with precision and care. She has demonstrated how to open the book, turn the pages, find the top and bottom. "Watch how I turn the page so it doesn't get all crinkly. Who else thinks they can turn a page without crinkling it?"

The children's vocabulary now includes terms like "margin," "line," and "binding." They have decorated their journals and attached name labels to the front covers, practiced writing on the lines of the first page, and learned to enter "Tuesday" on the top line near the margin before beginning an entry.

The drenching rain this morning prompts Ms. Nophlin's question, written on the chart: "What did you do to stay dry on this very, very rainy day?"

"Before we start," she asks, "who can remind me what we need to do to begin our journal writing?" The short reminders will help settle and focus the group.

"Look at the chart."

"Put our hands in our laps."

"Open our ears."

"Who sees our journal question for today?" Hands go up. Most now know where the question is even if they can't read all the words. First, with their teacher's help, they read in chorus, then a few do solos. Once more, they read in refrain, then begin to share their rainy-day mornings. In a burst of competitive zeal, four talk at once. Ms. Nophlin holds up her hand, signaling for silence. Myra continues to wiggle and whisper to her neighbor. "Myra, move over here, please," says Ms. Nophlin quietly, redirecting the child to a seat next to the teacher.

"Does rain have a sound? Let's listen," Ms. Nophlin continues, launching a discussion about rain, wet shoes, protective gear. Children are gathering ideas from this conversation that will be reflected in their journal entries. It is both rehearsal and a way to extend their ideas.

Before they move to their seats to write, there are a few quick reminders. "If you need to sharpen a pencil, what will you do, Dana?" Dana shrugs. "Who can remind Dana?"

"You raise your hand and wait."

"Show me. Pretend you are writing and your pencil point breaks and you need to sharpen it." Later, students will be encouraged to get up and get what they need on their own. For now, they are learning to stay in their seats and concentrate.

A pleasant hum settles over the room as the class gets to work writing about their day. Tyrone casts a critical eye at Jordan when Jordan starts his sentence on the same line as the date. "You're supposed to skip a line," Tyrone admonishes. Jordan looks as if he wants to argue, but he looks around at others' pages and then begins to erase furiously.

As the period continues, hands go up to ask for spelling help or permission to sharpen pencils. Jason's notebook remains unopened. He skates it vigorously over his desk until it bumps Leesha's arm.

"Look what you did!" Leesha cries. The disruption brings Ms. Nophlin, who helps Jason apologize and erase Leesha's smudged marks. Opening Jason's notebook, the teacher sees the jagged, unruly strokes that are his writing and realizes just how difficult this task is for him. She modifies the task, inserting some dots for Jason to connect into letters. Moments later she returns, has him dictate a sentence to her, and instructs him to trace the letters in it.

Ms. Nophlin continues to circulate, noticing, reinforcing, and asking questions. The egg timer on a shelf in the front of the room reminds students that there are three minutes to go in the twenty-minute writing period. They have almost made it—in their seats and still writing!

There is time for a few to share their work. The three readers stand tall in front of the class and wait until everyone is ready.

"The rain makes my shoes get wet," Alonzo reads.

"I like rain," reads Tanya, and she shows off a beautifully pencil-washed picture. "My brother likes to jump in puddles and he gets me all wet. I said Robert Stop. But he don't listen." An appreciative laugh greets her story.

"I got a new baby brother," Teresa reads. Everyone claps. It's not rain, but it's important.

Seventh and eighth grade book posters

During the first week of school, I started the seventh and eighth graders at Greenfield Center School in Massachusetts on a two-week project to help them learn work habits I hoped they would apply throughout the school year. I asked them to make a poster to promote a book they had read and "loved" over the summer, a book they wanted to recommend to their peers. The project taught students to create work in carefully sequenced steps, from a rough sketch or brainstorming, through several drafts, to a final product displayed proudly in the classroom.

Students needed to think carefully about how to convey their ideas using only a few words and chosen images. The project began with a worksheet asking a series of questions about the book. Students were asked, for example, to circle words that describe their book. Was it a fantasy or realistic fiction? Was it a mystery, horror, sci-fi, or historical fiction? What were some of the book's strengths—character, dialogue, suspense, action, interesting issues?

Students then created many drafts: first a small "thumbnail" sketch, then a larger, extended sketch including favorite ideas. Next, a written blurb or a few catchy sentences could be added. After this thorough preparation, students explored different art materials and approaches to adding color and collage to their draft. Next, they proofread and got a final okay from the teacher. Yes, the author's name is spelled correctly, there are periods in proper places, and the background and foreground colors are figured out.

Throughout this process, I circulated, asking questions, prompting, encouraging, and helping students find various resources to solve problems. To a lost-looking Myles, I said, "Who can show you ways to shade using Craypas?" To Wen-hai, I said, "Where might you find a good picture of a castle?"

I concentrated on how students did their work throughout the project. For example, when the class was about to leave their meeting area and go to a forty-five-minute quiet work time on book posters, I asked, "Before you go, what will you need to remember?" Students listed supplies such as paper, markers, and folders. I prompted them to recall the procedures for quiet work.

"Find a place where we can work."

"Not sit where we'll talk a lot."

"Get what we need first so we don't have to get up a lot."

I knew that students' social agenda was huge and that talking would easily become the focus. I also knew that while some of the students could talk and work at the same time, others needed a singular focus and very few distractions. A tone conducive to work had to be established for the good of the group. It needed to be industrious and quiet, with minimum movement.

Students got up, sharpened a pencil, asked a friend for an idea, went to the bathroom. Comments at one table appropriately accompanied the ebb and flow of work:

"I like your tree."

"May I have the black when you're done?"

"What's another word for exciting?"

At another table, whispers and giggles drew attention away from posters and into socializing. "I'm asking her about my poster," Justina cried as she saw me approach.

"I don't think so," I said. "I think this group is mostly chatting."

"I'm stuck and I don't like my draft," Justina whined. Stuck, she had diverted herself and others into the comfort of the social arena, a place of strength for her. To get past her frustrations, she would need redirection. I quickly realized that Justina often gave up quickly and digressed from independent work in the classroom. It would be a goal for the year for her to gain more confidence and improve her ability to concentrate. It was especially important to begin right away, before bad habits got established.

Justina was redirected to sit away from friends, closer to me. A brief conversation and a look at an earlier draft got her restarted. Several days later, she would complete her poster, proud of the design and shadings of color, a beautiful final completion to start off her year.

Morning Meeting

MORNING MEETING IS A DAILY GATHERING of the class that builds group cohesion and an attentive, responsive community. (See Figure 2.3 for the components of Morning Meeting.) *The Morning Meeting Book* by Roxann Kriete offers detailed explanations and descriptions of each component as well as specific greetings, activities, and charts.

....

FIGURE 2.3

Components of Morning Meeting

Morning Meeting is a fifteen- to thirty-minute class meeting at the beginning of each day. It builds community, creates a positive climate for learning, reinforces academic and social skills, and gives children daily practice in respectful communication. Morning Meeting consists of the following four components:

Greeting: Students greet each other by name. There are many different greeting activities that can be used throughout the year, including handshaking, singing, clapping, and greeting in different languages.

Sharing: Each day, two or three students share information about an event in their lives. Listeners take turns offering empathic comments or asking clarifying questions.

Group activity: All participate in a brief, lively activity such as singing, chanting, playing a game, reciting a poem, or dancing.

News and announcements: Children read the news and announcements chart that their teacher has written. Sometimes they read silently as a group, sometimes they follow as the teacher or a fellow student reads, sometimes they read aloud as a group. The news and announcements chart usually includes an activity that reinforces academic skills.

....

Children count on and internalize the consistent and predictable rituals of Morning Meeting: greetings; time to share personal news; a repertoire of games, chants, and songs; classroom news for the day. The strength of a Morning Meeting also depends on the capacity of children to take responsibility for the routines of the group—by listening actively, making relevant comments, playing enthusiastically, sitting still, raising a hand. There is a lot to learn.

Meetings vary from teacher to teacher and class to class. Each meeting incorporates the character and flavor of the group. Each teacher lets her/his own rituals evolve.

"It's time for meeting… It's time for meeting… " is the melodious signal in Ms. Porter's kindergarten-first grade class. The tune passes spontaneously as children drift over to the rug, their meeting area. "Where is Rosie, where is Rosie… there she is… there she is… ," they go on to sing.

In Mr. Jenkins's seventh grade group, students begin Morning Meeting by teaming up to move tables and chairs to form a space large enough for twenty-five adolescent bodies. They initiate their circle by naming all class members, without the melody. Every student is named, everyone is included in the circle with a resonant "Good morning," and everyone has the responsibility of greeting and including others. Noticing who has yet to be named takes keen attention and watchfulness. No one gets left out.

My third graders sometimes made number sentences for the calendar date. It is September 20th. We will need twenty sentences for the number twenty. "Who has one?" I ask.

"I hope we don't have school on the 30th!" someone whispers.

Molly says, "One-fifth of one hundred is twenty." Molly loves to be first and loves to demonstrate her superior skills.

Danny is next. "One hundred take away eighty is twenty."

It's Patty's turn. She says with hesitation, "Nine and nine is twenty." I notice Molly smirk and nudge her neighbor.

I say with strong feeling, "I like people to contribute in our circle. It's pretty easy to do that when you feel very sure of what you know. It takes courage to speak when you don't feel so sure. I want this to be a class where everyone feels they can contribute. Their math ideas, their singing voices, their stories—their sure things and their not-so-sure things. That's what's most important."

Often during meetings, someone gives an answer that is not correct. *This is an opportunity to teach "right behavior," not "right answers," a critical moment to set the tone and instill group ethics.* I am easily reminded of the childhood fear that lurked in my stomach every time I had to give an answer. So afraid to be wrong, I rarely volunteered. I dreaded those looks and barely smothered giggles. I was

afraid to forget seven times eight, the capital of Maine, the longest river, the last verse. Yet, though I hated being ridiculed, I was not hesitant to ridicule others, perpetuating the climate of fear in the classroom. Such fear stifles and hinders learning.

Now, as a teacher, I give a clear, direct, emphatic message to my students: *"I will not allow ridicule in our classroom."* Students transfer this learning to other parts of the day. Because we have established that put-downs are not acceptable in Morning Meeting, I can reinforce it with my eighth graders in English class. I can react to a sharp, sarcastic remark by one of my very articulate students as he disagrees with a peer's comment. Academic classes build on the social learning of Morning Meetings.

Sharing personal experiences in Morning Meeting

In our Morning Meeting, there is a time for sharing events and experiences that occurred outside of school. Morning Meeting serves as a transition, connecting lives at home to lives in school. In our routine, a student makes a brief report and then asks, "Any questions or comments?"

The rest of the group then becomes active. They may ask for more details, probe for more information, make reactive comments. They learn to respond with attention and authentic interest. When we permit the outward appearance of indifference (bodies turned away from the speaker, whispering to a neighbor, staring out windows), we encourage disengagement. When we expect the outward appearance of attention (looking at the person speaking, sitting still, a verbal response), we provide conditions for interest to develop.

Deidre reports that her mother got a new job. Deidre isn't sure just what the job was, but her Mom starts today.

"Any questions or comments?" No hands. Deidre is a quiet nine-year-old, apt to hang back and give a sour appearance. I raise my hand. Deidre calls on me shyly, "Ms. Charney."

"Are you glad your mother has a new job?"

Deidre replies uncertainly.

Janie's hand (at half-mast). "My mother got a job recently. She comes home tired and grumpy." Deidre smiles at Janie.

"What kind of job?" someone asks Janie. Before Janie can answer, I intervene and redirect the sharing back to Deidre by selecting a student and asking him for one more question for Deidre. He complies.

"Thank you for your interesting sharing. I'd love to hear more about your mother's new job, so let us know what you find out," I conclude.

In this meeting, I modeled a response with a question and comment. I also redirected the meeting when it began to shift away from the original sharer. Some children are naturally more outspoken and popular. Some command more attention from their peers. The group dynamics can be quite complex. The more comfortable and secure the group becomes, the more our quiet, reserved, or less popular children can risk coming forward.

Morning Meeting with older children

Many teachers of sixth through eighth grade students use a modified version of Morning Meeting that teacher, principal, and Northeast Foundation for Children co-founder Chip Wood named "Circle of Power and Respect" (CPR). Given positive direction and clear guidelines, older children relish opportunities for sharing.

I observed Ron, the class "outsider," tell a spell-bound audience in his Maine school an antic tale of a mishap on a hunting trip. "See, I had my cousin's three-wheeler, and I thought my Granddad said to take the right fork trail, only he didn't…"

"Did you see how everyone listened to you?" his teacher asked later, reinforcing his success. "They did?" Ron responded, a smile belying his question.

Older children also bring up subjects which spark important and intense discussions. When a student relates, with obvious relish, the events of a baseball game he watched that nearly erupted into a fan riot when a bad call was made, some students suggest beating up the umpires. The teacher intervenes and extends the discussion to violent actions at sporting events and the ethical questions involved.

When a sixth grader describes a weekend activity, a prank played on some female classmates that involved calling them sexual names, he explains it was just "fun." "See," he insists, "they're grinning."

"I'm having trouble with this," Ms. Ellison says firmly. "We'll stop and talk about this later." Morning Meetings provide a format and opportunity for these discussions that are just as important for older children as for younger ones.

DURING STAGE ONE OF THE FIRST SIX WEEKS, I introduce the areas of the room and establish routines and ways to use materials. We start a routine called "quiet time." Children choose an activity that they wish to do alone and quietly for a sustained period of time: puzzles, sewing, drawing, reading, independent math sheets. I observe as some students do elaborate things, others dream, and a few watch the clock.

During this stage, I set up an art activity or a new technique for using the pastels. We may go outside and sketch a tree in the schoolyard. I urge them to look at shapes, textures, colors. I ask, "What part of your sketch do you like the best? What part do you think you might want to do differently next time?" I am teaching children to self evaluate, to survey their own work before asking "Teacher, is it good?"

The children have to know the place for the stapler, how to carry scissors, where to find the bin for lined paper, the place for finished work, the proper storage for the paint brushes. I demonstrate. I explain. I model. One technique for opening the room during the first weeks is called Guided Discovery.

Guided Discovery

GUIDED DISCOVERY IS A PROCESS for introducing materials, opening areas in the classroom, and preparing children for different aspects of the curriculum. For example, teachers may use Guided Discovery to introduce journal books, the library area, or a "choice" period. The process sparks children's interest in the activity or classroom area while giving them opportunities to be creative and to practice making productive choices.

Guided Discovery lessons may establish routines for whole-class or independent work. They may take thirty minutes or only ten. In any Guided Discovery lesson, there may be the following objectives:

- ✦ Motivate and excite students by exploring creative possibilities.

- ✦ Stretch individual students toward involvement in new or extended areas of learning.

- Give information and ideas to guide and deepen the understanding of materials and activities in the classroom.

- Give instruction in the techniques and skills needed for effective use of tools and materials.

- Establish a common language and vocabulary.

- Share ideas and procedures for independent use of materials or areas. (These ideas may come from children who have invented or found alternatives.)

- Teach or reinforce social or cooperative guidelines.

- Teach and reinforce care and clean-up routines.

Importantly, Guided Discoveries may be used not only to introduce new materials or activities, but to stimulate new interest in familiar resources. One year, I used the process to get fourth graders to experiment with new techniques for using the number two pencil in sketching. The value of Guided Discovery is its power to excite children and help them unlock the potential uses hidden in a tool—be it a pencil, atlas, or microscope—while teaching them to use the tool with care and respect. (See Figure 2.4 for the steps in a Guided Discovery.)

TEACHING CHILDREN TO CARE

FIGURE 2.4

Steps in a Guided Discovery

In general, Guided Discoveries include the following steps:

1. Introduction—The teacher and children name the material or room area in a way that excites the children and motivates them to explore.

2. Generating ideas—The teacher helps children generate ideas for possible ways to use the material or room area, and the teacher demonstrates the uses.

3. Children explore—Children try their hand at using the material or room area in different ways, with guidance and encouragement from the teacher.

4. Sharing—Children show their work to the group, pointing out features they would like others to notice. The audience offers comments.

5. Clean-up and care of material or area—The teacher asks children to suggest and demonstrate good ways to clean up, establishing expectations for the care of classroom materials and areas.

6. Extensions—Children work in groups, pairs, or alone to continue exploring or discovering further uses of the material or room area.

Guided Discovery with a box of crayons

I often introduce a box of crayons with more than thirty different colors during the first week of school. Even with older groups, I deliberately start with a common material, one that is taken for granted. I want to extend possibilities, as well as model a considered approach to the resources of our classroom.

I have covered the box of crayons with a wrapper. "Who can guess what I have? I'll give you a clue—it's something we regularly use in school." Quickly, this six-year-old group, feeling and shaking the package, guesses correctly.

"Yes. It's a box of crayons. But how many? A few or a lot?"

"A lot," replies a chorus of voices.

"Well. What's a lot?" I write down some of the numbers, enjoying the ideas of quantity that vary so with this age. One thousand, some say. Twenty-hundred is another possibility. Eighty-eight, a more precise fellow suggests.

"How will we find out?"

"Open it," come the excited answers.

I unwrap the package, but I don't open the box. "Where does it tell us exactly how many?" As I hold up the box, different children try to locate and distinguish the numbers. Finding them easily, they are satisfied. And some will read them. But is it 46 or 64?

"Sixty-four crayons. That is a lot. Think now—are they all the same color? Are there sixty-four blue crayons? Sixty-four red crayons?" A quick poll shows that most are pretty sure there are sixty-four different colors. "Do you think you might be able to name ten… twenty?" Lots of nods.

Remember now, what we are exploring is a standard box of crayons, not a jazzy new product! By the time I actually open the lid in order to display sixty-four different colors, there is considerable interest, even drama. "Let's see if you can figure out ten of these fancy colors. I wonder… " The children eagerly begin to name first the obvious, and then silver, gold, turquoise. I put their inventory on a chart, locating the crayon with each given label. They name ten, then twenty, and are pleased with their own knowledge, excited by their discoveries.

Perhaps I will add one new color. "Here's a very fancy one… magenta, it says on the label. Can anyone guess what color magenta might be?" I wiggle it in the box, keeping it hidden. Guessing adds to the final pleasure of discovery.

"It's sort of like reddish-purplish-pink," someone says.

"It's like Kim's shirt."

"Magenta, magenta," someone else sings.

The concept that there are shades of color—that magenta is a shade of red—would be an interesting one to develop in another lesson, or it might be the focus for an older group. Now, I move on to using the crayons. I explain that later in the morning there will be a drawing time.

Everyone will have a chance to use these special boxes of sixty-four crayons. "Where do you think we should keep them?"

"On the art shelf."

"Why would that be a good place?"

"'Cause you use them for drawing and art."

"Yes. They are things that artists use."

"How do you think artists take care of their crayons?" I tell students that I've noticed how full the box is and how hard it can be to take out the crayons and find where to put them back. I demonstrate. "Should I just dump them all out, because I'm in a hurry?"

"You gotta be careful," someone tells me.

"Show me how you would be careful." A student comes up and gingerly extracts a single crayon. I make it tricky and shake the box, challenging her to then replace the crayon. She does. "How did you know to put it there?"

She smiles. "I could see."

"What could she see?" I ask the others. The rest of the class peers into the box, intrigued with this mystery. Others want to try, but I remind them that they will all have a chance when it's time for art (or "choice").

"I've noticed something else about these crayons. I've noticed that they have a pretty sharp point."

"It's kind of roundish, too," someone observes.

"What do you think will happen if I need to press down hard to make it dark?"

"It will break?"

"You shouldn't do it so hard."

"It gets flat."

"Suppose I want to make a dark sky and I press hard and it does break, but I want it sharp again. Does anyone know a way to sharpen a crayon? Can you sharpen crayons?"

"They get stuck a lot."

"They do get stuck in pencil sharpeners. Is there another way?" We might experiment with different types of crayon sharpeners at another meeting—a group of seven-year-olds once took off on a study of crayon sharpeners! But for now, I just introduce the tool.

Before finishing the day's Guided Discovery lesson, I may need to talk about sharing. As one of the children finds space on our art shelf, I ask someone to count how many boxes we have in our class. There are six. "Will that be enough for everyone? Suppose more than six children want to use them at the same time? Suppose the whole class wants to use them for drawing later? How will we do that?" This may be a good time to introduce, or reinforce, behavior and language for sharing.

"If I want the black, do I say, 'gimme it!'? What should I say? Remind me." I ask a child to demonstrate. I may propose other dilemmas. "What happens if the box is out of my reach?" or "What if we both need the same crayon at the same time?" I find that children need to go through this, even when they have heard it before, and even when they are ten years old. Managing these courtesies helps children be polite, kind, and helpful to each other, to visitors, and to teachers.

"Show me that you remember how to ask someone to pass over a marker," I say. "Who knows what to do if you have been waiting for the brown crayon for a long time? Is it okay to grab?"

As the children go to work with the crayons, or the math manipulatives, or their new readers, the role of the teacher is to watch. S/he reinforces the discoveries, notices the careful handling of the material, observes the behaviors.

"I see that you are trying both light and dark coloring."

"I like the way you are passing the box around the table."

"What nice words I hear… "

"You found another new color. What other color do you think it's like? Would you like to add that to our chart so others can look for it?"

And, of course, the teacher must remind and redirect when children "forget," because the process will always break down—for sixes and eights and tens and twelves. ❖

Guided Discovery with a dictionary

The following energetic and engaging Guided Discovery took only twenty minutes. Yet it instilled an interest and competence that lasted through the year with these middle school students. Ms. Foot gathered her group into a circle and in the center placed about eight different dictionaries, including one that was quite huge and weathered, which she boasted as a garage sale find. Her pleasure immediately infected the group. "What do you notice about these books?" she asked.

"They're all dictionaries."

"They're all different."

"Some are much bigger."

"You like the one you found in the garage sale."

Ms. Foot next asked students what they knew about dictionaries and how they had used them before. The many quick answers showed familiarity. She then assigned each student a partner and asked each pair to select one of the dictionaries to study. Each pair was given a "scavenger hunt work sheet" with about ten questions, including:

- What's the longest word you can find in the dictionary?

- Find a word that you think no one else in the class will know.

- What letter has the most (or the fewest) words?

- Find a symbol that is used and tell what it means.

- English words come from other languages. Find two words that come from another language. How did you find out?

In the process, the students worked at problem solving. "Medical words are always big. Let's think of a disease and look that up." Or to find the letter with the most words, one student wanted to get a ruler and measure. That strategy, overheard, quickly made the rounds. "'X' won't have hardly any," someone said. "Whoever heard of words beginning with 'x' anyway?"

"X-ray," someone quickly piped up.

"Okay, besides 'x-ray.'" There was a sudden interest in "x" words.

Students came back to the circle and combined results. In the final few minutes, Ms. Foot talked about where the dictionaries would "live" in the classroom and how she particularly wanted her favorite to be taken care of so it could "continue to grow old." ❖

Moving on from stage one

ALTHOUGH THERE ARE ALWAYS SLIPS, times when even the most basic routines and expectations need to be reestablished, I know that a class is ready to move on to stage two when they meet five simple criteria:

1. They group up quickly for meetings, story time, games, work periods.
2. They can locate and replace materials in the room.
3. They listen and make relevant comments at meetings.
4. Most can stay with an activity for the expected and appropriate period of time.
5. They can make simple choices.

During stage one, teachers need to see what is right in front of them, as the whole group learns expectations and routines. During stage two, when the class begins working in small groups and teachers must divide their attention among groups, teachers need to see everything—in the literal sense and in the sense of extending a feeling of security to all students. During this stage, teachers are expanding their expectations of the classroom beyond their line of sight and noting whether children are beginning to internalize those expectations.

STAGE TWO:
"Paradoxical Groups"

STAGE TWO OF THE INITIAL SIX WEEKS establishes expectations for group work. It's a time when children learn to function in two ways:

- ✦ In small groups, with the teacher

- ✦ Away from the teacher, with independence

I call the groups I set up during this time "paradoxical groups" because I pretend to teach the small group while I am actually continuing to teach the whole class.

It is essential that children work effectively in small groups as well as in a whole class. Small groups and independent work are ways to accommodate students' different levels and rates of learning. Small groups can generate interest and participation; they allow teachers to teach in greater depth and students to pursue individual questions and divergent lines of inquiry. As I teach a small group, I provide a model for cooperative, peer-directed groups as well.

When the teacher is teaching the group, the rest of the class still needs to work productively. I will not be able to concentrate on my group if I need to attend to disruptions and interruptions coming from the other corners of the classroom. If the rest of the class idles or can only handle "busy work" without the teacher's undivided attention, they miss a great deal of learning. A primary objective of stage two is for children to learn to be productive while the teacher teaches her/his group.

The basic goals for independent work away from the teacher are explained to the children and regularly repeated:

- ✦ You plan ahead what you will do.

- ✦ You decide what to do from clear choices. It is your job to know the choices. They may be posted or they may be announced at Morning Meeting.

+ You talk quietly.

+ You keep your mind on your work.

+ You stay in the area you have chosen to work in. (Fives and under may change areas more often.)

+ You try to solve problems on your own or with the help of your classmates.

My strategy for teaching these behaviors is to provide the small group with work that needs little of my attention while actually focusing on the rest of the class. At first, the teacher appears to be teaching a small group, but the real agenda is "I see everything." While the teacher is meeting with a small group, her/his chair is always facing the class. The teacher's eyes can see all the students.

A math group and a poetry assignment

The bell chimes, signaling that it is time to get ready for the next class period. Ten of the twenty-six third graders have a math group with me. The others are to finish copying and illustrating a poem, an activity that we began together. It still takes five minutes for many to make a transition. There are reminders:

"I notice that many of you get ready quickly."

"I see students ready with their notebooks."

"Jeffrey, you've chosen a good place to work today."

"Alice, will you really be able to see the poem from there?"

"Everyone needs to be settled now," I say. "Last chance—THINK. Remind me, what do you need so that you will be able to concentrate and work for this entire period?" There is a quick review of work habits. "Do I have everything I need? What will I do if I finish early? Have I found a good place to do my work?" In this case, children have choices about location—it is one of their responsibilities to find a spot for writing from which they can see the posted poem, or a place where they can concentrate on their drawing.

My math group is seated around the table. There is a single box of manipulatives on the table. A few children start to grab objects from the box. "How do you know what you will need?" I ask. Most shrug and remove their hands. "That's a serious question," I repeat. "How will you know what you will need to do for math groups?"

"You'll tell us?"

"Any other way?" I ask. My goal for this group session is to introduce written directions as a prompt for an activity. On the blackboard next to our table, I have written out directions. Someone notices and begins to read aloud: "When you think you know what to do first, show us by doing it." That sentence is followed by more directions, which I have made simple and easy to read. I observe how different children in the group respond differently. Some go right to work; some seem cautious and hesitant; one student looks puzzled. After a few minutes, I ask, "What could you do if you're not sure how to read a word, or if you don't understand the directions?" I take time to affirm the many resources available in a group. "You can ask a friend. You can read it again. You can ask the teacher."

We also talk about what it means to be helpful. I ask some of the children to model asking for help and giving the help. This takes only a short time, and soon the children understand the directions clearly and have the materials they need. They are ready to explore on their own. Now I can do the essential task for stage two. I can watch the students outside the group as they follow through with copying or illustrating the poem.

As my math group figures out different ways to combine and arrange the pattern blocks I have distributed, I circulate throughout the room and quietly reinforce these other students' efforts at working independently:

"I see very good concentration."

"I notice that people are using quiet voices."

"Thanks for helping Renee find an eraser."

"Kyle, I see you are being very careful with your writing today."

Usually, I need only a few moments to check in, to affirm and confirm the efforts I see. Still, my attention is necessary to validate the importance of independent work. No matter what we say, there is a sense that the real business is in the group, the place where the teacher is. It must be clear that the work done outside the teacher's circle is also serious and has purpose. Otherwise, children will be all business in the group, while outside of it, they will fiddle. There should be essential learning going on outside the group: planning, making choices, sustaining attention, solving problems.

We need to pay attention to the work the children do outside the group. We need to make sure it is real work, not "busy work" meant largely to keep children quiet. Busy work is mechanical, repetitious, and long. Real work is relevant, takes skill, provides a challenge, and may be interesting or fun. Copying and illustrating a poem that the class recites and enacts together has meaning. Writing it beautifully, centering it on the page, and illustrating its message take skill and pose a challenge for many eight-year-olds. Marcie wants to do the title in cursive. Jessica wants to do it fast and be done first. Carlos is fascinated with Emily Dickinson's line "The rose is out of town." He is working hard on drawing the rose.

Some of the children are already into the tempo and rhythms of their own industry. A cluster of children is copying the poem. A few recite it, practicing with each other. Others draw the gentle autumn scene evoked in the poem with ease and pleasurable concentration. Comments and spontaneous utterances create a wonderful hum.

I never object to talk. Instead, I want to teach children the distinction between distracting and productive conversation. The group working on the library rug, for example, chatters about a "cute boy on TV." Distracting conversation, I decide. They need reminding ("What do you need to be doing?") or redirecting ("Find another place where you will be better able to concentrate."). Some return easily to their work.

Others flounder. Meg writes one word at a time, looking around, flicking her braids. Her gaze wanders over her paper and about the classroom with an abstract, dreamy look. Jimmy has created his own hockey arena with select crumbs of eraser and a pencil. The goal is now Meg's adjacent paper. She becomes a willing goalie. Andrea monitors the room. "Teacher, someone's at the door," she informs me, seconds after a visitor arrives.

I remind and redirect Andrea:

"Andrea, you need to finish the poem. If you are looking at the door, your eyes can't see the chart. Where will you keep your eyes? I want you to try to concentrate for the next ten minutes. Eyes staying on your own work. Think you can manage that? Show me."

I redirect Jimmy and Meg:

"I expect to see the poem finished. What do you need to do so you can accomplish that goal?"

I continue to reinforce and encourage the class:

"So many of you are working on your poems. I see fine concentration. I see lots of people keeping their minds on their work. The quiet voices help us work. I notice the way Carrie found something to do on her own when she finished her poem. I liked seeing people help each other recite. You look happy with your illustration, Carlos."

I have not abandoned my math group. When I see they are ready for a new activity, I demonstrate a simple attribute game these students already know. The objective of the game is to guess the general category that someone has in mind by asking if certain shapes belong to the set. "Pick a shape. If it's in my set, I will say 'yes.' If it's not in my set, I will say 'no.' After you have five 'yes' answers, see if you can name my set. Let's try a round." They are quick to catch on and soon generalize from the collection of small yellow, red, green, and blue circles (both thick and thin) that my set is small circles. The next set is a bit trickier and involves three attributes.

They go around the table, taking turns questioning and inventing new sets. I am able to monitor the activity of both the group and the class. I see that this group is able to categorize by three attributes and to identify categories. I see they are anxious to get their turns and need reminders to go in order. When I change the game and assign them partners for the activity, I find they are more focused as pairs than as a small group.

Most of the children outside the math group have sustained their work and conduct for the period, though a few had trouble, and concentration got more ragged near the end. At the close of the period, the math group talks about other ways to use the math materials for independent activity. We also go over clean-up, placing (not pitching) the objects in the container, checking the floor, and putting the bin back in its place on the shelf.

The bell rings again, signaling the end of the period. I again compliment the class on their independent work. I remind them that if they didn't finish their poems, they will have another chance after lunch. I ask everyone to think about what they have next on the schedule. I am satisfied that we have made progress in stage two during this class period, in both small group work and independent work. ❖

Working in small groups: "Self-Portraits"

I use stage two to establish both work and social habits: how to look up a word in a dictionary, make a straight line with a ruler, revise a first draft of a composition, and study with a partner. During this stage, my instructional objectives in reading groups, for example, concern *how* children choose a book to read and a time and place to read, rather than *what* they know about main ideas or digraph blends.

One project I introduce during stage two is "Self-Portraits." In this project, students record facts about themselves, events they were involved in, and their personal feelings. They will tell about siblings, pets, and middle names and describe likes and dislikes. They will narrate a summer experience or reveal interests and hobbies. And they will study their image in a mirror, carefully noting shapes of eyes, shades of hair color, contours of lips, and textures of skin. They will draw themselves. It's a project well suited for paradoxical groups: I often meet with a small group on their portrait work while the rest of the class is busy with their portraits or doing another task.

Self-Portraits calls on a variety of skills that students will use all year long. It involves composition, art, and research. To answer the questions that arise in their explorations of self, children learn to use a number of sources, from a phone book to a parent—"How do you spell Grandma's name?"—and learn to think about whether the answers they find make sense.

The project may be done by kindergartners through eighth graders and may be repeated year after year with minor adaptations. Seventh and eighth graders can produce a wonderful portfolio by using a detailed interview procedure and precise portrait drawings.

In the course of compiling their portraits, students discover the satisfaction of sharing work in progress as they read and compare results. "I hate getting stung by jellyfish," Anthony writes, reading aloud as he works.

"You got jellyfish stings?" Christopher asks. Anthony tells Christopher about his day at the beach with jellyfish. Later, he expands the sentence into an entire story, prompted by the interest of a friend.

"I hate spinach and throw up," a younger child notes, to a gleeful consensus that erupts around the table. An appreciative audience is a powerful motivation for work.

Some pages from an eight-year-old's self-portrait

Jessica shows others how she blended the pastels to get shades of color for her portrait. Justin helps others punch the holes to bind the sheets of paper. The proficient readers help the uncertain ones. The skillful artists demonstrate ways to etch the eyes. The good spellers supply a word or two. The quick workers may help the slower ones. The group works on working together, a primary objective of the project.

As always, I remind, reinforce, and redirect:

"I notice the way Anita is helping Joey read the directions."

"What a good way to make a mouth. Will you share this idea with the class?"

"Remind me, how do the guide words in the dictionary help us find a word?"

"If you're not sure what to do next, how can you find out? Show me."

"How is this conversation helping you with your work right now?"

"I notice the good listening I see when people are reading their stories to each other."

Along with the other objectives, I see something else from the self-portraits. I see my children. I find out who likes horses, who likes to invent, who loves to draw. I find out about big brothers and new babies and special grandparents. I discover the things that intrigue children, their particular fascinations and expertise. I notice the way they do things—who helps others, who is first to talk, who is in a hurry, and who takes their time—as well as what they do. I have much more to learn, but this foundation will help the building.

It is still important that the demands of the small group do not absorb the entire focus of the teacher. As I work with a group on their self-portraits, I continue to monitor the rest of the class. The class is still learning to plan, stay in their seats, keep their minds on their work, control their voices, and work cooperatively.

Everyone will complete a self-portrait book. The books will be read aloud, cherished in the class archives, and shared with families. Everyone will have learned, or started to learn, the ways I expect students to work in my class. And we will all have learned more about each other. We know about Marsha's operation, Gerald's motorcycle ride, and Danny's dislike of bees. We even know Tommy's middle name. ❖

Moving on from stage two

BEFORE I CAN CONCENTRATE ON TEACHING NEW SKILLS, concepts, and content during stage three, the class needs to be relatively proficient in the following skills:

1. Children work independently for structured periods of time. They should be able to:

   + Choose an appropriate task

   + Choose an appropriate workspace

   + Stay on task for most of the work period

   + Moderate voice and physical movement

2. Children work in pairs or small peer-directed groups (for example, playing an attribute game or rehearsing a poem together). They should be able to:

   + Choose an appropriate task

   + Choose an appropriate workspace

   + Stay on task (illustrating, not tickling, for example)

   + Moderate voice and physical movements

3. Children work in teacher-led groups. They should be able to:

   + Come prepared and on time with necessary materials

   + Follow directions, written or spoken

   + Attend to group-given information

   + Cooperate with peers by sharing space, materials, and information

   + Cooperate with the teacher by listening, asking for help if needed, and participating in activities

STAGE THREE:
Independence and Responsibility

STAGE THREE LASTS THE REST OF THE YEAR and stresses independence and responsibility. The children are ready for content groups, which require undivided attention from a teacher and present new, challenging subject matter.

The goals for stage three are part of a continuous learning process. Depending on the nature of the classroom, you may expect students to be able to:

- Follow through with a plan for an entire work period

- Make an appropriate choice

- Demonstrate voice and body controls

- Solve a problem without the teacher

- Set up, care for, and clean up materials

- Be helpful and friendly when working with a partner, in a small group, or in the class as a whole

- Care for the rules of the classroom

When I am teaching decimals to a small math group, the rest of the class works independently. Some students are busy with a piece of writing. Some are busy with weekly assignments. A few work on an art project or play a game together. They are purposeful and engaged, using quiet voices; but if they forget—which they will—there are consequences (see Chapter 6).

Now that we are in stage three, I don't always stay in the back of the line or observe the progress of the children through the corridors. I no longer need to angle my chair and divide my attention as I sit with a group. Most of the time, the rest of the class is industrious and responsible, as most of the children have internalized their responsibilities. The words that remind, reinforce, and redirect, although never scarce, are more focused and particular.

If during the first six weeks we have patiently taught students how to manage, we can refer back to those basics at any time during the year. If children internalize the expectations established during stages one and two, we can generally rely on their behavior as they grow in knowledge, independence, and responsibility. (See Figure 2.5 for an overview of the stages, including some content and techniques discussed in this chapter and later in the book.)

FIGURE 2.5

General Stages of the School Year

Stage One: Whole-class learning (first six weeks)

Key goals and activities

+ Class members learn one another's names.

+ Children learn to listen, use kind language, ask questions, solve problems together, and have fun and enjoy jokes without teasing.

+ The class generates classroom rules and practices following them (see Chapters 3 and 4 for details).

+ The class holds a Morning Meeting every day.

+ Students learn the expectations for behavior during basic classroom routines, such as academic work times, meeting times, outdoor times, and trips to the bathroom.

+ Children learn activities, such as responding to the safety signal and circling up, that support basic classroom routines.

+ Students practice putting things away and making smooth transitions between activities.

+ The class does Guided Discoveries of materials (crayons, math manipulatives, etc.).

+ The teacher focuses on the three Rs—reinforcing, reminding, redirecting.

Criteria for moving on

+ The class gathers up quickly for meetings, story time, games, and work periods.

+ Children locate and replace materials in the room efficiently.

+ Students listen and make relevant comments at meetings.

+ Students stay with an activity for the expected period of time.

+ Children are successful at making simple choices.

Stage Two: Paradoxical groups (first six weeks)

Key goals and activities

✦ Students learn to work in small groups with the teacher, as well as independently away from the teacher.

✦ The class does Guided Discoveries of classroom areas (block area, computer center, etc.).

✦ Critical Contracts arc being created (see Chapter 5).

✦ The class discusses logical consequences for rule breaking (see Section II).

✦ Students learn how to use time-out (see Chapter 7).

Criteria for moving on

✦ When working without the teacher in small groups, in pairs, or alone, children choose appropriate tasks and workspaces, stay on task, and moderate their voice and movements.

✦ When working in groups with the teacher, children come prepared and on time, follow directions, pay attention, and cooperate with peers and the teacher.

Stage Three: Independence and responsibility (the rest of the year)

Key goals and activities

✦ Children continue to care for classroom rules and materials and to be helpful and friendly with each other.

✦ Critical Contracts are completed.

✦ Inappropriate behavior results in logical consequences.

✦ Children continue to practice making choices and work on following through with a plan for an entire work period.

✦ Students work on solving problems independently or through problem-solving class meetings (see Chapter 13).

SUMMARY

THE PROCESS OF CLASSROOM MANAGEMENT is based on the assumption that to feel safe, children need to be seen. Literally, we see children, observing how they do things, as well as what they do. But we also "see" more symbolically. During these first six weeks, we get to know new children and we get reacquainted with ones we already know. We show students that we see what they do by commenting on it in positive language. We give children the sense of security which comes from knowing that we see them as individuals and as a group. Then we work to "see everything," to extend this sense of security beyond our line of sight.

We articulate our expectations and make sure the children know and understand how to apply them. When children begin to internalize positive expectations, they are then free to learn in an atmosphere that fosters independence and responsibility.

I think of the year as divided into three stages. Stage one establishes expectations for whole-class routines and group cohesion—meetings, rules, circling up, "freeze," etc. Stage two focuses on small-group work ("paradoxical groups") and independent work away from the teacher. Stage three lasts the rest of the year and stresses independence and responsibility as children take on new, challenging subject matter.

Works Cited

KRIETE, ROXANN. 2002. *The Morning Meeting Book.* Expanded edition. Greenfield, MA: Northeast Foundation for Children.

RUDDICK, SARA. 1989. *Maternal Thinking: Toward a Politics of Peace.* Boston: Beacon Press.

WATSON, MARILYN. 1998. "The Child Development Project: Building Character by Building Community." *Action in Teacher Education: The Journal of the Association of Teacher Educators* (winter).

CHAPTER 3
Making the Rules with Children

Rules are what make the good things happen.

CHIP WOOD
The Importance of Child Development in Education

A LEARNING COMMUNITY REQUIRES RULES, and students at all grade levels are more invested in and respectful of rules they help construct. Collaborative rule-making can generate active cooperation, even when there is disagreement about a particular decision. Recently, I heard a sixth grade teacher challenged by a student about the classroom's rules. Fortified by years of teaching experience and a group rule-making process used earlier in the year, she responded with an assertiveness that was more than just studied optimism. "Well, Ruben, you helped to make these rules, so I guess you'll help us take care of them."

Creating rules *with* children is an important part of the work of the first six weeks of school. These rules help set the classroom tone for the year. They lead to greater growth if they are framed in the positive and are the result of a process which requires the true involvement of the class.

I know that classrooms are happier with a few rules that are honored than with many rules that are forgotten. I do not want rules to legislate every action. I want them to encourage reasoned thinking and discussion. I want rules that we like, not because they give license or permission, but because they help us construct and maintain a community that is orderly and safe. And I want rules that have meaningful applications to concrete behaviors—rules that require active participation, not passive submission.

Years ago I asked a group of teachers how they defined the word "rules." In their school, rules were always posted and consisted of lengthy lists of don'ts: "Don't push. Don't talk out. Don't run. DON'T…" Yet when these same teachers struggled to define their understanding of the concept of rules, they described positive guidelines rather than prohibitive laws.

Too often we think of rules as necessary evils, restraints which prevent our negative impulses from gaining the upper hand. I believe that rules can lead us in positive directions, serving as guideposts and guardrails as we move toward our goals and ideals. Rules help us strive toward social and ethical growth—they "make the good things happen."

Our rules should frame what we *do* want, and what we hope to achieve or become. We must, as teachers, envision our classrooms as places where children learn to be ethical beings—to act in ways that are fair, honest, and kind. When a student repeatedly shrugs a shoulder and says "I don't care," meaning "I won't" or "I haven't done it" or "So what if I fail," we as teachers must respond "We care and here's how we're going to help you."

This chapter begins with information and assumptions about the development of ethical and moral thinking in children and about their social understandings. Based on this knowledge and on teachers' experiences across the country, the chapter continues with some possibilities for making the rules with children.

FOUNDATIONS IN THEORY

*Social understanding and social responsibility are built on
children's desire to understand and feel effective in the social world,
to initiate and maintain connection with others, and to
reach out to those in distress. Researchers have found that
such basic components of social responsibility as empathy,
moral sensibilities, the understanding of social conventions,
and political awareness merge prior to the age of eight.*

SHELDON BERMAN
Children's Social Consciousness and the Development of Social Responsibility

Making rules with children takes into account what we know about their human development. Jean Piaget, Erik Erikson, Lawrence Kohlberg, and Carol Gilligan have conducted extensive studies on the development of ethical and moral thinking in children. (See the Recommended Resources list at the end of this book for works by these developmental psychologists.) They have observed children's capacity to resolve conflicts and abide by rules at different stages of growth. The following is a summary of my understanding of some of their basic ideas.

One underlying idea of the work of these developmental psychologists is that knowledge is actively constructed rather than passively received. Supplying children a list of rules does not guarantee that they understand or internalize them unless they are actively involved in applying the rules to their own experiences. Children learn by creating a construct of beliefs based on their own experiences as well as by internalizing the "correct" models that are presented to them. The constructs that children form are often wrong because children don't have enough experience to build accurate models. But by comparing their "wrong" ideas with the ideas of others—those of adults and peers—or by experiencing the inaccuracies, they progressively refine their conception of the world. When we allow children to encounter problems and to say what they think they can do about them, we help them acquire knowledge by refining their conceptions.

A second underlying principle of these psychologists' work is that children grow through predictable and progressive stages. These stages affect the way children think about rules and make decisions in situations of conflict. There are three basic stages, which can be roughly translated into age ranges. The first stage is most typical of the ages five through seven, the second stage is likely to include ages seven through eleven, while the third stage may begin anytime during adolescence and continue through adulthood. These stages also represent a progression of social and moral thinking.

Stage 1: Rules based on the power of adults

In the earliest stage, children see rules as based on the all-knowing power of adults. Compliance comes from the desire to please and gain approval from these adults, or from fear of punishments—"It's wrong to take things because my teacher gets mad and then I'll have to go to time-out."

Young children's thought is also characterized by their egocentric thinking and need for immediate gratification. Fear of punishment or wish for approval may mitigate their impulses. Still, rules are easily bent and twisted in the face of keen desires.

Leah, age five, wanted to go and pick berries, but knew that the rule was to ask permission first. Though a babysitter was in charge, her father was working at home and available if needed. Anticipating that her father would answer "no" if she asked whether she could pick the berries, yet knowing that the rule was to ask permission, Leah went instead to the garden, well out of her father's range of hearing, and directed her request to the occupants there, calling out, "Cabbages, can I pick berries?" Having followed the letter of the law, she then dutifully returned to the house, telling her babysitter that it was okay if she picked the berries.

Daniel, age two, was told over and over not to pull out the books from the bookshelves. He was found one day in a mountain of books, extracting one after the other, saying aloud, "No, NO, Daniel!" The words and deeds were still an unwed pair.

"Well, I want to…I need to…I felt like it…I just had to…" may begin the explanation of a lie, a grab, a push, a pocketful of objects belonging to others, or other misdeeds. The young child may solemnly tattle on a classmate or righteously cheat his way through a game, explaining, "It wasn't fair. He was winning and I didn't want him to."

The early years of school are marked by children's struggles to gain control over their bodies and to achieve a sense of autonomy while still earning the approval of their teachers and parents. Even at the height of testing limits, children yearn to be perceived as "good" in the eyes of the adult. A five-year-old wants to master the limits, then quickly wants to test the limits at six. A six-year-old's sense of adventure takes her into places she knows not to go. When teachers or parents confront children with their misbehavior, rule breaking, or loss of control, children may (according to Erikson) experience a sense of shame or guilt. When the confrontation is too harsh, there is a danger of stifling the growth of initiative and autonomy.

If, on the other hand, teachers or parents respond weakly or passively to children's misbehavior, the danger is that children will not develop an interest in restraint or ethical conduct. During early stages of development, I do not use harsh threats or instill fear when regulating children's behavior, but I make sure children's behavior does not escape regulation.

Stage 2: Rules based on social conventions

IN THE NEXT STAGE OF DEVELOPMENT, children see rules as based on social conventions rather than individual authority. Children become aware of the shared nature of norms and values that are necessary for the game or the group to work.

They struggle to make rules uniform and consistent, often at the expense of anything else.

Seeing rules as existing outside of adults, as part of society and its conventions, prompts children to consider factors besides the calculated risks or rewards of their most immediate intentions. Children at this stage have an interest in ethical matters, a concern for fairness and the well-being of others. However, they do not consistently or easily act on these concerns, especially if social claims tug them in another direction. But there is a growing capacity to travel both intellectually and morally—to see the legitimacy of a broader view that includes, but is not limited to, one's own needs. They are beginning to believe that rules are necessary for the game to work, for events to be fair, and for everyone to meet their obligations to the group.

If at five or six, children worry primarily that their teachers will dislike them if they are "bad," at eight or older, there is at least equal concern for peer approval and a fear of public exposure and embarrassment. But—and it is a big "but" for these children—there is an important second judgment. "Is the teacher fair? Are the rules fair? Do I get my say? Am I treated right?" While children are developing their own judgment, adults need to help them carry out their best intentions. At ten, Ricky announces that he doesn't like teachers who "let you get away with stuff," and Cameron says he likes that his teacher can "make" him do his work.

Stage 3: Rules based on ethical ideas

IN THE THIRD STAGE OF DEVELOPMENT, children may want to help their classmates, not just in order to earn stars or social status, but also out of a belief that it's best if people take care of each other.

This stage is marked by the movement toward autonomous thinking: the capacity to be governed by ethical ideas rather than by social approval and disapproval. During the growth of autonomy, especially through the critical periods of adolescence, children need opportunities to make choices on the basis of principled thinking rather than in submission to the authority of adults or the pull of peers.

I think of a sixth grade boy from a tough Washington, DC, neighborhood who gave up his chair in order to resolve a conflict. When asked if he felt okay about that, he announced with great pride, "I be makin' the peace."

We need to keep in mind that a critical factor for adolescents is an ethical sense of self, the desire to see themselves as effective and able to make a difference, and to be seen by others as "good people." Education professor Chris Stevenson points out that middle school students are dedicated advocates for idealistic and social causes and show concern for injustices and inequities (Stevenson 1998). They are readily engaged in curricula that study child labor history, the holocaust, slavery, and racism, as well as projects such as peer mediation and environmental protection.

Even at the age of thirteen, children are apt to "think globally, but still can't often act locally; i.e., [they are] often mean to each other," as Chip Wood puts it (Wood 1997, 157). I recall a group of eighth grade students from a recent class who gave generously to others in the community, visiting nursing homes, helping out in animal shelters, and volunteering in the school. Yet they flaunted exclusive concert dates and sleepovers so that those not invited were publicly hurt. When I spoke to them about disregarding the feelings of those left out, they retorted, "It's our social life! You can't tell us what to do with that!"

Giving children the opportunity to grow

WE STUDY DEVELOPMENTAL THEORY so that we understand children's behavior, and so that our expectations of them are reasonable and informed by what is appropriate for their age. We do not want our study to limit our vision of children's capacities or the experiences we offer them.

We are learning that children have the capacity to care about others and to act in socially empathic and responsible ways at an age much younger than earlier theory indicated. Sheldon Berman cites research showing signs of growing social consciousness from a very early age. Two-year-olds can respond to the distress signals of other children with empathy, and between three and five, children will begin to "empathize with another's life condition" (Berman 1997, 23). These responses may be motivated in part by the children's desire to please an adult they care about—teacher, parent, or caregiver—but they are also pleasing themselves.

We can call upon and enhance children's ability to feel and respond to another's emotions by providing opportunities for them to exercise this ability, and by offering recognition when they do show empathy for others. All growth, after all, reflects a combination of a child's inherent biology and external experiences. Whether and how quickly a child moves through the stages of development—from considering only his/her own needs to considering the needs of others, and then to deciding matters of right and wrong apart from external sanctions—partially depends on the child's opportunities for growth.

Opportunities that help children feel effective as caretakers and responsible citizens include peer tutoring, community service, and class meetings to plan, discuss, or resolve relevant classroom matters. In one public school, sixth graders are paired

with kindergartners or first graders as "Book Club Buddies." The older students have the responsibility to read to, listen to, and select books of interest for their younger charges. They learn to be patient, to encourage, to initiate. The younger children learn to show appreciation and give thanks. I remember an eighth grader coming back into the classroom with a big smile, showing off a drawing made specially for her by her buddy, a card with big hearts and a smiling figure stretched across green construction paper.

Carol Gilligan, in her book *In a Different Voice*, focused on the development of moral thinking in women. She identified two different ways in which people characteristically think about moral conflicts. One she called "the ethic of justice" and the other "the ethic of care." In the ethic of justice, thinking focuses on issues of equality and reciprocity; the main concern is that everyone gets a fair share. In the ethic of care, concerns center on the need for connections with people, on not leaving out, abandoning, or hurting others; critical values involve obligations to relationships and showing care for others. Gilligan found that these two approaches or "voices" are frequently identified by gender. Boys have a greater concern for issues of justice, girls for issues of response and connection (Gilligan 1983).

From an educational viewpoint, the ideal would be to encourage both an ethic of care and an ethic of justice in all students: to provide opportunities for girls, for example, to examine the merits of a situation, regardless of whether a best friend is involved; and for boys to face up to questions of attachment and caretaking.

COLLABORATIVE
RULE-MAKING WITH CHILDREN

THERE IS NO SINGLE RIGHT WAY TO GENERATE RULES WITH CHILDREN. I have used various processes successfully over the years and have seen many different approaches work in classrooms I've visited. If the result is a set of rules that the children and teacher feel are theirs, and if the climate resulting from application of these rules is one of respect, safety, achievement, and fun, then the process has been successful.

The process may be as simple as the teacher suggesting rules that the children amend or put into their own words. Or it may be fairly elaborate, with the children taking much of the responsibility for creating the rules. Teachers must consider their particular class and setting when choosing how they will establish rules. Sometimes, when students have used the same process several years in a row, variation can keep the approach fresh and the content genuine. No matter what the specifics of the process, the following common elements are key:

1. The teacher launches the process with a broad vision, a statement of the kind of learning community the rules must help create.

2. The process involves conversation in which children have a voice, identify their own hopes and dreams for school, and explore the purpose and meaning of rules. Children discuss how suggested rules would influence behavior.

3. The rules are positively stated and few in number.

4. Once agreed upon, the rules are posted and referred to often as the basis for actions in the classroom.

The next sections describe one process in depth and several others in less detail. Many of the types of classroom discussions and steps used in the first process—developing rules out of the class's hopes and dreams—are used in the other processes as well, so I have not repeated mention of them in the later sections.

Rules grow from our hopes and dreams

One approach to making rules begins with the hopes and dreams of students and teachers:

My hope is that you will all be a friend and have a friend this year.

—KINDERGARTEN TEACHER

My hope is that you will each learn to love something you do in school and be proud of an accomplishment this year.

—SIXTH GRADE TEACHER

My hope for this year is to be a good speller and not go to time-out.

—SEAN, AGE SEVEN

My dream for this year is for everyone to feel that they belong and fit in to our classroom.

—MARIA, AGE THIRTEEN

THE "HOPES AND DREAMS" APPROACH makes a clear connection between the achievement of group and individual goals and the positive behaviors described in a communal set of rules. I have seen it used very effectively by teachers in grades K–8 in classrooms with all sorts of demographics.

The teacher states her/his hopes and expectations

Making the rules begins with the hopes and dreams of the teacher, or a vision statement for the class that year. With this statement, we establish a positive view for the year to come and name core expectations we hope are promoted and nourished in the classroom. Depending on the group, a teacher may describe only the most general and generous hopes for a classroom community, or define more concrete, specific actions and attitudes s/he knows are critical for the group to make progress and work together that year. It often helps teachers to begin the process by asking themselves:

- ✦ How do I want my classroom to function together as a community?
- ✦ What social and academic learning tasks do I envision for students this year?
- ✦ How do I want to stretch this group's learning the most?

Answers might include resolving conflicts with words (for a group that is highly volatile); becoming independent workers (for a group that characteristically works only when under scrutiny); or working with a variety of peers, not just best buddies (for a group that tends towards cliques and exclusion).

Following, in addition to the ones above, are some examples of teachers' visions at the beginning of a year:

*My hope is that each of you will be the asker of good questions
and the discoverer of good ideas.*

—THIRD GRADE TEACHER

*My hope is that you will learn to take good care of yourselves,
each other, and your school this year.*

—FOURTH GRADE TEACHER

*My hope is that this class will be inclusive, have honest discussions,
do beautiful work, and take care of the things in the classroom.*

—SEVENTH-EIGHTH GRADE TEACHER

After establishing her/his hopes and dreams, the teacher translates them into more concrete behavioral expectations which children can understand. These expectations connect our hopeful visions to realistic classroom goals. Teachers can define their particular expectations by asking themselves more questions:

- ✦ If our hope is to be a community where people respect themselves, each other, and their environment, what are a few important things we must do this year in order to accomplish that vision?

- ✦ If our vision is that our class be more independent, what will make it possible for this class to be more independent?

We can then say to students, for example, "I hope that you will become more independent workers. I hope you will be able to say to yourselves, your teachers, and your parents that you are going to do your work at a certain time, and then get it done without anyone nagging."

See Figure 3.1 for a list of some common teacher expectations.

....

FIGURE 3.1

Some Common Teacher Expectations

Although expectations are by nature unique and reflective of the wide range of students, classrooms, schools, and communities, the following are some basic behaviors commonly expected in morally, socially, and intellectually responsible communities. Examples of possible teacher explanations are in italics.

+ **Listening to others**—Students will listen to their teachers and classmates. Teachers will listen to their colleagues and students. *My hope is that you will learn to respect yourself and each other this year. One way to respect each other is to be active listeners. That means to me that when others are talking, you will listen carefully and be able to ask good questions and make real comments.*

+ **Speaking to others using a respectful tone of voice**—Teachers and students will talk to each other with respect, ask questions, and share information even when angry or upset. *My hope is that we will have a classroom where people feel comfortable saying they don't understand something, asking for help when needed, and even telling someone that they are angry in a respectful voice.*

+ **Showing basic respect and friendliness**—We will be friendly to one another even if we are not all friends. This includes welcoming and showing interest in one another, and getting to know one another through sharing and cooperative work and play. *My hope is that we will be a classroom where everyone feels included. One hope I have is that you will invite new people to sit with you, and you will work with different people, not just the same people every day.*

+ **Having positive work attitudes**—We will concentrate and persist even on difficult tasks. *My hope is that you will become good workers this year. That means that you will do beautiful completed work, and the work process may include drafts, revisions, and careful proofreading.*

+ **Resolving conflicts**—We will work to resolve conflicts with fairness and active listening, and without recourse to violence. *My hope is that when we have a disagreement, we work through it peacefully. That means using words, not fighting. It means listening carefully to what each person feels and wants, and thinking of a way to solve the problem that everyone is okay with.*

+ **Relating to others without bullying**—We will treat others with respect at all times, even when things are not going the way we want. *My hope is that no one will use mean words or do mean things to others in our school, even when we're frustrated or angry.*

The teacher communicates both vision and expectations to students

"My hope is that school will be a place you want to be and that you will be able to do important work," I might begin, offering the class a welcoming statement early on the first day of school. My statement sets a tone that is positive and encourages participation in school. It is also intended to prompt my students to think about their hopes for the year.

"What do you think I mean by 'want to come to school'? What makes kids want to come to school? What do I mean by 'important work'?" On a chart I may list reasons that children want to come to school. I list their ideas about "important work." I want to get across these constructs of school as a "want" and a place for "important work."

As the week progresses, students will begin to generate their hopes for the year. "My hope is… What is your hope?" we ask our students in this second phase of generating hopes and dreams.

Depending on the class and the students, this part of the process may involve considerable teacher modeling and guidance. The teacher may have the class brainstorm possible hopes. She may also suggest some, so that students have patterns of language to express the concept. The result may be a simple sentence or picture or a complex vision with multiple parts.

When students extend their thoughts to explain the reason for their hope, they tend to move from the more general to the concrete, thus adding clarity and focus. "My hope is to be a better writer because I like to write stories and my grandma says they are good but she can't read all my words," wrote Frederick, age eight. We see his yearning for the competency that comes with gaining many kinds of skills. We can also see the strength of his desire to communicate and to reach a favored audience, his grandma.

Generating hopes with young children

It is not always easy for children to understand the question "What are your hopes and dreams for the year?" With young children the language of "hope" may be glued to getting presents or an out-of-school treat, and dreams mean you are fast asleep. Young children may need some patterns and language to draw on; they may need help distinguishing between in-school and out-of-school activities. Sometimes they haven't been in school long enough to have a repertoire of choices. One teacher I know has her K–1 students revisit their hopes and dreams in mid-year, which often results in children making specific, powerful revisions to their earlier statements.

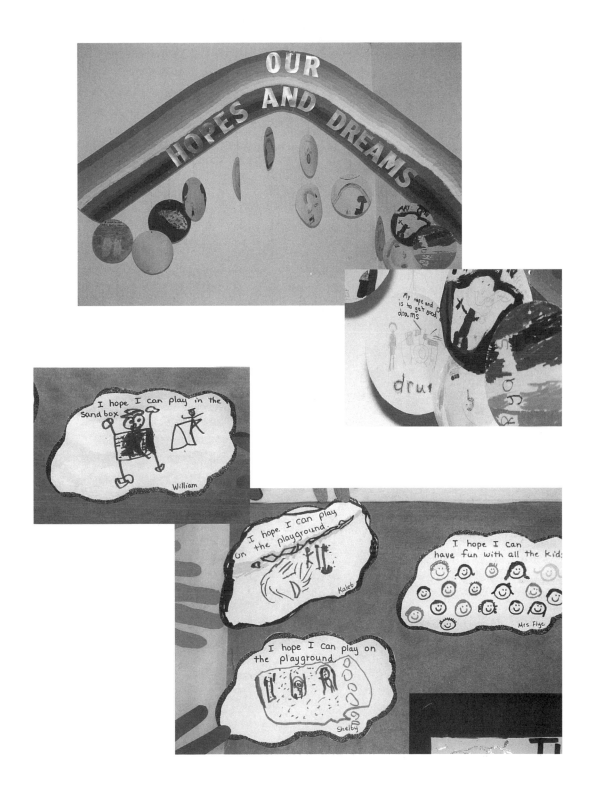

Teachers of young children often ask students to draw their hopes after they have gotten acquainted (or reacquainted) with areas of the classroom. Deborah Porter has her K–1's start with a picture of something they love to do in school. Jo makes a skyscraper and writes, "I love blocks." Marissa draws herself and her friends on swings. Big smiles and hearts fill the background. These favorite activities are recorded on a chart titled "What we like to do in school and why": "Jo loves to build with blocks because she likes to make things tall. Marissa loves swinging with her friends because they have fun."

During another meeting time, Ms. Porter asks her class to think about some things they do in school now or remember from last year that they don't like as well. "Are there any ideas?" Sarah says she gets stomachaches when she has to do lots of writing. Ben says he hates the time-out chair "'cause all you do is sit and sit. You get tired sitting." He adds, "and your body hurts." The class talks about how sometimes things are hard in school and sometimes they are even scary, particularly when they are new.

The children draw a picture of something that they don't like to do in school, or something that is hard or a little scary. Again, their drawings are shared and their dictations are recorded on a big chart. Finally, Ms. Porter asks each of them to think of a "hope and dream" for this year. Jo "wants to build the highest skyscraper ever and use all the blocks." Marissa hopes for "two best friends," and Ben hopes to be the "fastest runner" and "not go to the time-out chair." The pages—drawings of a favorite and not favorite thing in school and a dictated "hope and dream"—are collected and put together to form a personal "My Hopes and Dreams Book." These books are read and reread by each child throughout the year.

Creating Hopes and Dreams with Kindergartners

KERRIN FLANAGAN
Public school teacher, Boston, Massachusetts

I did a number of things with Hopes and Dreams last year in kindergarten. I started by having the children look around the room to see what they noticed. I asked them what kinds of things they thought we'd do in kindergarten; play and paint were at the top of the list. I added some of my own ideas, then asked the children to think about what they hoped to learn and do in kindergarten. They were able to focus much more on the "do" than the "learn," which was as expected for their age. They shared their hopes and dreams in the large group, after which I wrote their sentences on chart paper and had them draw themselves doing the things that they hoped to do. I told them to draw what it would look like if their hopes came true. I know a prekindergarten teacher who took photographs of her children "doing their hopes"—playing at the water table, doing a puzzle, climbing on the climber. For children who are not drawing representationally, a photograph works well.

My kindergartners' hopes were as varied as they come. Stephen hoped to ride the school bus; Lillian hoped to read; Shavar hoped to play outside; Tiffany hoped to draw; Joshua hoped to learn to run faster; Gryphon hoped to go on a hiking trip and see a turtle; Shannon hoped to learn to smell all the flowers; Christian hoped to paint; Ryan hoped to play with blocks; Joshua hoped to learn to sit down and listen to the teacher. Each of them brought different expectations about what this first year of school held for them. I mounted their pictures, printed their hopes on the computer as captions, and hung these works of art from a clothesline in our room.

I decided to repeat the whole process in January, after we returned from winter break. I knew that with a few months of experience in school, the children would likely have some different wishes for themselves. Their second hopes, which I called their "hopes for the rest of kindergarten," were decidedly more about learning: "I want to learn to read." "I want to learn how to write my numbers." "I want to learn how to spell many words." Hopes were also about caring: "I hope to help my friends." I think it was valuable for the children to revisit their hopes later in kindergarten when they had more shared knowledge of what school was about and more of a chance to think about what they had left to do in our community.

....

Generating hopes with older children

Older students, familiar with school and with the concept of Hopes and Dreams, may still struggle to generate hopes. When they are ten or eleven, students may resist investment, prepared only to slither through another term. Sometimes, with older children, we ask them to respond to three questions:

✦ What was something you accomplished and felt proud of last year?

✦ What was something you found difficult or didn't work well for you?

✦ What do you think is most important for you to work on this year?

During the first six weeks of school, students will revise their most important goal, adding an explanation of how they hope to work on it and what help they think they may need. (If Critical Contracts are used as well, this statement may be a foundation for the student's goal for the year. See Chapter 5 for more information.) Eventually, these goals are shared with the class as part of the rule-making process: What rules will we need in order for all of us to make progress toward our goals?

I often see older children referring to their hopes and goals all year long. In Island Falls, Maine, I was struck by Louann Richie's fourth grade bulletin board of student hopes, beautifully illustrated and prominent even in April. Six students working on a social studies project at a table adjacent to this bulletin board still referred to it.

Some eighth graders' Hopes and Dreams for the year

As one filled in the last touches on his assignment, he uttered to his neighbor, "I had trouble getting my work done once, but now it's no problem." Both boys cast their eyes over to his Hopes and Dreams illustration, which said "I hope I can get my work done on time." In the same school, a huge tapestry of stars stood in the corridor announcing the Hopes and Dreams of the seventh graders for all to see and read.

Sometimes issues other than age make it difficult for students to think of school as a place where individual hopes are kindled and nurtured. Not all children have hopes that are related to their school life. They answer "nothing" or "I dunno" to questions about hopes and dreams, and they may see school as obligatory, with little in it for them.

Psychologist Janie Victoria Ward points out that students who have suffered the effects of the racism deeply ingrained in our society often develop an attitude of complacency as a kind of resistance. She states that adults must acknowledge the issues involved in racism (particularly at the middle school level) while helping students find productive—not anti-education—strategies to deal with it (Ward 2000).

Kelly

Kelly comes into her eighth grade year with a very short reach. "I don't care," she says, avoiding all semblance of working on her goal statement. "I only come to school to be with my friends, and I know you don't want me to write that," she utters with a glare and a dark look. "Stay back," she seems to be saying to me. "Don't bother, don't push, don't expect more." But I must and I do, while recognizing that her prominent social agenda is natural for a thirteen-year-old.

I can accept her social needs, but I also want her to see how her keen social intelligence has value, even in an academic setting. I believe she can find connections with others through learning together, through sharing not only what to wear to the teen center next weekend but also what to make for a history poster, how to prepare for a mock trial presentation, or how students might form lunch partner groupings.

After a deep breath, I say to her, "I know you love to be with your friends. I think you're telling me that you're not excited about schoolwork this year. I hope you find at least one exciting project this year— maybe the drama workshops, since you like to act and you're good at it. That's my goal for you." I walk away deciding not to notice whether her glare recedes or gets worse. I know that her hopes are tangled up with her struggles. I hope to help Kelly see herself as a student and a friend. ❖

Moving from Hopes and Dreams to rules

If we want our classroom to be a place where we can do our best to achieve the hopes and dreams we have named with such care, what rules do we need? What rules will govern and reinforce our best intentions, our hopes for self and others? Note that this is a question, a real question that invites thought and participation. As teachers, we know some of the rules that might be necessary, but not all. And we do not know the issues foremost on the children's minds, or what words give these issues meaning and image. We are asking and not telling because we know that constructing rules together creates more ownership and acceptance. In the process, students learn and practice critical social skills and ethical thinking.

There are a number of steps that take us from a list of many rules, sometimes phrased in the negative (such as "no running in the halls"), to a final written class document containing a few well-chosen general rules phrased in the positive (such as "We will move safely in the halls and in the classroom."). This work will take place over several group sessions. Shorter, more focused lessons result in greater interest and more serious work than one marathon session. By breaking up the process into short, focused chunks that take place over many days, we give students time to reflect, to explain, to bat ideas around, and to revise. In doing so, we invite real participation.

The first step may be to brainstorm rules we believe will help us achieve the hopes we have named. Or sometimes I begin by asking students to think about rules they know and like from other years. I soon have a chart of many, many rules written in their words. "We listen to each other and the teacher, we clean up our stuff, we don't interrupt, we don't tease, we say 'sorry' if we knock someone down, we include everyone in a game, we are friendly… "

After this brainstorming, I ask students, "What is your most important rule to make our classroom a place where all of us can learn and work toward our hopes and dreams? And why?" The language used with younger children is simpler: "What is one rule you think is most important for you to feel safe and good in your class this year?" I ask this question in order to urge individual thinking and give greater significance to the list.

I give everyone time to think and put his/her ideas into words. Teachers often have younger students draw or dictate, if writing is not yet an option for everyone in the class. Often, with older students, this part of the process becomes a writing exercise, with students going off for fifteen minutes or more to write. Sometimes I extend the question: "What is your most important rule, and what do you think is the most important rule for the class?" Interestingly, the two rules are not always the same.

Rules

Do not push.
Do not hit anybody.
Do not hit anybody with puzzles.
No saying bad words.
No fighting over toys.
Don't kick.
Don't punch anyone in the face (eye).
Don't throw toys.
Don't snatch toys.
Don't break toys.
Listen to the teacher.
Don't scream.
Don't break crayons.
Don't slam toys.
Don't ~~~~ s of books.
~~~~ door.
~~~~
~~~~ le's feet, hands, fingers, toys.
~~~~ throom without permission.
~~~~ ush the toilet.
~~~~ ithout a grown-up.
~~~~ talking.

Rules – What to Do

Be nice to the class.
Be happy.
Ask in a nice way for crayons.
Use nice words.
Listen to the teacher.
Talk nicely.
Share toys.
Clean up.
Listen nicely.
Say "Good Morning."
Stop and freeze at the bell.
Be friendly.

Our Classroom Rules

Be nice to everyone.
Clean up.
Use nice words.

Asked to help generate classroom rules, this group of kindergartners— as is typical of all classes—first named a long list of "don'ts." With their teacher's help, they turned these statements of what *not* to do into statements of what *to* do, which they then consolidated into three general easy-to-remember rules, shown in the last poster.

Students next bring their most important rules back to the circle, and the teacher lists them on a chart. Sometimes individual responses lead to lively group discussions. Michael, age twelve, wrote that the most important rule for him was "More work, less talk." He continued, "I get distracted and then my work isn't done when I talk too much and then I miss choice times and have so much homework." Because he has difficulty getting work done when others are talking, he proposed the rule for the class that work times are silent. "What does that mean?" I asked. "Don't you like to talk and work at the same time?" This led to a good class discussion about conflicting views of concentration and quiet. Michael and the class ended up qualifying the rule to include individual responsibility when distraction occurs and not just a blanket rule of silence.

When all the "important rules" are charted, we move on to the next step. With younger students, or students new to this process, we work on going from the don'ts to the do's. Children often think in terms of "no's":

+ "No grabbing."

+ "No taking stuff."

+ "No talking when the teacher is talking."

+ "No saying bad words and saying kids are fat and ugly."

No's have their purpose. They put in place boundaries and limits that protect children from many dangerous impulses. It is critical that children know that their teachers want to keep them safe, and thus some of our underlying rules are non-negotiable, reactive, and prohibitive: no weapons, no threats, no hitting, no leaving school without permission.

But each class must also establish rules which are proactive, learning tools that give guidance about what is expected and what we do to make our classroom safe. To move from reactive to proactive rules, a teacher might ask the following questions:

+ "If we don't call people fat and ugly, what do we do?"

+ "If we don't grab, what do we do?"

Especially with younger children, this is a critical step and an important teaching time. They see a negative incident or interaction precisely, but they don't see or visualize the positive behaviors as clearly. While most children know the word "nice" or "friend," a vocabulary for positive behaviors and interactions is often very limited. We often need to help children develop the words along with the expectations. We start by naming and demonstrating what we do instead of grabbing, pushing, running, hitting, or name-calling. From these specifics, we also build up general expectations about using words, taking helpful and cooperative actions, taking turns, and sharing feelings, objects, and even good ideas!

"No running in the room"

A discussion might progress through the following questions:

+ "Who can tell me why 'no running' is an important rule in our classroom?"

+ "Are there some places where it is safe to run?"

+ "Who can show me a safe way to get paper or crayons in our room, so that we won't bump ourselves or someone else?"

+ "What shall we call what Megan just showed us?"

+ "So if we don't run, we will use our 'Careful Walk.' Is that a good rule?"

"No calling names or teasing"

Teasing is a given in schools. "No teasing" is also often the most important rule that students and teachers cite. If we don't tease, then what do we do?

Any rules we create about teasing need to be discussed if they are to be useful. Teasing can include many things. Children may, through teasing, be expressing humor, anger, or power. They may be doing instant replays of their favorite television shows, which may constantly model mockery, "dissing," put-downs, and confrontational language. In the classroom and in the larger world, the line between insult and joke is very slim. The tone of voice that distinguishes "I was just fooling" from intentional cruelty is also subtle and easily blurred.

Two children sit side-by-side drawing and giggling with pleasure as they utter silly words. "My picture is a boogie nose man!" Squeals of rapturous delight. "Mine is a doody head!" More laughter. But suddenly, without transition, the play on body parts turns and hits a nerve. "Your nose looks like a... " The joking quickly escalates until a picture is scribbled on, a paper torn. Teasing becomes taunting, and the response "I was just joking" is both true and yet not true.

"It was only a joke" offers opportunities for fruitful discussion. Maybe it was a joke to the utterer of the comment, but not to the receiver. What is hurtful and what is funny takes constant sorting out. Doing this sorting can help children of all ages develop perspective and empathy. "If we don't tease, what do we do?" In some cases, children readily come up with many responses:

+ "We say nice things."

+ "We have fun and say things that we agree are funny."

+ "It has to be funny for both people."

+ "We use friendly words."

In other cases, children need teachers to suggest words like "friendly," "put-ups," "compliments," and "kind words" to help them formulate and articulate ideas.

I have seen different classes come up with different ways of finally stating a "no teasing" rule that is unique to their group:

- ✦ "Use friendly words, and no teasing unless everyone agrees it is a real joke."

- ✦ "No teasing about things that people can't change, like appearance or family."

- ✦ "No teasing, and if someone says stop, you should stop, and the person who says stop should mean it."

- ✦ "Everyone makes mistakes. Don't laugh at other people's mistakes."

- ✦ "No teasing, and care about other people's feelings."

As stated earlier, sometimes teasing is related to anger. Therefore our efforts to curb teasing will also require teaching other strategies for conflict resolution. "If we are not going to tease when we are angry with someone, what will we do?" We want to encourage children to be assertive and use a strong voice. We want them to learn to use their strengths in ways that are respectful and also responsible. "If someone makes you angry, what can you do that shows respect for them and for you?" we might ask.

"Say I don't like it."

"If someone picks on you, tell them to stop, and if they don't, tell the teacher."

"Say it makes you mad when they tell a secret and you are right there."

Most children see retaliation as a show of strength. Any appearance of backing away may be seen as a sign of weakness. Many mediation and conflict resolution programs help work on these hard issues. (See Appendix B for more on conflict resolution in elementary school.)

When a student intern returned to work in the school that she had found so hurtful as a child, she said, "There is still teasing here, but at least the teachers pay attention." Our rules help us pay attention.

"No interrupting"

This rule affects how children take care of themselves and others in a group. An essential task of not interrupting is listening to others and attending to what they have to say. For young children, the impulse to shout out or the inability to wait one more second to say something is an attribute of their development.

But children—even young children—can and do learn to raise hands, to listen, and to "hold their good ideas in their head" until it is their turn. I even see groups that learn to keep their hands down until someone has finished their sharing. Then, hands go up. Expecting children to keep their hands down or to hold their comments supports active listening, an essential behavior if students are going to learn from each other and work together effectively. Children who do not listen to each other make mincemeat of cooperative projects and function poorly in peer-led small-group tasks.

If we don't interrupt, we:

+ "Wait."

+ "Raise our hands."

+ "Listen and think about what someone is saying."

+ "Look at the person who is speaking."

+ "Care about what the person is saying."

Combining and generalizing rules

Having rules which are positively phrased is important; so is having a list short enough that it can be remembered and used. More than five or six rules are easily forgotten—even by the teachers!

Students bring their most important rules to the circle, and the teacher writes each rule on the chart. Some of these rules are duplications. Others are only slightly different from one another. The task now is to combine the rules and generalize them. This process involves a discussion, which may include asking students the following questions:

+ "Let's read all the rules we now have. Are some of them similar?"

+ "What rules are about being safe, about taking care of ourselves... ?" (Teachers help children to see some of the sets or categories.)

+ "Do some of these rules fit together?" (Teachers show students how to link ideas and sentences.)

+ "Is there a word that covers all the rules we underlined with red?"

Most rules will fall into the three broad categories of respect and care for one-self, respect and care for each other, and respect and care for the school. (See Figure 3.2.) However, these three need not be—and often are not—the exact rules every class ends up with. It is a matter of teacher choice and judgment as to how broad or how specific to make the final few class rules.

I often ask older students, particularly those who have used this process for years, to write an important rule—"one that will really make the classroom a place you want to be"—on a small piece of paper from an adhesive pad. I tell them not to include their names. Allowing anonymity while assuring that all thoughts will be considered motivates genuine responses. Then all the individual notes are posted on large chart paper. Together we note and synthesize duplicates. We note categories and sort again. The final list is succinct and powerful.

Once there is a short list, there may be a "thumbs-up" procedure as each rule is considered. Can we live with this rule? Does it work for us? Final rules represent the class consensus of rules we agree to live with.

....

FIGURE 3.2

Our "Most Important" Rules

The following is a list of typical individual "most important" rules from a sixth and seventh grade classroom. The items are categorized according to whether they pertain to care and respect for self, for others, or for the environment. Later, they would be combined and synthesized into a final list of just a few broadly encompassing rules.

Respect and care for self

+ Do our best work.

+ Use the "I voice" when in a conflict.

+ Listen to others.

+ Ask for help when needed.

+ Participate honestly and with good effort.

Respect and care for others

+ Be friendly, even if people aren't your best friends.

+ Don't pass on secrets or gossip if you think it's going to hurt someone's feelings.

+ Work quietly and don't distract others.

+ Ask first and take things from backpacks only if you have permission.

+ Include anyone who wants to play in four-square and other games.

+ Play fairly.

Respect and care for the school

✦ Put things back where they came from.

✦ Do your clean-up job right.

✦ Pick up things that get left outside.

✦ Think of ways to make the room beautiful.

....

Regardless of the exact procedure for arriving at a final short list of rules, the important thing is that the rules are clear and can guide behavior. If, in the process of grouping and synthesizing, the rules are transformed into very general statements, children need to translate the statements into the language and detail of their classroom life. "Respect," for example, is a common word in students' general rules about caring for self, others, and their environment. But concepts like respect need to be "unpacked" and applied through class discussions to realistic situations with recognizable details.

Younger children need these discussions to help define the words; older children need them to make the words more than automatic, "please-the-teacher" responses. A seventh grader elaborated, "Respect means that when you invite someone to join a group, you really talk to them." A classmate contributed, "If you need a pencil, you don't just grab it from someone's backpack. You ask if you can use it." These specifics flesh out sincere, seventh-grade respect.

"Couldn't we just have eight?"

In a classroom in Maine, groups of fourth graders are clustered at tables, their attention focused on charts of the long lists of rules the class has generated. They are trying to figure out how to winnow twenty-six rules into not more than six, and their conversation is lively. At one table, there is a discussion about whether there needs to be a rule about "not interrupting" if "listening" is already a rule. Another group wants to eliminate rules that have to do with dress codes. "Whether we wear hats indoors or tie our sneakers is like a personal thing," someone says. "Besides," someone else adds, "we have a rule that says we should be prepared for school. That's like the same thing, isn't it?" At the third table, the students silently draw lines and arrows, as they saw their teacher doing, to show the rules they would combine or even eliminate.

After thirty minutes, the teacher stops the groups and asks them to bring their charts back to the whole group. They will share their suggestions and see how close they have come to the six rules. As they continue their work, they ask, "Couldn't we just have eight? That's close!" ❖

Posting the rules

To use the rules they've generated and refer to them as they go about classroom life throughout the year, children need to see the rules posted and know that teachers see them. The rules should be posted with pride. I suggest the following:

1. Have students copy and illustrate the rules in ways that are appropriate for their age. First graders may illustrate their favorite rule and add their own interpretation. Fifth graders may copy in their best cursive.

2. Send copies of the rules home for parents to read over with their children. Ask parents to add their own comments and sign the rules.

3. Write, or have students write, the final rules on a poster-sized chart or oak tag. Have all class members sign the poster, making sure their names are clearly visible and readable.

4. Post the rules in a central place in the room. Refer to them often, perhaps reading them together each morning during the early weeks of school.

Some other approaches to making the rules

THE NEXT SECTIONS describe some variations in rule-making procedures. Sometimes teachers simply begin by presenting a very broad, general guideline—one that, if followed, will let children achieve their goals.

Beginning with the Golden Rule

As you go through the life cycle, every stage of life has to add something to the possibility of being able to obey the Golden Rule.

ERIK ERIKSON
Interview, Boston Globe Magazine

For many years when I taught at Greenfield Center School, the Golden Rule provided a unifying school principle and was the starting point from which we generated classroom rules. I have seen this work well in many diverse school settings. The Golden Rule is so very simple, yet it can be applied to nearly every action of significance to children.

It's possible to begin by simply reciting the Golden Rule and discussing its meaning, but we ask parents to read a parable called "Horse" to their child before the first day of school (see Appendix A). It illustrates many faces of the Golden Rule as it tells how a big, strong horse, leader of the pack, is afraid to cross a bridge that the smaller creatures scamper across with ease. Finally, interdependence helps Horse to "cross his bridge."

We explain that the Golden Rule describes how we want to be with each other and how we want to be as a school. We have students state it in their own words. "The Golden Rule," Robby says, "means you gotta treat others as you want to be treated back." Ideas like this need to be anchored in particular actions and events for children to understand them, so we ask children to give examples of what it means and how to use this rule. Over time, we make up dramas and "what-if" plays:

- "What if I am trying to concentrate and you are talking to a friend, and I ask you to please be quiet? What might you say if you are using the Golden Rule?"

- "What if I accidentally bump into you? Do I say, 'Hey, watch out!'?"

- "What if I can't solve a math problem and it's hard for me, but it's easy for you? Do you say, 'You can't do that cinchy math?'"

- "What if you ask me to play, and I don't feel like it? What might I do?"

The Golden Rule is posted in the translated words of the students: "Do to others as you would have others do to you" or "Treat others as you would like others to treat you." Teachers may then construct, with children, the rules for particular areas of the program, such as Meeting Rules, Block Area Rules, and Computer Rules.

We invoke the Golden Rule to govern interactions all year long. When a group of nine- and ten-year-olds flees to the bathroom to "gossip," we invoke the Golden Rule. When there is a sudden problem with disappearing pens followed by casual accusations, we recall the rule. We remind students of the Golden Rule when Dolores is off by herself day after day, carelessly ignored by the rest of the class; when children are rude and disruptive with their lunch aide; when globs of paste or reams of paper are left for others to clean up.

Part of the strength of the Golden Rule is that it does not provide direct solutions to problems of missing pens or left-out children. Rather, it provides an ethical or moral reference point, a place to begin the search for different ways to act.

As we ask children to address problems themselves, we begin by asking questions. "What do you think it feels like to have your things taken?" "What do you think it feels like to not have anyone talk to you all through lunch?" "Is it right to pass the ball only to the best players? Or do you think everyone should have a chance?"

We desperately need to prepare children to examine questions of right and wrong for themselves and to see the consequences of their choices. Classroom life is rich in opportunities. Discussions come directly from the classroom, the playground, and the lunchroom, and children then have the chance to act on their choices. The Golden Rule can become a living standard, an operative rule in everyday life at school.

Rules for classroom workers

"We are all workers in school," I tell the children. "What are the most important rules we need to help us in our work?" Discussions follow, full of examples and applications, in similar fashion to the way the Golden Rule is introduced. We work on rules for our games and rules for our classroom. These rules can inspire mutual responsibility through the concept of school as a workplace. Rules are needed to help all class members accomplish their jobs. Here's an example of a set of class rules:

- ✦ "We are all workers in school."
- ✦ "We value our work and our workplace."
- ✦ "Good workers need to take care of their tools."
- ✦ "Good workers need to keep their worksite safe."
- ✦ "Good workers are helpful, friendly, and respectful of one another."
- ✦ "Good workers make mistakes."
- ✦ "Good workers don't laugh at their own or others' mistakes."

Note that these rules are stated in language that elicits strong, affirmative images—good workers, valued work and workplace, care and respect. The rules are general enough to be inclusive yet concrete enough to apply directly to experiences.

A third grade teacher, Debby Roth, described using this approach in her classroom journal:

We spent about two weeks discussing rules, writing down rules, revising our rules. The first day of school we discussed rules that the students remembered from previous years. I explained how we were going to write down our classroom rules for the year. For homework, the students had to write down one rule that they thought was important to have. We discussed positive and negative wording for rules. I modeled different ways of disciplining, using positive and negative wording. The students decided that they would rather have a list of positive rules to follow. The rule they brought in was to be a positive rule.

The next day, I shared with them my list of rules. The students shared with me their rules. I listed them on chart paper. We compared the two lists of rules to see if all of their rules were covered. We worked on this every day until everyone was comfortable with a final list of rules. It was a long process, but I feel it was a worthwhile one. I think the rules will have more meaning to students, since they were a part of them.

Rule-making tied to academic work

Teachers may also find interesting ways to make rules with children that are tied to academic work the children will be doing that year. Here are two examples.

A fifth-grade charter

One year I decided to construct a class "constitution" with a fifth grade class to initiate a unit on the American Revolution. With the aim of having everyone contributing to the content of the charter, the exercise quickly expanded into a valuable rule-making process.

"Tell me any rules you know," I began—although I might have gotten a truer response had I asked them to tell me all the rules they broke in a week's time! This was a class not known for its rule-abiding citizenry.

"You mean like no chewin' gum in school?" This from a boy whose cheek puffed with a wad of gum pocketed in one side.

"Yes. Like that."

"No running in the hallways."

"No fighting."

"Be nice."

I wrote down all the rules they said, which in the end numbered close to fifty. Most began with "no."

I copied the chart and gave everyone a copy at the next day's meeting. "Check the rules you like. Cross out the rules you don't like," were the instructions.

"Whattaya' mean?"

"Some of these rules you like. You might say to yourself, 'That's a good rule.' Some rules may seem silly or not important or even wrong. Cross those out or put an 'X' mark next to them."

"Most rules are dumb 'cause nobody can make you do stuff," Roger stated.

"You mean if you don't follow a rule, it's a bad rule?"

"Yeah."

"OK, but for now imagine what rules you might make yourself follow if you could boss yourself."

Roger nodded.

I decided to incorporate Roger's idea and suggested that we add a new notation. "If you like a rule, but think it's hard to follow, put a star beside it."

When I collected their papers, I was struck with the clear patterns. Rules that related to safety were "liked." Rules that had to do with personal styles (gum chewing, dress codes, swearing) were often crossed out. Rules that had to do with ethics and "rights of others" (stealing, fighting, cheating, name-calling) were good rules but qualified by the stars—hard to follow. I found it interesting that there were more stars or checks than cross-outs, even from this band of rule-shakers!

During several more meetings, we collected and collated responses. Students were excited about discovering the group reactions and regarding themselves as researchers.

After students reported the results and entered the information on a master list, I gave out a second worksheet with questions to help them begin to organize and classify the information.

+ What are the most popular rules?

+ What are the least popular rules?

+ What kinds of rules did people like/not like?

+ What kinds of rules had stars?

+ Which of these rules do you think would be the most important, if you could choose only one?

In the next day's discussion, children noted the popularity of categories that included ideas of safety, care, and fairness. Roger stayed with his enforcement concerns and divided rules according to how you might get caught. This raised issues of intrinsic moral conflicts as well as external sanctions. For example, what if you cheat and no one catches you? What if you fight outside of school?

The most vigorous discussion centered on question five, the one about the "most important rule." This was good, since the aim was to create our class charter by having everyone contribute a rule he/she agreed was important.

In order to avoid a long list of rules, I told students that they could combine or reword the rules from our charts. I then added one more thumbprint. I said that I didn't like rules that began with "no," and that

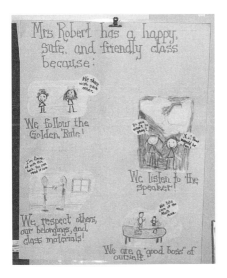

Examples of class rules that children generated with teachers' guidance. In some classes, children sign their names to show they agree with the rules and will try their best to live by them.

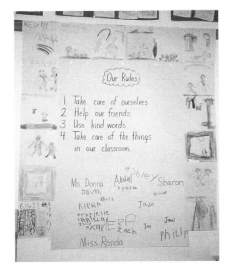

students needed to state their rules in a "yes." "If we don't run, what do we do? if we don't fight, what do we do?" We combined and honed, reworded and revised, until there were six rules:

1. We will treat each other fairly.

2. We will keep quiet when others are working.

3. We will help teachers or classmates when they ask for help.

4. We will walk in the halls and in the classroom.

5. We will try to solve disagreements by talking it over ourselves. If we can't, we will ask the teacher to help.

6. We will use only the things we need and put the tops back on stuff.

Not all of these rules worked. Some were vague, some narrow, and one used the word "fairly," which resulted in many discussions about its meaning. Yet it was a powerful beginning and instilled a sense of mutual responsibility. These students' interest in ethical issues was keen, even if there were moments when they clearly felt it was more to one's advantage to exploit others than to be fair!

"Cooperation leads to autonomy," wrote Piaget in *The Moral Judgment of the Child* (Piaget 1965, 195). Cooperation is rooted in the kinds of discussions that this fifth grade class had, arguing the rights and wrongs of their own issues, wrestling with whether it's right to hit back or mess up someone's paper if they messed up your paper. It is cooperation, Piaget asserted, that allows children to perceive not just results of actions, but the intentions behind them. Cooperation forces "the individual to be constantly occupied with the point of view of other people so as to compare it with his own" (Piaget 1965, 189).

Eventually, these fifth graders studied the United States Constitution. I recall Roger's brash pronouncement, "Hey, they did like us!" ❖

The class covenant: a sixth grade contract of binding rules

This process was referred to as building a "covenant," in keeping with the class's studies of King Arthur and medieval history. It involved selecting four rules that represented the perspectives of four constituencies:

teacher, students, parents, and principal. To gather these perspectives, the students conducted interviews, adding a research component to the process. Each group was asked the same question: "What's the most important rule, in your opinion, that we need to help students do their work and take care of themselves in class and in school?"

The teacher went first, modeling her perspective. "As your teacher, I think that the most important rule for this year is that you use your self-control to show independence and responsibility. That means you will manage yourselves well outside of the classroom, with other adults in the classroom, and when you work on projects with each other."

The teacher's response reflected the specific needs and developmental potentials of the group. This was a class devoted to their teacher, cooperative and responsible as long as she was in charge. They were more difficult to manage during recess, and they vigorously dispatched most substitutes. The teacher's "most important rule" was meant to stretch these children and to prepare them for the independence that they would need the following year as they moved on to junior high school.

Next came the students' interviews with their parents and the principal. They enjoyed preparing for these interviews and afterwards held rich and extensive "round table" discussions, comparing parent responses and exchanging their own ideas. The students worked to edit the parent responses, to synthesize and define the common objectives. They boiled down the responses to a single basic edict: "Do good work." Then they expanded it, believing that parents wanted to get examples of good work each week. The work would need to be neat, spelled correctly, and in good handwriting on clean paper.

The principal chose as his most important rule "decent behavior on the playground." The teacher asked students to give at least three examples of decent playground behavior. If they were to follow the principal's rule, what would they have to do? The children agreed that decent behavior involved taking care of the equipment, making fair teams, and solving conflicts without swearing or fighting. They reviewed these points with the principal, who then took the time to create routines and assign the students responsibilities in each of these areas. As the year unfolded, the class proved quite conscientious about care of the playground equipment, looking after the equipment with pride and devotion throughout the year. They had a harder time living by the rules about selecting teams and team captains, but they certainly had more interest than before in finding solutions to conflicts in these areas.

The rule from the last constituency, the students, was actually a request—to have "free time to do things we want to do as long as they belong in school." They argued forcefully that although this didn't sound like a rule, it was a rule because it included a rule, the "as long as... " clause. Eventually, the teacher edited this "rule" to say that during "choice time," students had to be responsible, get things they needed, and behave.

Developing this covenant helped this class consider others' thoughts as well as their own. The set of rules they selected was purposeful, meaningful, and brief. Papers did go home every week to their parents—almost without fail! The playground behavior improved, and if sometimes there was a fight, at least there wasn't a war. Both in their efforts to abide by their teacher's rule about managing themselves and in their quest for "free time," the students showed significant growth in independence. The class's experience was a reminder that it is the struggle, not the achievement, that is the true measure of learning. ❖

Rules in specials

IN MOST SCHOOLS, children spend time with art, music, and gym teachers. They go to the library and the cafeteria and have substitutes who come to their classrooms. As students change locations and negotiate different relationships, it is important that the rules remain the rules and that the expectations remain as consistent as possible. I offer the following suggestions:

✦ Invite specialists to share in generating rules in homerooms when possible. Encourage them to contribute to the group discussions.

✦ Have specialists sign the classroom rules before they are posted.

✦ Have specialist teachers name hopes and dreams that apply to their area:

From a physical education teacher: *"I want everyone to learn to play safely, play hard, and play fairly."*

From an art teacher: *"I expect all class members to share their art, and others to show appreciation and give positive comments."*

From a library teacher: *"My hope is that everyone will find books he or she loves to read."*

From a library teacher: *"My hope is that everyone will become a competent researcher."*

✦ Generate, during the first six weeks of school, particular rules that apply in the library, the art classroom, the music center, and physical education class. These are rules that apply in *addition* to classroom rules. Have students sign and post these special rules as well.

Monica

It is the first week of school for these sixth graders. I have sent them off in pairs on a scavenger hunt to learn about their classroom. They are searching for answers to such questions as "Where in this room would a Revised American Heritage live?" and "What is the most recently published book in this room?" and "How many safety features are in the classroom?"

I have set up the pairs, deliberately creating partnerships that students would probably not choose, but that I hoped would introduce new possibilities. I observe amid the animated chatter and movement that Monica and her partner, Shelly, are at opposite ends of the room. Shelly suddenly reappears next to Monica, showing Monica an answer she obtained. Monica nods, makes a notation on her sheet, then turns back to a cluster that includes her friends. Shelly drifts off again.

"This is not working," I think to myself. I approach Monica. "Monica, aren't you supposed to be with your partner?"

"Well, she's checking out different questions. We divided the stuff," she replies stiffly.

"What did the instruction say?" I ask.

"We're supposed to stay together, but... "

"Why do you think I asked you to do that?"

"So we would work together?" Monica knows the objectives of the activity and yet is pulled toward her friends. While I know that her attachments to her friends are to be expected for her age, the tendency for class cliques can be a major disruption in sixth grade. I want to set a different tone and provide alternatives.

"Do you remember what I said my hopes were for this year?" I ask Monica.

She nods, and states, "That we will be able to work with and get to know different people, boys and girls, and not just the same kids all the time."

"So you and Shelly are partners not just to make you miserable?"

Monica smiles, and I continue. "I know it's harder and less fun some-times, but it is also important. If we were all better at working with different people, we would have a great skill."

Monica gets my drift and goes back to her task with Shelly with a better attitude and resolve.

"Do you think the water fountain is a safety feature?" I hear her ask Shelly.

"Maybe," responds Shelly. "You need water to stay alive." ❖

Summary

"I thought the children made the rules," suggested one teacher who had learned about engaging children in rule-making. Not quite. While children are involved in making the rules, they do not do it alone. Generating rules with children is a collaborative process. Teachers play a crucial role—providing children with positive guidelines and a vision of a classroom in which care, respect, and responsibility matter. "Rules give students concrete directions to ensure that our expectation becomes a reality," says Marilyn E. Gootman (Gootman 1997, 34).

Children progress through predictable stages of moral and ethical growth. Their development and their potential for social consciousness, evident from an early age, can be enhanced by the experiences and opportunities our classrooms provide. It is important that our rules are created in a context of learning ethical behavior and self-discipline and are informed by our knowledge of children's development.

It is equally important that children are enlisted in this process of rule creation. Students' and teachers' hopes and dreams inspire the overall purposes of a learning community. Rules are generated together to ensure that everyone has a voice. We work together to define the concepts and behaviors required for a safe, caring, and respectful classroom. Whatever process is used to create a set of rules, the following statements apply:

- ✦ Rules are presented as a social necessity, a way of "helping good things happen."

- ✦ The teacher's vision (hopes and dreams) and expectations are key.

- ✦ Students' individual hopes and dreams are connected to the rules.

- ✦ Rules are translated into positive statements—from don'ts to do's.

- ✦ Rules are prioritized, combined, and generalized so that the final list is short.

Rules are not intended to legislate every action, but children must be clear about what is expected. When we say "respect," what do we mean? While the meaning may be defined in our discussions, it is truly established and internalized through the repeated investigations and ongoing interactions of everyday life in the classroom. Making and interpreting the rules can provide powerful lessons as children grow toward ethical, autonomous thinking.

Works Cited

BERMAN, SHELDON. 1997. *Children's Social Consciousness and the Development of Social Responsibility*. Albany: State University of New York.

COMER, JAMES, AND CHIP WOOD. 2000. *The Importance of Child Development in Education: A Conversation with James Comer and Chip Wood*. (Video) Greenfield, MA: Northeast Foundation for Children and New Haven, CT: Yale Child Study Center School Development Program.

ERIKSON, ERIK. 1987. Interviewed in "Partners for Life." *Boston Globe Magazine* (March 22).

GILLIGAN, CAROL. 1983. *In a Different Voice: Psychological Theory and Women's Development*. Cambridge, MA: Harvard University Press.

GOOTMAN, MARILYN E. 1997. *The Caring Teacher's Guide to Discipline: Helping Young Students Learn Self-Control, Responsibility, and Respect*. Thousand Oaks, CA: Corwin Press, Inc.

PIAGET, JEAN. 1965. *The Moral Judgement of the Child*. New York: The Free Press.

STEVENSON, CHRIS. 1998. *Teaching Ten to Fourteen Year Olds*. Second edition. New York: Addison Wesley Longman, Inc.

WARD, JANIE VICTORIA, EdD. 2000. *The Skin We're In: Teaching Our Children to Be Socially Smart, Emotionally Strong, Spiritually Connected*. New York: The Free Press.

WOOD, CHIP. 1997. *Yardsticks: Children in the Classroom Ages 4–14*. Greenfield, MA: Northeast Foundation for Children.

CHAPTER 4
Teaching the Rules

*Research on classroom management has found that
effective educators teach behavioral rules… in much
the same way as they teach instructional content.*

DAVID SCHIMMEL
*"Traditional Rule-Making and the Subversion of
Citizenship Education," Social Education*

THE PROCESS OF MAKING THE RULES is an important way to build a learning
community. But after we work with students to make the rules, we need to teach
the rules proactively, rather than simply waiting for the carefully created rules to be
broken. Whether we frame our rules in terms of broad ethical and social principles,
or more specifically in phrases that unpack the ideas of respect or care, we must
follow through—by reinforcing and redirecting behavior, by teaching and reteach-
ing the broad principles and specific actions, and by imposing consequences when
our rules are broken. By consciously teaching the rules, we affirm that rules need
to be what we do, not just what we say.

I check in with the class frequently in the beginning of the year and continue
all year long by asking "How are we doing following our class rules?" Even after
the rules have been created through a lengthy collaborative process and posted on
beautifully written and laminated charts, they need to be taught, practiced, and
learned in the context of our school life. Students need to understand what it means
to care for and respect each other in all types of situations—to pick up a playground ball even when it isn't "their job," to share the one absolutely necessary
brown crayon when they both need it first, to introduce new people to our class

and welcome them into the hub of activity (not just leaving them on the margins), and to greet everyone, even those who aren't their good friends, in friendly ways. As teachers, we need to be ready to follow through when the rules are broken, and to seize these moments as opportunities for students to solve problems and learn behaviors.

And most importantly, as teachers we need to remember that we teach the rules by how we ourselves live the rules. We are always setting the example. Middle school students are particularly alert to inconsistencies in what we ask of them and what we ourselves do. I recall two middle school administrators from Minnesota recounting a situation in which students had generated "Rules for Teachers." Topping their list were "No sarcasm," "Calling us on stuff privately, not publicly," and "Listen to the other side." It was an echo of what the rock group Pink Floyd pronounced in its 1979 song that was to become a teenage anthem of angst: "When we grew up and went to school, there were certain teachers who would hurt the children in any way they could, by pouring their derision upon anything we did, exposing every weakness, however carefully hidden by the kids…We don't need no…dark sarcasm in the classroom!" When teachers all honor the rules that they and their classes set up together, such desperation on the part of students is more apt to be the exception than the rule, and students are less likely to need to develop a separate charter for teachers.

The process of teaching the rules begins with the creation of the rules. But during the first six weeks of school, we continue to demonstrate, define, and live the rules. Modeling and role-playing can be effective dramatization techniques that make rules come alive.

MODELING

WHEN WE MODEL A BEHAVIOR, we demonstrate the actions and language patterns we want children to learn. I use the following sequence to model behavior:

1. Demonstrating

2. Noticing

3. Summarizing and reminding

4. Repeating the noticing by having students demonstrate the behavior and getting responses to the student demonstration

5. Having everyone practice

Modeling good listening and not interrupting

Demonstrating

In demonstrating an expected behavior, I set the stage and ham it up a bit. I say, "I am going to demonstrate good listening, so imagine that Ms. Jones is sharing a story at meeting time and I am a good listener. Watch me." (Ms. Jones is the assistant teacher and has been recruited for this modeling.) Ms. Jones begins to tell about her trip to the museum. I sit still, facing her, and when she finishes, I raise my hand and ask a question.

Noticing

After Ms. Jones answers my question, I ask the class, "What did you notice I did as a good listener?"

"You looked at Ms. Jones," one student says.

"You didn't fidget or anything," says another.

"Yes. I kept my body still."

"You raised your hand," a child points out.

"When?"

"You waited until she was done to raise your hand."

"You asked a question about something she said." This is an observant class.

Summarizing and reminding

I summarize and remind students of the discussion that just took place. "Good listeners are still, look at the speaker, and raise their hands with a question after the speaker is finished. Remind me, what's one thing you do when you listen? Who else remembers something?"

Have students demonstrate

Now it's a student's turn to demonstrate. "Who thinks they can show us how to be a good listener?" I ask. (I may reset the stage with a new speaker or use the same exact setup as before.)

Repeat noticing

I then ask the class for responses to the student's demonstration. I might ask, "What was one thing you noticed that showed Alisha was listening?" or "Who noticed something Alisha said that showed she listened?" To stretch children's observation skills, I ask, "Who noticed one more thing Alisha did to show she was listening carefully?"

Everyone practices

The lesson isn't complete until everyone has a chance to practice the behavior. In this case, it is easy to have everyone practice listening in the circle. Sometimes the behavior is practiced later, in the context of the day.

Paradoxical modeling

AFTER CHILDREN "GET" THE APPROPRIATE BEHAVIORS, it may be effective to model how *not* to do the behaviors, using real examples we've seen from the class. I never cite names or make fun of individuals, but when I model what is clearly them, they are amused and know that I've been watching. I might use examples like the following:

- ✦ "Is this good listening? Why not?" (I model rapt concentration on my shoelaces.)

- ✦ "Is this good listening?" (I wave my hand madly throughout the presentation.)

- ✦ "Is this good listening?" (I send hand signals across the room to a friend.)

- ✦ "Is this good listening?" (I ask a question that the speaker has already answered.)

I KNOW THAT TEACHERS often struggle with the poor listening skills of their students and frequently compensate in ways that become automatic. We repeat directions frequently. We "voice over" other students. We talk louder and more slowly. And yet what we most need to do is teach children the critical skill of listening.

In Morning Meetings, the Sharing component is a time for students to practice listening and to show they are listening by asking relevant and real questions. The kinds of questions and comments that demonstrate good listening may also be the subject of a lesson.

Deepening listening skills

After brainstorming wonderful questions that listeners could ask to add detail or clarification, or to show connections to a speaker's story, Ms. Jenkins conducted the following exercise. She handed each of her third graders a slip of paper from a sticky pad. She then reported briefly on an incident that happened to her. "I was hiking with my dog, and all of a sudden lightning and thunder started. My dog got so scared he froze and couldn't walk. I'm ready for questions and comments." Each student then wrote down a question or comment.

As Ms. Jenkins responded to the students' questions and comments, the story grew in delicious depth. She helped them see how good questioning expands and deepens the interaction. She invited them to use this system when sharing events and to post their slips on the chart to be answered later by the sharer. The system improved the general level of listening and questioning during meetings and worked equally well when transferred to reading and social studies groups. ❖

IN THE BEGINNING OF THE YEAR, I tend to do a lot of modeling of the specific and concrete expectations that help students take care of themselves, each other, and our environment. What I focus on depends on the nature and needs of the children. Some groups are highly attentive and considerate but are more reluctant to show initiative, ask questions, and take risks. Other groups are inventive and live-ly but have short attention spans and are very impatient. The overall behavior of a class reflects the children's developmental characteristics, which don't always coincide with their grade level or chronological age.

It is important to work with children where they are and to stretch them accordingly. Modeling is a way to help children learn and practice, stretching their capacities for appropriate behavior. The expectations teachers can model include basic social and study skills, such as:

- Asking for something in a respectful voice

- Waiting patiently for a turn or for someone's attention

- Filling out a heading on a paper (name, date, topic...)

- Organizing a notebook, a backpack, or an assignment book

- Inviting someone to join a game

- Asking to join a game

- Fixing a mistake

- Correctly using equipment and tools (pencil sharpener, glue stick, etc.)

- Following the procedure for going to the bathroom or walking down the halls

- Responding to all safety systems and signals (fire drill, hand signals, and bell signals)

- Going to time-out properly

- Maintaining acceptable noise levels in the room

Modeling in general—so important to group building—and techniques such as Guided Discovery in particular (see Chapter 2), are part of setting up the routines and procedures of the classroom. Teaching the rules by modeling takes time initially. But it saves much more time later when lessons and activities aren't continually interrupted.

ROLE-PLAYING

ROLE-PLAYING HELPS CHILDREN ANTICIPATE familiar and problematic situations and act out a number of appropriate ways to apply the rules in order to take care of themselves and each other. In this way, it helps children develop perceptions, interpretations, and judgments. Students learn ways to respond if there are accidental spills, pushes, mistakes. They learn how to name and identify a range of feelings. They learn strategies and skills for conflict resolution and ways to initiate

FIGURE 4.1

Steps in Role-Playing

1. The teacher describes a situation in detail.

2. Students volunteer to act out the situation.

3. The class discusses what happened, using some of the following questions:

   ✦ What's the problem here?

   ✦ What do we need or want to happen?

   ✦ How might we do this in a way that uses the _____ rule?

4. Students volunteer to act out appropriate ways to handle the situation.

5. The teacher summarizes the ideas and reinforces them by encouraging practice.

Tips for Success

✦ Keep the role-play short—no more than 30 minutes. (Some role-plays last just a few minutes.) Continue on another day if there's more to cover.

✦ Sometimes try out ideas that you don't think will work.

✦ Show that you notice students' attempts to use the positive alternatives in spontaneous interactions outside of the role-play.

✦ Return to a discussion of the issue if the problem that was role-played persists.

....

interactions and react to them: how to make a new friend, or let someone know when they need help, or say that they don't agree. I use role-playing early in the year to help students think proactively about common dilemmas:

✦ What are ways to be honest and not give excuses when you don't have your homework?

✦ What can you do if you see someone making fun of someone else?

- What are some options if you suddenly realize you don't have a pencil and see one sticking out of a classmate's cubby?

- Imagine that you don't understand what the teacher means, but all your classmates look like they get it. Do you fake it or dare to ask a question?

- You see classmates playing a game and having fun. You want to join, and you move even closer to watch, but no one invites you to play. What can you do?

Role-playing is a way to give students relational tools and help them develop stronger social skills. It is a way for them try out cooperation, assertion, honesty, and kindness. It is a way to show them, as their teacher, that you see their daily experiences and are willing to help. I frequently use the steps shown in Figure 4.1.

"Mario and Lisa": a role-play

I want to work on the rule for sharing because most of our classroom materials are in limited supply and must be shared efficiently. I notice that once the children are absorbed in activity, they don't listen to others asking to use certain materials, and they don't put materials where they're convenient for others. Fights occur when children take what they want without thinking.

The class is gathered in a circle while I briefly describe the following scene, using made-up names: "Imagine that Mario has the bin of markers at his table, right next to him, and is using them with intense concentration. Lisa comes and sits down, also planning to work on her illustration. She reaches across the table to get the bin of markers, jostling the table and causing Mario's careful writing to smudge. Angry, Mario glares at Lisa and utters a threat.

"Both Mario and Lisa are full of good intentions and purposes. They both want to do their work. But now instead of work, there are bad feelings, an argument, or even a fight brewing. So what went wrong? What do the rules say?

"Who wants to pretend to be Mario? Who will play Lisa?"

Students are selected to play the parts, and a table and materials are set up in the center of the circle. "Mario" saunters over to the table, gathering his supplies and taking up his concentrated work stance. He acts the part with great poise—head and eyes glued to the page, markers at his elbow, humming a bit. "Lisa" strolls over to the table in a businesslike manner, laying out her clean sheet of paper with precision. We watch her pull up a chair and position herself just so. We see her reach over and tug the markers toward her side of the table. "Mario's" hand jiggles and his writing gets knocked off-center. "Dummy! Look what you made me do!" he cries. "Now I have to start all over again. I'll get you for this."

I ask the class to share what they noticed about the actors: actions, gestures, words. They named several nitty-gritties:

"Lisa didn't ask for the markers."

"She could've asked Mario to pass them."

"She wasn't careful that Mario was working there."

"She didn't say nothing…she just sat down."

"It was an accident."

Noticing and recognizing possible feelings helps students develop insights and empathy. I want children to understand and be able to recognize themselves in these situations without fear of judgment or criticism. We all forget, make mistakes, need to learn ways to take better care of ourselves and of each other. What might Lisa and Mario be feeling? The students are insightful:

"Lisa is thinking about her own picture."

"Mario is concentrating."

"Lisa forgets to ask for things" [and after I ask why] "because she is so busy with her own picture."

"Mario is mad" [again I prompt why] "because he likes his writing and is sad to have to do it again."

"Mario thinks Lisa did it on purpose."

The discussion continues with a brainstorming session to think of alternatives. What could Lisa do differently? What could Mario do differently? The students call out ideas and I list them on a chart:

"Lisa could tell Mario she's going to work at the same table."

"Lisa could ask if it's okay to work at the same table."

"Lisa could say, 'Please pass the markers, Mario.'"

"Lisa could wait till he does and not just reach over and grab."

"Mario should listen and pass the markers when Lisa asks."

"Mario could move the markers closer to Lisa before she even asks."

"Mario should tell Lisa calmly that she made him mess up, instead of yelling."

"Lisa should say she is sorry and say it was an accident."

"Lisa could offer to help him start over."

Again I ask for volunteers, this time to act out a few of these proposed alternatives. "Show us how you would approach Mario if you were Lisa." "Show us how you would handle the accident if you were Lisa." "Show us how you would conduct yourself if you were Mario."

I find that when children act out positive alternatives, self-realization occurs, perceptions shift, skills are acquired, and responsibility develops. In this example:

✦ Lisa shows consideration of others by asking rather than taking.

✦ A distinction is made between accidents and deliberate hurts.

✦ Impulse control is practiced when Lisa asks and Mario listens.

✦ Conflict resolution begins when Lisa admits her mistake and Mario listens.

I wrap up the role-play by summarizing the ideas. I encourage students to practice the ideas and suggest when they might practice. "At the next choice period, I hope that people will remember to say 'hello,' to ask for materials, and to listen to each other's requests." Then, when I see children attempt these positive behaviors, I show them that I noticed by giving a gentle pat, an encouraging word. I might check in directly: "How's it going with our ability to share materials in the room? Who has noticed something that is working (or not working)?" ❖

116

"Dissing" in middle school

As students act out or watch others act out a situation, comforts and discomforts become more evident and often prompt more realistic insights. I remember when I joined a seventh grade role-play in a school I was visiting. The role-play grew out of a class meeting on lunchtime teasing. After listening to the good intentions and righteous tones of students asserting that "dissing" was wrong, I engaged their teacher in a casual bout.

First, I asked the class if I could do a role-play with their teacher. They were ready and eager! We used the same issue that most distressed the students—appearances. I teased their teacher about his shoes; he teased me about my sweater. As the encounter continued and got more direct, I was struck by the laughter and encouragement that an appreciative audience provided for us, pushing us into ever more dangerous territory. I realized the central role of the audience, and that if this behavior were to stop, the audience had to behave differently.

"Your face..." Mr. Rainier began.

I broke out of my role and turned to the group. "Why is everyone laughing?" I said. There was sudden silence. "What else could you do?" I asked. A productive conversation began about the reactions of the audience and realistic alternatives to laughter.

As I left the room that day, I apologized to Mr. Rainier for making fun of his shoes. "I really do like them," I said. He smiled, but another student then admonished him, "Tell her you really do like her face," she said.

He did and I smiled. ❖

AN INDIVIDUAL PLAN FOR THE RULES

ANOTHER OPTION FOR TEACHING THE RULES, one that works especially well with older students, is to have each student prepare an individual response to them.

This process involves several discussions. Initially, we talk about how easy the rules look on paper and how difficult they sometimes are in real life. For example, my seventh and eighth grade students readily agree that they should take care of materials, put papers in their notebooks, do their room job well. But they also acknowledge that at the end of the day or when they are in a hurry to get to a class, they shove papers anywhere, grab anything, and leave a mess in their wake. And, okay, it wouldn't be such a mad dash if they hadn't stopped to talk, but they HAVE TO talk to their friends!

As a class, we acknowledge that it is hard to make transitions smoothly and keep our room beautiful. In this discussion, I want students to recognize that certain rules are harder for some people and easier for others. For those who struggle against internal and external chaos, keeping track of their books and schedules is a constant battle. Their poor organization is a constant threat to their success in school. For those who easily tidy and ready themselves, who have no trouble packing the right books to go home, recalling when work is due, and getting notes signed and returned, this rule is easy. But they may be the ones who struggle with respecting others or asking for help. During this discussion, I ask students to think about their own behaviors using the following questions:

+ What rule do you think is easiest for you to follow? Why?

+ What rule is hardest for you to follow? Why?

This becomes a writing assignment. As students draft their thoughts in writing, I circulate and start brief individual conferences in which I may acknowledge or prod. Generally, I find students very honest and self-aware. My impulsive students usually are quick to say they have trouble keeping their mouths shut or their hands to themselves. They get frustrated and throw stuff or say things they shouldn't.

"I have trouble with respecting someone when I'm mad at them," a thirteen-year-old girl wrote. "I know I shouldn't, but I talk behind her back and try to get my friends on my side and against her." Others write about their struggles with "doing your best work," about putting off homework and then doing it at the last minute. It took some digging for Todd, so focused on his continuous struggle to get to his work in a timely way, to realize that he also had strengths. Eventually, he wrote, "I'm good at setting up fun games and including people." The recognition that they contribute as well as struggle is a critical insight for many children.

As I circulate and talk with each student, I also ask the important question "So, how will you work on that rule, and how may I help you?" For the students who need the most help with internal controls, this is a chance for me to declare my intention to be helpful and start the year with a plan for working together. Later, when I see Mira begin to lose it, to argue, and to push, I can say, "Remember our plan? Do you need my help now?" Our plans are not always going to work, but they do encourage a relationship of mutual support.

After each student has written an individual response and plan and we have discussed it (which may take a week), the plans are copied over carefully and placed in each student's file. We will share them at parent conferences, amend them as necessary through the year, and celebrate what works.

Following through on the rules

WE CONTINUE TO TEACH THE RULES in many ways during the school day. Two students are whispering to each other while another is presenting information. The teacher stops the entire group. "When someone is sharing, what is it that we all need to remember? Who recalls our rule?"

"I was just telling Marion…"

"Yes," the teacher affirms. "Sometimes we all just bubble over with something we need to add or tell, but why is it important not to chat with neighbors and to wait till later to tell your personal comments?" We stop the group, not because we want to scold or doubt the good intentions of particular students, but because we need to reinforce respectful listening.

We need to encourage and notice our students' positive behaviors as well. "What good questions for your interviews…how quietly and quickly everyone walked through the halls…I noticed that teams really cooperated during the scavenger hunt. Does anyone want to share a strategy they used?"

Being consistent

A TEACHER FROM A PUBLIC MIDDLE SCHOOL in Fitchburg, Massachusetts, talked about how easy it is to forget our own rules. Because of some muddles that had occurred, her class had created a very specific rule about asking questions and getting help. The rule said "Stay in your seat and raise your hand if you have a question. Wait for the teacher to come to you."

Eduardo raised his hand, but his teacher was busy. After a few seconds—seconds that felt like hours to him—he got up and went over to her. He waited restlessly while she helped another student. Then, seeing him, she said, "Eduardo, what's our rule?" He repeated it word for word. She nodded and then said, "Okay. What's your question?"

Then it dawned on her and she cried, "No. Go back to your seat, Eduardo, and then I'll come to you." We must follow the rules, too, if we want our kids to "do them right."

Using the rules to examine problems

AS THE YEAR PROGRESSES, we can use the rules to help us interpret and manage those times when serious problems occur with individuals or in the group. It is important to remember that our rules are guidelines and not perfect formulas for behavior.

Vital contradictions and complexities may exist, even for young children, as they seek to interpret a rule that includes, for example, the phrase "be nice." Do you include someone who bullies or intimidates you? Joan Goodman asks this question in her very provocative article "When Being Nice Isn't Good." She writes, "Although of course we want children to be caring, considerate, tactful and understanding of others, we also want them to be honest, strong-minded and bold. We want them to resist peer pressure, to speak out against wrongfulness, to refuse to go along, even at the cost of offending. An honorable child, standing by the truth, must risk hurting, perhaps alienating another." (Goodman 2000, 30, 34)

Sometimes we need to help students make connections between their actions and the concepts of respect, care for others, or "treating others as you wish to be treated." They may not see or "get" the connections. They may not think twice about the fact that no one ever goes to sit next to one certain student, leaving a huge space next to her in the circle, in line, or at tables. Or they may not think anything is wrong about the boys circulating a list titled "Cool Girls."

The "Cool Girls" list

The "Cool Girls" list happened in a fifth grade classroom. The list ranked the girls in the class according to the preference of three boys in the class. By the time the list landed on the teacher's desk, every student had seen it and read it. While no one said anything directly to the teacher, someone had navigated the list to his desk. He decided to ignore it, crumpling it and tossing it into the wastepaper bin but reporting it to colleagues, who told me the story.

I repeated the story to my own class of seventh and eighth graders and asked them what they thought. I said the list really bothered me. Several boys immediately spoke up: "It's funny." "It's just a joke." "Everyone does it." Their remarks were honest, perhaps defending boyhood and possibly contesting the teacher.

Then one well-liked boy changed the drift. "I don't think I'd like to be on that list." Others joined in. "I'd feel awful if I were ranked low." "I'd feel bad if I were high and my friends were low." We went on to talk about lists, about ranking, about exclusionary clubs in our society, and about a recent news item about a golf club that excluded African Americans.

By the end of the discussion, it was clear that making lists was something most of the students did at one time or another, but most now saw that the lists could hurt, and that, even if they started out to be "funny," they weren't "just a joke."

I wish that the teacher of the fifth grade had also seen the value in a discussion with his class. Students are figuring out their place in a group, learning how to assert power, to claim status, to sort out friendships or cliques. Mistakes are inevitable; processing them can yield profound learning. If respect, kindness, and empathy are to be our rules, not passive phrases, we must sort through these issues with our students, helping them define and act in ethical ways. ❖

SUMMARY

IN THIS CHAPTER, the focus is on teaching the rules. We use many strategies in this teaching: discussion, modeling, role-play, and written responses. We need to be consistent and to take advantage of opportunities to use the rules to examine tough or confusing classroom situations.

By explicitly teaching the rules and following through consistently, we continually build a community which reflects the hopes and dreams of teachers and students. We create the rules with students and teach them in a conscious and concentrated way in the early weeks of the year. Continuing to refer to and teach the rules is a critical part of our ongoing curriculum all year long.

Works Cited

GOODMAN, JOAN. 2000. "When Being Nice Isn't Good." *Education Week* (September 20): 30, 34.

PINK FLOYD. 1979. *Another Brick in the Wall, Part 2.* Vinyl single. Columbia-USA.

SCHIMMEL, DAVID. 1997. "Traditional Rule-Making and the Subversion of Citizenship Education," *Social Education* (February): 70–74.

CHAPTER 5
The Critical Contract:
A Student's Individual
Goals for the Year

DURING THE FIRST SIX WEEKS OF SCHOOL, students are adjusting to their school and their teachers. Teachers are getting to know their class, developing and articulating goals for the year, and making and teaching rules that will help support the attainment of these goals. After we get more comfortable and establish some basic understanding and respect in the early weeks, we can also work on setting individual goals for each child for the year in a process incorporating the input of individual children, their parents, and the teacher. It is a way to help set a positive, productive, and cooperative tone for the year.

At Greenfield Center School, where I taught for years, the written expression of these goals is called a "Critical Contract" because it answers "critical" questions for each student: "What do you most want to work on this year in school? What is most important to you?" The contract contains answers to these questions from three perspectives—child, parents, teacher—phrased as goals for the year. Here are some examples:

My most important work this year is to make friends.

*My parents think that the most important work for me this year is
to enjoy going to school.*

*My teachers think that the most important work for me this year is that
I enjoy my first year in school.*

—DARRELL, AGE FIVE

My most important work this year is to work on reading, because
when I read words, it makes me feel all grown up.

My parents think that the most important work for me
this year is to enjoy my new class.

My teacher thinks that the most important work for me this year
is to share my good ideas with my classmates.

—NINA, AGE SIX

My goal for myself this year is taking care of myself
and not being sent to time-out.

My parents' goal for me is to follow directions better.

My teacher's goal for me is to be an interested worker.

—KEVIN, AGE EIGHT

My goal for myself is to make friends.

My parents' goal for me is to read more and enjoy it.

My teacher's goal for me is to learn math and enjoy it.

—RACHEL, AGE NINE

The most important thing for me this year is to gather two or three
more friends. My parents' goal is for me to be a helpful and
thoughtful friend to classmates.

My teacher's goal is for me to be an honest worker,
to do what I say I'm going to do.

—JAMAAL, AGE ELEVEN

My goal for myself is just to be a good person and keep to my own standards
and not lose control, like getting behind and forgetting things.

My parents' goal for me is to work on my spelling.

My teacher's goal for me is to be able to spend time with a lot of people
in the class and not just my best friends, and not to be cliquey.

—ANDREA, AGE THIRTEEN

The Critical Contract is another way to know children—to know their wants, their hopes, even their fantasies for themselves in school. The more children feel known in school, the more we can be their teachers. We use the Critical Contract to help shape our expectations and objectives for each student for the year.

FOCUSING ON WHAT MATTERS MOST

THE PROCESS FOR MAKING A CRITICAL CONTRACT begins with a leading question. Of parents, we ask, "What do you most want your child to achieve this year?" Of students, we ask, "What do you most want to work on this year in school? What is most important to you?" The respect implied in this question is critical. When we ask students the question, for example, we demonstrate our belief that if we invite them to think seriously about their education, they will. In the beginning, it is not the answer but the question—a question for each student to study and ponder—that I most prize.

The question is *not* "What do you need to do better?" or "How should you improve?" and is not directly related to following classroom rules. Instead, the question asks about the area of greatest interest, what matters or is most important. To form their answers, students must reflect on themselves and the upcoming year. They must make a personal investment in school and take responsibility for the work of the year.

The process of creating a Critical Contract requires the student—and the parent and the teacher—to focus. To name a goal and follow through, we need to set priorities and organize our time and energy to devote to those priorities. Often we fall short of our resolves, not because we try to do too little, but because we try to do too much.

The process also requires making a judgment. When we ask children to think about what they most want to work on in school, we're asking them to take a serious look at themselves. Even our fives and sixes, given time to think, respond with discrimination and self-possession. Their responses to the question remind us that even young children find serious questions a validation of their involvement in school. As children get older, their ability to reflect their own needs and aims is often impressive. This statement was written by a twelve-year-old boy:

At first when you told us about the Critical Contract, I immediately thought of writing, to get it under control so I could be a well-rounded student. But after a while, I got to thinking that the reasons why I haven't had much luck with it is that I either put it off, or lose it and have to do it in a rush. And the same with lots of other subjects. Also I kept losing my notebooks. So I realized that I need to organize my work and get things in order.

Not all statements will be as practical or insightful as this one, but rarely will children be glib or silly. To be able to single out one thing that is most important to work on involves judging what is doable as well as desirable.

Teachers must make judgments, too. Instead of presenting children with generic laundry lists of expectations, teachers define a specific goal appropriate for an individual student. We reveal our understanding and awareness of each student in various contexts by naming a unique, verifiable area of growth for that child. It is important to be clear about the reasons for the goal. Do we want to see a child stretch—take a risk and move beyond a familiar pattern, make new friends, or try out a new skill? Do we feel a student is ready to improve specific competencies, responsibilities, or habits of work? Do we want to see a change in how the student behaves with others or in his/her role in the group?

"I'd like to see you complete more of your projects this year," I might say to one student. Yes, I think to myself, I want this student to continue to read, write, and get along, but an important issue will be to finish more of what gets started without all the delays and digressions. "I'd like to see you write a story this year," I tell another student, recalling her strong interest from last year and knowing her need for a satisfying project for this year. "I'd like to see you work hard on some of your projects and feel good about working hard," I might state as a goal for a student who is easily frustrated and discouraged.

I want to affirm the growth and strength of the student. It is much easier to form these goals when we have two-year classroom cycles and children return to us for a second time. But it is also possible to draw on observations from the first six weeks of school or by a selective review of records, as long as we are careful to balance what was true with what we currently see.

Parents also need to make judgments to identify their special issue or aim for their child. Parents are generally very aware of their children's strengths and weaknesses and have many hopes for the coming year. But we ask them to single out one special goal and we help them express that goal in positive wording. Their focus may reinforce or diverge from the teacher's goal for their child. For example, both the teacher and the parent may want the student to develop independent work habits in school and at home. Or, the parent may single out math competencies, whereas the teacher's focus is on study skills.

Sometimes, teacher and parent goals appear incompatible. For example, a teacher may want to focus on getting a reluctant writer to write more willingly, whereas a parent may want to emphasize spelling. Forming the contract offers a chance to discuss educational decisions. We may need to find ways to phrase the goals so that they are not contradictory or divisive. "Your parents want you to bring home a paper every week that shows beautiful spelling" and "Your teachers want you to find five topics you are excited to write about" may be a way to reconcile expectations.

The process of discussing the goals allows teachers and parents to think aloud together, to discuss points of view and reasons. The aim is not to contest or argue, but to understand and communicate. Children witness this serious consideration in educational planning, but they are participants as well as listeners. The partnership of school and family can be one of our most powerful unions, and one of the most difficult to establish. A Critical Contract helps build cooperation and trust.

GUIDELINES FOR MAKING CRITICAL CONTRACTS

THERE IS NO SINGLE CORRECT PROCESS for making a Critical Contract. The process is modified according to age and developmental level. The following steps are generally included for all ages, although the order may be slightly different:

1. A query before the start of the school year (or during the early weeks of school) asking parents to state their goals for their child.

2. Students work on drafts of their goals (generally after the first six weeks).

3. Teacher-parent conference to discuss parent goals and current teacher and student goals.

4. Parents discuss their goal with student.

5. Teacher discusses her/his goal with student.

6. Student prepares contract.

7. Contract is sent home for signature and copied for home and school.

8. Contract is reviewed—continuously or at specified times.

I trust that readers who find Critical Contracts a tantalizing and practical idea will experiment and adapt the process to best meet the conditions of their community and group. In the following pages, I offer some suggestions for using this process, with examples drawn from my own teaching as well as from the experience of other teachers at Greenfield Center School.

Listening to parents' goals

AT GREENFIELD CENTER SCHOOL, teachers meet with parents before the start of the school year. In many schools, teachers are not able to meet before school begins, but they schedule conferences in the very early fall. At that first conference, they ask parents to think about their priorities for their child. "What do you feel is most important for your child to work on this year in school?"

When teachers in Island Falls, Maine, started using preschool conferences and asking parents this question, they reported a significant and very positive impact on parent/teacher relationships. Often parents share compelling insights, pertinent history, lingering anxieties, and deep aspirations. We find out about children's interests, habits, attitudes, and struggles. Parents feel part of a team from the beginning of the year.

We are all sometimes afraid for our children, fearful that, lacking certain accomplishments, they will not hold their own in the world. These worries and hopes can produce a flood of demands on top of numerous existing teaching prescriptions that assess and measure discrete skills. If we are not careful, we start the year

A Critical Contract for a kindergartner

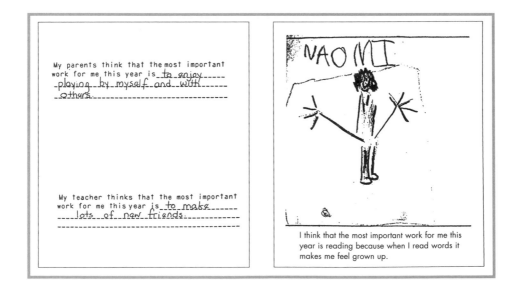

My parents think that the most important work for me this year is to enjoy playing by myself and with others

My teacher thinks that the most important work for me this year is to make lots of new friends

NAOMI

I think that the most important work for me this year is reading because when I read words it makes me feel grown up.

TEACHING CHILDREN TO CARE

preparing for a marathon. When we ask ourselves and parents, "What is most important?" we intend to shorten the list and highlight a plan. The more we identify a focus, the better able we are to devote attention and effort to a course of improvement. And the more tangible successes children experience—and parents and teachers witness—the more pride and hope we create.

Children are responsive to the concerns and expectations issued by their parents and teachers. "I don't like the math we are doing right now," explained Tyrone, "but I know it's important for me." He "knows" because his parents have emphasized his need to improve his accuracy and proficiency with operations. He cares, not because the material provides intrinsic satisfaction or interest, but because of his authentic desire to please. It is the collaboration of interests and perspectives that makes the Critical Contract strong.

Helping students formulate goals

HOW DOES ONE COME UP WITH A GOAL FOR THE YEAR? Where does one start? Students often need help formulating a clear goal statement out of disorganized wants and needs, likes and dislikes. I see several possible ways to help students.

One way is to have students think about a strong interest. "What do you love to do and want to continue to do this year?" "What are you interested in finding out this year?" Another way, related to this, is to have students think about stretching themselves in an area they seem to have potential in. A colleague, fond of baseball metaphors, explains to his sevens that Nomar Garciaparra is a great hitter, but perhaps not as skillful at stealing bases. Becoming a better base stealer might therefore be a goal of his one year. If a student is good at solving math equations, getting better at math story problems might be a goal this year. If a child did well in drama activities last year, s/he might want to try harder roles this year.

Yet another way to help children is to have them envision a personal change. "Last year I was…This year I want to be more…" Many older children articulate "change" goals that involve social issues—having more friends, becoming more outspoken in a group, being less "cliquish." One eleven-year-old stated that he didn't want to be the class clown. A girl wanted to be friends with boys. A teacher of fives and sixes noted that many children in her class came up with goals related to ways to use the Golden Rule. For example, one child said, "To tell when you are mad, so they can say 'sorry,' and say you're sorry when you are mean to somebody."

Finally, teachers can help students articulate a wish to improve a skill or attitude—to write better, to learn to spell, to get work in on time, to be organized. "You know that you do well in math, but this year you want to see if you can do better in art," a teacher might say to help children think beyond their strengths and interests to areas that might need improvement.

Helping parents and students express goals positively

WE MUST HELP PARENTS AND STUDENTS to put their goals in positive terms. We want expectations that will inspire and help us establish guidelines for desirable behavior and purpose. When we tell a child to stop being sloppy with his work, we are scolding. Instead, we can say, "I remember your goal was to turn in really neat final drafts. How can I help you make this essay look like your most careful work?" When we use this language, we are reminding them of their own goals and abilities and encouraging their positive accomplishments.

Making goals specific rather than general

WHAT DOES IT MEAN TO BECOME "organized" or "independent" or "good readers" in first or fourth grade? Does "independent" mean to know how to come by a sharp pencil on your own, to go to the bathroom on your own, to find answers to questions, or to use free time? If we are concerned about a social issue such as bossiness, for example, how will we specify what it means *not* to be bossy? To find the right wording, I often visualize classroom interactions. I can see, for instance, a child's tendency to give orders during a cooperative activity. I can then visualize what I would like to see in concrete terms that help me express my goal to the child. "Be a good partner who gets the scissors instead of telling others to get them, and who not only contributes ideas but accepts other people's as well." The more we clarify what we mean by "consideration," "organization," "friendliness," or even "active reading," the easier it is for children to grow.

BELOW ARE EXAMPLES of how to adapt the goal-naming process for students of different ages.

Fives and sixes

With children this age, the process usually begins in late October, when children have had time to become familiar with school and with classroom routines. The process involves children using drawings to answer three questions.

The first question is "What do you like to do in school, and why?" Children brainstorm as a group to generate ideas. Each child then draws a picture of his/her favorite activity. Fives usually dictate an accompanying sentence for the teacher to write. "I like to play in drama because it's fun and I like the hats," a child might say. Sixes usually write their own sentences, using invented spelling for the first draft.

The second question is "What is one thing you don't like to do in school, and why?" Again the group brainstorms, reviewing the different things they do during the day. They may even sit in the area of the room where an activity takes place to help recall what doing that activity felt like. Then each child draws a picture and dictates or writes an answer to the question. "The place in the Prime Blue room that I don't like is math meeting because it's too long," one child wrote.

The third question is "What do you think is the most important work you have to do this year, and why?" It's more helpful if teachers give children a way to think about this question, rather than provide lists of examples.

"What do you think I mean by 'most important'?" a teacher might ask.

"You like it a real lot."

"Like if you want it and your mom says you can't have it, then you really get mad."

"Yes. 'Important' is something that you care a lot about," says the teacher. "What do you care a lot about working on in school? Before you think, let me ask one more thing. You know that word I used just now, the word 'working'? Well, that's also a special word. What do you think it means to do important work in school?"

"You learn stuff."

"You get better at knowing things."

"You can do things you couldn't do before."

"You know things and your mom is proud of you."

"Like you do hard things, like count to a trillion and stuff."

"These are all very good ideas about important work in school," the teacher affirms. "You told me that you learn new things and get better at things. People are proud of you for doing this important work. And perhaps most of all, you feel proud of yourself. So now I want you to think about something you want to work on this year in school that is important and that will make you proud of yourself."

The children may still need some modeling and some examples. Teachers often share something important they want to work on. One teacher described how she really loved art and thought it was a very important way to show feelings and thoughts. She didn't teach very much art the year before, she told the class, and wanted to teach it more this year.

Teachers might also demonstrate how to think about the question by thinking aloud for students to hear. "I wonder if it is important that I work on my writing," a teacher might say aloud. "Well, that's OK, but I don't know. I really wish that I had more friends… "

Once ready to work on their individual goals, the children begin with the drawing. Again the fives tend to dictate the sentence that goes with the picture, while the sixes tend to write their own, using invented spelling for the first draft.

Finally, each child binds all three pages—the page showing what s/he likes about school, the page showing what s/he doesn't like about school, and the page showing her/his goal for the year—into a folder. The folders are presented to parents during a November conference.

One teacher who used this method noted how seriously the children took the goal-naming. "No one talked about lunch or endless recess," she said. One six-year-old wrote, "The most important work for me is the Golden Rule because that's everything." Other students talked about doing projects, building strong model buildings, making friends, and learning to read. All children gave voice to important work, something they cared about doing in school and something to share with classmates, teacher, and parents.

Nines and tens

With nines and tens, I use three steps:

1. Mapping

2. Representing

3. Reviewing and producing final drafts

1. Mapping

The process of forming goals starts with an exercise of mapping the classroom. The idea is to enable children to visualize their classroom and see themselves in relation to it. Children are asked to draw a rough map of their room. They are given large sheets of manila paper with crayons. Large paper and crayons suggest broad strokes and strong lines. It is a sketch rather than a lesson in precision mapping, although a wide range of mapping skills is needed. Some children reveal a keen sense of scale and proportion. They capture a bird's-eye view and a three-dimensional field. Others draw a side view, with everything anchored on the bottom of the page. I set time limits to release children from over-investment in the mapping task. Most

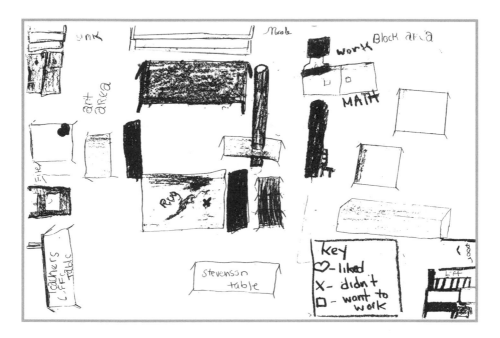

In this map of the classroom, drawn as part of a process of creating a Critical Contract, the student is showing that she likes working on art projects, doesn't like meetings (because they're too long), and wants to work most on math this year.

will do a "final draft map," giving more care to the drawing. It takes one or two forty-minute periods to work on the maps.

When the maps are complete, I ask the group three questions:

- ✦ What do you like to do most and find most interesting in school?
- ✦ What's one thing you don't like or tend to avoid in school?
- ✦ What do you think is most important to work on this year?

The class as a whole discusses each of these questions. Students brainstorm and share interests, likes, and dislikes. This is usually a lively and animated discussion, with increasing specificity as ideas are generated. If some children like only recess, I may prod them, but generally the input from other classmates sets a tone of positive responsiveness. A few hold out. There is nothing to like in school. "I hope this year is better," I will suggest, and then go on.

I tell students invent a symbol for each of their three answers and to locate the area of the room that's related to each. Next we have a short lesson about what map keys are. Students then go off to make keys for their maps.

For a first-time contract, it works better to discuss each question and then identify the corresponding area on the map before going on to the next question. A clump of tables symbolized "group work" for many children. The meeting area represented feelings about meeting activities. For most of the children, the maps were a springboard, a chance to remember.

Discussing each question will also help clear up any confusion between what activity students like and the physical entity of the map. Some children are so literal that they will take the question about likes and dislikes to be about a kind of furniture or a part of the room arrangement.

The third question, the goal-setting, always involves discussion and examples. I will model various kinds of goals. Because many parents' and teachers' goals will stress improvement or change, I like to encourage children to think about stretching themselves and developing strong areas of interest. I want to make sure children understand that a goal is not always getting better at something.

I may model this on a map that I draw. I point out that last year I didn't teach much science, and I explain my reasons. But my new goal is not to focus on science. "I really want to work on playwriting. I am excited about teaching people to write their own plays." I encourage them to choose goals that involve expanding and developing their interests, but they don't always take the hint! Many children still choose improvement goals.

The students have now drawn their map. They have included a key and created symbols. They have placed their symbols in the proper areas of the floor plan.

2. Representing

Representing is a way that children may extend and revise their thinking by sharing their work. As they explain the points on their map to others, they are making the inside become the outside, giving an appearance and stability to an inner logic. And as they communicate, they organize and edit, finding words, order, and reason. As they listen to the sharing of others, they find commonality and difference. In short, they construct and transmit knowledge.

We start the representing in pairs. I assign partners to describe their maps to one another. Then—and this is the "hard part"—students will explain their partner's map to the whole group. I have two children model this interview.

"I like the science observation table."

"Why?"

"I think the crickets are fun to watch."

The partners take turns and switch roles. The challenging part is to listen carefully and recall the information. Time limits are effective ways to help children stay on task and remain focused. I allow about ten minutes for this part of the representing, before asking them to return to the circle. As the partners are conferencing, it is a good time for me to reinforce cooperative learning—quiet conversational voices, attentive listening to your partner, focus, and mutual regulation.

Now, in a meeting of the whole class, the students are interested in each child's choices and decisions. They see the maps. They listen to the content of the answers to the three questions. It is important that this sharing is respectful and that ground rules for representing have been previously established. Students who have drawn maps very crudely and speakers who forget some words receive help only if they wish it. The job of the audience is to listen and to ask a question if necessary. But it is probably enough to hear and learn what others are thinking.

3. Revising and producing final drafts

After the representing meeting, children may wish to revise their goals because of a new idea or recent insight. Changes are a part of the process, as long as they are not merely the result of children attempting to conform or to rebel, but the result of true further reflection. There is also time for personal conferences between each child and the teacher as children work on finalizing their maps and copying over their goals for the contract. This is a chance for the teacher to check in and help if some students need help clarifying or defining.

Children complete the statement "My goal for myself is _____ " in their own words and handwriting. After teacher and parent goals are discussed with the student, the student prepares a contract that includes all three goals. In the final draft, both content and form must be satisfactory. Maps are mounted for display, and the contract is ready to share with parents. With middle school students, teachers sometimes have the students write a letter to their parents incorporating their three goals.

Elevens and twelves

One teacher of a seventh and eighth grade class designed a format to build Critical Contracts that involved letter writing. At the beginning of the semester, the students were told that they would be expected to set up a goal for themselves for the year. They would have time to reflect and consider during the first six weeks of school. Then they would compose a letter to their teacher stating their goal, their reasons for selecting it, and how they plan to accomplish it.

The students were given a choice in how to get others' reactions as they developed ideas for their goal. Some preferred conferencing privately with the teacher. Others relished peer feedback and recognition. Once they had formulated their goals, students were also given a choice in how to share their goals with others. Students could either read their letters to a classmate or share them individually with the teacher. This sharing of goals was an important part of the process, one that allowed children to be known and that allowed the teacher to become a better teacher.

Most students were able to formulate powerful goals using this process. "What I want most for myself this year is just to be a good person and keep up my own standards and not lose control, like getting behind or forgetting things," wrote one twelve-year-old.

Another stated, "I want to be more respected by other kids this year, and I guess that means I have to say what I think more, not be so quiet all the time."

"I want to know I can do hard work and not have to be pushed," proclaimed Erik, who often delighted in last-minute dashes or flippant attitudes about tests and papers. Erik's goal was well grounded in the reality of his transition year before high school.

The next step in the process was for parents to write a letter to their child and the teacher, and for the teacher to write a letter to the student. Both letters would state the adult's goal for the child. This communication of parent and teacher goals may be the second most vital incentive for the learning to come. The first, though, is the student's own sense of contribution to the plan.

In one seventh and eighth grade class, the creation of Critical Contracts involved this exchange of letters between the teacher and student.

Mandy,

My goal for you would be that you would have a real friend who is a boy who doesn't have to be a "boyfriend." I want you to know boys without it having to include coyness, flirting, and silliness.

Dear Mr. Lord,

I think that sometimes I need help getting my work organized. Like when we have a full schedule of work, for someone to sit down with me, maybe Mary-Beth, for a short time at the beginning of the week. Designing my week by having me do work for particular classes during free periods.

My teacher would like me to work on having more boy friend boys who are just friends.

Offering realistic strategies for achieving goals

TEACHERS SHOULD OFFER TO HELP CHILDREN by suggesting realistic strategies whenever necessary. "How to do it" may be a separate issue from setting the goals. Sometimes students have their own ideas, but sometimes they need help. Joel wants to become more organized, to not lose things so much, but he may need help with a system to make order. I observe how Joel organizes himself now. When he wants to straighten his desk, he dumps all the contents out and is confronted with a huge mess, a chaos that dismays him. I ask his parents how he cleans up his room at home. Does he go about it randomly, or does he start with all the toys and then the clothes, categorizing as he works? Strategies may accompany the Critical Contract or evolve during the year.

Evaluating and sharing progress

GOALS CAN BE ACTUALIZED only if there are realistic opportunities to act on them. Therefore, there need to be ways to accomplish the goals we specify. But the goals in a Critical Contract are not meant to be behavioral objectives. I think it is counterproductive to try to measure children's performance precisely in relation to these broad goals. If we limit these goals and evaluations to objectively measurable behaviors, we risk scaling down the goals to what is most easily graded.

Instead, I suggest that we review the goals periodically, and revise and reinforce them. We can help children get to their goals, but we must be careful to show patience with less realistic claims and difficult challenges. Our assistance may consist only of noticing: "I see you are trying to finish your work before you start on something else." Or we may need to nudge a bit: "Remind me how you're coming with your important work of taking turns in groups." Teachers also need to notice and reinforce the growth children make with the goals posed by their teacher and parents.

As part of a regular midyear progress report in one class, nine- and ten-year-old students reviewed their contracts and commented on them with these guidelines:

___ I am working on my goals and think they are appropriate.

___ I need to change or revise my goals.

___ I want to choose as a new goal: _____

Not all goals need to be continued throughout the year. Sometimes by midyear, children shift because they change their minds or have finished with something. If a goal is difficult and the student shows a keen avoidance, I want to redirect the student rather than erase the goal. I may need to break it down into smaller steps or provide additional support. "You told me that you wanted to learn to read better, but I don't see you reading. What do you think can help you meet your goals?" "How can I help?" is not replaced with "You have to…" If children work toward improvement, rather than perfection, they will often be able to accomplish what is most important for them that year in school.

Finally, we must notice and celebrate the achievements and accomplishments. In some cases, as soon as the times tables have been learned, it's best to continue the momentum right into long division. At other times, it's better to practice and enjoy the fruits of victory before beginning the next campaign.

SUMMARY

CRITICAL CONTRACTS help build a learning community by identifying different perspectives, establishing the importance of cooperative effort, and presenting a positive vision of growth for the year. The process of making a Critical Contract involves parents, teacher, and child in a conversation that articulates goals for the school year. It provides the teacher with much information about the needs and expectations of students and their families. It also respects and fosters the investment of child, parents, and teacher.

The process begins even before the school year, whenever possible, with a question asked of parents, and continues through the first weeks as teacher and students get to know each other. The actual contract is usually finished in early October, but it is referred to often during the school year, reviewed and sometimes revised during the middle of the year, and incorporated in end-of-the-year reflections. A Critical Contract can be a motivation and a reference point throughout the year.

SECTION II
Making the Community Work

Introduction

SECTION I focused on building the foundations of a learning community during the early weeks of school—establishing the expectations, routines, rules, and goals that guide our social and academic pursuits throughout the year. This essential work explores teacher and student ideals and provides structures to help us build a learning community where individuals and the group can find success.

But teaching and learning is accomplished in the actions and interactions that make up the fabric of each day. In some cases, lofty ideals and sterling goals are lost in the din of children's inattention and disruptions, the rude remarks and clandestine schemes, the confrontations and conflicts which are bound to happen in every class in every school. Our best intentions cannot survive if we are not prepared to make the community work through a considered and consistent approach to discipline.

This section explores ways to protect the integrity of groups and individuals by helping children stop dangerous or disruptive behaviors. At the same time, we can help them understand and repair the effects of their actions.

- ◆ Chapter 6 presents logical consequences as a foundation for responding to the inevitable testing and rule breaking that are part of children's growth. Logical consequences are a way to stop unacceptable behavior and to help children learn about themselves and about the requirements of a classroom community.

- ◆ Chapter 7 discusses one type of logical consequence in depth—time-out. It involves a consistent routine for helping children regain their controls without disrupting the work of the classroom. Guidelines are presented along with examples taken from everyday situations.

- ◆ Chapter 8 addresses some of the issues teachers face with the minority of children who don't respond to logical consequences and time-out, the children sometimes called "the five percent." Their demands are often so great that teachers must sacrifice some of the attention and energy which the rest of the children need and deserve. Approaches are discussed for children who are engaged in power struggles and those who lack appropriate cognitive and social skills.

✦ Chapter 9 details some ways that teachers and schools can work together to ensure a consistent and effective approach to discipline in different school environments. By working together with parents and others within the school, teachers can help build a cooperative community where children feel safe and productive.

Making the community work requires confidence in the importance of the rules and the learning opportunities which are created when rules are broken. A firm and caring approach to discipline is not superficial or peripheral, but rather is an integral part of social and academic learning and the development of community and self-control.

CHAPTER 6
Using Logical Consequences When Rules Are Broken

Where did we ever get the crazy idea that in order to make children perform better, we must first make them feel worse?

JANE NELSEN
Positive Discipline

Consequences are like walls. They stop misbehavior. They provide clear and definitive answers to children's research questions about what's acceptable and who's in charge, and they teach responsibility by holding children accountable for their choices and behavior. When used consistently, consequences define the path you want your students to stay on and teach them to tune in to your words.

ROBERT J. MACKENZIE
"Setting Limits in the Classroom," American Educator

ONCE WE HAVE CREATED RULES with the class and practiced them and defined positive goals for the year, we can sit back and rest assured that everyone will behave. Yes?

No. Everyone will not behave. Children will break the rules, even rules they cherish and respect because they helped create them. The way we manage the rule breaking is critical to the development of community. The way we attend to children when the rules are broken is critical to the development of discipline.

In fine schools, I still witness children who do not listen to each other or their teachers, are easily frustrated by their own mistakes, and are quick to taunt others who make mistakes. Of course, for all children there are times when impulse overrides sense, when limit-testing replaces caution, or when a retaliatory shove substitutes for respectful assertion. However, repeated interruptions and distractions, habitually inattentive pupils, and an atmosphere of insult and inaction in the face of disorder divert and compromise the best efforts of teachers to teach and of children to learn. In this chapter, I will discuss logical consequences as an approach to what happens when children break the rules. And they will.

When we invoke logical consequences, we want children to learn from their mistakes. Making a mistake, however, doesn't ensure learning. In order for children to learn from a mistake, we need to help them understand the relationship of their actions to an outcome or consequence—and we need to help them figure out different courses of action when the situation occurs again. We learn, as Dewey pointed out, not from experience alone, but from comprehending the experience (Dewey 1963). Helping children see the connection between their acts and the consequences—beyond dismay at getting caught—helps them think about what went wrong in a situation and what alternative strategies are needed. Stopping behavior that is not constructive and ensuring logical, reasonable consequences for that behavior help children process the experience of rule breaking—and therefore, to learn from it.

Our intentions in using logical consequences are to make clear the connection between behavior and consequence, to support children in figuring out how to behave differently, and to communicate to them our belief in their ability to make better choices. When we invoke logical consequences, we intervene to stop unwanted behavior, but we also listen, guide, coach, and, if necessary, nudge our children along an alternative route.

NEITHER PUNISHMENT NOR PERMISSION

LOGICAL CONSEQUENCES ARE REASONABLE AND RESPECTFUL, neither punishment nor permission. They help students assume responsibility and try again. As psychologist Robert MacKenzie explains, they are structured learning opportunities (Mackenzie 1997).

How we handle rule breaking helps to differentiate consequences from punishment. For example, either a consequence or a punishment may involve a time-out. The time-out will be seen as a punishment if the child is arbitrarily sent out of the group, and the teacher's manner is sarcastic or derisive. It is more apt to be perceived as a consequence if it seems a result of the child's choice to continue to whisper to her/his friends during meeting time, and if the manner of the teacher is firm but respectful. Students often have input in the process of logical consequences through discussion that looks for solutions. They are a part of a cooperative process designed to support and protect individuals and the community.

Logical consequences are intended to help children take stock of their own behavior, not to humiliate or hurt. I remember Alex, a twelve-year-old boy quick to act, slower to think, and apt to get into frequent trouble. We were in an impromptu class meeting, called to talk about a Civil War medal belonging to Carola, missing after the previous night's class play. Carola had volunteered it as a prop. As the meeting unfolded, we talked about the missing medal, its sentimental value to Carola and her family, and its irreplaceable nature. Carola, a highly composed and private girl, wept. We talked about the inclination to take things that don't belong to us, an inclination that many of us could identify with at different times. "Sometimes we act without thinking because we want something badly," I said, "but it's wrong and harmful."

All students were sent to check their backpacks—just in case. In moments, with no attempt at concealment, Alex handed me the medal. I sent him to Carola and watched him apologize, head down, expression somber. She wiped her tears and smiled. Later, I heard a student say, referring to Alex, "That took such courage." And it did. Basically, I considered the incident over and responsibility accepted, although Alex, his parents, and I talked further and decided that Alex would make an "apology of action." Alex used money he had earned to buy Carola flowers and accompanied them with a sincere and tender note.

Logical consequences are related to the rule breaking. When Suhalie distracted neighbors during a work time, she had to work by herself for two days. When Robbie threw tissues all over the bathroom stall, he had to get a bathroom pass from the teachers and have the stall checked after his visits for two weeks. Generic consequences, such as missing recess, do not help children rework and learn to manage difficult situations.

Missing recess may sometimes be a related consequence, though. For example, Stephie used recess to make up the homework she didn't do the night before, and Luis, who did not follow the rules for safe touching during recess games, needed to stand with the recess teacher the next day and observe safe play rather than playing himself. Related consequences provide timely feedback and refer to appropriate choices.

While punishment is not productive, neither is a permissive approach in which teachers see external controls as a hindrance to internalized motivation and understanding. When using a permissive approach, teachers explain, lecture, and convince, not once in the beginning, but repeatedly with endless reminders, warnings, and appeals. The rules become negotiable, the limits unclear and inconsistent. Children increase their efforts to manipulate and rationalize, to test and stretch the limits. Their actions are begging their teachers to stop them, to DO SOMETHING. When teachers finally do respond, the response is rarely a reasoned or controlled one. When children lack the development and skills to govern themselves, adults have a responsibility—one that they must not abdicate—to enforce the rules. When adults do abdicate this role, chaos and anarchy are more the norm than learning and growth.

It is not easy to build and use a consistent, respectful approach when rules are broken. Many of us feel some ambivalence, simultaneously believing that punishment is an effective deterrent and that "nice words" should work with no further action. Our ambivalence can show up as anger or inconsistency or as guilt that we are being unkind. It is critical to remember that our intention is to help our children learn to make better choices. Real kindness involves helping children meet their responsibilities.

Logical consequences are effective not because they intimidate or deprive and not because they deal out rewards or threaten punishment. They work because they reinforce children's desire to be in control of themselves and to enlist in the ethics of community. This desire and commitment are strengthened by relationships with caring teachers. I often hear frustrated comments from dedicated teachers faced with numerous complacent students. "Some of these kids just don't care when you tell them to go to time-out," report the teachers. When children don't seem to care, letting them know that we care may be the only response, the first step in the children's ability to reconnect and to care about themselves.

In a seventh grade math class for struggling students, I watched the teacher hug and high-five every student who earned a passing test grade.

"What'd you get, Tanya?" she asks.

"An 84," whispers Tanya, head down.

"WOW! A 'B', that's great!" hollers Ms. Bryant.

"Yeah, that's good, huh? I gotta show my mother," cries Tanya, grabbing her paper from her teacher and demanding that she enter it into her grade book faster.

"I'm real proud of you," Ms. Bryant continues, "but slow down and remember your respectful words." We show care through our high expectations, and through our accessibility to help children achieve these expectations.

NATURAL CONSEQUENCES

SOMETIMES CONSEQUENCES OCCUR NATURALLY, without adult input. A student who forgets his lunch may get hungry. A child who is a bad sport may not get chosen to be on teams. A student who doesn't do her work may get behind. I say "may" because often adults intercede to protect children from their mistakes. Parents scurry into school with forgotten lunches. Teachers find a place on the team for the poor sport, with a mild warning. And we all needle and cajole children to complete their work, rather than allow them to fall behind.

Often our intercessions are necessary because natural consequences are not productive in the ways we might hope. The hungry child takes a classmate's lunch. The bad sport dominates the game. The nonworker becomes more and more discouraged and loses all motivation to participate. Clearly, teachers need to establish and implement a system of logical consequences to help children learn and grow. As my colleague Pamela Porter says, "Logical consequences are invoked by adults to protect children from natural consequences." We need to protect children from the natural consequences that failing to acquire skills, for example, might cause.

The importance of the "Stop Step"

OUR FIRST STEP IN RESPONDING to rule breaking must be to stop the behavior. In a recent workshop on discipline, a kindergarten teacher who believed in non-punitive discipline described a recent situation in her classroom. "I handled this badly," she confessed, "but I didn't really know how to do it differently." The other participants were all ears as she told the story.

Five-year-old Joseph, high-spirited and strong-willed, exploded into the classroom one morning. Typically, he sped off the bus, making a beeline for the classroom, anxious not to miss a minute's worth of activity. That morning, many children were already at work. Joseph entered the room with cyclone force, bumping and jostling others in his excitement. The inevitable collision occurred. He knocked into Dylan, toppling the intricate design of colored pattern blocks he had so carefully balanced in a "fairy kingdom."

"Hey," Dylan called out in distress as the blocks tumbled.

"You made me," retorted Joseph, suddenly crouched and tense. "Besides, it's ugly," he added defiantly. Within moments Dylan was crying. Joseph's fists were up, and the entire class was expectantly silent.

"What do you do?" the teacher asked her workshop colleagues, real frustration in her voice. "I know it sounds like a simple case, but everything I did just made it worse."

Her audience of teachers identified easily with the situation—the peaceful morning punctured by explosions of five-year-old violence, a volatile child who needs help, a weeping child who needs consolation, and an entire classroom in need of assurance and direction to regain the momentum of a good morning. There is one teacher and one moment, and it isn't simple at all. It is a balancing act that juggles many priorities and competing claims, all important.

In the workshop we role-played the parts of teacher and children to explore different scenarios. Someone crouched down and embraced "Joseph." Others offered ideas for helping "Dylan" fix his tower. And someone urged Dylan to tell Joseph how he felt.

But what was most primary slipped our minds. No one said "Stop." Before anything else—before interpretation, consolation, or reparation—must come "Stop." The upset Joseph, the upset Dylan, the silent (and maybe upset) class all need to hear us say "STOP. It is not okay to hurt people in our class. We take care of each other here."

Then we must enforce that notion with actions. We might take Joseph's hand and, keeping him safely by our side, remove him from the activity that he disrupted.

We might then ask a colleague or assistant (hopefully, we have one) to remove Joseph from the classroom until controls are restored and an appropriate entrance is renegotiated. We want to take time to redirect the others and to comfort and reassure Dylan before we think about Joseph.

Later, we may plan interventions to help Joseph go from bus to class with more ease and control. We may find him a partner, perhaps an older student to walk with. Maybe we will help him practice his entrance to school. "You come into our room in a way that keeps you and others safe. You walk. You stop and think. You look. And if you forget…"

For each of our "Josephs" there are numbers of options to explore. For each of our Josephs, there must first be stop signs. The journey to self-control begins with acceptable choices and predictable limits. It is not simple at all.

When the Stop Step is enough

THERE IS A LADDER OF INTERVENTIONS—a progression of responses to misbehavior that begins with small, subtle signals to a child who is a bit chatty or needs a reminder. When the rule breaking is minor and the child responds to such a signal by regaining control, that is usually enough. We do not need to follow up every small incident with further consequences. Teachers need a repertoire of small interventions that help to refocus and remind children.

Marcos whispers to his friend while Jose is presenting a report to the group. The teacher may use the following:

- **A look:** A brief moment of eye contact, a quizzical you-know-better facial expression.

- **A glare:** A stern look (well practiced) that conveys "Stop it—I mean NOW."

- **A gesture:** A head shake, thumbs-down, finger waggle, finger over lips (sshh), flat palm over fist that means "Cut it out" or "Stop."

- **A few words:** The individual's name is spoken softly, as in "Marcos, listen please" or "Let's wait, please, Jose, until everyone is listening." "Meeting rules," Mr. Lord often said to his seventh and eighth graders, pausing for a moment for a few to refocus their attention.

- **A touch:** A firm but friendly hand on a shoulder, meaning to calm down, slow down, recall rules. I have held someone's hand for a few moments as a way to calm, steady, or keep hands from tickling, poking, fidgeting.

- **A few gestures:** Perhaps eye contact, a whispered name, a signal for Marcos to move his seat and come sit next to the teacher or away from distractions.

- **Removal:** Using silent gestures and signals, the teacher pockets a distracting object or holds it for safekeeping.

When misbehaviors continue or are part of a pattern of repeated behavior, or when the child progresses to a slightly more disruptive behavior, then we move up the intervention ladder, presenting clear verbal reminders and options to the student. We may present choices or issue a "final reminder":

- "Use the markers correctly, or I will hold them for the rest of the period."

- "Quiet voices, or no talking—which is it?"

- "Stop arguing and agree on rules, or the game ends for today."

- "Find a fair way to include everyone, or I will make the seating arrangements for today."

GUIDELINES FOR IMPLEMENTING LOGICAL CONSEQUENCES

WHEN SIGNALS, A REMINDER, AND REDIRECTION DON'T WORK, and after we have taken action to stop the misbehavior, logical consequences are the next step. Here are some guidelines for using logical consequences in a reasonable way:

Logical consequences are respectful of the student and of the classroom.

This is an essential criterion proposed by Rudolf Dreikurs in *Maintaining Sanity in the Classroom* (Dreikurs 1982). It entails giving students input into possible consequences and including some choices about the specifics of the consequences. For example, asking "Do you want to get that homework done at lunch or after school?" implies that the homework will get done, but allows the student some say in when. Logical consequences are not intended to humiliate or hurt.

Logical consequences need to respond to choices and actions, not to character.

The message is that misbehavior results from poor judgment or bad planning, not from poor character.

Logical consequences need to be put into practice with both *empathy* and *structure*.

Empathy shows our knowledge of children and our willingness to hear what they have to say; structure establishes our capacity to set limits and provide appropriate direction. Jane Nelsen, in *Positive Discipline,* talks about the need to be both kind and firm. Kindness, she says, shows respect for the child; firmness shows respect for oneself (Nelsen 1996).

Logical consequences should describe the demands of the situation, not the demands of the authority.

This helps avoid power struggles. "For our classroom to feel safe, you need to contribute in a more friendly and agreeable way. When you put down other people, it doesn't feel so safe anymore."

Logical consequences should be used only after the teacher has assessed the situation.

Misbehaviors may result from expectations that are not appropriate to the developmental needs of the child, or from expectations incompatible with the child's individual needs. The best alternative may be to restructure the environment and readjust the expectations. For example, sustained periods of quiet work take significant control for children even as old as ten or twelve. If they are then released to go to the bathroom, they can't be expected to stay in straight and silent lines. Instead, they release pent-up energy; they tap dance, chatter, and tickle. Do these children need a consequence, or do they need breaks and outlets for movement and social contact? By providing a fifteen-minute activity or social period, or relaxing the hallway rules, we may make the problem disappear.

When Kyle copied from another student on his spelling test, he was compensating not for a lack of study (he had studied), but for an inability to memorize twenty new spelling words each week. He was a student with a specific visual memory weakness, and the class expectations, despite his efforts, were not within his grasp. When he was given a portion of the list, and was able to succeed, the cheating stopped. He needed the expectations restructured, rather than a consequence for cheating.

Confronted with misbehavior, we first ask ourselves questions: Are my expectations appropriate to the needs of this age group?...to the individual needs and abilities

of the student? Do I need to restructure the environment or modify individual expectations?

Teachers need to "Stop and Think" before imposing logical consequences.

Teachers often need time to think, not just react. Confronted with aggravating behavior, our first responses may not be the most logical. We may also need time to decide on a consequence that is reasonable and realistic for the child and for us—manageable within the schedules and demands of the day and the resources of adults and students. "Your rudeness is not acceptable. You need to go back to your desk, and we will both need to think about this for a while. I will talk to you later (or after lunch, or tomorrow morning)." The message is that students may not go on when behavior is unacceptable. The next step will be decided when the teacher has time to think and respond appropriately.

Logical consequences help to restore self-control and self-respect through actions, not just words.

I see fewer recurrences of misbehavior when children have the opportunity to make amends through some type of action that goes beyond the words of an apology.

THREE TYPES OF
LOGICAL CONSEQUENCES

I'VE CATEGORIZED THREE TYPES OF LOGICAL CONSEQUENCES and their relationship to broad areas of behavior: reparation, loss of a privilege, and forfeiting participation through time-out. These categories and their accompanying examples of consequences are meant to illustrate, not to dictate, what every teacher must do. I've provided just a few examples. You will quickly think of others.

Reparation: "You broke it. You fix it."

REPARATIONS GIVE CHILDREN OPPORTUNITIES to face mistakes and actively repair the damage they caused, providing children integrity. The process involves practicing critical social skills, including honesty, responsibility, cooperation, assertion, empathy, and self-control. It allows children to take responsibility and right their wrongs, and to be a part of the solution, not just the problem. Reparations also provide an opportunity to learn from what happened by seeing the impact of one's own behavior and, with assistance from teachers, to figure out a better alternative. Teachers often need to help children practice the specifics of the words, gestures, or actions which are needed.

Importantly, reparations also give students who were harmed a chance to speak out and explain what happened to them. It may give them a voice in what will help fix the wrong. Do they want help in rebuilding the knocked-over structure?...help rewriting a paper that was torn? What does Karin think will help her feel safe on the team after Terry deliberately made fun of her playing ability? A principal reported dealing with a bus bully by asking the victim what he needed from the other student. Both were present in her office. "I just want him to be nice to me," the fourth grader replied. "Can you do that?" asked the principal. "Yes," was the emphatic reply. And he was, after also giving up bus rights for a week and practicing some "nice" behaviors.

For both the rule breaker and those who are upset by the incident, a voice in what should happen gives reassurance and provides a constructive use of power. In some cases, reparations may be invoked to help reassure and reestablish trust with an entire class. In one seventh grade class, Seth, a popular class leader, brought a thermos of liquor to school and made a display of drinking it during bathroom breaks. By the time the teachers were aware, many students were distracted, distressed, and conflicted by their sense of loyalty to friends and community. Seth's breach of rules involved serious consequences, including suspension. It was also important for teachers to help Seth reenter the classroom in a way that involved him in restoring integrity to the conflicted and upset class. The teachers gave the group a chance to talk about how the incident affected them and to suggest a way to restore trust. They decided to ask Seth to listen "so he would see that it was hard for them too, and then not want to do it again."

Reparations often include an apology, either a verbal apology or an apology of action. To use an apology of action, teachers guide students to think beforehand about ways to show they are sorry when they hurt someone. The class discusses ways to make amends that are realistic and would make the apology meaningful. On a chart, they post a number of possible "actions," including writing letters, offering to do a special favor, and sharing a treat. They practice using "I statements" to state when they feel wronged and to make their apology. "I'm sorry I didn't listen to you today," began a letter from a fourth grader to a guest teacher. (See Appendix C for a full description of apologies of action.)

The following pages list some situations in which reparations might be useful. I offer some possible ways to respond in each situation.

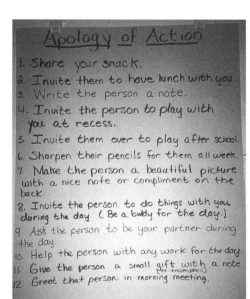

Left: An apology of action, such as making a card or writing a letter, is one possible logical consequence for physically or emotionally hurting someone.

Right: In many classes, students generate and post a list of possible apologies of action. Anyone who needs to make an apology of action can then refer to the list for ideas.

TEACHING CHILDREN TO CARE

Individuals making reparations

A student spills milk, paint, glue, collage pieces, etc.

The teacher might simply say "I'll help you find a sponge so you can clean it up."

Or the help might come from other students. In an active primary classroom where many materials were available and spills were frequent, the teacher organized what she called "spill teams." When someone accidentally spilled something, he/she asked for help from the team, and together the team and the spiller wiped up glue, squeegeed paint off the table, or collected the scraps.

A student accidentally knocks over another child's block building.

"Ask Mark if he wants you to help build it back up," the teacher might say.

A five-year-old uses a mean voice, commanding instead of asking.

"Move over," Kazu yells at Maurice, who is sitting very close to Kazu in the circle.
Maurice complains, "Ms. Chadderton, Kazu used mean words."
"But he's touching me," rejoins Kazu with frustration.
"How can you tell someone to move over in a kind voice?" asks Ms. Chadderton. Kazu whispers the words to her and she nods approval. "Tell Maurice now."
"Move, please," he repeats.
"See, he fixed it," Ms. Chadderton tells Maurice. "Thank you, Kazu."

An older child uses a negative tone when speaking to someone.

"Use the rewind button and say it again," I tell older children when they need practice using an appropriate tone of voice.

Kendall often boasts about his accomplishments after someone shares about a feat. "I won a race, too," he says after Johnny shares about winning a race.

"Kachink. Rewind." I use the signal that Kendall knows means he needs to make a relevant comment that is not a boast.

"I'm glad you did well in your race," manages Kendall.

A child trips a classmate on the playground.

The reparation here may simply be to stop and offer help if needed. "Did you stop and see if he's all right, or if he needs any help?" I ask the child who did the tripping.

A student laughs when a classmate makes a mistake.

The teacher directs the child to stop and apologize using an "I statement."

"I'm sorry I laughed when you missed that word. I make mistakes, too, and it would feel bad if someone laughed," the child says to the classmate.

A student fools around in class and doesn't get work done.

"You wasted fifteen minutes of your learning time. You need to decide when to make it up today. Do you want to stay fifteen minutes after dismissal or bring your lunch here?" the teacher asks.

A seventh grader trashes the bathroom.

The teacher and student agree that a reasonable reparation would be to clean up the mess and help the custodian clean the bathrooms for the following week.

A group making reparations

A group has been socializing rather than doing its work.

"Your work isn't done because you have been chatting," says the teacher. "You owe yourself a thirty-minute work time today. When will you make it up? It needs to be done before you go home."

A group becomes argumentative and noisy while working on a map, getting very little work done and disturbing the rest of the room.

The teacher names the problem and offers a choice: "This group is disturbing our classroom and also getting very little accomplished. You need to quickly divide up the jobs and work alone. Do you want to do that right now or should I?"

The class is rude and unruly with a substitute, or "guest teacher."

Upon returning to class, Ms. Ritchie calls a class meeting to discuss the problem. "Yesterday afternoon, many of you were upset. It sounds like some of you didn't take care of yourselves with our guest teacher. What did you notice?" she asks. Everyone noticed something. Students noticed that someone had yelled "party time" and then lots of people were out of their seats, not doing their jobs, barricading the door, erasing and writing on the board.

"I didn't listen to Mr. Montgomery," someone adds.

"I feel sorry for Mr. Montgomery," someone spontaneously offers. "It's like we made him invisible, like he wasn't even there and we didn't hear him."

Ms. Ritchie asks students to think about a time when they were ignored. One student volunteers, "It makes me remember when I was telling something in class and people weren't listening and I didn't want to be here any more."

The children think together of ways they want to be more helpful, and offer a few suggestions to make it easier for their guest teacher the next time. As a first step they decide to write him a letter of apology. It concludes, "We hope you will come back and teach us social studies again. You are a good teacher."

Breach of contract:
"If you are not responsible, you lose a privilege."

"THE GOOD THING ABOUT GETTING TO BE IN MIDDLE SCHOOL," some children reported to their new peers, "is you get more freedom." Then they quickly added, "Of course, you get more responsibility, too." The children perceived having more choices and decisions, greater independence, and wider boundaries as "freedom." These are also "privileges," to be used in responsible ways.

A privilege is not a reward for students who finish their work. It is not when the well-behaved get to be the hall monitors. In order to learn to be reliable, everyone needs opportunities to be the hall monitor. Everyone has a chance to learn the connection between responsibility and privileges.

Younger children might get to deliver a message to the office with a partner or to go on their own to the sink and clean the paint brushes. A group of older children get to choose among different ways to study their spelling words—with partners or alone, making a word maze or using the computer, with the teacher in the classroom or independently out in the hallway.

Part of our contract as a learning community is the expectation that children will act responsibly. We help them learn responsibility by offering practice on tasks integrated into the daily arrangements and design of our classroom. We expect and trust that children will tell the truth, do their jobs, take care of property, and treat each other with respect, fairness, and friendliness. A breach of that trust includes telling lies, disregard for others' rights or feelings, and disregard for materials in the room.

When those instances happen, we reteach, remind, and invoke consequences when necessary. When the trip to the bathroom turns into a romp, when the pattern blocks are left in a heap, or when homework is not done, we narrow the choices, reorder the steps, or try smaller chunks until students are ready to try again. Losing a privilege is the consequence when children "blow" a responsibility.

Individuals losing a privilege

A student says her work is done when it isn't,
in order to play games or avoid a task.

"I won't be able to believe what you say, or trust you to follow routines for finished work. You will have to show me your finished work every day this week."

A child leaves the room to go to the bathroom, fools around in the
bathroom, and doesn't return in a reasonable period of time.

"You're not taking care of yourself in the bathroom, so you won't be able to go by yourself for the next two days. You will have to wait until a teacher is free to go with you," the teacher might say to a young child. Or, to an eighth grader, the teacher might say, "You will need to get a bathroom pass with a set time on it for the next week."

A student leaves the room on an errand and gets into
a water fight at the fountain in the hall.

"You're not taking care of yourself when you leave the classroom; therefore, you will not have the privilege of leaving the room on your own for the rest of the day (or week), until you show me you can follow rules of the classroom again."

A child cheats when playing games.

"When you cheat, you make the game less fun for others. You will need to leave the game until you are willing to play by the rules," the teacher says. Students are also encouraged to stop a game if there is cheating and to say, "If you continue to cheat, I don't want to play with you."

A student is rude to a teacher, ignoring a request
not to interrupt and then making a face.

The teacher confronts the student. "You ignore me when I speak to you, which tells me you don't care to be in my group. You are welcome to return when you are ready to show respect." The student may need to give examples and demonstrate respectful responses before returning to the group. Role-playing situations may also be helpful.

A child makes faces or sarcastic remarks to peers
during an activity or group.

"I see you are not ready to work in a friendly way in this group," says the teacher. "You will need to leave until you are ready to use kind words, or show you know how to respect the good ideas of others in our group." The student may need to write out and give examples of respectful and kind responses.

After several reminders, a student still leaves
computer disks scattered on the table.

"You have been mishandling the computer center. You won't be able to use it by yourself until you show me that you are ready to follow all the procedures," the teacher says.

A student pushes to get a place in line.

"I see you push people to get in line. You'll have to get out of the line and wait in the back with me, until you show me that you know how to line up safely."

A child requests help from her teacher using
a demanding and unpleasant voice.

"I don't like people talking to me in a rude voice. I do not talk to you in a rude voice. If you want me to answer your question or explain something you don't understand, you need to use a pleasant voice and nice words, or I won't feel like helping you." The teacher walks away.

A student comes to class without homework.

"Your homework is your ticket to class. You need to leave the class and get your work done. Come back when you have your ticket." The student may work in another classroom or a quiet area.

A group losing a privilege

A group playing four-square applies the rules of the game
unfairly to exclude or intimidate certain classmates.
"The game is over. If you want to play tomorrow, you have to let me know how you plan to use the rules in ways that are fair for everyone. I want a written plan signed by the following players…"

A group lesson becomes very noisy.

"You are still not remembering to use quiet voices. Now there is no talking at all."
Or: "There are a lot of people talking to each other instead of listening. I'll wait.
I won't talk when you're talking. I do not plan to continue until people show they
are ready to listen." In some instances, students may have to make up lost instructional time with written work.

Room clean-up is sloppy and difficult.

"You have not been cleaning up with care, so for the next few days the art, library,
and science centers are closed. You will have less clean-up to do. Then you can
decide if you want the responsibility for these centers."

*The class is particularly rude
and unruly with a guest teacher.*

In addition to reparations like those suggested earlier in the chapter, the teacher
may offer the following choice: "I will have to be away again, so I'll give each of
you a choice. The choice is to remain in your classroom and follow the rules, or to
go to another room with a teacher you know. If you feel you can't manage with a
guest teacher and will do better elsewhere, that's a good decision. If you choose to
stay in this room, you are choosing to take care of yourselves. I will be angry if you
choose to stay and then don't manage. The next time, I will not be able to believe
you, and I will make the decision. Think about it."

There is a misuse of class supplies.

"This class has been using so much paper that we are almost out of a month's supply. Since you are not able to regulate it now, I've put out what I think is a reasonable quantity. When that is gone, there will be no more drawing paper for the
week."

Children come to their math lesson unprepared.

"I see that many of you do not have your work done or do not have what you need
for this lesson. I will go do other things. When you are ready, let me know. I am
sorry that you will miss some of your valuable math time."

Time-outs: "You must forfeit participation."

SOMETIMES WE REMOVE A CHILD FROM A SITUATION temporarily to stop disruptive behavior or as a logical consequence of a child's disruption. Sometimes (though not always) the words "time-out" and a specific procedure are used, a process discussed in detail in the next chapter. Some basic examples of appropriate uses of time-out follow.

Individual time-out

A child talks continually to a neighbor during a group activity.

"You're disturbing us. You need to leave and come back when you're ready to follow the rules."

A student bangs his pencil and drums on the table.

"You are making it hard for others at your table to concentrate. You will need to stop or leave the group."

A child takes extra turns or pays no attention when it isn't her turn.

"You have to pay attention to the game or not play."

A child makes negative and sarcastic comments.

"Time-out. Come back when you're ready to contribute helpful comments."

*A student refuses to work with a partner or participate
in a shared project unless she gets her way.*

"Time-out. I want you to think about one thing that is important for you to work on and one thing that your partner wants to work on. Come back when you have figured that out, and when you are ready to cooperate."

Group time-out

Class transition is shoddy.

"This room is not ready to go to recess. I'll be at the table working. Let me know when you think you're ready."

A group is not able to cooperate.

"I hear a lot of bickering from this foursome. It sounds like you haven't figured out how to work together on this project. Take a time-out and think what you might do to make it work better. When you come back, I will hear one solution from each of you."

Heather's assignments

Heather is getting behind in her homework for "seminar," an English class open to any eighth grader who elects a more challenging curriculum. "I know, Ms. Charney," she says each time I get near, "I'll have it tomorrow…My dad's computer…It's in my backpack. I'll go check." Her excuses are accompanied with a pitiful voice, a scurry of activity, and faith that her teacher is easily waylaid, distractible, and gullible.

In truth, she doesn't have the assignments; they are not in her book bag and will not be done the next time. Heather is in a rut, and the further behind she gets, the deeper the hole. I've gotten into a rut as well, accepting Heather's excuses rather than immediately checking in with her and demanding results. We are approaching a long weekend, time for her to catch up. I say to her, "Heather, it needs to be on my desk on Tuesday or you are out of the English class. You've already missed two assignments, and you know that is the limit."

"I know, " she says in an annoyed voice. "I'll have it, " she promises.

I expect and truly hope she will. I like Heather and want her to succeed, to learn what she is truly capable of accomplishing if she gets down to work. I also enjoy her presence in class, her beautiful artwork, her lively character improvisations, her sweet and supportive compliments to others. I also know that she procrastinates, works slowly, and makes many excuses to avoid what is challenging and hard for her. I have accepted one excuse too many already.

First thing on Tuesday morning, I check my desk, expecting to find Heather's missing assignments. They're not there, and I am disappointed. I know I have to follow through and expel her from seminar. I speak to her directly, privately, before class begins. "Your actions tell me that you choose not to be in the class." I try for a matter-of-fact tone, but I know that I am abrupt and unsympathetic, steeled as I am for the task.

Her face tightens, turns red. "Okay," she cries, "I won't be in the dumb class." She storms out of the room and heads for the bathroom, where I hear a mix of weeping and ranting, as she accuses me of every kind of unfairness. She is furious and sad, and I am the one at fault.

She does not come to class that week. She mopes and broods, and yet somehow decides that she really does want to be back in seminar. On the following Tuesday, I find a letter on my desk asking if there is any way she can earn her way back into the class. I write her back asking her to detail a plan to make up and keep up with assignments without having to be nagged or reminded. I will not accept even one more excuse.

After several drafts, her plan outlines a specific schedule, time after school, fewer breaks, and set hours every weekend. The plan is initialed by her parents. She returns to the class, her attitude and effort greatly improved.

As the year progresses, the initial relief and good intentions bump head-on with her old habits of sidling out of what is hard for her. But she meets her commitment, even taking herself out of extracurricular activities in order to make sufficient time for her seminar work. In May, she writes about her conflict and struggle. "I learned I could do something if I really wanted to, and that makes me stronger." ❖

OVER AND OVER, MY STUDENTS SHOW ME THEIR WILL TO LEARN, to improve their work, to assert controls, and to reveal empathy and self-respect. And, yes, sometimes they show me their ability to make poor choices. It takes my best efforts and teaching to confront missing assignments, inappropriate T-shirts, the suspicious clutch of students hovering at the edge of the playground, the ugly words in the note passed secretly, or the unmistakable threats that occur during a class activity.

And over and over, I learn that when I do pay attention, enforce limits, and use consequences, a mutual respect and alliance grows. Teachers need to hold "high expectations and be accessible," asserts Chris Stevenson in *Teaching Ten to Fourteen Year Olds* (Stevenson 1998, 14). Accessibility allows us to get to know our students, to listen to their "hopes and dreams." High expectations help us guide and protect those hopes.

"You were strict," Zack tells his sixth grade teacher during a surprise visit back from high school, "but you'd hang in with me." We have to "hang in" with limits and consequences that embrace our students and help them embrace their own best intentions.

SUMMARY

WHEN CHILDREN BREAK RULES, teachers need to respond in a way that is neither punitive nor permissive, but that holds children accountable, keeps them safe, and helps them construct learning from the experience. Our responses to rule breaking are incremental, with levels of intervention ranging from subtly signaling a child to stop a behavior, through various consequences that include reparations, loss of privileges, or temporary removal from an activity.

When implementing logical consequences, teachers must first stop the misbehavior, give themselves time to evaluate the options, and then provide a specific workable action related to the problem, often with student input. Teachers should use language that helps children see the choices they make and the connection between privileges and responsibility. Logical consequences should be respectful in content and tone, reasonable in demand and duration, and related to the problem.

Logical consequences help children see the connection between what they did and the damage that happened, offer them a chance to repair the damage as best they can, and support them in learning ways they might behave differently in the future.

Works Cited

DEWEY, JOHN. 1963. *Experience & Education*. First Collier Books Edition. London: Collier Books.

DREIKURS, RUDOLF, FLOY C. PEPPER, AND BERNICE BRONIA GRUNWALD. 1982. *Maintaining Sanity in the Classroom: Classroom Management Techniques*. Second edition. Philadelphia, PA: Taylor & Francis, Inc.

MACKENZIE, ROBERT. 1997. "Setting Limits in the Classroom." *American Educator* (Fall): 32–43.

NELSEN, JANE, EdD. 1996. *Positive Discipline*. Revised edition. New York: Ballantine Books.

STEVENSON, CHRIS. 1998. *Teaching Ten to Fourteen Year Olds*. Second edition. New York: Addison Wesley Longman, Inc.

CHAPTER 7
Time-Out:
Establishing Boundaries and Promoting Self-Control

"TIME-OUT" IS ONE PART OF A SYSTEM of logical consequences. All children, in the natural course of things, explore limits, test boundaries, lose control, act out, defy authority, and "forget" the very rules that they uttered just five minutes ago. Used correctly, in combination with other techniques, time-out permits children to make mistakes and test the limits well within the guardrails of adult controls. It is a system which is protective, and which at the same time supports the child's own struggle for autonomous control. Time-outs can establish the safety nets and boundaries of rules, while promoting the dignity of self-control and the incentive to achieve it.

Time-out in fourth grade

Ms. Bush's fourth graders are a diverse group, some still learning English, some struggling with other skills. They are familiar with the practiced routines of the class and need only a few words from their teacher to prepare for language arts time. In moments, chairs slip under desks, books go back on shelves, and a circle forms around the standing easel. Ms. Bush signals for silence and the comfortable chatter subsides.

"Today," she begins, "we are going to work on ways to show what you have learned about verbs. Yesterday I asked you to think of ideas, and I thought of a few ideas, too."

For the next fifteen minutes, possibilities ranging from "a verb ABC book" to games like "verbopoly" and "verb trivia" are suggested, described, and written on a chart. Evan, seated strategically next to his teacher, begins to skate around the floor, sliding into his own orbits, bumping into a neighbor. Her voice barely above a whisper, head bent toward Evan, Ms. Bush says, "Time-out, Evan." She turns immediately back to the group as Evan gets up, walks around the edge of the circle, and takes a seat at his desk a few yards away. He slouches, head resting on extended arms, his face turned toward the class. When a plan sheet is passed out, he starts immediately to write. He has not missed a thing and rejoins the circle a few minutes later when Ms. Bush signals him to do so.

A few minutes later, Elise talks with a neighbor while a classmate is describing his idea. Ms. Bush mouths "time-out" to her, almost imperceptibly, and Elise goes to her desk with little disturbance. Like Evan, she clearly keeps track of the continuing discussion while there.

Students disperse to their seats, fill out plan sheets, and begin to work. Half an hour later the class is still focused and engaged. An eager, purposeful hum fills the room as partners pass rulers, sharpen pencils, read over drafts, enjoy each other's wit, and share spelling skills. Evan is working with Jaime on their verb "Pictionary" game. "The boxes have to match," he comments as he eyes his work critically, erases, and lines up his ruler again.

These students are learning and demonstrating discipline. They are expected to follow through on a plan and enjoy the benefits of productive activity. "Power is the ability to frame purposes and…follow through," says John Dewey in his definition of self-control (Dewey 1963, 64). ❖

THE IMPORTANCE OF TRUST AND CONNECTION

DURING THE LAST TEN YEARS, as a teacher of older children and as a consultant in many schools, I have advocated time-out and used it in my own classrooms. I have seen it help teachers create a safe, orderly atmosphere in which children can take risks and learn.

I have also observed the misuse of time-out. It does not work when teachers see it as a punishment tool, or when it is used to shame, threaten, chastise, or segregate.

It does not work when it is used over and over again for the same child; nor does it work when teachers become overly frustrated or resentful of a particular child. For time-out to work, teachers have to believe in and feel capable of implementing it as a strategy that enhances autonomy and classroom participation.

At best, time-out is a useful way to teach children to refocus and return to successful participation in class activity. Importantly, it preserves the integrity and fluidity of the work of the room. At worst, when it is seen as simply punitive, time-out kindles resentment and escalates foolish or defiant behaviors.

Psychologist Sally Crawford, who greatly supported Greenfield Center School teachers' work with middle school students, believes that for time-out to be effective, children must trust that the adults who put them in time-out ultimately (if not at the exact moment) understand the reasons for their behavior. One student acts up because he can't stop himself. Another may be unsettled and in the midst of a family unhappiness. A third may be distracting attention from inadequacies. While each student may be given a time-out, the sense that their teacher knows them and their lives helps keep them attached to the community.

Sheila Kelly, another child psychologist with whom I've worked, once described time-out as "a life-long skill." It is a challenge, even for skilled adults, to monitor their own behavior and give themselves a bit of a breather in order to regain controls they feel slipping. As with learning other valuable life skills, children need adult help and intervention to acquire the skill of time-out. They need practice in developing self-awareness and strategies to help them stay in control and be productive even in stressful moments. A system of time-out administered in a way that is matter-of-fact, not blameful, helps children to identify times when their behavior is unproductive and to practice ways to recapture self-control.

GUIDELINES FOR A TIME-OUT PROGRAM

IT SHOULD BE REMEMBERED that time-out does not work for every child. A small percentage of children need other strategies, as I discuss in depth in Chapters 8, 14, and 15.

For most children, however, time-out does work if used appropriately. The following guidelines describe an effective time-out program in the classroom. Each will be discussed in depth.

1. There is a familiar, predictable, and consistent procedure for classroom time-outs, and it is taught and practiced until students are familiar with it.

2. "Small things—time-out." The key is to pay attention to minor disturbances, rather than waiting for the work of the classroom or the controls of a child to deteriorate.

3. Time-outs affirm the integrity of the school rules, of the work of the group, and of the disruptive students.

4. Time-out is a direction, *not* a negotiation. The appropriate times for explanations are before and after the consequence, *never during.*

5. Check in with the student after the time-out. A check-in is a brief but important conversation to reestablish rapport and mutual understanding.

6. Time-outs are democratic. They are as appropriate a consequence for spreading gossip as they are for rambunctious pushing and shoving. And teachers must observe the classroom demographics to make sure time-outs are not being used disproportionately with any particular ethnic, gender, or racial group.

7. "I like you. I don't like that behavior." Time-outs focus on the behavior, not the character of the student. Teachers need to reassure children of acceptance when rules are broken and show empathy for rule breakers.

8. Time-outs emphasize choice and *faith.* Most children choose to follow or not follow the rules. Teachers express faith in the ability of students to return and follow the rules again—and again.

9. Time-outs may be carried out in another classroom with support from other teachers or administrators.

10. Teachers need to show empathy for rule breakers.

1. A familiar, consistent, predictable procedure

MARTY GETS UP FROM HER SEAT and goes to the time-out chair, located in a visible (not central) area of the classroom. She sits for five minutes, or until she receives a gesture from her teacher to return to her group. Signaled by her teacher's nod, Marty quietly returns to her place. There has been no explanation, no discussion. The unstated message is "You know the rules. You know you are disturbing the meeting. You will be able to recover your controls and return as a member of the group." Later, the teacher will check in to make sure that Marty does understand why she was sent to time-out.

The time-out chair

Time-out occurs in a designated, visible place in the classroom, away from a door or busy aisles and activity centers. It is not adjacent to the easel or blocks and is never in the hall or a dark corner. One teacher of eights used a time-out pillow instead of a chair. Children liked the idea of being less conspicuous and more comfortable. Recently, I saw a fifth grade in which a large reclining lounge chair was used for time-out. This chair enfolded the bodies of even the largest students in the room and seemed to soothe and help them regain equilibrium. Though it was highly appealing, the chair was used appropriately and carefully throughout the day.

For older students, time-out is often a single desk or worktable positioned off to the side, allowing privacy and quiet. It is not out in the hall or out of teachers' sight. It is not a "conversation pit" with other students or adults. Students may write or sit quietly as they recover controls and remember the rules.

A standard length of time

Time-outs are generally two to three minutes for five-year-olds and five minutes for ages six and older. The duration may depend on the nature of the misbehavior and the ability of the student to regain controls and properly return to the group.

With students in upper elementary or middle school grades, the duration of time-outs can vary depending upon the nature of the disturbance. Whether the duration is five minutes with permission to "Come back when you are ready" or the remainder of a period depends upon whether the behavior is an overflow of excitement, for example, or an intentional act of meanness. I believe that as children get older, we need to really weigh in on acts that affect the social well-being and emotional safety of the classroom as well as those that affect physical safety and classroom routines. If we hope to help children move toward self-control and enhance their ability to take on academic challenges, we must be vigilant about noticing and responding very strongly to behavior that endangers students' ability to ask questions, to concentrate, to tackle new material—behavior that hurts themselves or others.

A standard way to be released

Children may be released from time-out in several ways. It's best to be consistent once you choose a way.

With fives, the teacher tends to release the child using her voice: "Laura, you may come back now, and remember your quiet voice." She names the expectation and appropriate behavior. With sixes, sevens, and eights, a signal from the teacher is preferred—a nod or hand gesture. There is still a brief contact between the teacher and student, a recognition and confirmation that the student is ready to return, which assures the student as well as the teacher.

With older students—nines through twelves, familiar with time-out—I prefer a procedure which shares decision and responsibility: "Return when you know you are ready to follow the rules" or, more specifically, "Return when you know you are ready to make helpful comments to your math partner."

Even with older students, the responsibility is shared, not turned over. If I see a student return and resume the misbehavior, then I will determine readiness next time. (Remember that it takes practice and learning for children to have a clear conception of time. The child who darts right back may actually feel as if he/she was in time-out for an hour!) If certain children frequently return before they are ready to participate successfully, we may not want to leave them with that decision. Some students may need help to change their goals from just coming back to coming back ready to work. A "contract" (see Chapter 15) to specify the skills needed to return to the group and resume work is needed for some students.

Some teachers like to use timers, such as sand timers, which are quiet and don't attract attention. Often children like the timer, which gives them a sense of control, although it must also be understood that the task is not merely to bide time, but to recover controls.

Time-out is carefully introduced

Teachers introduce time-out to the class during the first week of school as part of the process of establishing rules and consequences. I present time-out as a way that grown-ups help children to get back their controls. Children can also teach themselves to get back their controls, quiet and calm their bodies, and remember their rules.

Some teachers prefer to present time-out as a time to "take a break" or "stop and think," and they call the chair "the thinking chair." A word of caution about this term: It is not a requirement that every child use time-out to think. The goal of time-out is for the child to regain his/her best controls. Some children may need to do this by thinking. Others may not—they may simply need to be in a quiet, removed spot. A few, even, are better able to regain their controls by doing some small, simple activity, such as finger knitting or doodling. The critical factor in time-out is that a space is created for self-control to be regained.

I stress that time-out is a job; it is work to recover self-control. With older students, I talk about the angry or bad feelings time-out may evoke and about appropriate ways to channel frustrations. It's a hard job to return to your work and also express upset feelings in a timely and respectful way. I also explain that other people have a job to do when someone is in time-out—to help the person concentrate by not disturbing or making fun of him/her.

Over and over, I remind children that time-out doesn't mean teachers don't like you. "Everyone forgets their controls sometimes, and everyone forgets the rules sometimes. Children forget the rules; so do teachers and parents. Our rules make it safe and good for everyone in school: not just me, not just one or two other people—everyone. So, it's very important that we respect the rules and use them. When we do forget or choose not to use a rule, we need to remember. We need a time-out. *Time-out is a chance to recover the rules* so we can keep our classroom safe and gather our own controls. Then we are ready to come back and join the group."

Role-playing

From ages five through eight, students love to role-play and practice the steps of time-out. Students rehearse how to go to time-out, regain control, and return to the group showing the appropriate behavior. It is also important for the other students to rehearse their "jobs" when a classmate is in time-out.

I act the part of a student who sits in the time-out chair banging her feet and chanting provocatively. "Is this the way to be in time-out?" I ask. Students respond with a no. "And why not?" I continue. I want to make sure that my class understands the purpose of time-out.

"You're not supposed to make noise," one student replies.

"Why not?" I want to reinforce the idea that time-out is for getting back in control. "If I see you banging your feet and chanting, I'm not sure that you are really working on remembering your controls," I might say. "Now, who can show us the right way to be in time-out?"

Another time, I might play the part of a student who grabs a pencil from a partner. Another student, acting the part of the teacher, says, "Time-out." I start to argue and fuss. Then I ask the class, "Is this what to do when the teacher says 'Time-out'? Who can show us what to do?" We will also go over what to do if we want to talk to the teacher. "If you have special reasons for needing a pencil, when may you tell the teacher?" Reassurance that there will be a check-in lets children know that they will have a time to share information and register their feelings.

Later, Margie acts out going to time-out and I act out the part of another pestering classmate. "Whattaya doin', Margie?" I whisper, and start to play with her. "Am I doing my job now?" I ask the class. I reinforce that the job of classmates and friends is to help the person in time-out to concentrate. "How do we help our friends when they are in time-out?" I will ask. Eventually the answers come:

"Let them be quiet."

"Let them concentrate."

"Let them be alone."

It is critical to remind children that they can be helpful, not hurtful, after a time-out. "You can welcome friends back to the group after a time-out. You can show them what the group is doing. You can give them a friendly pat on the back."

Let students share feelings about time-out

It's important for children to talk about how time-out feels. Most often it feels bad, although that is not the objective. Five-year-olds tend to feel bad because they strongly want the approval of teachers. Sixes are more apt to experience pangs of guilt, stemming from confused desires to do good and also to do bad. With sevens, the children are vulnerable to self-criticism and criticism from adults, and sometimes an exaggerated fear of disapproval. At eight, peer visibility and the resulting embarrassment surfaces. Issues of fairness and justice (particularly the teacher's) appear by ten and eleven, and students regularly take sides or make judgments about their own and others' time-outs. They are more apt to be angry at the teacher or at classmates.

Here are some examples of typical feelings:

"You feel bad in time-out 'cause you wish you were good." —(AGE FIVE)

"The worst thing about time-out is you get sent away from everybody and you can't talk." —(AGE SIX)

"Time-out feels angry. I'm angry at myself for doing what I did, like punching." —(AGE SEVEN)

"I'm embarrassed because the whole class was there." —(AGE EIGHT)

"You feel embarrassed and that you've done the worst thing in the world! Especially if the teacher yells at you and then everyone stares." —(AGE NINE)

"Time-out feels bad, because it takes time out of your day with friends or important things that you have to do." —(AGE TEN)

"It's a quiet place if I know what I did to get there. It's an angry place if I don't know what I did." —(AGE ELEVEN)

"Sometimes time-out is OK. I mean, I feel bad when it happens, like when I'm hyper and I have to go to time-out. But sometimes I think there should be other things too, 'cause kids don't really learn that much from time-out when they get older anyway." —(AGE TWELVE)

2. Small things—time-out

TIME-OUT IS THE STEP that follows a reminder. The key to using a time-out system effectively is to pay attention to the small disruptions, the minor infractions and misbehaviors. We take action before the lesson is in ruins, before self-controls—the student's and our own—deteriorate. When we wait for things to get worse, we are rarely disappointed.

We don't allow the minor drumming on the desk to reach a crescendo. The nagging and nuisance behavior does not go on until finally all our "buttons" are pushed. The background whispers and snide teasing are not ignored until fists fly or tears pour.

When we wait for an explosion, we risk ugly confrontations. It can be very difficult for children to reenter their group and recover a sense of goodwill after making a scene. The eruptions tend to be frightening and isolate the child from peers. They may also threaten the relationship between the teacher and the class. I recall, once, a child hurling scissors at someone. In a rage, I yanked the child out of the room.

A little later, at a drawing and writing time, another child showed me her picture. It depicted a large lady with a terrible frown holding a smaller person with tears. The caption said, "Miss Charney taking Michael outside." It was a scary picture.

The hope is that we will be able to intercept Michael before he throws things and before our patience is gone. We must deal with the small things so they don't grow. We try to deal with the rude remark rather than the physical fight, with the distracting gesture rather than the outburst that stops a lesson, with the whispered secrets rather than established cliques.

A pattern of casual "shut-ups" is not allowed to grow into one of constant insults. Noah may not call Mark "Fatty," even if he claims he's joking. Kevin may not use his superior size to push others aside, take a pencil, or reserve first place in line. The group lesson might be stalled if I say "Martin, the blackboard is this way!" for the fiftieth time between clenched teeth instead of saying "Martin, time-out." The small sideshows will not devastate the lesson, or the temper of the teacher. But, unless they are confronted, these "small disturbances" add up to constant noise and interruptions which drain and divert the best intentions. Often they are the very things we pretend not to notice.

Every teacher could make an endless list—during instruction, Tracy spaces out, Romero fiddles with his shoes (loudly ripping the Velcro straps), Katrina waves her

TEACHING CHILDREN TO CARE

hand while someone else is talking, Jules smiles and winks in secret collusion with his friend Marc. Alex regularly careens around the room—his idea of walking is full-speed-ahead. He's a large boy, and he frequently bumps into the furniture, other children, and even largish teachers. He's quick to say "sorry" and express genuine regret, but if he slowed down, he would hardly crash at all, and no one would get hurt. Why make a fuss? He's only ten—he can't help it. But the fact is that he *can* help it! He can move slowly and with planning—or not move at all.

It is important that children understand that they can help it. Minor disturbances are within their control. Tracy is able to listen, Romero to disregard his shoe straps, and Katrina to put her hand down while someone else is talking. We know that at age two the ability to inhibit behavior is lacking. At age four, wants may still win out over shoulds. But at age ten, Alex can tell himself not to run, and he can follow his own directions. If we focus on "small things," the poke does not turn into a punch, and the poking child is still very much in control of his/her own body. With help, children are able to pull themselves together, to regain self-control. When we intervene before the behavior escalates, we increase the chance for self-regulation, and we protect the child from outbursts which threaten self-respect.

Noah may not call Mark "Fatty," even if he claims he's joking.

"Time-out, Noah," says his teacher.

Later, Noah reflects on the experience.

3. Time-outs protect the integrity of school rules, the group, and the disruptive student

Donny

Christie is speaking. She is telling the group about a week-long visit from her cousin. She confesses that it wasn't so easy to have to share her room, her possessions, her parents. She further admits that she didn't want to let her cousin ride her bike, and her father made her. "That was just so unfair. I had a terrible weekend." Donny, meanwhile, is fidgeting with an eraser, which he has balled up so that it rolls. He begins to roll it, making an inclined plane with his leg. He watches with rapt attention as the eraser-ball travels one leg, then another. He is so intent on his own activity that Christie and the group have momentarily ceased to exist. As the ball gathers momentum, he looks around, catching the eye of another classmate, a giddy grin spreading across his face. "Time-out, Donny," I say quietly.

Donny gets up and leaves the group. He looks back, making a face. The group stays riveted on Christie. A few initial displays from Donny, as he settles into the time-out chair, are ignored. After several minutes, he appears to relax, tension subsiding. His attention—he is still within earshot of the circle—returns to the meeting. A nod lets him know that he can return. He takes his seat. The group is still questioning Christie.

"What did your father do when you grabbed your bike away from your cousin?" the class wants to know.

Donny raises his hand. "Did your cousin get mad at you, too?" he questions. Donny has rejoined the class. ❖

SEVERAL THINGS HAVE HAPPENED. The teacher has preserved Christie's turn to speak. She has followed through on the expectation that children respect each other's "turn" by actively listening to one another. She has also intercepted Donny before he receded further from the meeting or became disruptive. The short time-out allowed Donny to redirect his energy and take charge of himself, making it possible for him to reinvest in the group. The brief exchange between teacher and child did not distract from Christie's story or divert attention from the sharing to the misbehavior. The time-out ritual is not intrusive, and it leaves Donny's action as

Name: Erin

Group: _____ Age: 6

1) Why do you think kids go to time-out?

tery Boo [to friends]
tery hyret Pre)PI's   Fieiings

2) What's good about time-out?

Y
    Lren   kiбS   how to   can
Canterl   tcme Sckels

3) What's the worst thing about time-out?

Yoy   Can't
take

Translation:

They are bad to their friends. They hurt people's feelings.

Kids can learn how to control themselves.

You can't talk.

inconspicuous as possible. There is no need to admonish or scold. The objectives—to safeguard the group and ensure individual conduct—were met. Donny's behavior did not progress to the point where it upset Christie, the teacher, or Donny because the teacher reacted to "small things."

A "small thing" that is frequently observed among students of middle school age is the exchange of come-backs, put-downs, and "dis you" comments. It has become almost a mark of adolescence, part of the process of coming of age. However, it is not conducive to open and honest discussion and instruction because it tends to silence questions, especially from the more hesitant and self-conscious questioners. Sharp-tongued students can dominate and intimidate. It often means that girls—though not only girls—are less apt to raise their hands, participate in class, or share their views. When that happens, despite our intentions to encourage expression, it means that those students with confidence and plenty of social currency dominate.

I have seen remarkable changes when teachers confront these behaviors and set up the ground rules for respectful interactions, particularly for how to talk, listen, joke, and have fun. Once the tone and expectations are clear, time-outs protect the work of the group and the individual.

4. Time-out is a direction, *not* a negotiation

IN THE IMMEDIATE ENFORCEMENT of time-out, lengthy verbal explanations and negotiations are strictly avoided. Imagine if instead of the directive "Time-out," the teacher had said, "Donny, you need to go to time-out, because you are rolling a ball and not listening to Christie." Donny, now the center of attention, would be apt to argue, "I *was* so listening…" An argument might lead next to a confrontation, and Christie's sharing would quickly take second place to the duel between teacher and student.

If the teacher had just reached over and taken the ball from Donny, called his name, or nudged him gently back into the activity, with no mention of time-out, wouldn't that be as effective and easier? Not likely. Too many reminders (more than one) allow small disturbances to keep erupting like popcorn—one after another—and keep taking the attention of the teacher and the group. Time-out sends the message that you are *truly* expected to follow the rules.

There is a strong urge in teachers and parents to justify and defend their enforcement of the rules each time an incident occurs. We want to be clear and to be sure that children understand, and we also want them to agree. This justifying and defending may encourage children to use a form of "blackmail." Children will use whatever language is effective, such as "You're a bad teacher. You're not nice" or even the "H" word: "I hate you, Teacher. You're mean."

When we hasten to convince children that the rules are right, fair, and necessary, we shift attention from the misbehavior. It is vitally important that children understand what is right, fair, and necessary about the rules, but they don't usually understand those concepts at the moment a rule is invoked. In a meeting circle, my students brilliantly explain the meaning of respect and defend the concept, but when a student is caught shoving someone on the playground, it's usually the other person's fault, the referee "stinks," and the rules are "stupid."

Gabrielle

Gabrielle was a fifth grade student who had developed negotiation to an art, often to her own detriment. She came to work with me on her reading, delayed for her age, and was presented to me as a difficult but appealing child. "She has tantrums," I was told kindly by the principal. I could expect at least one tantrum a week, which showed progress because they had once been more frequent.

Along with tears and blubbering, Gabrielle hurled selected insults, which revealed a knack for the precise words to hurt and offend her teachers. To the kind, mild-mannered principal, she yelled, "Child-molester!" To her stern but fair-minded classroom teacher, she yelled, "You're picking on me. You pick on me 'cause I'm not your pet!" And to another, warm and affectionate teacher, she spat out, "You think everyone likes you, but they don't."

Usually, in the din of comforting this wailing child, in quieting her accusations and offering reassurance—"course I like you"—no one remembered what had started the tantrum in the first place. The trigger was always the same. Gabrielle was asked for some piece of work, work that she couldn't—or wouldn't—do. The tears and stomping stopped the minute the threat of the work was removed. She was hardly out of control. She was effectively manipulating teachers to hide her real deficits and fears.

The vulnerability of the adults helped to establish this pattern of behavior. Gabrielle was skilled at creating a sense of doubt and loss of clarity. It was easy to over-explain and reassure her with affection. In the end, she was not asked to come through with her work or required to use self-control like other children. Always, her academic program was modified and reduced, in hopes that another tantrum might be averted.

With her parents and the principal, I made a plan. The next time Gabrielle erupted, I told her, "You have two minutes. Get yourself back together, go back to your work, or you go home." Sobs, tears, loud cries, insults. I counted. I pointed to the timer. Two minutes. Through the blanket of red eyes and writhing motions, she watched me. At the two-minute buzzer, the principal entered, according to our prearranged plan, and took Gabrielle, crying and cursing, to the office. Her mother was called immediately, according to the second part of the plan, and she went home. Gabrielle returned the next day, cheerful and composed. The day went fine, the week passed without event. The second week she told me the work was too hard and began to whimper.

"No whimpering, Gaby."

"You're supposed to understand," she said puckering her mouth, jutting out her lips in disdain. "You're supposed to help us kids, and not be so mean."

"Time-out," I replied. "Two minutes."

I was very prepared for this student. I had school and parent support. I knew her history, her deflated self-esteem. I'd seen her bluff and fake.

I struggled with my own controls, to appear calm and to keep my mouth shut. I would not say "Yes, I am understanding. No, I'm not mean. I do this for your own good." I would not try to convince her that she could do her work, or try to explain, reason, or argue her into compliance. It is not a disgrace that this young, willful girl could create such a rush of anxiety and doubt in the minds and purposes of adults. Certainty is seldom found in teaching, and it can take a while to put the pieces of a puzzle together.

It is not remarkable that this girl never went home again, that she returned after one and a half minutes to her work, mindful of the timer. She looked grim and wary. She snarled and glowered, but she sat back at the table, beginning a long journey, through syllables and vowel utterances and Judy Blume's captivating stories, to achieve some degree of reading success. The next couple of years were good for Gabrielle with all her teachers, although the onset of adolescence and new social pressures again took their toll.

Gabrielle helped me realize my obligation as a teacher to insist that children draw on their own controls—and not to apologize. She was not the ordinary student, testing and experimenting with the boundaries of the world. She was erecting a shield for what she saw as failures and inadequacies. Time-outs that let her know I believed she could gather her controls and get to work helped her put aside that shield. Negotiations and explanations had not. ❖

5. Use "check-ins" as a procedure for inquiry and reconnection

AT THE RIGHT MOMENT—after a time-out—explanation and discussion help students construct meaning and take responsibility. At the wrong time—while a rule is being enforced—discussion stimulates evasion.

Check-ins consist of a five-minute inquiry at the end of the morning or the day, covering the following points:

- ✦ Do you know why I sent you to time-out?

- ✦ What was going on for you?

- ✦ Do you understand why that behavior is a problem for our class?

- ✦ Do you need any help following the rules next time?

Even when an additional explanation about the rules is not necessary, a check-in helps to reestablish connection and rapport. If time-outs have been repetitive, I might start a short conversation by saying, "I notice that you have been in time-out several times this week. You seem to have trouble taking care of yourself during writing period. What's up?"

This is the time when I listen. "Tell me why you think you had a time-out today." I am willing to hear the other side and even to negotiate— "What do you think might help you during writing time?" or "What do you think might help you avoid quarreling with Maggie?"

Our goals are to air any misperceptions, build shared perceptions and understanding, establish agreements, and reconnect and "shake hands." We emphasize that it is the behavior that is a problem, not the person.

"I wasn't making a face," Reena explained when I checked in with her. "I was just confused."

"When you are confused and then you scrunch up your mouth and roll your eyes, it makes me think you are making fun of what someone is saying. Do you see how that could happen?"

It is important to acknowledge differing perceptions and understand the different perspectives. Check-ins allow teachers and students to ask questions, clarify intentions, and offer explanations. I am struck with how often students harbor resentments for those times teachers were "wrong" and never gave them a chance to explain. And yet students readily forgive mistakes if teachers listen to an honest explanation and, when appropriate, apologize.

Recently an eighth grader recalled a time when his first grade teacher had been explaining about gravity. Utterly baffled at the concept of a spinning earth, Matt had asked, "Why don't we all just fall off?" He said, "I thought it was the smartest thing I'd said all day and I felt proud of myself. To this day I have no idea why she sent me to time-out." Remembering Matt at age six, his penchant for wisecracks already well developed, I could imagine his teacher's interpretation. But, honestly, Matt couldn't, and an opportunity for empathy and connection went ignored. Imagine Matt's first grade teacher saying, "I thought you were making a wisecrack. I see that I was wrong this time and I'm sorry. Next time I will try to remember to ask you first."

Cindy

A discussion on current events was underway in my seventh and eighth grade class. Cindy, socially awkward and intent on being heard, was again quick to raise her hand and offer her opinion. Brittany turned to her friends and whispered a comment that sent them into a spasm of ill-concealed giggles. Cindy was clearly the object of their mockery. Although I could not hear the comment, I could tell from their expressions that they were making fun of an awkward classmate.

"You need to leave the meeting," I said to them sharply. They got up quickly to find seats in adjacent areas of the room.

After the meeting, I went to check in with them, to see if what I had observed was correct. "Were you making fun of Cindy?" I asked. Brittany answered first and made no attempt to deny or evade responsibility. But she started to cry when she said, "I'm so tired of Cindy." The other girls broke in with similar claims of mounting irritation and resentment. They had tried over and over to include Cindy with little success and felt overwhelmed with the job of being "nice." While mocking Cindy was not acceptable, for these girls it was an understandable release from complex and frustrating social responsibilities.

While my first response was one of anger and a desire to protect a vulnerable student from the sometimes cruel reactions of peers, by checking in with the other students I became aware of their perspective. Protecting socially awkward children from ridicule and exclusion is a tricky process. The circle had to be made safe for Cindy, but Cindy also needed to acquire social skills for interacting with her peers. And while she was acquiring them, I needed to help both her and other children—some of whom had been trying very hard to reach out to Cindy and were exhausted by their efforts. Later in the day, we made time to talk about ways to assert their needs with Cindy without being mean. ❖

6. Time-outs are democratic

"I THINK THAT KIDS GO TO TIME-OUT FOR FOOLIN' AROUND. Well, that's boys. Girls go 'cause they're talking when they're not supposed to," said Peter, age eleven. "I guess you could say that girls are loudmouths and boys act goofy."

Time-out needs to be applied equally to the chronic troublemakers and the occasional rule breakers. Anyone can misbehave. Time-out applies to the boys who are most likely to tumble from chairs and flick the pattern blocks across the floor. It applies to the girls who may be more apt to tell secrets and make snide remarks. It is used for the sneaky as well as the obvious misdemeanors. It applies to Gretchen, who loves to sit next to Seth, who is so easy to engage. Given any little poke or tickle, Seth flops and writhes flamboyantly, quickly catching the teacher's eye and getting sent to the time-out chair. But the teacher must also notice Gretchen's provocation and say "Gretchen, time-out."

Some children struggle more with self-control and therefore have more time-outs. But if we pay attention to the subtle provocations as well as what Peter called "goofy" behavior, we would see that most children forget the rules at one point or another. Time-outs need to be there for Gabrielle's outbursts, for Alex when he bumps a path through the classroom, and for Dinah, who is usually a "model student."

Dinah

Dinah, as a fifth grader, was cheerful, took her work seriously, adored her teacher, and got along with her classmates. She was a class leader and an ardent contributor to every project. She loved to play and loved to work. She was tearful when her best friends left her out, and she tried to be a better friend when she was the one who excluded others. She put in overtime as a school tutor, enjoying her role as a teacher and counselor for younger students. To a casual observer, therefore, it might have been something of a surprise to see Dinah a year later in the time-out chair in her sixth grade classroom. Dinah? In time-out?

But Dinah herself seemed energized by the experience. "I went to time-out today!" she announced with a twinge of boasting in her voice. It was her teacher's unfair handling of a classroom situation that started it all, Dinah explained. "She blamed Angela, but Angela didn't do a thing," she stated righteously.

"So what did you do?"

"I told her she was a jerk. Well, she was!"

For the first time, Dinah had dared to challenge authority. It was in part a function of her age and development. By age eleven, most children are eager to try out a small act of rebellion, to question and judge the fairness of elders. So it was with Dinah. Her unquestioning devotion to teachers had given way to feisty defiance.

It would have been simple for her teacher to dismiss Dinah's behavior, to pretend she hadn't heard. But it was important that Dinah got sent to time-out because it demonstrated the teacher's self-respect. The teacher's response conveyed the message "I don't insist that you like me or agree with me. I do insist that you show respect."

Time-out provides a way for children to test limits while still maintaining the structure and order of the classroom. It is the child's deed, not the child's character, that is at issue. Time-out is there for all children and keeps them all safe. ❖

7. "I like you, but I don't like that behavior"

"I LIKE YOU but I don't like it when you hurt other people."

"I don't like it when you don't listen to directions, but I do like you."

"I like that you have so much to say, but I don't like it when you keep interrupting."

These statements preserve the knowledge of the teacher's ongoing approval and secure the child's own sense of inner approval. I've done something "wrong," but my teacher still likes me—and I can still like myself. If either statement is lacking, children may become utterly discouraged. I go out of my way to reassure children, particularly when time-outs are frequent or hard, or if I feel angry. Angry or intense feelings, calculated or not, can have a strong effect on children.

"When I sent you to time-out today, I was feeling angry at you. It makes me angry to see you act silly at every meeting. And I think it makes you feel bad when I get angry. Is that true?" (Student nods.) "I get angry because I want your good contributions at meeting, and I want to see not the silly behavior but the smart behavior I know you have." I acknowledge my anger and the student's response to it, often a combination of anger and upset. I also want to convey the idea that my anger comes from positive expectations. The aim is to affirm, by recognizing and naming the strengths that we see in students, while holding them to the limits.

Children are particularly vulnerable to criticism and to consequences at certain ages. I have seen seven-year-olds react severely to time-out and teacher disapproval of any kind. The reactions often grow from a heightened fear of any criticism and a need for immediate reassurance. I don't eliminate time-outs from the classroom, but I do make a concerted effort to use a mild manner and to provide many assurances, often at the end of the day. "I see you really made the art shelf look beautiful."

Children entering adolescence also tend to be highly vulnerable. Adult rebukes become easily exaggerated, as do many other things, particularly when children are in the throes of finding everything from their hair to their parents unacceptable. While there is often a surface disclaimer, such as "Who cares," I am convinced that most children care deeply and need repeated reassurances. I find that they need to hear that they are liked and that they are likable, in specific and realistic terms.

There are some children, at any age, because of their make-up or temperament, who find time-outs especially painful. They are sometimes our most difficult children, yet they must be protected from becoming unlikable to themselves, their peers, and their teachers. My approaches to these children are detailed in Chapter 8, "The Five Percent."

Time-outs work best when a reliable message is given, in words and body language, that teachers accept and like their students, even when they don't like some of their behavior.

8. Time-outs emphasize choice and faith

WHEN I SAY "TIME-OUT," I am responding to a choice that the student has made. The choice is either to follow meeting rules or to go to time-out. It is a true decision. When I remind a child who has started to whisper to her friend instead of listening, I restate that choice. Sometimes the child decides to stop whispering and plugs in to the meeting. Sometimes she doesn't, and a time-out is enforced. The child has chosen not to cooperate—this time. Next time the choice may be different.

The vocabulary of time-out establishes over and over the choices available and, importantly, the consequences of those choices. "You can speak quietly to your partner or, if you get loud and silly, you go to time-out. Your choice."

When we state the choices for children, and stress their essential role as the choice-maker, we state our faith in their ability to achieve self-control. One eight-year-old boy made daily rampages to be first in line. He pushed, he ran, he calculated his timing to the second so he could always be first. Finally, after several time-outs, he was told, "You can continue to try to be first in line, and to shove or push and then go to time-out. Or you can decide that being first isn't always so important, and probably then you won't go to time-out. It's your choice."

After a few days, there was a noticeable shift in his behavior, as if he were testing out a new mode. A few more days after that, he quietly confided to his teacher that he didn't think he had to be first every day anymore. It really wasn't *so* important, but he still wanted to be first once in awhile.

It was important that the teacher did not attempt to argue the objective importance of being first in line with him. The teacher could and did establish the boundaries, but she could not establish the essential meaning of being first in line for this child. That was his choice. He was allowed to come to a meaningful decision and then to take charge of that decision for himself, even though it meant giving up something he cared about. That, I feel, is a perfect example of self-control.

When there is not a real choice, I will modify the expectations until there is a choice. For example, when I feel that a child cannot choose to sit and attend for a thirty-minute period, I might say, "You can sit and pay attention for ten minutes." This affirms the controls that exist in all children and our faith that each of them can make the choices to use those controls.

Brendan

Brendan was a second grader in Ms. Freeman's Washington, DC, classroom. He was a boy with a winsome desire to please and a maddening capacity to displease. In his fear that he might miss something, might not be chosen or noticed, might not get his own way, he was apt to push, grab, call out, and throw things, including a convenient tantrum. He tended to listen only when absolutely necessary or when compelled.

By late September, I could see that he responded to his teacher's quiet and firm manner, her patient repetition, and her insistence that he do things over and get them right. Still, most days included at least one time-out. As the year went on, he stayed by his teacher's side and placed his chair next to hers, often by choice. Much later in the year, observing the class getting ready to go to lunch and recess, I noticed Brendan in step with the routines. He was responding to his teacher's faith in his abilities by making choices and directing himself, often out loud.

As the class lined up, Ms. Freeman listed off the things to remember: lunch boxes, meal tickets, jackets, and "Does everyone have their SSR book on a table?" Brendan reacted with a jolt. "My book," he said and speedily ran to his cubby, pulled out his reader, and hastily plopped it down on a table. Then he stopped. Words again: "No. That's Steven's table...I'll get in trouble. I don't want to get in trouble." He moved his book to a new spot and ran to the end of the line. ❖

9. Time-outs may be carried out in another classroom with support from other teachers or administrators

ALTHOUGH THE MAJORITY of time-outs are handled exclusively by the primary teacher, time-out outside of the classroom may be necessary if:

   ✦ A child's distracting behaviors (banging feet, calling out) continue while in the time-out space and are disrupting others.

- The stimulation of the room continues to overwhelm or agitate the student.

- The misbehaviors repeat even after one or two time-outs in the room.

- The teacher needs a time-out from the student.

- The message needs to be sent to the student that this misbehavior is serious enough to warrant more than a momentary pause within the room. Contemptuous, taunting behavior is one example.

Ways that teachers act as "buddies" to support classroom and community rules are discussed in Chapter 9, "Working Together to Support the Rules."

10. Teachers need to show empathy for rule breakers

ONE THIRTEEN-YEAR-OLD DEFINED, for me, an empathic response to children when he explained why he liked his teacher, why all the kids did. "'Cause he doesn't let you get away with stuff, like not doing your work, but if it's raining and he knows you're restless, he'll let you run around awhile."

Having empathy does not mean pitying or making excuses for the child. It means trying to understand the child's experience in the way that s/he experiences it. It means listening to what the child is saying, even when we do not sanction the behavior. We may not accept a child's lie, but we recognize its humanness. We show empathy for our rule breakers when we welcome them back to the group, express faith in their capacity to improve, show that we see their strengths as well as their weaknesses. Empathy cements the bonds between teachers and children and allows teachers and children to learn, not in opposition, but in mutual trust.

ADAPTING TIME-OUT FOR
STUDENTS OF MIDDLE SCHOOL AGE

I USE TIME-OUT with sixth, seventh, and eighth graders. I do not use it often, and I do not use a time-out chair. Often, I do not even use the words "time-out." It is the action, not the wording, that is critical, and older children, particularly those who associate the words "time-out" with their own younger student days, may bristle at the phrase.

There are a number of ways to modify time-out to be more effective with older students, to insure respect for the rules and also to keep the relationship between teachers and students viable. Because most older students are quick to pick up and respond to subtle signals, I use time-outs with them only after signals are ignored or when behavior is deliberately hurtful or provocative. For example, when the class discussion slips into chit-chat, merely saying the phrase "meeting rules" generally refocuses attention. When I see a twosome off and running on their own agenda despite the on-going lesson, a snappy look or "I need your attention now" will usually work. A head shake reminds Casey that legs don't go up on adjacent chairs or lets Robbie know to stop rummaging and rustling papers. Usually, a few words, a look, a light touch, or a raised hand reminds and refocuses distracting or inappropriate behaviors.

Older children also have a critical need to "save face," and I often present them a choice, then walk away for a moment, giving them the chance to make their decision without confrontation. "You must focus on your note-taking at this table, or I will move you to a place where there are fewer distractions," I say quietly to a student who continues to whisper and giggle after I have already made eye contact and given her the "Sshh" signal. I walk away, check in with another student, then walk back close enough to ascertain that she is diligently writing in her notebook, her finger locating her place on a chart in the book she is using. She has made her choice.

Most students, at this point, do know the rules and need time-out as a periodic reminder, not as a repetitive pattern. Bouncing in and out of time-out does not build self-restraints. I recall one year when sixth graders, busy further undermining an ineffective teacher, had contests to see who could go to time-out the most. One claimed a record of fifty-two! It may be necessary to establish a "contract" with a specified number of time-outs in a day or a week. After two time-outs, there are sequential next steps: other classroom, parents notified, etc. (See Chapter 9, "Working Together to Support the Rules.") There are always exceptions. Some children will benefit from more frequent "breaks." Some will not benefit from any.

Time-outs are appropriate when misbehavior is continued after a reminder or when students are provocative or dismissive of one another. Here are some examples from middle-school-age classrooms:

- ✦ Peter makes sarcastic statements when peers say things he disagrees with during the discussion.

- ✦ Alicia continues to show off her nails or to set off giggles, disrupting a quiet work period.

- ✦ Jamal continues to blurt out answers in math class despite reminders.

- ✦ In response to a teacher's request, Margaret makes a face, saying, "Why should I?"

- Leila pretends not to hear the teacher and keeps sauntering about the room.

- James throws his pencil at Liddy.

- Erin and Claudia whisper and snicker while others are talking.

- Khary grabs Kim's hat and won't give it back.

Teachers are permitted to establish their authority as students test the limits. But even when authority is not the issue, time-outs with older students are important to maintain their respect for one another. Holding children to the limits usually elicits respect. Talking over discipline problems, at an appropriate time, creates accessibility, mutual respect, and empathy.

TIME-OUTS DO NOT WORK
FOR ALL CHILDREN

TIME-OUTS OFTEN DO NOT WORK for those children who have poor adaptive skills and have not developed the capacity to "shift gears," according to child psychologist Ross Greene. He describes particular children as "inflexible and explosive" (Greene 2001). Others are easily overwhelmed and frustrated by even minor or trivial obstacles and demands. Teachers may need to use time-outs to protect the work of the group, while also seeking other strategies to help these children learn (see Chapters 8, 14, and 15).

Most often, time-out does not work when children are engaged in power struggles, discussed in depth in Chapter 8. Again, teachers may need to continue to use time-out to protect the work of the group, while seeking other strategies. Generally, we need to question the effectiveness of time-outs if we see mounting or lingering signs of resentment, withdrawal, or insecurity. In some cases, we may want to reevaluate our class or individual expectations to make sure they are appropriate. When a child truly can't make an appropriate choice or meet an expectation, time-out will discourage, not encourage, discipline. Other approaches are needed.

Sometimes children come to school or back from recess already upset—fists clenched, bodies aggressively in motion. A teacher described one of her five-year-olds who began the day kicking, punching, and knocking over anything or anyone in his path. These children need a "time-in" rather than a time-out. They need comfort and holding, a time to build up or recover a sense of self, which is necessary to using self-control.

Summary

MARTY POKES HER NEIGHBOR during a meeting. "Marty—time-out."

Rachel interrupts…again. "Rachel—time-out."

Tyrone shoves ahead of the line to get out first.

Janie continues to draw after the signal.

Maggie tells Paul, "Shut up, moron."

Simmie and David are pencil-dueling during math lesson.

"Why should I?" whines Gorky when the teacher asks her to pick up her things.

The teacher responds each time. "Tyrone, Janie, Maggie, Simmie and David, Gorky—time-out."

Time-out redirects the rude remark, the impulsive action, the disruptive interruption, and is an effective strategy to reinforce rules and maintain limits. When rooted in an effort to promote accountability rather than blame, and when implemented with deliberate, practiced authority, time-out helps teachers preserve the well-being of the classroom and of individuals. Both reminder and reinforcement, time-out helps us remain firm and kind, to "do" the rules and not just say them.

Works Cited

DEWEY, JOHN. 1963. *Experience & Education*. First Collier Books Edition. London: Collier Books.

GREENE, ROSS W., PHD. 2001. *The Explosive Child: A New Approach for Understanding and Parenting Easily Frustrated, Chronically Inflexible Children.* Second edition. New York: Harper Collins Publishers.

CHAPTER 8
The Five Percent

To be effective, you must dare to start over—
to search for a whole new set of tools to reach through the
façade of misbehavior to the troubled child hiding within.

L. TOBIN
What Do You Do with a Child Like This?

KATY IS DELIBERATE AND ARTFUL in her provocations. Asked to hurry, she dawdles. She is the last to come to line and to circle up, slowing down her preparations in response to the readiness of the group. Asked to use a quiet voice, she makes airplane landing noises. Asked to wait a turn, she shoves ahead. Rather than appear oblivious or in a daydream, she defies with a gaze riveted on the teacher. If her first gestures are ignored, she does it again—and again. A smile crosses her face when her teacher finally bursts with impatience.

Nolan's eruptions are frequent and intense. If he gets called "out" in a kickball game, he hurls himself to the ground, pounding the pavement with coiled fists and letting go with inconsolable sobs. When Alana, seated next to him at a table, accidentally spills the container of markers, Nolan reacts with a powerful sideways shove, sending the astonished Alana to the floor, both her feelings and the arm she landed on bruised.

Mariah quickly appoints herself boss of her math team. No one protests. She is a fast thinker, vigilant as a scorekeeper, and intimidating with her tongue. When others' tallies conflict with her own, she corrects their additions with a snap. If a team member seems unsure of an answer, she mouths impatient, rude hints or utters loud expressions of disdain. When one of her own answers is wrong, she lashes out, cursing the game, her peers, and the teachers alike. Guided gently out of the class-room, she returns five minutes later and grabs the score sheet from a teammate, crosses out his sums, throws her pen on the floor, and begins to pull charts and papers from the wall. Later, after school that day, she replaces the displays with tidy and precise attentions, sweetly humming to herself.

WHILE TIME-OUT IS PART OF A PROCESS that begins where children are and takes them in the direction of self-control, it doesn't work for all children. In schools everywhere, teachers consistently identify a core of their children, "the five percent," who take so much of their time and energy that they feel the other ninety-five percent are neglected or shortchanged.

The behavior of the children they describe is often extreme and repetitive and persists despite consequences. Sometimes the severe behaviors numb us to more ordinary infractions and allow a tolerance for misbehavior to infect the tone of the classroom. We must figure out ways to manage our five-percenters—ways that involve limits, direction, and guidance. We must weigh carefully the needs of the community and the needs of the individual, perhaps our most difficult balancing act.

The five-percenters may follow time-out with a show of remorse or with a shrug of indifference; either way, the disruptions soon begin again. The five percent comprises two different groups: those who intentionally engage in power struggles and those who lack the emotional or cognitive skills to exert their own controls. Katy is a power struggler; Nolan is an "inflexible-explosive child," a term used by psychologist Ross Greene (Greene 2001); Mariah has a significant family history of abuse. Their behaviors stem from very different roots and require very different strategies, although time-outs are not likely to be helpful for any of them. Time-outs may still be necessary sometimes in order for the class to continue on course, but time-out will not be the strategy that helps our Katys, our Nolans, or our Mariahs improve their behavior.

Because the usual approaches do not always work effectively with these children, we need to explore alternative approaches and strategies. Both groups of children require flexibility from their teachers, along with some engineering and creative designing of classroom situations that will let such students experience and build upon success.

This chapter begins with two variations on the time-out strategy which help us deal with the power struggles of our more obstinate scrappers—using a "Time-Out Place" and "Bargaining." Some general guidelines for working with children lacking appropriate emotional or cognitive skills follow.

One word of caution: It can be very hard to tell whether a child behaving in an oppositional way is intentionally engaging in a power struggle or simply lacks the emotional or cognitive skills to behave differently. In other words, it can be hard to tell whether a child won't or can't behave well. Based on his many years of work with different kinds of children, Greene has come to the conclusion that most oppositional children fall in the "can't" category. "Children do well if they can" is the philosophy he holds in mind as he begins working with a child, and the assumption that he urges teachers to start with. (Greene 2001, 310)

POWER STRUGGLES

CHILDREN STRUGGLING WITH POWER challenge the teacher with defiance and insurgence. Teachers must find ways to break the cycle of negative attention that these children's adversarial relationship with authority generates. These are children who often trap us into arguments, usually to justify their claims that teachers are unfair and mean if we win, and that we are pushovers if we lose. We must recharge their relationship with authority, often by structuring elements of choice into situations that might typically not have choices, and by finding ways to listen and interpret without turning over the controls. Noting that sometimes power struggles have their origin in children's insecurity about their ability to succeed, psychologist Sylvia Rimm offers an approach that teaches "anti-arguing" strategies that hold children while preventing ceaseless cycles of argument and blame (Rimm 1997).

Doug

Doug, eleven, comes to school tired, often tardy, and in a negative mood. Getting him to bed and up in time for school has been a battle for years. His mother has long given up any say over bedtime or schedules. At school, Doug spends much of his energy on a steady pattern of evasion and trickery with teachers and classmates. Asked to produce the reading assignment he claims is done, he pretends to hunt for it, slowly and deliberately fumbling through his backpack and binders, hoping to play the scene out long enough that his teacher will be needed elsewhere and will forget. His maneuvers are particularly frustrating because Doug is very capable, and his work, when finally "extracted," is often of superior quality.

Though Doug's own work is frequently missing or hurried or unfinished, he is quick to comment on the insufficiencies of others' work. "You only did that much?" he guffaws, looking over at someone's paper. He is always ready with a snide comment or an assertion that he has a bigger computer, went on a better trip, or knows more facts. When confronted about misbehaviors, he denies, argues, and blames. He usually presents his situation as the fault of the school and the teachers. "They don't make me do my work," he blusters with a sly grin.

"Can we make you?" I ask.

"Not really," he answers. ❖

DOUG, LIKE KATY, is engaging his teachers in a power struggle. Sent to time-out, they are hapless victims of their teacher's disfavor. At the same time, if their misbehaviors are ignored or overlooked, they increase the pitch until the teacher or fellow students become *their* victims. The prize, in either case, is a disturbance and disruption, usually at the expense of the intended agendas of work and play.

Time-out will not improve the behavior of Doug or Katy. They have no rules to remember because it was "the teacher's fault" or it was "unfair." Doug will go home and tell his parents that he spent all day in time-out because his teacher is "so mean." His parents are opposed to time-out and make that clear to the teacher. A home-school conflict is added to the stress.

Still, while time-out may not improve Doug's behavior or attitude, it may sometimes be necessary to secure the well-being of the group and prevent Doug from browbeating other children or continually occupying the attention of the teacher. It is important that other children and teachers not be permitted to get so angry and fed up with Doug or Katy that they start to dislike them. It is important to rescue these children from the ingenuity of their own alienation. But, because Doug perceives the time-outs as "unfair"—more evidence that his teacher or classmates or the school "picks on" him—he will disturb the class again and again. Time-outs are not creating self-control.

Is it possible in a school setting to help Doug or Katy develop self-control rather than to let them control others? Or should we be satisfied with a patient and consistent use of external structures and sanctions? I find that while children such as Doug or Katy respond in the short run to stiffer sanctions—they lose the power struggle, and the authority appears to gain the upper hand—this approach defeats and discourages them in the long term. A defeated or discouraged child is not transformed into a productive one. It is more likely that the battling will continue, even through eventual suspensions. Doug, in fact, imported the power struggles from home into school primarily when he approached adolescence and when the academic challenges became harder. He was less able to keep up and compete with his peers without more personal investment of time and effort, and homework was generally out of the question.

So somehow we need to alter the terms, to refuse to win the power struggle, to decline the war. And this in itself is a slow, arduous, and protracted struggle. It takes inspiration and stamina and outside support, most importantly from the family. When the family only pretends to cooperate, privately agreeing with the child that the school and the teacher are terrible, *they* have to be turned around before the child can be turned around.

One aspect of changing the terms is to try to relocate a legitimate source of power. Often the children I see trying to boss me, their parents, their peers, or the rest of the world are most at a loss for a sense of place—what psychologists call a sense of significance. They are not children who seem to solve problems or overcome frustrations or fears. They are often the first to quit when something is a little hard or doesn't come swiftly and easily. Despite many mental or physical resources, they give up right away. Children who have high self-esteem associated with positive assertiveness show a sense of persistence in the face of a hard problem, some inner conviction that they can jump a hurdle. We need to help children who persist in power struggles to rediscover a constructive use for their power, or learn to conquer their own fears and insecurities.

The time-out place

KATY AND DOUG ARE NOT SENT to the time-out chair. Instead they go to a time-out place they have selected. It is a place they choose in the room where they can be quiet and peaceful, a place where they can recover their controls. They can return from their time-out place when they are ready to cooperate.

Katy lies down on the floor during circle time, strumming her fingers on the floor, humming lightly while Maggie attempts to read the chart.

"Katy," the teacher says, "you are showing me that you are choosing not to cooperate. You may either join the circle or go to your time-out place." Katy bangs her foot and scowls at the teacher.

"I see you are choosing to go to your time-out place."

At this point, Katy removes herself from the circle and goes over to a table, taking with her a specially designated bin with prearranged work. She goes grudgingly, she pouts along the way, but she goes. She takes out the booklets that contain a maze or a dot-to-dot and slowly begins to draw. She stops to glance at the teacher or catch the eye of a classmate; unsuccessful, she returns to her own tasks. But after a time, the tasks engage her, and her body appears to relax. She will soon be done, returning for the very end of the morning circle time, silently resuming her place in the circle, as if she had never left.

When Katy was presented with the plan, emphasis was placed on Katy's own choice to cooperate or not to cooperate. If she decided not to cooperate, the teacher explained, she would go to a time-out place. It was up to Katy to pick the time-out place, a place in the classroom where she liked to be. She would need to be quiet and alone in her place, but she could select some special work to do there that would help her relax and feel peaceful. Katy chose a table that was fairly central, often used as a work space for drawing or looking at books. It was understood that when Katy was in her time-out place, it was hers alone. At other times it could be used by classmates. Katy could leave her time-out place when she was ready to return, showing her readiness by cooperating with her teacher and classmates.

It was also understood that if she chose not to cooperate, she would go to her time-out place by herself, and in an appropriate manner. If she did not, she went home. In this case, the parent was supportive, willing to work with the teacher to improve Katy's behavior. During the first week of the plan, the parent was available and expecting a phone call. It came, and Katy went home. She did not go home for further punishment, although she did not go home to television and treats either. The message was that she showed she wanted to be in school by cooperating and by using her time-out place when she didn't choose to cooperate. Otherwise, she was showing her teacher and her mother that she wanted to be home. So, home it was.

Katy, despite her negativity, her outbursts and defiance, went home only twice for the rest of the year. The need for the time-out place diminished, although there were sporadic upheavals. Her willingness to embrace school improved measurably.

Doug also had a time-out place. When he was presented with the decisions of place and time, and with the language of choice, his sense of control increased. Conversations with his parents helped them support the plan, and their timely involvement (when he needed to go home or when they checked in weekly) also developed a visible web of communication for Doug. The lies and attempts to manipulate were intercepted, which was a key for his adjustment. Like Katy, his behavior and acceptance of school improved markedly.

In some cases, children are not sent home but to the principal's office or to another classroom. If parents are unable to leave work but are supportive and will meet with the teacher at their earliest convenience, this has been an effective procedure. Without parental support, the procedure is less effective.

As much as possible, we need to enlist our parents as allies, not against the child, but as part of a team working toward the child's happy and productive school life. I remember one student who often blurted out, was inconsiderate, and dominated the class. I made very little headway with her because her parents and I could not come to agreement on acceptable intervention.

Without strong parental participation—or even with it—we may need to move to the next alternative, which I call "Bargaining."

Bargaining

I OFTEN COMBINE A TIME-OUT place with an approach I call "Bargaining." It is an attempt to try to enlist cooperation, or establish a "negotiated peace." The notion of bargaining is taken here from my grandmother. As a child, I used to go along on her grocery expeditions, first to the butcher, then to the bakery, and finally to the grocer. The best was the butcher. The butcher saw her coming. Here my grandmother became the seasoned haggler to get the freshest cut, the tenderest piece, the best price. She left only when she was convinced of her shrewd buy. In all her years, she would never buy her meat any other way, never wrapped in cellophane, prepackaged, or prepriced. Bargains were everything.

I have never enjoyed negotiating my marketing, but Grandma's training turned up in my teaching. I use it to avoid a power struggle. In order to bargain, it's important to remember Grandma's skills:

- Be clear—know what you want.
- Be specific about a bottom line—know what you won't accept.
- Establish a good mood and use a sense of humor.

Grandma says, "So, what's good today, Louie? Don't tell me everything 'cause your stories don't interest me today. I want we should have some nice lamb chops, but some you can see, fat ones, Louie, thick like your head! Yes? You got?"

Louie replies, "For you I got."

Steps in a bargaining conference

1. **Naming**—stating the problem with specific examples
2. **Emphasizing the student's choice**—"I can help you, but I can't make you. It's your choice."

3. **Bargaining**—setting a friendly tone and establishing a "fair deal"

4. **Sealing the bargain**—a contract with clear expectations and consequences

1. Naming

"Louie, what you sold me yesterday, you call that tender? You could break your jaw, it was so tough. What do you think we are, tigers, for such chewing?"

In a private meeting, I tell the student what I have noticed. For example:

"When I ask people to come quickly to group, I notice that you go in slow motion."

"When I ask for your work, you tell me that it is lost."

"When I need your help to get the room in order, I see you whiz around with the broom stirring up noise, not dust."

"I leave the room, and when I come back, I find you fooling around."

"I hear you call people mean names like 'fatty' and 'retard'."

"I notice that you make faces and whisper to friends when some people are presenting in the group."

These are my rules of thumb for naming:

+ Examples are real and specific. Don't use generalizations such as "I notice that you lie (or bully, or never do your work)." They may be true, but they overwhelm the child and tend to elicit rebuttals and more power struggles. Usually, I will cite only one behavior and a few examples of that behavior.

+ Use "I statements." "I notice that…" or "I see that…"

+ Use a manner and voice that is as objective and businesslike as possible—neither angry and blameful nor cozy and cuddlesome.

+ Be brief. This is not a lecture. If I use specifics, children tune in. If I don't, they are expert nonlisteners.

2. Emphasizing the student's choice

"Louie, I know you got some extra good meat, special, for my son-in-law. You take a good look before you show me something, yes?"

Here, I try to withdraw from a power struggle by pointing out the choices and responsibilities that belong to the student. My responsibility, as teacher, is to state clear expectations (and limits). The student's responsibility is to choose how he/she can work on them. Some examples:

"I want you to enjoy being in the group, but I can't force you to do that."

"You are the one with the power to 'push the right buttons,' so you can use kind words or take care of your work."

"I want to help you, but you are the boss of your own self, so you have to decide 'Yes, I want to contribute to my class.'"

"I'm not so strong that I can make you want to do your best stuff. Only you are that strong over your own self."

"I know you have a lot you might share with us and that you could contribute a lot to our class, but that's your decision to make. However, I won't let you hurt others."

3. Bargaining

"You know me for all these years, Louie, and you still think to say such a price? You know I pay a fair price—but that much, never! Tell me a dollar less."

I try to set up the lively spirit, humor, and savvy of bargaining. I want to use specific terms and language that reinforce mutual effort. It is "our problem" or "our good deal": "We need to figure out a fair deal" or "I'll trade you this for that."

Beginning bargaining

When you begin bargaining, remember that it is the butcher's meat, not the butcher, that is sometimes tough:

  ✦ Avoid analyzing and explanations.

◆ State clearly what you want from the student:

—"Be on time for groups."

—"Have your work done and in your notebook."

—"Contribute good ideas or nice comments."

◆ Be prepared with a specific, definite, and concrete demand. Again, choose one behavior and give two or three examples:

—"I want to see more independent work in class. That means you know your own assignments, get your work done without several reminders, and check your own completions for accuracy and neatness."

—"I want to see you use your serious thinking in class. That means you ask good questions in math group, you write full-page compositions during writing, and you help solve problems during class work."

—"I want to see the friendly Sheila come to school. That means you say 'yes' when someone asks to join your game; you offer nice comments and make positive suggestions about the work of your classmates; and you share your own good work without bragging."

Helping students bargain

"I might consider those chops you're holding if they didn't cost the Brooklyn Bridge. How much, Louie? Remember you're not talking to the Rockefellers here."

"This is what I want," says the teacher. "What do you want to trade me?" We need to be prepared to help the student bargain, to figure out what the student wants and how to put it into words. To help children understand the concept, I sometimes use the story "Jack and the Beanstalk" and use symbolic objects—a toy cow and beans. I have the beans. The child has the cow. I want to get the cow. The actual trade of the cow for the beans provides a role-play and drama which is both fun and meaningful, even with older children.

To help students figure out what they want, I often use the "could it be" question format from *Maintaining Sanity in the Classroom* (Dreikurs 1982, 28–31):

"Could it be that you would like extra time to read or to work on the computer?"

"Could it be that you would like a special time to work on an art project?"

"Could it be that you would like an extra reminder or signal when you start to get silly?"

"Could it be that you need a special time to relax and listen to music on your Walkman?"

"Could it be that you would like us to know that you are an expert on motorcycles? How might I help you share that with the class?"

To help children "deal," I use my knowledge of their interests, skills, and needs. The "bargain" validates one of the child's strengths and satisfies a child's preference in return for asking the child to endure a "hardship." Bargaining (not bribing) sets up an exchange which allows children to *accept* what is given and then to *give* in return.

Jon, who regularly disrupted school assemblies, bargained to skip one of the two meetings each week and to manage the other. Interestingly, after about a month, he attended all of them and no further incidents were reported. Tammy decreased her incidents of aggressive behavior because she bargained to retreat into her Walkman. Marcy was permitted to do a morning job instead of joining the meeting circle before she felt ready. Lester chose to help the teachers with class reading, which reinforced his excellent reading skills and "helped" his teachers.

Verna took charge of stapler repairs and Lenny became a "class curator," arranging a bulletin board to make *our* room more beautiful. Mary Beth learned to play jacks and will soon be ready to teach others how to play. She has to practice not just picking up two's and three's but being a nice teacher, especially when someone "goofs up."

This bargaining process is often a part of an individual behavior contract (see Chapter 15). One special educator tells the story of an oppositional eight-year-old who kicked chairs out from under children, ripped up his and others' work, and tore things off the walls in his fury. She drew up a behavioral contract with him, the terms of which allowed him to earn Pokémon cards for intervals of acceptable behavior. After just a few weeks, his behavior improved and his card deck grew fat. When the teacher encountered him months later, when his contract was no longer necessary, she asked, "How's it going? I don't see you much any more."

"I still have all those Pokémon cards you gave me," the boy remarked.

"That's great," the teacher said.

"I don't need any more, so I guess I can go back to my old ways," the child said with a sly smile.

"I think not," she replied. "I think you like the way you are now."

"I guess." He nodded. "I still have all my cards, too," he added as he strolled down the hall.

4. Sealing the bargain

When Grandma nodded her head once and began to open her pocketbook, the deal was done. Neither Louie nor Grandma would consider changing it once they had agreed.

The classroom bargain is sealed with a handshake, a smile, or a written, signed contract. The contract restates the agreement—what the student agrees to try to do and what the teacher agrees to try to do:

- ✦ Gretchen will come to group on time.

- ✦ Gretchen will have the special job of taping stories for our listening center instead of attending Morning Meeting on Wednesdays.

It's important that the contract is worded in specific language. Does Gretchen have to show her good faith by coming to group on time three days in a row before beginning her special job? And, what does "on time" mean? Is she on time when she is sitting in the right place but has to get up to get her book and pencil? If the contract isn't specific, children will say (rightly), "But you didn't tell me that!" It may be necessary to amend the contract to say "Gretchen will come to group on time, with all her materials."

Consequences need to be an integral part of the bargain because the expectation is that there will be improvement, not perfection. The bargain will not always be kept.

Lester does his work without arguing every question or losing every assignment now. But during art group, he flicks his paint off the brush into someone's hair, chortling, "Rain painting."

"Time-out, Lester."

Consequences may need to include a time-out. Lester will help clean up his friend's hair and the sprayed paint. He will also lose the privilege of painting for that day. We continue to set limits, even as we extend a special bargain.

The contract is signed by the student, the teacher, and the parents. Again, without parental support, the success of our new rapport and "deal" will be weakened. Parents need to be enlisted to support the arrangements of the contract and the consequences.

Some teachers worry that striking a bargain that gives a child a special option (such as listening to a Walkman) reinforces the misbehaviors or is unfair to the rest of the class. "Why does she get to listen and we don't?" a child asks.

"Janey needs to listen to the Walkman to relax. You don't." Differing needs, interests, and skills are admissible facts of school life. They are valued and respected. "This is a way we can help someone in our class feel good," I point out. "When you need a special consideration, then I will help you, too." In this definition of *fair*, we extend opportunities to children to help them get what they need the most in order to work and feel good in school. Children understand.

CHILDREN WITH
BEHAVIORAL SKILL DEFICITS

OUR CLASSROOMS ALSO INCLUDE children with severe behavioral problems who do not seem to benefit from standard disciplinary approaches, yet are not engaged in power struggles. While these students "know who is boss," their behavior is not improved by repeated time-outs, motivational incentives, or whatever consequences we devise.

"Minutes after I send her to time-out, the same behavior occurs."

"'I don't care,' he says when I tell him he's about to fail."

"I'm so tired of long meetings after school, trying to figure out what to do."

"If I respond to all of his actions that disrupt, interrupt, infuriate, or are inappropriate, he'd be in time-out all day long."

"Nothing I do seems to make any difference. I end up dreaming about these kids and getting so down."

In contrast to those who struggle with power, the struggles of inflexible-explosive children are not with authority. Instead, these children lack some of the skills that are necessary to negotiate the day. They may not have developed the capacity to anticipate, for example, and cannot make the kind of subtle adjustments to signals and situations that most children make fluently. They also have learned patterns of dependency and withdrawal from tasks that make them uneasy. Even after a series of well-planned and consistent attempts to help them function within the rules, they are unlikely to stay in their seats, take turns, proceed through a transition smoothly, follow a direction safely, or complete a task. Rather than structuring more choice into situations, our job with these children is often to name limited acceptable choices before situations that we know will challenge them, thereby cueing them to succeed.

Ira

Ira was an engaging and bright sixth grader; he was also aggravating and often in trouble. He was a thoughtful and insightful contributor to class discussions, a precise and painstaking artist, and often a generous friend. Yet it was a mistake to lose sight of his whereabouts for very long. Ira was easily frustrated, sometimes by a particular academic task and sometimes by the constant social demands of the classroom.

When he was frustrated, bored, or confused, he tended to provoke someone equally provokable. He might snatch a pair of glasses and toss them around in a makeshift game of keep-away. Most of his peers knew to ignore Ira and wait for him to tire of the "game." If confronted straight on, particularly with a counterattack, he might swear or retaliate with harder physical shoves and kicks. Over the year, this behavior lessened, although he continued to pick on a few classmates when agitated and frustrated.

Near the end of school, there was a moment when Ira was sitting around doing nothing, avoiding a play rehearsal, afraid he didn't know his lines. When Maureen walked by, he threw a pencil, narrowly missing her face. I sent Ira to time-out in the office, the expected consequence. This time, I was determined to teach him a lesson and decided not to deal with him until I was finished with rehearsals. I left him waiting there with nothing to do but sit for well over an hour, past his lunch period.

Clearly, "teaching him a lesson" was motivated by my own anger and frustration. By the time I was free and able to talk with him about the incident, he was taut and reticent. Although he said he was ready to return to the classroom, within a half hour he exploded, cursed and hit someone else, and was then sent home. ❖

IN RETROSPECT, several things become clear. Ira's ways of dealing with his own frustration were not constructive. My ways of dealing with Ira's frustration were not constructive, either. All teachers are confronted with Iras in our classrooms. We despair of some of our own methods and yet are only slowly learning new approaches.

"The Explosive Child"

ROSS GREENE SUGGESTS THAT THERE ARE noncompliant children who do "not choose to be explosive and noncompliant any more than a child would choose to have a reading disability…" (Greene 2001, 12). To understand their behavior, we have to realize that it is not intentional or planned; it is also not manipulative or attention-seeking. Unlike children who seek out confrontation, these children have no wish to challenge authority or get in trouble. These are children bounded by cognitive delays in the social and/or thinking skills needed to manage frustration and interact with the world appropriately. They tend to cling to the moment rather than looking ahead and seeing the potential results of their own behaviors. Despite negative results, they often persist in rigid and irritating patterns.

I believe we all have moments when our facilities to deal with frustration break down, and we verge on the explosive. Not long ago, I was lost in Paterson, New

Jersey, looking for a particular school. I had a map and written directions, but nothing was getting me there. Suddenly, I felt lost forever, catastrophically and irretrievably. I was close to a tantrum when I said to myself, "Stop and look at what you're doing. Stop the panic and think." I pulled into a gas station and made a patient worker give me directions five times over!

The capacity to step back and gain perspective helped me get a grip on my alternatives. This episode gave me great insight into the lives of children without the cognitive resources to adapt, children caught in the throes of such panic over and over again.

Faced with an immediate obstacle, reasonable or utterly illogical, these children are unable to adapt, to shift gears, or to think coherently. Attempts to advise, reason, or warn may only escalate their furious or distressed reactions. Threatened consequences often increase rather than stifle the coming confrontation. But adaptive and regulation strategies can be taught, according to Greene. With consistent help, children can learn to modulate their feelings and behavior in incremental stages. There is hope, though no quick cure.

Helpful interventions focus on both adaptations in the environment and direct skill-based instruction with the student. I think of a student, Josie, who often spoke to others in a rude, abrupt tone in limited social exchanges. Asked in a friendly way "How are you?" Josie replied "Fine," and then turned back to whatever she was doing. End of discussion. For a very long time, both adults and peers misinterpreted her intentions, assuming deliberate indifference. Interventions based on this misunderstanding not only didn't improve interactions but often made her feel rejected and guilty. When we realized that her manner reflected a nonverbal learning impairment and was not intentional, we were finally able to begin to provide more technical assistance.

"If someone asks you what are you reading," she was coached, "you explain and then you ask them a similar question. Let's try it." The name for this skill is called "turn-abouts," the teacher explained. To change our approach from consequence to adaptation, we need to remember that the children's behavior is not manipulative or intentional. Following are a number of suggestions for working with these children, incrementally building their skills.

Adapt the environment

TEACHERS MAY BE ABLE TO ADAPT the environment to become, as Greene puts it, "user-friendlier" (Greene 2001, 264). This involves both standard special needs assessment procedures and teacher observations to identify parts of the day or tasks that are particularly troublesome for the child. Once these trouble spots have been identified, the teacher can often make changes to make things easier for the student. For example, s/he might suggest ear phones to help with distractions or inner turmoil, allow an extra break time for moving about, or narrow an activity's choices to two if a student is overwhelmed with four choices.

Create a support team

IT IS CRITICAL THAT TEACHERS do not feel alone or out of the loop. All the adults—regular classroom teachers and specialists, principals, parents, aides, and special needs providers—should be aware of intervention strategies and be included in them.

It is important to include other students in the "classroom team." I find that my students are much more helpful when their peers have difficult times if they realize that they can help and that the behavior is not always intentional.

When students have physical impairments, the fact that they can't play soccer or talk clearly is obvious. My students were eager to help David, a peer who uses a wheelchair, even though they needed ongoing suggestions of ways to interact with him. On the other hand, they were less tolerant with Deborah, who had social issues and often said or did inappropriate things. They needed help understanding that Deborah was not being annoying "just for the fun of it" before they were able to be more inclusive.

Try to keep everyone involved with regular conversations and progress reports. Change is often slow and unsteady. It is hard to see what is going right and easy to see the next thing that is breaking down. We are more likely to see and continue the positive when we share concerns and support progress.

Communicate with troubled students

IT IS IMPORTANT TO LET STUDENTS know that you realize certain things are particularly hard or difficult, and that you understand they don't want to make people mad or get in trouble. State your desire to help, perhaps naming ways that you might work with them on the problem. "I see how hard it is for you sometimes in school," I might say. "I want to help you not get so frustrated when you don't get the math." Or "I want to help you find other ways to tell me you need help besides calling me names."

It helps also to develop a shared vocabulary of clear, nonjudgmental words and phrases to name feelings, needs, and specific problem behaviors. "You get frustrated" or "You get easily stuck in math and can't think how to get unstuck" or "You sometimes get very antsy and can't hold still." The child can feel "frustrated" or "confused" instead of "bad" or "stupid."

Naming the problem in concrete and qualified terms ("I get frustrated in math class") identifies something specific and manageable with possible solutions, whereas a global statement such as "I hate school" leads to more frustration, even despair. Conversations naming conditions such as "frustrated" help children know and "read" their bodily states. Identifying a specific problem also helps both student and teacher to identify warning signs for problem behavior—a necessary prerequisite for averting explosive behavior and learning better ways to handle hard situations.

Establishing a common vocabulary also helps in setting goals with the children. "I want to see you handle frustration better. Do you want to work on that, too? Would you like me to help you with that goal?"

Develop strategies to respond to troubling situations

TO TEACH CHILDREN NEW SKILLS, we break down the larger behavior into discrete actions. For example, if we are teaching a class how to move their chairs efficiently and safely into a circle, we teach how to pick up the chair with two hands, carry it in front, look ahead, move slowly. To teach some of her children how to make smooth transitions, first grade teacher Julie Cash found success with a technique called "Mouths, Bodies, Materials (MBM)". Each time there was a transition, the teacher gave specific instructions about what to do with each component. She might say "Mouths are silent, bodies are in our chairs, materials are pencils." While it is beneficial at times for all children to have steps and actions made as discrete and specific as possible, it is critical for children with learning impairments.

A crucial time for most children is the transition from time-out back into the classroom flow. Psychologist Sally Crawford pointed out that, for some children, when we release them from time-out without any check-in or tell them "come back when you're ready," we set them up for failure because they honestly do not know when they are ready. They may not be able to read their own body language; they may not read social cues; or their ability to "de-escalate" their own behavior may be underdeveloped. They need more attention and coaching, not isolation, in order to regain control.

Sometimes the missing skills can be identified, named, and taught to children so that a restructured form of time-out does help them. The teacher can help by explicitly naming indicators of readiness to rejoin the group. "I'll check in with you in a few minutes to see if you can use words to say you're ready now." Or, kneeling next to a child, "Let's see if you're ready—if your body is quiet now." Or "Tell me what you will need to do next to be in math group. What materials will you need to get?"

Create "frameworks for solutions" as a team

In *The Explosive Child*, Greene outlines a "basket" concept for prioritizing needs, a concept that is highly pragmatic and familiar to classroom teachers (Greene 2001). Teachers and parents sort a child's behavior into three categories, or "baskets":

Basket A is for non-negotiable issues, such as those of safety, over which it is worth inducing and enduring a meltdown. Hitting other children would be in Basket A. No matter how frustrated the child is, he/she is not allowed to hit. If stopping the child from hitting brings on a meltdown, you endure it because keeping the class safe is so important.

Basket B is for important but negotiable issues that you're willing to take some time to work on. Basket B is where the child learns the important skills of problem solving. Judi, a very bright but impulsive and domineering eighth grader, was in the habit of blurting out comments before being called on during group discussions. Half the time the comments came out sarcastic and thoughtless, casting a negative tone throughout the class. Whenever her teacher would try to shut off her comments, she would explode in a fury. The teacher decided to work with Judi during calm times on raising her hand and waiting to be called on before speaking, a method that bought Judi time to think about what others said and to find more considered and civil ways to phrase her own comments.

Basket C is for things to ignore for now while steps in the learning curve are being built. Having a basket C helps remove many unnecessary frustrations for the child so that he/she can concentrate on the important issues. For example, we might choose to ignore Melissa's off-the-shoulder blouses, even though they grate on us, because we realize that in the scheme of things they aren't that big a deal. Basket C is for behaviors that are neither worth inducing meltdowns over, nor important enough to spend the child's, teacher's, and class's limited emotional resources on right now.

The point is not to follow a prescription for what to put into which basket, but for teachers to decide based on the unique capabilities and needs of the child, the teacher, and the rest of the class. I am apt to put not only issues of physical safety into basket A, but also those of emotional safety such as name-calling. In basket B, I would most likely put behaviors such as not listening and not following directions. Sloppiness, being disorganized, and doodling during lessons tend to be basket C items for me.

Does putting things in baskets mean we permanently excuse the child from important behaviors? No. We can and should increase expectations of the child as his/her skills for handling frustration increase. As a team, teachers, parents, and other adults in the child's life begin to help the child have appropriate conversations and interactions with adults and peers. We develop clear, measurable goals and a plan with the student. We celebrate successes and allow time for mastery before moving on to the next goals.

Administrative and economic support

WE URGENTLY NEED PROGRAMS that make it possible to balance the special needs of individuals with those of the larger learning community. Classroom teachers or specialists need support in order to work with children who have severe and constant behavioral problems. We need additional knowledge, and often we need staffing resources, such as trained aides to work individually with children. We also need classes that are a manageable size and balance of students, so that teaching is not tantamount to chronically putting out brush fires—after which the teacher burns out.

We also need respite, perhaps time just to observe, to help us remember that for many children, their own unruly actions are painful and mysterious. They do care what others think and feel, even if they don't act as if they do. At age five, Marina says her hope is "that everyone will like her." At age thirteen, Michael writes, "I want teachers to know I don't mean to say bad words and I really want to be nice to everyone."

SUMMARY

SOME CHILDREN STRUGGLE with behavior problems that persist despite our use of logical consequences. We must develop different strategies to help these children and remember that the difficult behavior of some children stems from specific skill deficits, not motivational problems or struggles with authority.

With children who are entrenched in power struggles, we must change the rules of the game to let them "win" by choosing a positive alternative and following through with it. A positive approach builds on student strengths. It also helps them to work hard on those difficult tasks they most avoid, thus allowing them to gain some of the confidence they may lack. By using a consistent approach and enlisting parental support whenever possible, we can avoid the power struggles which threaten the community we are trying so hard to build. As psychologist Sylvia Rimm suggests, we may also need to develop "anti-arguing" strategies for adults and students (Rimm 1997).

Along with effective strategies, we must give ourselves permission to be flexible, particularly to aid our work with inflexible children. We do not forfeit consistency or fairness when we give children what they need, even if what they need is something different from their peers and different from what they think they want.

"Fair is getting what you need," we tell our children over and over. "You're lucky," I tell Jennifer when she complains that Danny gets to use earphones at study times. "You don't need earphones to keep yourself focused on your work." I recall having to advocate for my own special case when I went in to a seventh grade classroom to teach a writing lesson. The group had just decided that all would sit on the floor rather than have to wrangle over the insufficient space for thirty chairs in the circle. I brought a chair over and sat down. "No one gets a chair," one student quickly piped up. For a moment, I wavered. Then I replied, "I need a chair. My older body doesn't do well teaching on the floor." The class began.

Works Cited

DREIKURS, RUDOLF, FLOY C. PEPPER, AND BERNICE BRONIA GRUNWALD. 1982. *Maintaining Sanity in the Classroom: Classroom Management Techniques.* Second edition. Philadelphia, PA: Taylor & Francis, Inc.

GREENE, ROSS W., PHD. 2001. *The Explosive Child: A New Approach for Understanding and Parenting Easily Frustrated, Chronically Inflexible Children.* Second edition. New York: Harper Collins Publishers.

RIMM, SYLVIA B. 1997. "An Underachievement Epidemic." *Educational Leadership* (April): 15–18.

TOBIN, L. 1991. *What Do You Do with a Child Like This? Inside the Lives of Troubled Children.* Duluth, MN: Whole Person Associates, Inc.

CHAPTER 9
Working Together to Support the Rules

WHEN ROSA HAS A BLOW-OUT in the classroom and gets sent to the principal's office, her teacher, principal, and parents meet to figure out how to help her control her frustrations before she returns to business as usual.

When Akira gets in trouble at recess for kicking and pushing, his classroom teacher and the recess teacher talk together with him before he is ready to participate again.

Micah sits around the table with all his teachers, including his reading and math tutors, and explains that he hates to miss choice time every single day, and that's why he "hates" tutoring and has been hiding or refusing to budge when it's tutoring time. The teaching team listens and acknowledges Micah's wishes and needs. They juggle the schedule to honor both Micah's wishes and his needs for special assistance.

Although the majority of logical consequences and time-outs are handled by the primary classroom teacher, some children and some situations require a team approach. The team may consist simply of two teachers who agree to cooperate during routine time-outs so that a child not managing in her/his own room has another place to recover controls. Or a team might consist of many concerned individuals working in concert.

Sometimes a team approach is a spontaneous occurrence. When Mr. Joiner passes some of "my" children fooling around in the hall, he stops their shenanigans and sends them back to class. At other times, teamwork involves more planning. When one of "my" students gets in trouble on the bus, the bus driver lets me know. At some point, she and I, along with the principal, will talk with the student, devising a plan before the student is welcomed back on the bus.

"My children" signifies a relationship and a responsibility that exceeds the four walls of the classroom. But "our children" signifies our common charge. When we turn to others for help with certain children—choosing to send a student to another classroom or to the principal—it is not from lack of skill. It is not a personal failure, not evidence that teachers cannot manage their own classrooms. The message that "I see you" and "we see you," in the schoolyard, on the bus, in the gym, is one of mutual care and safety. A process that includes both holding on to our children when they are out of our particular rooms, and also trusting others to know and share in the arrangements, is a critical part of school-wide discipline.

When we actively work as a team, we reinforce our hopes and expectations for community. Importantly, teachers and students feel less alone. A consistent approach to discipline throughout a school not only helps teachers with immediate support in particular crises but reinforces the basic values of self-discipline and community for all the children.

This chapter looks at team efforts, particularly when students need to have time-outs in another teacher's classroom (a buddy teacher system) or need to be sent to the office. In these situations there are a number of constants. A time-out is used to stop the disruptive or inappropriate behavior. A team (including only the teacher and the student, or also specialists, recess or lunch teachers, administrators, and parents) meets to figure out a solution. The student is welcomed back into the classroom and is expected and encouraged to exhibit new behaviors, at least most of the time, or "in math class each morning." Expectations might be for Maura to use a more respectful tone, stay in her seat, keep her hands to herself, wait for a turn, or use the new checklist to remember her books.

In this approach, it is critical that the classroom teacher is part of the problem solving and discussion, even if the student was disrupting a setting outside the primary classroom—the bus, the recess game, the art teacher's lesson, an extracurricular activity. The teacher's knowledge and relationship contribute to the best problem-solving efforts for her students.

Megan, for example, has a hard time shifting gears, and although she is fine with her regular teacher, she does not adjust well to the different expectations and routines in music. A chance to anticipate the changes through a short check-in conversation with her teacher before music class emerges as a possible tactic during a team conference. Most of the time, it helps. "Remember, in music you have a required seat. In music, Mr. Giantino needs you to stay in your seat...you can do that, right?" Megan nods. Most days now she does manage music class and is actually starting to like playing some songs on the recorder. Both teachers are helping

a rather rigid child learn to adjust and adapt, a critical step in the development of self-management and self-control.

TIME-OUTS USING A BUDDY TEACHER

SOMETIMES TIME-OUTS are best completed out of a student's home classroom and involve a prearranged system using a buddy teacher. Teachers need to use their judgment and consider their unique teaching situation to decide when to use time-outs outside the classroom. Whether to respond to a foolish moment with a wrinkled nose and a slight head shake, to utter a warning, or to issue a time-out depends on knowing the children and taking the pulse of the room. Our reactions vary according to whether an incident is a single or repeated event, is relatively trivial or important. We also differentiate between rules that cover social conventions and those that affect the physical and ethical safety of the community. A physical threat must be treated more seriously than leaving the markers scattered on a table would be, and it may result in time-out in another classroom. A child may need to leave the room when:

+ The distraction continues while the student is in time-out.

+ The student repeats the same behavior soon after returning from time-out.

+ The stimulation of the room continues to overwhelm or agitate the student.

- The teacher needs a time-out from the student.

- The behavior is unusually serious.

All five conditions should be anticipated during the course of a year. Some children may try to use time-out as an attention getter. Others may initially test the process by leaving time-out or by refusing to leave it. Sometimes a child is already too aroused or overloaded to recover and continues to call out, cry, or carry on while in time-out. A child may repeat a deliberately mean comment to another student. Last, but not least, a child may have stripped the patience of the teacher by flicking a wad of eraser one too many times or making one too many insolent remarks. Before losing her/his control, the teacher enlists the help of others.

The buddy teacher is usually across the hall or close by. Sometimes teachers prefer to use a different grade level classroom; an older class may quiet a younger student more readily by providing less stimulation and more anonymity. Sometimes a particular buddy classroom is arranged just for one student if a sibling is in the usual buddy room or if there is some other conflict of interest. Sometimes several buddy teachers may be agreed upon in anticipation of needing to send more than one student out at a time, although this is an unusual occurrence.

When a buddy teacher is required, the procedure is direct and simple. The disruptive student does not commandeer the teacher or spoil the lesson; in fact, at that point, the less the teacher engages with the student, the better. The teacher initiates the time-out and selects another student to get the buddy teacher.

"Time-out to Ms. Daniels," the teacher says quietly to Lucia. "James, please tell Ms. Daniels that we need her."

James goes across the hall and speaks to Ms. Daniels. "Ms. Charney needs you," James reports. Ms. Daniels leaves her own class temporarily to come and get Lucia. Such a request is treated as a priority.

Note that James's message is brief and without explanation. Carol Davis, a fourth grade teacher, even used laminated cards with students' names on them. She would silently hand a card to the student messenger, who would silently hand it to the buddy teacher. The buddy teacher would then know to come get the student.

In the case of Lucia, Ms. Daniels enters the classroom after getting the message, gestures for Lucia to come with her, and escorts her to a suitable table or resting spot in her classroom. Generally the interaction takes only a few minutes, causing only a momentary lull in either class. (When a buddy teacher feels that even that brief stepping-out time is too risky, another adult needs to be on call to accompany a student across the hall.)

When the buddy teacher enters the room, the classroom teacher says, "Lucia, you need to go with Ms. Daniels now." Lucia leaves, escorted by Ms. Daniels, but without conversation. Ms. Daniels does not ask Lucia what happened, does not express sympathy or scold in any way. She ushers Lucia to a quiet area of the new room, one that is visible to the teacher and not by the door. Lucia's controls may be borderline at this point. It is important that she is not left alone in an empty room or hallway, or out of sight of the teacher.

Older students may be presented with a "check-in" or "reentry plan sheet" to fill out when they are ready. The form provides a written outlet for the student to think about what occurred and tell her/his side of the story. Initially, it signals to the classroom teacher that a student is ready to return to work. Later, when it is time for a conversation, it will provide a beginning reference. Writing, rather than talking, often produces less defensiveness, and is a safer way to vent. Some students will write the bare minimum, although the questions themselves may facilitate constructive thinking. Questions can help direct attention to problem solving and away from angry recriminations: "Why do you think this happened?" "Were the directions (rules) clear?" "What will help you next time?"

It is important that the classroom teacher continue with whatever s/he had been doing with the class during this time, confining "time-out" directions and interactions to the routine. There are several reasons for this. Disruptive behavior should not commandeer instructional time. Also, the teacher's focus upon the lesson limits and defuses engagement and prevents power struggles and negative displays. The student is accompanied by another adult so that there is no temptation to play along the way, to engage anyone else who happens by, or to go anywhere but the expected destination. The second adult also provides a neutral intermediary presence.

Some teachers worry that this procedure will disrupt the buddy teacher's class because the buddy teacher has to leave, reenter, and bring in an upset child. In fact, most teachers report that the results are well worth the brief disruption their absence may cause. The majority of children go quietly and settle in quickly. They do not have the same impulse or stimulation to engage in this new setting. Of course, students in the second classroom must know their "jobs," and not provoke or interact with the student. When prepared, they are usually highly considerate, and recovery occurs quite seamlessly.

Very rarely a student may refuse to leave or may make a scene in the second classroom. Then the principal is called and is prepared to accompany the student to the office. In one such instance, I told a student quietly but firmly, "You have a choice. You can get up and go with Ms. Clayton, or you can go with the principal. Your choice. You have one minute." I walked away. In this case, the student went grudg-ingly, but under his own steam, with the buddy teacher. In the event of serious melt-downs, teachers have been known to take the rest of the class somewhere else—to the library or for a quick outside time—while other adults deal with the tantrum. This resistance is certainly the exception.

When the time-out is over

THE TEACHER COMES TO GET THE STUDENT, releasing the child from time-out after about fifteen minutes. The teacher assesses whether the child is ready to return and helps him/her reenter gracefully. "Do you think you are ready to return and follow the rules of the room?" If the child says yes, then teacher and student return to the classroom. If necessary, I have children wash their face and straighten themselves out so they can return to the classroom collected and composed.

If the child starts to cry or attack the teacher, the teacher might say, "It looks like you need more time to gather your control before you can choose to return to our room" or "You don't seem ready. Do you need another five or ten minutes?"

Sometimes it is not the child who needs more time. One child observed, "The worst thing about time-out is that sometimes teachers forget about you!" We certainly do "forget" when we are suddenly treated to peace in our classroom and relief from an obvious strain. I think there are times when our memory is jostled only after we have properly recovered our own controls. The demands that certain children place on teachers and on the class are not to be minimized. If a half-hour break allows everyone to regroup and rejuvenate, it's a useful and effective procedure.

"You're right, I did forget," I admit to Anton, who had sat dutifully in another classroom for forty-five minutes. "Suddenly I noticed that it was too quiet in the room, no one was arguing, and I realized we were missing Anton!" Anton grinned. I grinned.

There are two cautions. First, don't try to process the incident with the child right when he/she returns. Generally, children are ready to return before they are ready to discuss. Returning to work allows the child time to settle down and the anger or upset to subside, so there can be a productive dialogue later. We may soothe or hold a child shortly after an incident, and a quick hug, pat on the back, or appoint-ment to talk later usually facilitates recovery better than discussion. Both student and teacher may need some distance to think through a problem. (With younger children, "distance" may be only fifteen minutes.)

Second, teachers must monitor the response of other children during time-outs and establish a respectful tone, not a shameful one. This is done by introducing and reinforcing time-out as a serious task, and by modeling a quiet and considerate manner. Children in both classrooms must do their job. Their job is to let the person in time-out concentrate and then to receive him/her back into the group.

Follow-up discussions

WHEN CHILDREN ARE SENT OUT of the room for time-out, it is best to have a discussion later that day or the next morning. The goals of the conference are to try to work together to find a way to prevent the problem from recurring, and to reestablish a friendly flow between teacher and student. These are similar to check-ins after an in-class time-out, but are usually a bit more involved and may explore the problem in more depth.

In these meetings, there is an exchange of views and an exchange of ideas. It is not necessary for teacher and student to figure out exactly what happened or to reach absolute agreement. It is less important to try to figure out causes and cures than to listen, to try to understand the other's perspective, and to come up with a realistic alternative which is acceptable to both. The teacher must offer to help the child manage better and to show that s/he is an advocate, not an adversary. In general, the following areas are discussed:

- ✦ "What happened and why did you need time-out?" or "Why do you think I sent you out of the room?"

- ✦ "What rule did you break? Why is that a problem?"

- ✦ "What do you need to do to be able to stay in the classroom and not lose the privilege of participation? How can I help you?"

- ✦ "Do you understand the consequences if it occurs again?"

In the student-teacher conference, specific actions and possible solutions are generated. Tiffany agrees to use a checklist to help her keep track of her assignments. Her teacher will go over the list at the start and the end of each day until she is able to be independent. Arden will have a special signal (he decides on "the hitchhiker") to remind him when he needs to say what he has to say in a friendlier manner. Alice, whose utterly random ups and downs are distracting, gets three "chits" each day that she may use to get up and walk around the room, as long as she doesn't bother or interrupt people who are working or speaking. Alex decides to invite a peer to lunch as part of an apology for his name-calling.

Conferences often allow teachers to gather information and help remediate a situation. Tina's clowning and defiance in math class is traced to academic difficulty, though she wants so much to be in the same level as her best friends. Together, Tiffany and her teacher figure out instructional support. Talking to Matthew individually, his teacher noticed how much he squints and avoids reading anything unless up close. A sharp change in his vision coupled with a reluctance to appear uncool had interfered with his ability to participate. New eyeglasses and getting his cooperation to use them improved his behavior.

Middle school students may be required to write a letter detailing their responses to the questions listed above. The letter may be their "ticket" back to the classroom. Though the teacher may not conference at the reentry point, s/he will read the letter and make a plan to meet when convenient.

I usually call parents when children need to be sent out of the classroom. Sometimes I alert a parent that this step may be necessary soon, or I may inform them afterwards. This helps avoid misunderstandings and encourages a united effort to help deal with the issues. Generally, parents are supportive and are concerned about their children missing classroom work. The effectiveness of time-out can be greatly increased with parental approval; parental disapproval often makes the system counterproductive. Indeed, *nothing* works if the parents aren't working with you.

Middle school teachers express concern that some of their students want to go to time-out, and use it to avoid work. Making up the missed time may be a reparative consequence. "You owe yourself fifteen minutes of work. When do you want to make it up, at recess today or after school?" Sometimes this reveals that a student was avoiding the task because of difficulty with it and may lead to other interventions. Middle school teachers also note that some students repeat the same behaviors days later, with little improvement over the previous time. While we hope that the conference after the earlier time-out leads to positive strategies, sometimes the first conference doesn't produce enough insight or an effective recourse, and sometimes improvement simply takes time. It may be necessary for students who continue to act out to go to the next step, a time-out in the principal's office or a time-out center.

FURTHER STEPS
OUTSIDE THE CLASSROOM

ASSISTANCE FROM THE PRINCIPAL or use of a supervised time-out center may be necessary if other steps have been tried without success, or when the misbehavior is more threatening than usual to the equilibrium of the learning community. These more severe disruptions may include physical or verbal threats to a teacher or other students; a significant loss of self-control and disregard for limits; students placing themselves or others in danger; or a breach of trust, such as students being absent from where they are expected to be, stealing, or deliberately destroying property. The office time-out may also be the third step after a stipulated number of in-class or buddy teacher time-outs. This step involves a longer period of time out of the classroom and a conference to establish a workable plan agreed to by the school-parent-student team before the student returns to the classroom. The strength of this procedure is in this group effort to figure out constructive solutions. The task is to reach consensus rather than to assign blame.

Office time-outs include a safe place for students to remain when not in the classroom. Teachers know that when a student is sent to the office, certain things will happen. The student will be looked after, parents will be notified, and a conference will take place before the student returns.

Time-out for the remainder of the day

THE PROCESS BEGINS when the teacher sends for someone from the office or time-out center. The student is escorted to a quiet place in the office or center, protected and insulated from distraction. It is important that this space is secure and private. This time-out is intended to remove the student from a difficult situation. It is not a time for discussion or other activities. Later, the student is given specific jobs to complete: writing (or dictating) a letter which states what happened, why, and what the student needs to do differently to be able to return to the classroom.

The primary teacher or the principal informs the parents and sets up a time to discuss problems during a reentry meeting scheduled for the next day. Parents are asked to participate in order to help everyone understand and construct positive outcomes. The hope is that in working together, we can establish a tone and presence that is unified, consistent, and supportive. "We understand that you don't like homework (or writing…or certain classmates), but we won't allow you to act this way. Let's figure out how to help you get through the homework (or do good writing…or deal with certain people when they get on your nerves)."

Our clarity and unity are underlined by our use of "we"—"we all want to help you and make this work." We provide a critical safety net for all students, which is particularly important when they get themselves into trouble. I realize that unity is often an ideal and not the reality when people feel confronted or resentful, defensive, or even apologetic. However, a system that structures such follow-through at least names the ideal and prepares all of us to come together.

The reentry conference

THE GOAL OF THE CONFERENCE is to agree upon a plan of action that includes specific consequences and contracts. The group also establishes how success will be measured and what will happen if misbehavior recurs. Parents and the primary teacher agree on a way to check in, so that parents can stay informed and can help with reinforcement and follow-through. A regular behavioral report card might be helpful, for example.

Sometimes the meeting takes place in two parts, with the initial part involving fact-finding and the determination of immediate consequences, including in-school or out-of-school suspension or detention. The principal and teacher may meet briefly to determine and implement this policy. The second part involves creation of a plan or contract that brings the student back to school or class. Older students are expected to make up work that they missed. It is important that students not use time-outs away from the classroom to escape from studies, though the misbehavior may signal study-related problems. Providing students with a work packet to complete during their absence is helpful, though work may be made up after the student returns if teacher help is needed.

Before the child returns, a team consisting of the primary classroom teacher, specialists, assisting staff, principal, and parents may first need to meet without the

student to review the issues and brainstorm possible alternative approaches. This is essential if the student needs consistent expectations and consequences for success.

When the student meets with the team, it is important for him/her to be given an opportunity and support to talk about what is not working. Students may need help giving their version of the events and problems. They are encouraged to think about what will help them come back to their school and follow the rules. Older students may read their letters.

The plan or contract drawn up by the teachers and parents is presented to the student. This may be a time for clarification, for changes or additions, or for choices. "What signal do you want when I see you beginning to get out of control?" Mr. McLean asks Rudy. If Rudy can't think of any, Mr. McLean is ready with options.

The meeting details consequences as well. These may include a loss of privileges, an apology of action, specified school service, proactive interventions or assessments, a schedule for making up missed work, reparative actions, and steps to regain lost privileges. For example, if the disturbance occurred in the hallways, the student may not be permitted to change classes or move through corridors without supervision for a specified time. There must always be a reasonable time limit on the consequence, and privileges must be restored afterward. Students need an opportunity to earn and restore trust.

Specific measures of success are important also. For example, if Kara shows she knows how to make pleasant and kind comments for the next two weeks, she will be allowed to contribute to group discussions without checking in first with her teacher. When Lee demonstrates that he plays fair in games led by the teacher, he will be able to choose different recess activities.

When stronger measures are needed

IN A FEW CASES, students continue to defy, oppose, or resist the limits. Testing and oppositional behaviors may continue after the first suspension because of entrenched and deep-seated needs that will change only over time. If outside circumstances are contributing to the problems seen in school, change may require family and therapeutic services as well as consistent school interventions.

For these students with severe behavior problems, we need to evaluate progress and explore our options carefully. For older children with severe behavioral needs, alternative middle school programs may be a necessary bridge after a three-day suspension. In Saint Charles Parish, New Orleans, the school system has a special facility for suspended students that provides counseling and special academic services.

I believe that some children, by acting out, are saying that they do not want to be in school as they know it. More creative planning and programming may be what is required to keep them learning and keep them safe. For example, Trailblazers Academy, a charter school in Stamford, Connecticut, works with at-risk middle school students by providing small student-teacher ratios and a family service staff. Outdoor and work-study apprenticeships are other interesting possibilities.

Some basic concepts for working together

The primary teacher is always involved in the process

IT IS THE PRIMARY TEACHER who manages most interventions within the classroom, and who must teach a child after the child returns to the classroom. Although this teacher may get support and assistance from a variety of others within the school community, the primary teacher is always central to the process. In most cases, s/he acts on the misbehavior, contacts and informs parents, and determines with the child and the support team the appropriate consequences. The teacher assesses and measures progress afterwards and helps adjust plans or implement new strategies.

The principal and others support the teaching team

WHEN STUDENTS ARE SENT OUT of the room for supervision by another teacher or by the principal, it is the other adult's job to reinforce the teacher's responses. The principal and others (teachers, counselors, etc.) may be a vital part of the intervention team, meeting with parents, reinforcing and reminding students, and offering a hug or handshake for every inch of success. But they can't and shouldn't replace the immediacy and efficacy of the primary teacher. Principals and others need to take the same approach to discipline as classroom teachers, emphasizing choice and faith, using empathy and structure to show that they like the child but not the behavior. They can make important connections with the child and help the child meet the high expectations of the classroom and the school.

When Manny appears at the door of the principal's office, he calls out, "Hey, Mr. DiPasquale. I was good today. You proud of me?" Mr. DiPasquale smiles encouragement.

If a principal believes that an irresolvable personality conflict exists between a teacher and a student, the principal might consider another class placement as a way to help everyone involved. Handled in the right way, such a change can make a positive difference for the child and the teacher. However, if the change subverts the authority of the teacher or is seen by the child as a way to evade responsibilities, it can cause more harm than good.

We need to work with—not against—parents

TEACHERS AND PARENTS need to be on the same side and working together. Parents are a crucial part of rules and discipline. The adults in a child's life are much more apt to succeed when we feel we are all working for the good of the child and not as adversaries.

One approach is to include parents early in the year in constructing and endorsing rules and in creating hopes and dreams for the year through activities such as the creation of "Critical Contracts" (see Chapters 3 and 5). When parents and teachers are working together, they can answer questions such as "How can we help your child manage…make school a place your child wants to be…help your child learn to use controls…take care with her work…share ideas in kind ways?"

Informing parents at the outset of the year about the school's approach to discipline is also critical. (See Appendix D for a sample policy statement called "Steps to Self Control.") It is far better to explain and answer questions about our expectations and the ways we intend to address problems before any incidents occur.

Teachers can let parents know the small successes, the strengths, and the efforts they see children make during the first six weeks and throughout the year. And when a problem occurs, parents are enlisted to help strategize and implement solutions, not to assign blame.

Getting off the bus

Dora, a lively fourth grader, was in a hurry to get off the bus one morning. Heedless of the small child in front of her, she pushed her way out, kicking the other child out of her path. The two assistants on morning duty saw this and confronted Dora, determined to hold her accountable for her behavior.

Their determination was fortified by recent staff meetings in which the entire staff listed behaviors that would not be tolerated in their school community. Threatening language and physical violations such as grabbing, pushing, and knocking people down stairs were occurring too frequently. Together the staff had established clear consequences and empowered the assistants, who had previously been unsure of their authority and role, to act decisively in such difficult situations.

Dora was given an in-school suspension for the day. Her mother, arriving after school to pick her up, was furious and claimed that Dora didn't do it and "must have been provoked." The principal, supportive of her staff's actions, agreed that she would talk to the other child, but insisted that Dora's behavior was not acceptable.

The next day, the parent returned with an apology. Dora had admitted the push, even the kick. Dora was sorry. She would try not to do it again. "We are both learning to think twice," Dora's mother said. ❖

SUMMARY

THE PRIMARY TEACHER IS ALWAYS CENTRAL to the process of supporting rules with logical consequences, including time-out. S/he has the greatest opportunity and responsibility for making the learning community a place where both individual and group needs are considered and addressed. But the primary teacher is never alone in this process. When consequences within the classroom aren't working, or when the child's behavior is especially dangerous or detrimental to learning, a time-out with a buddy teacher or elsewhere in the school may be necessary. A team—which may consist of two teachers working together or a larger group made up of primary teacher, student, parents, and other teachers and staff—then needs to join efforts to address the situation. A team effort is also often needed when disruptions occur outside the classroom—in special classes, at lunch or recess, on the bus, or after school.

When a teacher needs help in responding to a particular child or behavior, it is not a failure or shortcoming of the teacher, but rather a reflection of the simple fact that some children and some situations need greater intervention than a single person can provide. A cooperative and united approach is essential in these cases. The focus of the team's effort remains on helping the student meet his/her unique needs while being a contributing and caring member of the learning community.

By enlisting parents and others within the community in a cooperative effort to support the basic rules of respect for oneself, for others, and for the environment, we give children the message that classroom rules don't stop at the classroom door. Our hope is that children internalize the basic values reflected in our rules and carry them throughout their school days and beyond.

SECTION III
The Voices of Teaching

Introduction

The hockey game

The group of about twenty twelve- and thirteen-year-olds is bursting at the seams, full of excitement and dread in anticipation of the first hockey game of the year. Some sit in stony, pale silence, while others are constantly moving at a feverish pace. The desire to do well in this game is palpable as they make their way into the locker room. There is bustle and expectation, last-minute fix-ups, final arrangements, a review of tactics.

"Gene, I want you to watch that mouth," the coach warns. "There'll be no tripping. Hold positions. Everyone ready?"

The team stumbles out of the locker room, gear still trailing behind, and on to their rink-side stations. Just as they are about to begin, the coach raises a hand for one last word.

"What is it I expect you all to do when you get out there—the most important thing you have to remember?"

There is a hush as the children wait. The grown-ups wait too, poised to hear this last directive, the final word, the most essential tactic.

"No fighting?" blunders one naïve player, unaware this is not a question to be answered blindly. The hush continues for a moment more until the coach shouts out for all the stadium to hear, "LISTEN. LISTEN. I expect you to listen." ❖

GENERATIONS OF COACHES, parents, and teachers add their voices to this injunction—the most important advice, the most necessary of all tactics—generations asking, reminding, demanding that their children *listen*. This section is about talking, which means it's also about listening. First, it concerns the ways that teachers listen and talk in the classroom. There is a vital relationship between the ways that teachers listen and talk and the ways that their students listen and talk. In both cases, we want to cultivate active listening—hearing what others have to say and showing that we hear and are trying to understand the intended meanings. Listening then becomes a willful act of respect and interest, rather than a passive stance of obedience.

Cultivating the best habits of listening is inseparable from the task of building respect. Rightfully, teachers expect respect, but they also must teach respect. This section focuses on methods that encourage mutual listening and mutual respect.

The central tool for this instruction in listening and respect is the tool of language—the way that we talk and listen. The teacher is the model and initiator of conversations based on the idea of "attentive love," a concept that belongs at the heart of teacher-student interaction. According to Simone Weil, as quoted in *Maternal Thinking*, attention consists of two attributes—"knowing" and "loving" (Ruddick 1989, 120).

The act of knowing comes from seeing children as they really are in real situations. We see children throw food to get attention, cry because a game is lost, make snotty faces when they're crossed. We see children disregard their work, tell foolish lies, and be mean to the frailest one in the group. We observe also their struggles to do "good." We "know" real children as they really are in the world, not fictional children or false, sentimental projections. We "love" these real children when we see them through a lens of acceptance and compassion rather than denial.

Weil describes attentive love as saying to someone "How are you?" and truly caring to know the answer. Picture the teacher at the door each morning, greeting her children and truly listening to their morning tales of adventure and mishaps, noticing and recording their trophies, new hats, and small Band-Aids. Attentive love withstands the frailty and limitations of human nature. It is an affection that allows us to look at children as more than beings to shape according to our own ideals and images. They are independent beings who may just as well resist and refuse our best attempts to shape them at all. Our use of language strives to communicate attentive love, to give children the sense that they are both known and cared for.

"Teachers should be strict sometimes, but they should also know when you need a break. They want you to come through with your work, but also, like you're in a bad mood one day, they should know you may need to talk to your friends," explained Tara, age thirteen.

When children talk about respecting a teacher, they mention a number of interesting things: challenging assignments, self-confidence, "not letting kids get away with a lot of stupid stuff," a teacher who is strict but also nice. But like Tara, they often express a wish that teachers know them and recognize their needs.

"They listen to you."

"They know things about you, not just like if you do your work."

"They greet you," one eleven-year-old said. She went on to explain that she knew a teacher didn't like her because "when I see him in the hall, he never even says 'hello' or anything."

"Maybe he's tired," reasoned a friend.

"He could just say 'hello.'"

Our words matter. The theme of this section is language, an essential component and tool of teaching. What we say and how we say it often take thought, practice, even rehearsal. Over the years, I have learned to speak more effectively in the classroom, much as someone acquires public debating skills. We can make the most effective use of the tool of language when we learn to be more direct and specific, to simplify and encourage, to choose the right times for open-ended questions and the right times for narrow ones.

It is often necessary to speak less and listen more—to learn economy of speech as well as active listening. Our natural temptation is to repeat and repeat, to become a persistent "voice-over" like those deep-throated announcers in cleaning commercials. All too often, what teachers say to children is in the form of commands and directives. I certainly recognize those days when almost every word from my mouth is of the "do/don't do" variety. There are times when I hear showers of words and realize they are all mine, choking out the voices of children. Sometimes I notice how quickly I provide an answer after asking a question, allowing too little time for anyone to think. When teachers simply expand the time allowed for answers, children's responsiveness improves substantially.

The three chapters in this section describe different ways to use language in teaching:

- ✦ Chapter 10, "Empowering Language: Say What You Mean and Mean What You Say," explores the powerful link between words and actions.

- ✦ Chapter 11, "Stress the Deed, Not the Doer," covers the use of specific language by children and teachers. It also explains "Pretzels," a group activity that permits children to express positive and negative feelings with specific language while keeping individuals and the group safe.

♦ Chapter 12, "The Voices of Authority," explains the different voices that teachers can use to invoke authority: the voice of principle, the voice of procedure, and the personal voice.

Work Cited

RUDDICK, SARA. 1989. *Maternal Thinking: Toward a Politics of Peace.* Boston: Beacon Press.

CHAPTER 10

Empowering Language:
Say What You Mean
and Mean What You Say

EARLY IN MY TEACHING CAREER, trying to learn how to discipline, I observed a master teacher at work. Rose Thompson was known for her orderly classroom and her industrious children. Even more, she was known for a quiet dignity which radiated from her person and enveloped her classroom. I wanted so much to understand how she did it, this powerful woman, so small in stature. I observed in her room whenever possible. I noticed the quiet voice she used even when addressing the whole class; I noted the clarity of her instructions. I noted her attention to detail and the firmness of her expectations. And one day, I observed a crucial lesson, although at the time I was shocked.

The class was ready to make Halloween masks, abuzz with ideas and excitement. Ms. Thompson had just handed out sharp scissors for groups to share. She carefully demonstrated how she wished to see them held: point down. "How will you hold them?" she asked. Darrell showed the class again. Point down. The allocation of paste, the bins of paper, the place for finished work were all reviewed before the start of the activity. "I expect to see you use things correctly," she cautioned, "or I will have to take them away for today" And then the children got to work.

Ms. Thompson watched quietly, occasionally commenting or giving assistance. She was watching when Michael walked across the room, the scissors dangling precariously from one pinky. Michael was not holding them safely, the point was not down, the grip not firm. Ms. Thompson beckoned to Michael. She quietly reached out her hand. Without a word, Michael placed the scissors in her outstretched palm.

He had lost the right to use the scissors for the rest of the period—no more cutting for that day. Michael went sadly back to his seat.

I watched, stricken. I wanted so much to restore the scissors, to give Michael another chance, to see the glow and smile return to his face. I am sure Ms. Thompson did, too. After years of disciplining my own children and my students, I sometimes believe the cliché "It hurts me more than it does you!" And if not more, at least it hurts.

But Ms. Thompson didn't give in. She knew better. It was not only the safe handling of the tools that was at stake, it was the true handling of her words. Her class believed her. And because they believed her, they trusted and felt safe. It was an extraordinary gift she gave them. It required some extra thought and effort from a seven-year-old, but the gains were worth it.

When she spoke, the students listened, and never because she berated them or used harsh threats. Michael got the use of scissors back the next day, and I imagine that he and everyone else thought harder before they moved an inch. Michael and others learned to think carefully about most of what Ms. Thompson said to them. They learned something about the value of words when they're used to say important things, and that some adults can be trusted to say what they truly mean. I was beginning to understand that compassion did not necessarily mean negotiating or relenting. It meant dignifying my arrangements with children by honoring my own words.

We tell children that when the bell rings (or the triangle sounds, or the lights flicker, or the teacher's hand goes up), the rule is to stop everything and listen. Stop. Listen.

The bell sounds. Immediately, the room is hushed, children look up from their writing or their books, cease conversations, stop moving around, and turn to look at the teacher—except for a few, who continue their conversations, their drawing, or their trip to the water fountain. A few more face the teacher but continue their chatter or their work on a project. The teacher begins her/his message, disregarding the activity in the room.

What will the two simple and concrete directions "stop" and "listen" signify if we accept such loose translations? My own answer is that if we allow children to sort of stop and kind of listen, we encourage the destruction of meaning. Our language becomes a shambles—and our classrooms may not be far behind. Rather than relying on a common and precise language, we develop a negotiable and idiosyncratic one. It doesn't matter how many times or in what tone of voice we say "stop" if we don't attach it to a specific way of acting. We need to say what we mean and mean what we say. In general, the less we talk, the more children listen.

Children need to know that words have meaning. They need to understand that words correspond with actions. Here are some guidelines for using language to affirm meaning and action:

- Keep demands simple and short.
- Say what you mean, and make your demands appropriate.
- Mean what you say—dignify your words with actions.
- Remind only twice. The third time, "you're out."
- Speak directly. Tell children "non-negotiables." Don't ask.
- Use words that invite cooperation.

KEEP DEMANDS SIMPLE AND SHORT

SHORT, SIMPLE DIRECTIONS ARE ESSENTIAL if we expect specific actions. Here are some examples of times when simple demands are especially important.

To guide children through transitions:

- A reminder about how much time is left helps children anticipate: "You have five more minutes."
- Thinking about what comes next helps children sequence: "Who can tell me what you do next?"
- Asking what is needed to clean up or complete a project names a process: "I want everyone to think to themselves, 'What do I need to do to finish up now? What do I need to do to clean up?'"
- When it's time to get ready for the next activity (lesson, class): "What do you need to do to get ready to go outside? Who can tell us? Think to yourself what you will do."

To restore the proper noise level in the room:

- "It is too noisy. You need to use your 'indoor' voices (conference voices, private voices)."
- "It is too noisy for our work time. Who can show me what a working voice is?" [Child demonstrates.] "Now, everyone ask a question to a neighbor using your working voice. I expect those voices for the rest of this period."
- "It is too noisy. If the bell rings again, it will mean no more talking."

To introduce changes in room organization or schedule:

✦ Describe the change: "At one o'clock, Ms. Marder is going to come in to do a special art project. She is going to show us ways to do watercolors. She will do it with everyone."

✦ Anticipate and reassure basic continuity: "I know that we usually do writing at that time. If you are in the middle of a story, don't worry, we'll figure out extra time for you if you need it. I think you'll all enjoy the art today, even if you have never done watercolors before."

✦ Ask children to repeat or paraphrase what they understand is going to happen: "Can someone tell us what is special about today? Are there any questions?"

To stop inappropriate behavior and redirect children to positive expectations:

✦ "You need to stop bickering (fooling around, chatting, etc.) and get on with your work."

✦ "You need to follow meeting rules."

✦ "I expect to see you use a kind attitude or this group stops."

✦ "I expect to see fair play or the game is over."

✦ "The yarn has become snarled and messy. Use it just the way you demonstrated before."

There are times when the brief, neutral voice must be abandoned. The magic and power of those times are in direct correlation to their infrequency. The fewer the sermons, the more powerful they are. A teacher of adolescents gathered them in a circle and spoke to them in a manner that cascaded from soothing to fiery for an entire hour. He spoke about their lack of kindness to each other and their need to speak up and stop each other rather than wait for the teacher to step in. The students sat transfixed, rolled their eyes, and wept. This type of guidance and moral authority must be there for children, as long as it is used with prudence on issues that they can't figure out for themselves.

SAY WHAT YOU MEAN

IN THE HEAT OF THE MOMENT, it's easy to say things we don't really mean. Severe threats or ones we simply don't mean (or want) to carry out put teachers in a bind and discourage children.

Jeremy and Danny

Each day, a class of first graders went back and forth to the back hall where coats and lunches were stored. A heavy door separated the hall from the class. The hall was not heated, so the door was kept closed in the winter. The children were unseen as they put away jackets and stashed lunches at the beginning of the day or got ready for recess or to go home.

Jeremy and Danny were spunky six-year-olds. On their way from the meeting rug to the reading table, it was common for them to stop for a quick romp and wrestle. They were savvy enough to look to see if the teacher was watching, and mostly she was. However, by midyear, they realized the potential of the back hall for excellent adventures. On some pretext or another—to check a pocket, return a mitten, find a note— they ventured out again and again. Finally, one rowdy and mischievous activity left coats tumbled and lunch pails scattered. The boys got caught, of course. The utter shambles and mess upset the teacher. The poorly concealed grins of mischief incensed her. "Do this one more time," she uttered, her voice low and threatening, "and you will miss recess for the rest of the week. Understand?"

The two heads nodded in unison. But what Danny and Jeremy really understood was that the teacher had issued a challenge, a test of their derring-do. The teacher had set herself up for disaster. What would she do with these two if she had to keep them in at recess? How would she deal with their energy and high spirits then?

The next day, Jeremy and Danny approached the back hall with renewed intensity and dedication. Coats were tossed to the floor, boots rocketed across the room. Lunches fell helter-skelter. Of course, it was not long before their exploits were discovered. There could be no appeal. Recess had to go. The imps were chastened and deprived of their playtime. The teacher was chagrined, left to manage the spirits of her boys indoors. In addition, the children were resentful—and so was the teacher. The boys complained bitterly to their parents. Eventually, the parents were mollified and the boys repentant. They had learned their lesson, and the back hall was left alone.

But suppose they had been more persistent? The pranks would have continued, followed by more lost recess time. And then what? Both the teacher and the students would be victims of growing frustration or defiance—certainly not the ideal attitudes for the classroom.

This was not a case of endless warnings or futile speeches. But did the teacher mean what she said? Did she say what she meant? We don't always use our best logic or logical consequences in a moment of anger.

In this case, I would suggest two logical consequences. "You mess it up. You clean it up." Danny and Jeremy would take their free time, possibly their recess time, to return the coats to the hooks, line up the boots neatly, arrange the lunch boxes, and also sweep and tidy the back hall until it was beautiful. That might discourage them from messing it up again.

Second, they would lose the privilege of going into the back hall. "If you can't take care of yourself in the back hall, you don't get to use it." In spaces such as the back hall, bathroom, or corridors, children must exert their own controls. They make decisions about whether to spray the water, toss the toilet paper, play tag in the halls, or take care of business. When behavior is not appropriate, they lose the privilege and trust for a period of time. Their coats and lunches would have to stay in the classroom for the rest of the week or the day. The privilege of using the back hall would be returned when the teacher agrees they are ready to be responsible for the care of the hallway and of themselves. ❖

WE NEED TO ANTICIPATE PROBLEMS in order to be able to say what we mean and mean what we say. We do "mean" to express anger and disapproval at key times, but we don't mean to carry through on the threats that anger alone may induce:

"No recess for a month."

"No more trips for the rest of the year."

"Stay after school and finish, and I don't care if you miss the bus and have to walk home."

And finally—"I'll kill the next person who opens their mouth." Tempting, but not so realistic!

When we anticipate problems, such as the invisible spaces that become irresistible to six-year-old testers, we are better prepared with logical consequences and a calmer, more rational mind. (For examples of common problems at various ages and developmental stages, see Appendix E.)

MEAN WHAT YOU SAY

DIGNIFY YOUR WORDS WITH ACTIONS. If we ask children to freeze, it is not acceptable for them to continue to draw or talk to a friend. That's not what we mean when we say "Freeze." If we ask children to work quietly, it is not acceptable for them to call across the table and laugh loudly. If we ask everyone to listen to a classmate read his/her story, we do not allow staring out the window or playing with a neighbor's fingers. That does not meet our expectations for attentive listening.

If we expect our children to follow through on their verbal commitments, we must follow through on ours as well. "The bell rang. What do you need to be doing?" the teacher asks. "Show me," s/he might say early in the year. "Time-out," s/he says later in the year because by now children know the routines and are expected to follow them. Consequences are more effective if they are made clear ahead of time and are anticipated. But, most importantly, we must be prepared to do what we say we will do.

There are times when actions communicate more clearly than any words. One class is highly familiar with the rules and conduct for a trip outdoors. As soon as we are outside, their voices get loud and partners begin to wander. I stop the class and have them return to the classroom without a word, signaling for the next period's

activity. I see no need to lecture or review the events. The problems were clear; the alternatives are also clear. The next day, prior to the excursion, I might ask them to think what they will each do differently in order to enjoy the trip. My assumption is that they know the words; they now need to behave appropriately. It important to communicate to children that we know that they know. It is a way of giving them credit. It is also a way of giving ourselves credit and respect.

Sometimes, repetitions and incremental steps are the best way for learning to occur, but there are also times when learning must be put into practice and used. If behavior at meeting is silly and disruptive, discontinue the meeting. If the line-up is noisy and rowdy, sit down and wait. If writing conferences are giddy and unproductive, stop them for the day. It's often better to try again tomorrow.

REMIND ONLY TWICE

Ronald

Children were lining up to go outside. Ronald continued to work at his desk. The class would be kept waiting again as Ronald slowly continued his work. Usually, I repeated my instructions personally to Ronald, hustling him along, nagging, or yelling. Today I waited. The class, taking its cue from me, grew still. We all waited to see what Ronald would do. Ronald did nothing. He continued on as if either he, or we, were invisible. After an eternity, I silently advanced toward his back. After no more than a few steps, Ronald, who had not lifted his gaze from his papers, sat up and suddenly scurried off to get his jacket. Not a word had been exchanged. How did he know I was there? Or was moving toward him?

Ronald knew all along that we were waiting, and from prior experience he assumed he was waiting safely for the daily torrent of words that roused him to action. The words, repeated especially for Ronald each day, had become a ritual. I realized that in many situations, repetitions had replaced the original message of the words. The words had lost their meaning because they were used too often. My classroom needed a change.

"Ronald," I recall saying, "teachers and mommas have patience, but only so much patience. They will ask you once NICELY. The second time they will ask in a stern voice. And the third time they will be angry." I realized again how irritating it was to repeat even the most routine expectations. Irritation eventually becomes sarcasm, shouting, or outright anger. Too often, we keep doing the very same thing.

As I spoke to Ronald, I realized that I had the rapt attention of the silent line of first graders. I turned to the class and repeated my now confident message, one which I use regularly: "Teachers and parents say things once nicely. The second time they will be stern, and the third time, you are out. They will not say it again." ❖

SPEAK DIRECTLY—
TELL "NON-NEGOTIABLES"

LORRIE IS JOKING AND FOOLING AROUND instead of doing her clean-up job. "Would you please do your job?" the teacher asks. Is this what the teacher means—"Would you"? Is it a choice for Lorrie to do her job, or is it a "have-to"? Is it even a question? If it is a question, Lorrie might answer, "No, I would much rather talk." In an effort to be courteous and pleasant, the teacher has delivered a confused message.

"You need to get the job done, Lorrie" is direct and honest. There is no mistake or confusion—it is non-negotiable. Non-negotiables are an integral part of every classroom and every community, although they vary from class to class, teacher to teacher, community to community. We need to make them clear and direct—they are declarations, not questions. We are not asking; we are telling. We need to declare what we need the child to do, what the group needs the individual to do, or what the child needs to do for her/his own good:

"You need to sit down now."

"The group needs to come over quickly so we can start."

"You need to get ready now."

"You need to keep your hands to yourself."

"You need to get this work done."

"I need your help to get the room ready."

"I need your help to solve this problem."

"This class needs to listen to Becky now."

"The rest of the class needs you to be attentive now."

Use words that invite cooperation

THE WAY WE TALK to children may invite participation or, unintentionally, resistance. I solicit cooperation with three techniques:

- ✦ Making it fun
- ✦ Asking for help
- ✦ Providing choices

Making it fun

TWO TEACHERS ARE TRYING to settle their class after recess as the children line up before going inside. The teachers know that the transition from outdoors to indoors is hard for some of their children. They prefer to have them regain their controls outside rather than charge back into the building.

One teacher, standing in front, begins to name all the inappropriate behaviors she sees. "Seth, turn around. Molly, stop talking. Dan, keep that ball still. Craig, hands to yourself." But it's like popcorn popping. As soon as Molly stops, Jennifer starts. As soon as Craig stops pinching Bobby, Bobby starts pinching Craig.

"Bobby," cries the teacher.

"But it wasn't me. He started it. What about him?" There is unbridled glee from the ones who didn't get caught, and they smirk at the ones who did. The ones who are ready to go are frustrated. Often the teacher gives up and takes the class in mild disarray upstairs. It takes another ten minutes before they settle down. In general, the naming of misbehavior does little to inspire good behavior.

Children, particularly in a transition, need to have a positive focus, one that sets the stage for immediate affirmative feedback.

A second teacher waits patiently for about three minutes, ignoring the bouncy bodies and gabbing, giggling voices. Then she says, "I'm going to close my eyes and count to ten, and when I open them, I expect to see a straight, quiet, beautiful line of fourth graders all ready to go back to their work."

Ninety-seven percent of the time this works! It works today, except for Randy, who needs his own glance or hand from the teacher. Why does this familiar gimmick work so often? Perhaps it's the challenge of the "clock," the bounded amount of time to compose and ready oneself. It is finite, predictable, and authoritative.

"Count to five and then I'll dive into the water," I always told my daughter, who begged me to swim with her and was always impatient as I stepped gingerly into the cold water. "You didn't say four-and-a-half or four-and-three-fourths," I would needle her. She would comply, but I knew that five would come and I would have to do it!

Teachers use this strategy for many activities. A count of three settles the class for meeting, as they move from chatting with friends to quietness. A count of twenty gathers a class from the four corners of the field into a circle. A count of five readies the group to leave meeting and go to their next activity, remembering their "walking feet, thinking brains, and quiet voices."

Even much older children respond to the challenge of preparing surprises for the teacher, surprises such as a quiet room, a perfect line, an orderly presentation. We encourage a pleasant complicity with phrases like "I'm going to close my eyes…" When we close our eyes, we transform duty into a contest. We avoid reprimands, inspiring instead a challenge—one in which there are two winners.

"I'm going to walk out of the room for two minutes, and when I come back in, it will be quiet, and everyone will be at their desk ready to work."

"Let's see if we can walk upstairs so quietly and enter the room so silently that no one will know we are here."

I suspect that when we close our eyes, momentarily, we get children to open theirs and figuratively watch over themselves. If we want children to rely on their own controls or skills, we must stop hovering. This challenge often works because we show implicit confidence in their abilities.

When I am ready to close my eyes, and I know that my Randy or Sylvie or Grady will not be able to manage, I take them with me, literally or figuratively. We close our eyes or step out of the room together. My hand may clasp Grady (and Randy too), or I may encourage them with a whisper or by bringing them near me. For the majority, the count of ten is plenty of time to recover the necessary controls.

Asking for help

SOMETIMES IT MAKES SENSE to invite cooperation directly. A teacher of a seventh and eighth grade group stands waiting for a few minutes as his class assembles and begins to slow down before returning inside.

"I need some help now," he says firmly. To Jess, who is still tossing the ball around, he says, "Jess, some help please." He doesn't say what help because he doesn't need to. Jess and all the children know. Most children willingly help adults who care for them, when they are asked directly. Asking for their help reinforces the reciprocal nature of the relationship and pays them respect. In fact, we do need their help. When they hold the ball still or hold on to themselves, they are helping the class and the teacher.

"Thanks for your help," the teacher responds.

Providing choices

CHOICES SET BOUNDARIES. They mark out what *is* possible—the sky is not the limit! At the same time, they give children some control and encourage responsibility. Early in my parenting career, I learned the importance of defining the parameters of a choice. "What do you want for breakfast, Daniel?" invited the response "pizza" or some other selection I was not prepared to grant, often launching an irritating and unproductive exchange. "Cereal or eggs?" named real possibilities and gave my son some say. Choices are best presented in direct, short, specific statements that avoid sermons or lectures:

TEACHING CHILDREN TO CARE

"You can either work together and get done quickly, or drag out this room clean-up and miss time later. Your choice."

"You can either quiet down and follow meeting rules, or meeting will be stopped. What will it be?"

"You can either do independent reading, or draw quietly at your desk. Talking is not a choice."

"You can either get it done now or later, but it needs to be done before you leave today. Your choice."

"You can stay with your group and choose to follow the rules, or leave and work by yourself. What's your choice?"

If there is a clear consequence involved, it should be expressed as part of the choice. We ask children to decide. If necessary, after a few moments, we say, "I see by your behavior that you have decided not to continue working with the group. You need to leave." And if the teacher has a clear preference, it too can be expressed— "I would like you to decide to join the group, but you need to figure out if you are ready."

SUMMARY

OUR WORDS MAKE A DIFFERENCE. We need to be clear in communicating what we expect, and we need to honor our words by doing what we say we will do. If we use language precisely and honestly, we can expect the same from our students. Too often we're in the position illustrated by Holden Caulfield in *Catcher in the Rye:* "I'm lucky, though. I mean I could shoot the old bull to Old Spencer and think about those ducks at the same time. It's funny. You don't have to think too hard when you talk to a teacher" (Salinger 1951). However, we need to think hard when we talk to children.

Work Cited

SALINGER, J. D. 1951. *The Catcher in the Rye*. Boston: Little, Brown.

CHAPTER 11
Stress the Deed,
Not the Doer

"I HATE HER!" Vinnie's strident words rang out and filled up the space in the principal's office. He had been sent there to calm down after an outburst at his classmate Cheryl. "I hate her! She's so neg!"

The principal sought to understand his last word. "She's so what?"

"Neg." Still a blank look from the principal.

"Neg, you know, always dissing stuff...this is no good, that's no good...stuff a person likes sometimes. Nothing's any good to her."

The principal got it. "You mean you don't like it when she says bad things about other people?"

"Yeah, exactly," responded Vinnie, somewhat mollified at being understood.

"And this has happened before, that Cheryl says things like this, but sometimes she's OK?"

"Well, yeah, sometimes she is."

"STRESS THE DEED, NOT THE DOER" is a technique that helps both teachers and children. It is a specific approach to our use of language, but it is also an attitude that expresses respect for people even though their actions may disappoint us. Stressing the deed is a way to express individual praise and criticism, appreciation and disapproval, compliments and complaints while keeping the class safe. The focus of the praise or compliment, the criticism or disapproval, is on the deed, not on the character or the personality of the doer. The emphasis is also on specific attributes or actions, rather than on generalizations:

- "Thank you for making our art shelf look so beautiful."

- "It was considerate to include new people in your game."

- "I don't want to work with you when you are interrupting and disturbing the lesson."

- "I don't like it when you make up excuses and don't tell me the truth."

- "Your story really presents an interesting problem."

- "Your patient explanation of the assignment really helped people get it."

- "I like the way you added shading to give depth to your drawing."

- "I don't like it when you take things from my desk without asking for permission."

When we name the deed, we preserve the doer. "I like you. I don't like this behavior." And when we define the deed, we help to clarify expectations and set boundaries. As we narrow, define, and specify, we show children what constitutes a caring or considerate deed, a good piece of writing, an independent worker, a good friend.

By pointing out the specific behaviors that work and those that don't work, we begin to take children beyond just the general categories of "good person," "bad person," "good student," or "bad student." When children come to see themselves as "bad," they often become defiant, defeated, or both. Many of our "incorrigibles" disrupt and distress our classrooms from beneath the weight of a broad, undifferentiated definition: "I am bad."

TEACHING CHILDREN TO CARE

While there are moments for heartfelt, global statements of praise or anger—"I just loved seeing how you took care of yourself today" or "I get angry when I see that sneaky stuff!"—we must be careful about labels and grandiose implications. "You were considerate to include new people" is different from the label of "considerate student." "You did a sneaky thing" is not the same as calling the child a "sneak." Labels, even the favorable ones, tend to constrict and shrink potentials. We want to avoid imposing unnatural or unrealistic expectations for behavior. What happens if, the next day, the child isn't considerate? We want to let children know that we like them—not because of their accomplishments, and in spite of their failings.

USING THE "I VOICE" IN TEACHING

WHEN COMMUNICATING either encouragement or disapproval, categorical judgments or commands are seldom helpful. I try to be specific ("smudged and crumpled-up math assignment") rather than general ("sloppy work") and to use an "I voice" to speak with children. When we use the "I voice," we take responsibility for our opinions and assert the importance of personal feelings. We are also calling upon connections we have established with students.

Note that this is distinct from the "do it for me" tone that can sometimes creep into our dealings with children. We are not asking them to behave "for" someone else. Instead, we are giving them feedback about the effect of a specific action of theirs, and we are adding our personal perspective and authority to the application of rules we have established together:

- ✦ "I don't like it when you choose not to listen to my words" rather than the more automatic response "You'd better learn to listen, young lady!"

- ✦ "I feel angry when you make faces if I ask you to do something" rather than "You'd better wipe that look off your face."

- ✦ "I want to see you go down the stairs without bumping anyone else's body" rather than "Walk down the stairs and don't touch anyone."

- ✦ "I want to know how you plan to get along with Sharon for the rest of the week and not hurt each other" rather than "You and Sharon better stop fighting."

Using the "I voice" has helped me not jump to conclusions too hastily or make too-quick assumptions, especially with middle schoolers. I think about a time when I wrongly accused a student of slacking off on an assignment in which everyone was to make a poster illustrating a book the class had read. For her poster, this student had brought in a large photograph of a house to represent the one in the book. To me, the photo didn't look or feel like the house in the story. I quickly assumed that the student didn't put much effort into this project. I told her she needed to do more work on it, only to find out later that she had spent hours and hours canvassing the neighborhood, picking exactly the right house to photograph. She even developed and enlarged the photo herself. My mistake, especially because it took place early in the school year, was not easily fixed.

Had I said, "I'm surprised at this photo because I don't think it looks like the one in the story" rather than "You need to do more work," I would have provided an opportunity for the student to explain her choice of house. She would have been able to point out similarities that perhaps I had overlooked, or even make a case for depicting a house that contrasted with the one in the story. Had I used an "I voice," I would have gone down the road of inquiry—holding a constructive conversation about the student's intentions—and not down the road of accusation.

Helping children "stress the deed"

NOT ONLY DO WE NEED to be vigilant about our own language with children, we also need to help them develop and practice constructive language. We do this in several ways. We model appropriate techniques in our own interactions with children; we provide regular opportunities for students to practice their skills in noticing and affirming others' efforts; and we use everyday situations to teach skills.

In the brief conversation between Vinnie and his principal, the principal helped Vinnie move from "I hate Cheryl" to "I hate it when she trashes something I like." Vinnie's negative focus has moved from the doer to the deed, and he has identified the specific trigger for his anger. These significant steps are a foundation for conflict resolution. When children understand only the surface feelings, they often feel overwhelmed and confused. They are stuck in an unpleasant situation with an explosion as a frequent result. When they explode, they are apt to reject themselves, their work, their school, their classmates, their EVERYTHING.

"Stressing the deed, not the doer" requires two skills. One is the skill of noticing the detail and specificity of behavior (the deed, not the doer). The other involves naming and commenting on the behavior with the use of the "I voice."

Children can learn to notice and comment on the details of interaction. While our culture abounds with put-downs, complaints, and blame, and we note the "trash-talk" common in lunchrooms and playgrounds, there are also many words of appreciation and affirmation. We must note and support the use of these words among students. Many teachers counter negativity in their classrooms by helping children pay attention to and comment on the positive cooperation and sharing that occur in the course of each day. When children are more aware of positive behaviors, they are more apt to behave positively.

Children can also learn to express feelings of appreciation and anger using the "I voice." They thrive on the praise and encouragement they receive from one another and attend carefully to the criticism. Children need help expressing praise of people other than their best friends and about things beyond interesting clothes or coveted possessions. They also need help expressing anger without using inflammatory words and abusive names.

To help children to stress the deed, not the doer, we use several techniques:

- ✦ Building a common, age-appropriate vocabulary that describes feelings and social skills. In middle school, we might use the term "flexibility," whereas at younger levels we say "taking turns," to describe the way the class respected Kathy's choice of an activity that was not a class favorite.

- ✦ Naming the gestures, words, and actions of welcome, cooperation, and sharing in school. Teachers may ask:
  —"What are ways that we show we listen?"
  —"What are ways that we show respect for different points of view?"
  —"What are respectful ways we can express frustration or disagreement in school?"

- ✦ Noticing instances and examples of social skills in action. Teachers might say:
  —"I noticed people raising their hands and waiting."
  —"I noticed that when Devon bumped into Mark, she apologized."
  —"I noticed that Carrie gave someone half her sandwich because that person forgot her lunch today."

- ✦ Helping students tell "what" they like, rather than "who." Teachers can help students say:
  —"I like it when people give me time to think of an answer."
  —"I like it better when people tell me I can play next round rather than just saying 'No, you can't play.'"
  —"I like it when teachers give you some choices."

—"I like it when we go around in a circle."

✦ Helping children learn to narrow and specify—to name the deed.

—With help, a student goes from saying "I like you" to "I like it when you let me join your conversations."

—Student to a classmate: "I liked being with you today because you didn't act like a jerk." Teacher: "What do you mean about acting like a jerk?" Student: "Like you let me make up some of the rules for our game."

—Student: "Thanks for being my friend." Teacher: "Can you explain how he was a friend to you this week?" "Well, thanks for being my friend and helping me catch up when I was absent the other day."

✦ Helping students to use their "I voice." With help, students can learn to say:

—"I liked it that you remembered to say "Good morning" before asking me a question."

—"Thanks for helping me with that problem. I like the way you explain stuff."

—"I felt bad when you didn't let me play" rather than "You never let anyone play."

✦ Helping students acknowledge a compliment with a smile and a "thank you."

✦ Helping students to "listen" to and accept criticism by practicing not arguing or rebutting. A teacher might say, "Listen. Don't argue. It may not be what you see or remember, but it's what your friend (teacher or classmate) recalls. See if you can just think about it. You may say 'I'm sorry' or 'I'll think about that.' But you don't argue."

HELPING CHILDREN to develop habits of encouraging and direct language, to "stress the deed," and to notice the positive occurrences in their classroom takes practice. Much of this practice is integrated into the day-to-day work of the classroom. But many teachers also use special "rituals" or events to practice noticing, commenting on positive interactions, and expressing a range of feelings in appropriate, constructive ways.

"I statements" in fifth and sixth grade

Paula Denton's fifth and sixth graders practice using "I statements" in class meetings. She presents the formula "When you _____, I feel _____ because _____, so what I would like is _____."

The class practices filling in the blanks first in playful ways and then by drawing on realistic situations. Importantly, she also works with her class to expand their vocabulary of feeling words and to associate them with specific occurrences. The "I statement" formula is put on a chart and broken down into its sections, with new words and phrases continually added. Children often refer to the chart as they struggle to put their thoughts into words. "I feel irritated when you tell me things over and over because it makes me feel dumb," a student told her partner after much fussing. "I wish you would tell me once and give me time to do it." The partners worked better with each other after that. ❖

The Compliment Club

Some years ago, I started a group for children ages nine to eleven with poor self-images (primarily children with learning problems) called a "Compliment Club." One task of the group was to give each other a weekly compliment. Names were picked from the hat. Each child wrote out a compliment, in a letter-like format:

- ✦ "I think you have improved your cursive a lot."

- ✦ "I think you did good in math this week."

- ✦ "I liked the drawing you did. I think you are a good artist."

- ✦ "You were a good friend this week. You helped me a lot with my reading assignment."

- ✦ "I'm glad you picked me to be on your team. I like playing with you."

Several things were clear in the first months of this club. First, the children noticed and recalled real things, just as previously they had ranked on each other by noticing real faults. Now they picked up each other's true (not fabricated) accomplishments. Second, they quickly developed the knack of offering specifics:

"You are a good friend."

"Can you tell what made him a good friend this week?"

"Well, he picked me for his team."

Third, I was struck with how much they cherished the compliments they received. The letters were folded away, and I would see them pulled out, read, and reread. It was a central part of building the esteem of individuals and also of creating a friendlier spirit in the group. The success of "compliments" depended on the capacity to notice and honestly describe by focusing on the concrete and specific. ❖

Adapting the process of giving compliments

TEACHERS HAVE ADAPTED THE PRACTICE of giving compliments in a variety of ways and settings to build community in the classroom and develop social awareness.

LuAnn Richie, a teacher from a public school in Maine, adapted Compliment Club to meet the needs of her fifth grade classroom. On Monday morning, students drew the name of a classmate or of the teacher from the hat. During the week, their task was to observe and look for "good things." "Good things" had been carefully defined and charted at the start of the year to include acts of sharing, kindness, accomplishment, and cooperation. The definition had expanded and become more specific during the course of the year. Children cherished the compliments they received at the end of the week, and the tone of the classroom became friendlier and more trusting.

A similar ritual is what some teachers call Appreciation Circle. Some classrooms use Appreciation Circle for ending the week on a positive note. Students pick a name at the start of the day and then observe "their person" in order to notice something positive the person does. Appreciative comments are shared in a closing circle with a handshake and a thank-you.

Rick Ellis, a kindergarten teacher in New Jersey, used compliments to teach a "language of noticing" and the skills of social observation (Ellis 1999). Ellis began with his own compliments to individuals and to the class, modeling both patterns of language and how to notice the particulars of helpful behaviors. For example, one day he complimented the class for taking care of the markers. "All the lids were put back on tightly, and now the markers won't dry out." He focuses on a specific event (care for the markers today), a concrete action (the lids were on tight), and a result (the markers won't dry out). After a few weeks of modeling, he asked the children to give compliments during their morning circle time, starting with a few children.

K–1 teacher Arona McNeill-Vann in Washington, DC, used a "catch a partner sharing" activity (Charney 1997, 37–51). When she observed her five- and six-year-olds having trouble sharing and taking turns, she designed this activity to help children notice and report on their classmates' ability to take care of each other, rather than noticing all the negatives—the pokes, name-calling, and irritability.

Zalika picked Anita that day as her partner. It was Zalika's job "to catch Anita sharing." At the afternoon meeting, Zalika filled out the "certificate" she would read in a presentation to Anita. It said, "I noticed that Anita shared with Jamal when they were playing on the playground."

As the children became better observers and namers, they came to understand their valued role as caretakers. And as they felt more noticed and effective as "sharers," affirmed by their peers, they gained empathy. They became more caring because they were recognized as caretakers.

"Representing" or "work sharing" meetings

"REPRESENTING" OR "WORK SHARING" meetings also help children learn to notice and appreciate. In these focused meetings, students bring selected pieces of work to the circle to share. It is the responsibility of the other students to notice and comment on particular aspects of their peers' work. Responses are structured and guided to be specific and constructive. This can have a profound impact, whether it is a five-year-old sharing a block building or a thirteen year-old reading selections from a short story in process.

In a fourth grade classroom in Stamford, Connecticut, a student reads her report about alligators. "Any questions or comments?" she asks. "I thought it was good the way you put in the details about how they take care of the babies," is one response.

In a seventh grade art class, a student holds up his etching. "This is my picture. A problem I had was the purple didn't scratch well." Everyone looks carefully; then hands go up. "I like the background colors you used," a classmate says. "I like the way it looks jagged," someone else notes. "How long did it take you to scratch all the scales on the turtle out?" "Four classes," the student answers honestly. "It was hard."

When children represent their work in this way, teachers promote a reciprocal "language of noticing," so that a way of examining work together is established. Students frame the discussion around their own questions, or what educator Linda Crawford calls "points of interest." Children, in general, come to be more observant and constructive in their critiques of their own work as well as the work of others. Attention to the figures of one drawing, the shading of another, the background of a third also develops a richer vocabulary around work, one that goes beyond "good" or "bad." With this approach, students focus on specifics and details, on intentions and process, on successes as well as obstacles. With the focus on effort, problem solving, and particular attributes of a composition, critical thinking expands.

"I need help with a title," says Jeffrey, age eight, as he prepares to read his story to his writing group. When he finishes reading, the class suggests title ideas. A fourth grader begins her report by commenting, "I don't think the introduction works." "I don't know why you don't like the introduction," a classmate says after listening carefully. "I thought it worked OK."

EXPRESSING ANGER

CHILDREN ALSO NEED HELP expressing a range of feelings, including anger, without calling names. We've all heard exchanges like this verbatim record:

"You're a total smelly jerk."

"So? You're a nerdo wimp creep."

"So? You're so ugly even a cockroach looks good."

"Yeah. Well you're such a shrimp, you gotta watch out or you'll get stepped on. Squish…"

Sometimes the one-upmanship gets so ridiculous it leads to laughing fits. Sometimes it hits too close to home, and sometimes it ends in a physical fight. What can you do if someone calls you a "creep" (or worse)? What can you expect from a creep, anyway? Both sides are stuck. The creep is not likely to say, "But I'm not a creep, I just acted like one." Children need to be able to name the ways they are creeps to each other, and they need safe ways to respond. Children can learn these skills through modeling by teachers, but primarily they will learn from doing. One way I involve children in "stressing the deed" is by using a special ritual in my classroom called "Pretzels."

"Pretzels"

IT IS VERY IMPORTANT TO ACKNOWLEDGE that in the course of a day together there are bound to be accidental misunderstandings and intentional hurts, and to stress that there are appropriate ways to express anger and frustration. We need to help children name and identify their hurt and angry moments, and we need to help them assert their feelings using direct and constructive words. "Pretzels," in which rewards and reparations are objectified in the form of pretzels, helps children to express both appreciation and anger in a safe way.

I invented Pretzels many years ago to develop stronger social skills in a particularly feisty first grade class. A day didn't pass without tears, tattling, and teasing. In addition, a special threesome bullied classmates out of lunch treats, playground balls, and small change. I was actually inspired to come up with the idea of Pretzels by observing the keen bartering powers of some of the children ("Give me that and I'll pick you for my team") and by reading the book *Reality Therapy* by William Glasser (Glasser 1965). The technique proved effective for this class and on other occasions when I have used it for group building.

Based on feedback from teachers using Pretzels over the past decade, I have revised some of the original details. I now recommend conducting Pretzels in two stages. In Pretzels I, only positive behaviors are noted. Only when the group feels safe and when the children are really able to notice the details of caring and friendliness in their class does the teacher introduce Pretzels II, which adds the component of noticing negative interactions. Figure 11.1 and the following descriptions include both Pretzels I and II.

FIGURE 11.1

Guidelines for "Pretzels"

Goals

+ Help children identify and name positive social interactions

+ Create, model, and reinforce friendly and kind interactions in order to build group trust and cooperation

+ Provide a safe and concrete form of appreciation when children help each other

+ Help children identify and name interactions that made them feel bad or angry (Pretzels II only)

+ Provide a safe and concrete form of reparation when children hurt each other (Pretzels II only)

Procedures

1. Getting ready

The class circles up, and the teacher passes out ten pretzels (or counters in place of pretzels) to every student in the circle.

2. Statements

Pretzels I: Going around the circle, each student may make two statements. In the first statement, students thank someone for helping or for a special kindness to them that week. In the second, they tell about an act of cooperation or consideration they observed that helped the class or others in the class.

Pretzels II: Going around the circle, each student may make two statements. In the first statement, students thank someone for helping or for a special kindness to them that week. They may use the second statement to tell about a hurt or upset caused by someone in the class.

3. Gestures

Pretzels I: Going around the circle, each student makes two gestures. First, students offer a pretzel (or a counter) as a thank-you or token of appreciation to the person who helped them. Second, students offer a pretzel (or a counter) to the person who contributed to the class.

Pretzels II: Going around the circle, each student makes two gestures. First, students offer a pretzel (or a counter) as a thank-you or token of appreciation to the person who helped them. Second, they may collect a pretzel (or a counter) as a token of apology or reparation.

4. Counter Exchange

If counters are used, students exchange the counters they have at the end of the session for real pretzels.

Rules

+ We all need to take time to stop and think in order to recall a special kindness (or hurt, in Pretzels II).

+ We may talk about what happened during this week only.

+ We may talk about only things that happened to ourselves or that we actually observed.

+ In Pretzels II, we use a "tagger's choice" rule. If someone thinks that you bothered him/her, it is what he/she feels, so you pay. You do not argue.

+ In a case where there is clear misunderstanding, the teacher may collect the pretzel from the alleged "wrong-doer" and agree to talk to both students further about the incident after the session is over.

+ Pretzels is confidential. That means we do not talk about what happens in Pretzels with students in other classes. "Will you say to your cousin in the fifth grade," I ask, "'Guess what happened in Pretzels today!'?"

+ Pretzels is over when everyone has taken his/her turn, and the teacher announces "Pretzels is closed." Discussions are finished.

Using Pretzels

In introducing Pretzels to students, I emphasize my positive goals for them. "We are going to begin a new activity, which has a kind of funny name but is really for a serious purpose. It's called 'Pretzels,' and pretty soon you will find out why it has such a funny name. Pretzels is a way for us to learn to be friendlier and kinder to one another in school, which I think is very serious. I believe that in order for us to do our best work, we all need to feel safe and good in school, and teachers can't make that happen alone. Only when we do it all together do we make it safe and good. That is what I want us to learn, and that is why we are going to try this serious activity with the funny name.

"I see people act in friendly and kind ways in our class. I see people help others open a thermos that is too tight. I see people say nice things like 'I like your drawing of the house.' Who else has noticed nice and friendly comments or actions?"

I chart the responses under the heading "Ways We Are Helpful and Friendly":

"Sometimes Sheila shares her jump rope with me when I ask."

"Glenda asks me to play a game with her sometimes."

"John lets me hold his markers."

"People help you when you don't know some things and they tell you stuff."

I teach the steps in Pretzels I, and we focus on noticing and rewarding positive interactions. With the aid of teacher modeling and reinforcement, children come to love noticing the kind and friendly contributions of their peers. They are highly observant and able to be very specific in their comments.

If, after a few months, I feel that the class is ready for the next stage involving noticing negative interactions (see Figure 11.2), I review our chart "Ways We Are Helpful and Friendly," then move on to introduce ways that we do not take good care of each other or our class.

"Sometimes, I also notice ways that you hurt each other physically or with your words. I see people push in line. I hear name-calling and teasing. I notice tattling and bossiness. What do you notice that we do in this classroom that hurts other people and isn't kind or friendly?" I do not want to get lists of accusations, so I just list key words, such as "unfair," "teasing," "put-downs," "bossing," or "bullying," on a chart under the heading "Ways We Hurt Each Other," with a few examples for each key word:

"Sometimes people say they hold seats, and you can't hold seats."

"Kids pick their friends to be on teams."

"Kids take your stuff and don't ask."

"Kids say you're stupid if you don't know how to do something right."

We read over both charts.

"My goal is to help, not hurt," I say emphatically. "What is your goal? What do you think makes us all feel good and helps us like to be in school? What do you think?" I ask different children directly. Eventually, everyone responds unanimously, "Our goal is to help and be friendly."

I then teach the children the steps in Pretzels II, which include naming hurts and collecting reparations.

When some children had difficulty keeping to the rules of Pretzels at first, I exempted them from the group, allowing them to observe but not to participate. In some cases, I set up a "pretzel bank," which accepted and paid pretzels on behalf of nonattending children. In all instances, after one or two times, students asked to return to the group and acted appropriately.

When I first started Pretzels, I felt that it was a risk. I wasn't sure what would happen when children were singled out consistently for hurtful behavior. I worried that there would be an increase in resentments and retaliation. I also worried that children would be too intimidated by the bullying to be able to confront it. Mostly, I worried that there would be far more complaints than compliments and that Pretzels would turn into endless gripe sessions.

My fear that some children would be singled out was accurate. Martin and a couple of other classmates went into "deficit-pretzels." They quickly paid up with pretzels until they were empty-handed.

At the same time, it was also evident that hostilities were decreasing rather than increasing. The class seemed more appeased, and Martin, particularly, appeared to be generally less aggressive.

I recall paying Martin a pretzel one week for helping me clean and set up the paints. Other children followed suit, so that Martin received a number of pretzels for helping others out. Some time later, he exclaimed with obvious pride, "Look, Ms. Charney, I got six pretzels this week." And then he did a funny thing. He went over to another child and handed over his pretzel stash. "Here, you can have these. I don't like pretzels," he said. ❖

FIGURE 11.2

When a Class May Be Ready for Pretzels II

Teachers might consider moving on to Pretzels II if Pretzels I sessions are characterized by the following:

✦ Children notice specific acts of friendliness.

✦ Children notice real behaviors.

✦ Statements give details—not just "You're the best teacher" but "You helped me understand the math problem yesterday."

✦ Pretzels are given to different people in the circle and not just to "friends."

✦ Children are comfortable receiving their "appreciation" and are able to nod, say "thank you," or smile.

✦ Children seem to enjoy the circle and are able to follow the rules and procedures with few reminders. That is, there is a tone of respectful participation. If there is a lot of whispering, jiggling, face-making, it may mean that there isn't a real comfort level, and Pretzels may not be working. This is a sign to stop and reconsider and not to add the more difficult part of noticing negatives.

✦ The teacher feels that there is a need to address the negative behaviors and that the group is ready to learn the following skills:

　　—To use the "I voice"

　　—To notice specific behavior

　　—To expand their vocabulary of feelings

　　—To listen to each other

　　—To accept responsibility for their actions and give a "pretzel"

SUMMARY

WHEN TEACHERS STRESS THE DEED, they preserve the doer: "I like you. I don't like this behavior." Using this approach requires noticing actions that contribute to a positive learning environment and those that don't—a task that takes careful attention and constant practice. When we encourage children as well to stress the deed and not the doer, we sharpen their skills of attention and social discourse. In activities such as Compliment Club, "representing" meetings, or Pretzels, and through our everyday work in Morning Meetings and in group and individual work, we help children use language precisely and intentionally to express their likes and dislikes, their satisfactions and frustrations, in constructive rather than destructive ways.

Constructive expression requires noticing and naming details. Teachers and students must learn to notice and name the specific behaviors that work or don't work, rather than to rely upon general impressions or global judgments of "good" or "bad." Repeatedly, I am struck by the keen powers of observation in our students. When we encourage students to use these skills and to voice their observations, we help them solve problems peacefully as well as appreciate each other and themselves.

Works Cited

CHARNEY, RUTH SIDNEY. 1997. *Habits of Goodness: Case Studies in the Social Curriculum*. Greenfield, MA: Northeast Foundation for Children.

ELLIS, RICK. 1999. "'Have You Noticed?' Building Skills of Social Observation." *Responsive Classroom* (Fall): 4–5.

GLASSER, WILLIAM, MD. 1965. *Reality Therapy*. New York: Harper & Row.

Chapter 12
The Voices of Authority

All teachers use different "voices" of authority in the classroom. We must use these different voices selectively and in the right contexts for them to be most effective. I use three voices of authority in my teaching; they are distinguished by the source of power, or type of rules, they call upon.

- ✦ The voice of principle (the Golden Rule, in my case)

- ✦ The voice of procedure (rules for safety and order)

- ✦ The personal voice (personal rules)

Although the voice of principle is the broadest, and actually serves as a foundation for the others, all are important and legitimate voices, essential in building and maintaining a true learning community.

THE VOICE OF PRINCIPLE

When we call upon a higher and more inclusive authority to guide our behavior, we invoke the authority of ethical standards. These are not unique to one teacher, or one class, but are principles which ideally guide and bind us together as human beings. Such a moral and ethical force guides us to become better individuals and better citizens of our school, our community, and our world. We have faith—not that we always do what's right, but that we *try* to do what's right.

I call upon the Golden Rule, though it is not the only such statement of principle. The essential "authority" of the Golden Rule comes from its capacity to inspire faith. It helps us stretch our imaginations—we see ourselves, others, and our community struggling to meet the highest ethical standards.

The Golden Rule doesn't tell us what to do. It lacks all specifics. It doesn't say that it's wrong to tease or call names. But the teaching and understanding of such specifics, growing from children's real-life experiences in school, powerfully involve children in ethical growth.

"What can you do if you accidentally knock someone down? [Shrug.] What would make you feel better if someone knocked you down? Can you say you're sorry? Help the person up? See if the person is hurt?" I don't necessarily expect five-year-olds to know what to say or what to do. Left alone, many would do just what we hope. Others might hasten away, either guilty or oblivious. But all of them can learn.

At eight, there are other important issues. The class is collecting toys and clothes to give away to those in need at Christmas. Some children bring in old, broken toys or torn and shabby articles of clothing. Again, I invoke the authority of the Golden Rule. "If we use the Golden Rule, how will we decide what to give to another person, even someone we don't know? Do we give what we don't want—or something that we guess someone else might like?" We present a germ of an idea—that the sacrifice of giving up something is rewarded with the satisfaction of caring for others and the self-respect that comes from a true act of generosity.

I often remind older children that as we get older, the Golden Rule gets harder, not easier. As adults, we live in a society that too often holds the self-interest of a few far above the common interests of the others. And as we increase our social involvement, social conflicts usually increase as well. It isn't a simple task to be able to take another's perspective while preserving our own autonomy.

I see this approach as moral teaching, not moralizing, because the act requires a choice by the student. The Golden Rule provides a principle, but it also provides choices. One must choose to use the Golden Rule and, further, must choose how to use it. A child must actually choose whether to contribute a still-treasured doll or an outgrown one that sits neglected in a closet. Even if, for now, the choice is the latter, we plant the seed for the next time.

I believe that we need to provide children with a higher moral and ethical authority, such as the Golden Rule. It is up to the teacher to help children recognize and name the possible choices. The Golden Rule is one voice of the teacher, but the teacher is not the Golden Rule—s/he didn't invent it or its practices. The teacher accepts its authority and therefore gives it her/his voice, encouraging children to add their own voices to its power in the larger community.

"When I see people in this class talk to the same friends every day and I see new people in our class not included, I think we are not using our Golden Rule. What does the Golden Rule tell us?"

TEACHING CHILDREN TO CARE

Later, we hear a child's voice. "Would you like to join us and play a game?"

As students get older, they are drawn to academic and social concerns that tap ideals of social justice and altruism. Adolescents, particularly, are eager to repair social ills, to participate in service work, to take principled stands. A study of labor history, for example, was enlivened when it linked inventories of students' own outfits and some current sweatshop conditions. The connections motivated them to research, write letters to the makers of sneakers and jeans, and share information with peers.

I also worked with a group of eighth graders who took action when a false but hurtful rumor about a classmate's drug use was passed around through e-mail "chats." The victim of these rumors was highly sensitive about substance abuse issues because of a painful family history. He was so distraught by the rumors that he banged his fist into a wall so hard that he broke his hand. Class discussions provoked recognition of the hurt caused and of the fact that everyone, even students barely involved in the episode, was responsible. The group realized that few had resisted the impulse to pass on the rumor, and few had actively tried to stop it. They decided as a class to write a letter to their peers about the harm that rumors can cause, and to send the letter to the local newspaper for publication.

The voice of procedure— rules for safety and order

"You need to be able to walk through the halls in a line as a class." That isn't a rule of grand principle, nor is it my personal rule. It is a school rule, a procedural rule. Children need to understand that there are rules that govern the well-being of the school and the community. The teacher recognizes and upholds these rules, but they are not specifically the teacher's. They are the rules that make for safety and order. Sometimes they are official, school-dictated rules; other times they are rules the children and the teacher have articulated together for their classroom. We often refer to them when we say "The rules say…"

It is important to be able to use a set of rules which are not arbitrary, but which are not individualistic or readily negotiable, either. If I want to play kickball, I need to follow the rules. These rules, like ethical rules, are for the common good, but they regulate practical matters such as physical safety, game procedures, and the allocation of rights and privileges. Permission or constraint comes from the authority of the rules, not the authority of the teacher.

✦ "You are out," says the teacher, "not because I say so, but because the rule says so."

✦ "The rules say you have to wait your turn in this game, even if you know the answer. That's not my rule. That's the rule of the game."

✦ "The rules of our school say that if you want the right to chew gum, you have to wait until you're in the oldest class. That's the school rule." "But that's not fair," protests a fourth grader. "Well, whom could you speak to if you want to question that rule?"

I think that it's important for children to understand the source of laws or rules that govern their society. It's useful for them to learn that rules are human-made constructions and therefore changeable. It can be an important exercise for children to pursue the reasons for such specific rules as no gum chewing, having to have bathroom passes, or having to stand in lunchroom lines. In the process of exploring, children may begin to understand why rules are not always for individual convenience or satisfaction. If children's questions about rules are taken seriously and then followed up with a disciplined, orderly study, the quality of school life can be improved. Positive changes can be made in procedures in the lunchroom, the halls, or the locker room. When children are involved, even on the classroom level, they generally gain respect for the process of shaping and making the rules.

When I use the authority of the rules, it is not my personal authority. When a child draws graffiti on the walls, I avoid saying, "I don't like it that you wrote on the walls." Instead, I might say, "In our school, we need to keep the walls beautiful" or "The rules say we need a clean place to work and play." If children cheat while playing a game of checkers, I might ask, "What do the rules say about jumping?" And then, "If you want to play this game, you have to do what the rules say." If a child argues with the referee, the rules says that the referee's call is final.

A group of six-year-olds is playing a game of Capture the Flag. One child says, "Teacher, I tagged him and he won't go to jail."

The teacher asks both children, "What's the rule?"

"Tagger's choice."

"But he didn't tag me."

"The rule says, 'If the tagger says he tagged you, you are tagged.' What do you do now?" If the "tagged" child chooses not to follow the rule, he loses the privilege of being in the game. These rules provide safety and order. The teacher facilitates and safeguards the rules, but it's the rules that "say," not the teacher.

PERSONAL RULES

THERE ARE TWO WAYS that I use the personal voice of authority. One has to do with personal "quirks" or preferences; the other has to do with matters of strong personal conviction.

There are a few rules I insist upon out of strong personal preference and that I ask for compliance with based upon consideration rather than moral choice or respect for the law. For example, I can't bear rock and roll music early in the morning, but when my children were at home, they not only could bear it, but liked it. I asked (actually insisted) that there be no R&R music within my earshot in those brutal waking hours. My authority did not stand on morality. I couldn't argue that it is bad or harmful to human dignity—not logically anyway. I also couldn't invoke the rules of the state or legal proceedings. I could only say that it bothered me and disturbed my well-being. I needed their consideration and respect as their parent.

I think it is important to request, even demand, consideration as long as the request is reasonable—something that is appropriate, that children can manage, and that truly reflects personal meaning. I wouldn't ask children to do their best work or to be nice just to please me. I would ask them to show personal consideration by turning down the radio, letting me talk undisturbed with a friend, or helping me with a chore.

One of my personal rules for the classroom is "no war games." I do not make it a matter of ethics. It is not a school rule either, although it could be. I present it as my preference, something that I do not like or allow in my classroom.

Noise level is also a matter of personal consideration. I like it quiet in the morning. I need it quiet. Invariably, I begin the day with a quiet social time. Yet, one year I co-taught with a wonderful teacher who loved music and kept a piano in the room, which the children loved to play—endless four-handed beats of "Chopsticks" in the morning! My co-teacher didn't mind at all and often joined in. It didn't work for me, so out of consideration, quiet music ruled the morning and "Chopsticks" the afternoon.

I also use personal authority for matters of strong personal conviction. These are most honestly expressed in the "I voice." When I use this voice, I am not reminding about the procedures of the school or simply translating the Golden Rule, but I am conveying my thoughts, convictions, and knowledge. These convictions are related to matters of principle, but I am choosing to add my personal authority based on my relationship with the children:

> ✦ "It matters to me that everyone participate."
>
> ✦ "I really care that everyone feels included in this class."
>
> ✦ "I really want to see you finish a book this year. That feels very important for me."

These convictions may apply to goals for the classroom or for specific children. When we have developed relationships of trust and respect with children, our personal authority is often our strongest voice with them—as long as we don't overdo it.

"I can wear whatever I want"

Through sixth grade, Chris had liked to sit close to her teachers and took pride in doing her work well. Then adolescence hit with the impact of a strong gale. Now the back, not the front, of the room was her spot, "cool" was the critical definition used for sorting all things, and her homework, still beautifully done, was handed in with a scowl, as if quality work was a defect to be concealed. By late fall, her "in-your-face" tone had escalated. The inevitable confrontation occurred the day she took off her sweatshirt to reveal a very tight T-shirt sporting the face and lyrics of a rock star known for his hate-mongering and degrading messages.

I drew her into the privacy of the office, took a deep breath, and plunged in. "Chris, I'd like to talk about your T-shirt. Is this a good time?" Arms folded, head down, body coiled, she appeared utterly unreceptive, but she didn't walk away. I continued. "I notice your T-shirt, and I wonder if you forgot you had it on?" Fat chance, but I wanted to offer her an out.

She didn't take it. "I can wear whatever I want," she snarled.

I told her that I knew about the musician's songs attacking women and people of color. I told her that I knew that she was always concerned about fairness and wondered what she thought.

"No one gets it," she responded. "It's just anger and stuff. Besides, it's my choice, and I can wear what I want."

"That may be true at home, but in school we have rules about respecting all people. Is it possible that this T-shirt might be offensive to others in the class?"

Chris's defiance was mounting, and the tension between us was rising. Time to stop. I told her that at the moment, I was convinced the T-shirt was inappropriate. She had three choices: to put her sweatshirt back on; to turn the tee inside out; or to stay in the office for the rest of the day. When I returned for her answer a few moments later, she had put her sweatshirt back on. She resumed her classes in a silent fury.

Dress and appearance are often ways to try on identities and to assert individuality. It is an ongoing challenge for teachers (and parents) to respect our children's explorations, however stridently they are carried out, while also honoring our own authority and responsibility for maintaining boundaries of decency and safety. While it isn't productive to battle over trifles, I find that ignoring all signals only increases distance between teachers and students. Besides, clothing endorsing messages of violence and degradation of groups of people isn't a trifle.

With Chris, I followed up our encounter with a letter to her in which I talked about social justice, and explained that when people used derogatory words to describe others, "it offended me and perhaps her peers, and that was not okay." While she didn't see the details of this issue as I did, Chris respected my conviction and appreciated a letter which spoke to her in grown-up terms. With her mother's support, Chris grappled with the idea that her particular "rights" were superseded by the rights of the group. For the rest of the year, her outfits continued to assert her nonconformity. Her dark lipstick remained intact, but her T-shirts were neutral. ❖

Summary

VARIED VOICES OF AUTHORITY serve as tools for the teacher. Sometimes, using the voice and principles of moral authority helps stretch children's power to care and attend to others. Procedural rules provide the permission and constraint of an external order. They give consistency and safety to the common ground. And finally, there is the personal authority of the teacher, which expresses both conviction and knowledge. Used carefully and sparingly, there is no stronger voice than the personal. It is the natural authority of a confident teacher—it springs from the teacher's inner strength and grace.

SECTION IV
Further Strategies for Difficult Classroom Behaviors

Introduction

CAREFUL AND THOROUGH COMMUNITY BUILDING, clear communication, and paying attention to small problems as they arise help prevent many potential classroom troubles—many, but not all. Each year, as we get to know our groups and our individual children, we spot issues that require concentrated efforts. Sometimes an issue is unique to a particular child, impeding the child's growth and requiring individualized work. Other times, issues involve many children and affect the whole group climate. To address these effectively, we use strategies involving the entire group.

A colleague describes a fifth grade class that struggled to play well together. Day after day, they returned from recess tense and disgruntled. The class had generated rules for their classroom, and they got along well when indoors. They had discussed how their rules applied to outdoor games. Their teacher had questioned them repeatedly to give the rules more muscle: "What do you need to do so that everyone will be safe in elimination dodgeball?" "How are you going to choose teams so that there are fair sides?" She had monitored their play with vigilance in the early weeks of the year and addressed specific violations. She was an experienced teacher and expected some ups and downs in the process of a new group of ten- and eleven-year-olds learning to play together. Yet at a point in the year when she typically saw emerging cohesion and spirit, each day brought growing tension after an outdoor time.

The teacher saw that this issue posed particular challenges for this class and decided it was time to name it and involve the class in problem solving. Because it was an issue that affected the whole class, she began with a class meeting.

In addition, since her observations of recess time had revealed that a couple of students consistently acted as catalysts in nasty interactions, she also worked with those two students individually. She held social conferences with them to reflect what she saw, hear their perceptions, and think together with them about what they could do when they felt "people weren't playing right."

With one of the students, she went on to involve the parents. Teacher, parents, and child eventually drew up a specific contract naming specific behaviors they all agreed the student would try. The contract provided a way for the child to gauge her performance, a concrete way to note and recognize her growth.

The anecdote above illustrates how a teacher may draw on several techniques—class meetings, social conferences, and an individual contract—all focused on improving one significant area. More often, teachers will use one strategy for one issue, another for a different issue. In a given week there may be a class meeting on problems in sharing the art supplies, a social conference with Robby about his scornful attitude spilling out frequently in Morning Meetings, and ongoing monitoring of Anya's contract about being ready for class.

All the strategies presented in detail in the following chapters have common elements. They all involve naming a problem with children and inviting and really listening to the children's perceptions. They involve the children in figuring out *how* to tackle the problem—while conveying the unequivocal message that improvement is possible and will happen. The strategies also help children to envision what progress will look like—sometimes in very concrete and specific detail.

✦ Chapter 13 discusses problem-solving class meetings, which can be used to address a wide variety of group issues for different age levels. By involving the class as a whole in solving a problem, these meetings encourage students to become workers toward a shared goal.

✦ Chapter 14 presents social conferences as a way for teachers to act as mirrors for individual students, lovingly and clearly reflecting their behavior back to them in the service of growth. In a social conference, the teacher helps a student identify and understand a problem the student is having, helps the child note his/her strengths and challenges, and works with the child to generate or choose a strategy that the child thinks will help. Social conferences give students a chance to state their point of view and a voice in their own problem solving.

✦ Chapter 15 focuses on specific contracts drawn up for individual students and agreed to by the teacher, the student, and the parents. They are helpful for children who need more concrete and frequent reminders of a new behavior they need to adopt, children who need a more concentrated "dose" of adult guidance. By identifying specific goals and stating a plan for making daily assessments of the student's progress in reaching them, the contract helps children make the connection between general classroom rules and what they themselves are doing this day, this minute.

CHAPTER 13
Problem-Solving Class Meetings

Essentially, class meetings are times to talk—a forum for students
and teacher to gather as a class to reflect, discuss issues,
or make decisions about ways they want their classroom to be....
Class meetings also take faith—faith that kids who may never have assumed
responsibility for their learning and behavior are capable of doing so.

DEVELOPMENTAL STUDIES CENTER
Ways We Want Our Class To Be

IN RECENT YEARS, I have been fortunate to observe and conduct many interesting and vital class meetings. Some of these class meetings anticipated problems and helped students become more self-governing in their classrooms. For example, Carolyn Bush, a Stamford, Connecticut, third grade teacher, asked her students in a class meeting early in the year to think about how to be good partners for their academic work, since she would often expect them to work cooperatively with partners. Months later, I watched her students generate a list of exciting ways to show what they knew about adjectives, decide on a method to use for their project on adjectives, then choose a partner with a similar interest. The selection of partners was seamless, the choices diverse. Girls chose boys, boys chose girls, the nimble allied with the deliberate, the good spellers with those who needed help. "It hasn't been easy," Ms. Bush noted, "but it is working."

Class meetings are also useful when things are not working well. They can initiate and instruct problem solving when the limits or boundaries fray as children grow and expand, wander and wonder. Problems occur even when the rules are in place, even when many challenging social and academic tasks are negotiated with skill under a watchful teacher's eye. As part of their learning, children make mistakes and choose poorly. Yet if children are given the opportunity to solve problems, these very mistakes can provide them an opportunity to develop moral and ethical thinking. Teachers can use children's mistakes and "problems" as fertile ground for learning in class meetings, just as logical consequences use rule breaking for further learning. The following are fragments from a few meetings which illustrate preventive and reactive problem solving.

WHEN MR. KWAME-ROSS took over a sixth grade class midyear, he knew he had to pull the group together. Gathering them into a circle and starting a class meeting, he asked them not to picture the class as they currently knew it, but to create a vision. He set them on what he called "the high ground." "Come up the mountain with me," he urged. He asked them to "draw a picture of what a classroom could be if everyone was good to each other, took care of one another, worked hard together." Step by step, he proceeded with his questions and the students' information. "What would it take?" And of course he proceeded with his faith: "I know you can do it."

MS. JOHNSON'S FIRST GRADERS returned from lunch and recess exhausted and irritable. They tattled, complained, showed bruises, and sought endless comfort. It was hard to get them focused on math or reading, impossible to begin a group activity. "Recess is supposed to be fun, but everyone looks mad when they come back from the yard," Ms. Johnson observed to the group. Using a class meeting, she helped the group describe "fun" and "not fun" games. She helped them recognize and name the current activities. While stopping a current, unsafe chase game, she also helped them find new games and new ways to rotate the job of game leader. With more structure and guidance, recess improved.

MS. COOPER BEGAN THE CLASS MEETING with a question. "Lately, many of you have been coming to me to tell me you feel hurt. What do you mean by that? What does it feel like when you are hurt?" "Like I'm not important," one child said. "Like there's a pain on my mind," another added. Ms. Cooper helped her students to identify and name feelings and, importantly, to act on them. "What can you say, Michelle, when someone doesn't even answer when you ask to join the Double Dutch game?" "What are you going to say, Dawn, when Michelle asks to play? Are you going to say, 'Girl, I'm playing. Get lost'?" With their teacher, students role-played and chanted words and actions.

SOMETIMES THE CHILDREN name the problems that occur; often it is the teachers who notice in the countenance and behavior of their students that things are not okay. They note the scrappy attitudes after recess. They hear their own nagging voices issuing too many reminders to complete work. The custodian informs them that the bathrooms are trashy, or the bus driver complains about bus behavior. However the problems surface, the ways we bring the problems to our children affect their willingness to take responsibility. Class meetings provide a ritual and routine, a structure and procedure for both inspiration and instruction.

Class meetings work at all grade levels, with appropriate adaptations. They are highly effective with middle school students, who are keen to feel their own agency and capacity to effect change. Critical at this age is the sense of purpose and "vision." It is an age at which children are idealistic, deeply interested in the social implications of fairness or justice. And, of course, children this age love to argue. With this age group, strong facilitation and clear procedures are important in order to keep pace and deter argument.

Years ago, William Glasser wrote in *Schools Without Failure,* "Given little help, children tend to evade problems, to lie their way out of situations, to depend upon others to solve their problems or just to give up" (Glasser 1969, 124). Without our help, children will "solve" a problem by manufacturing an excuse, blaming someone else, or providing an empty promise to teachers so they will shut up. But children are motivated to find just solutions when we give them tools to deal with what matters in their lives.

I use a problem-solving class meeting format taken largely from the pioneering work of William Glasser and Rudolf Dreikurs and adapted successfully for today's classrooms by many in the field.

PURPOSE OF CLASS MEETINGS

*The two main purposes of class meetings are to
help each other and to solve problems.*

JANE NELSEN
Positive Discipline

THE FIRST GOAL OF CLASS MEETINGS is to provide a constructive format for students to contribute to their classroom by helping each other. Honest discussion allows children to have a say in their classroom and to give appropriate input into some (not all) of the arrangements and decisions. We set up and teach a process that gives children an opportunity to express different opinions and to know that divergent voices will be respected. We must also give permission for children to say what they really think, not what they think we want to hear. A nonjudgmental tone and carefully selected and framed discussion topics are essential for honest and open discussion.

The second goal is to develop children's capacity to solve problems. In the process of dynamic discussion, students learn to recognize and name their own feelings, and to see and respect other perspectives. Students are learning to negotiate and compromise in order to reach not "their" solution, but a "just" solution. In a class meeting, it is the students, not the teacher, who must propose and choose the solutions that they think will work.

The solutions often work because students are invested in them, not because the solutions are so brilliant. Other times, solutions will fail, and must fail. But a failure can produce an even greater educational dividend—the process of revising and learning from mistakes. "I worry that there isn't time for failure," one teacher cried. And that may be one of the greatest failures of our schools—the lack of time we give children to learn from necessary mistakes.

SETTING THE TONE FOR CLASS MEETINGS

IT IS IMPORTANT TO SET UP an environment for class meetings that invites both participation and responsibility. We want to insure that students are comfortable, but also that they are attentive and focused. We want to encourage individual expression, but also respectful listening and acceptance of different opinions. How we come together and talk is as important as what gets said. When we facilitate a class meeting, we maintain the attitude and tone needed to search for solutions and to build community membership, a sense that we each belong and matter. It is critical to begin each class meeting with a positive note, to have and enforce a few clear and consistent rules about meeting conduct, and to have an appropriate and focused agenda.

A positive tone may be created by reflecting on something that works, by a round of compliments to the class, or even by a quick playful activity. The fourth graders poised to talk about the debacle with yesterday's guest teacher were very serious. They sat forward in their chairs, silent and still. Knowing that negativity is a nine-year-old characteristic, Ms. Ritchie began with a round of compliments.

"What do you think is working in our class right now?" she asks. "We work well with different partners," someone says. The eighth graders gathered to discuss lunch policy were ready to go, leaning forward, "up." Ms. Foot began by asking this class to think of one good reason for the current lunch policy. The group of first graders seated on the rug after a hard recess period looked anxious and uneasy, eyes bent on shoelaces. Their teacher started with a quick playful activity, "Zoom."

Establishing a few clear and consistent rules reassures the children that the meeting will be safe. Reviewing the rules at the outset of the meeting provides an opportunity for the teacher to frame and secure the tone and to gauge student buy in. A quick summary of the topic and a quicker show of "thumbs up" help the teacher know the mood and spirit of the group. (The "thumbs up" also permits some children to decide not to participate if they are not ready.) It is always important for the teacher to be the gatekeeper of these rules. S/he may give a few reminders but should stop a meeting if students are not listening to each other or are becoming too fierce. The teacher may suggest coming back to the discussion after students have had a chance to think about "how to have strong feelings but also be respectful."

In addition to determining which topics are appropriate for the agenda, teachers provide a helpful focus by defining the problem in a way that is inclusive and establishes the human nature of the problem. "We all sometimes forget to…try to…" The teacher also affirms the overriding goals of making the classroom a safe and good place for everyone. The teacher listens carefully, gathers information, and, when necessary, refocuses the discussion. Going around the circle, giving children extra time to think, allowing a student to pass now but contribute a short time later, and making sure to check in on certain students are ways to encourage participation. The goal is a group discussion, not a student-teacher back-and-forth.

Pace and timing are also tone setters. Sometimes it is important to slow down and wait so that others can find their words and ideas. Sometimes it is important to limit answers to prevent the discussion from being repetitive and dull. A discussion that is losing momentum may be stopped at any point so that the tone does not disintegrate because of restlessness or waning attention. It is also important that meetings do not drag on, even if there is keen interest in a topic. Everyone should have a chance to be heard, but eye contact or signals that show agreement also express participation. Careful facilitation and attention to the tone keep the more assertive and vocal students from dominating meetings.

Finally, the teacher closes the meeting on a positive note, recognizing and affirming the best efforts of the group to "actively listen to different ideas," to "take risks," to "explore new solutions." Even if the meeting has not been highly productive, it is important to let students know that you believe they can come back to this. "Think about how we can make this discussion work better next week," or "Let's think about it and try again." We may have to revise the question or topic so that we can say to children as their teacher, "I know you can do this." Many teachers like to close the class meeting with a quick go-around that allows students to evaluate or briefly comment on the process.

RULES AND SKILLS FOR CLASS MEETINGS

THE FOLLOWING RULES WERE DEVELOPED by the Mediation & Training Collaborative, an organization in Greenfield, Massachusetts, that helps individuals and groups resolve conflicts and improve communication (Mediation & Training Collaborative 2001). Students agree to:

- Try to solve problems

- Support one another and not use any put-downs—physical or verbal

- Listen to each other and not interrupt

- Use the "I voice" when speaking ("I have trouble concentrating when…")

I present these to the class as the four important ground rules for class meetings, but I ask if they think we need others to help solve problems, speak honestly, and "make sure everyone is heard." Sometimes students suggest going around the circle. In recent years, I added a rule of confidentiality. "We agree that our discussions are for our class and not for friends at recess. Of course, we can share with our parents."

Each rule needs to be discussed as well, since each teaches us skills of listening and talking to one another. When I say "us," I genuinely mean adults as well as children. Our own ability to model good listening or to paraphrase the best intentions of a statement will help children learn.

In the beginning, we model and demonstrate some of the skills that accompany our rules. For example, it is useful to talk about the possibility that solving problems as a group may mean giving up one's own ideas when others' seem better. I have often modeled this, because children can get into a contest over the ownership of an idea. "Suppose I have a solution and Terry has a solution. How should we decide what solution to use?"

I also demonstrate and role-play nonverbal put-downs, such as making faces, rolling eyes, exchanging glances with a friend, or showing indifference with body posture. We all need to practice respectful ways to express our disagreement or agreement. Class meetings are not intended to be debate societies or popularity contests. Since we want children to feel that they can offer thoughtful—if not fully thought-out—ideas, their ideas must be welcomed and not dissected.

Students also need to practice making "I statements." These are an essential tool in any problem solving or conflict resolution: "I had a hard time listening" rather than "they were talking and talking" or "I want to..." rather than "We should..." Children are learning to share by exchanging ideas and views. An important aspect of their participation is learning to communicate their own feelings or attitudes rather than criticizing and blaming others for the problem. Is it just the fault of the lunch aide that bedlam breaks out? Can this class of eleven-year-olds move from saying "She can't control us" to "What can we do to better control ourselves?"

"I statements" are a way to say what you feel without blame or accusation. ("I feel _____ when _____.") They also help us recognize and name a range of emotions and the degree of feeling, although often children need help with vocabulary and with how to sense the variables of feelings. "I statements" also help maintain personal investment. Using them takes practice and more practice, work that needs to be done before a situation that calls for their use arises. We want children to understand that they can take ownership of their own behavior even if they can't control what others do. We want them to say to themselves, "What can I do about the noise...or mess...or teasing?" rather than telling others how to improve and act. "I don't like it when you grab things from my desk" is direct but not as confrontational as "You'd better stop grabbing."

Active listening is another necessary but difficult skill. It involves paying attention to the meanings and intentions of what someone is saying. It includes the ability to paraphrase or repeat back the main points of a speaker. It easily transfers to many academic tasks, including science investigations, peer writing conferences, and note taking. In a wonderful strategy called "partner chats," students practice listening by exchanging ideas and then reporting back to the group, telling one or two things their partner said.

In a class meeting, we are teaching (as well as exercising) vital skills in cooperation and problem solving. We will need to be patient and encouraging. Figure 13.1 provides an abbreviated list of problem-solving skills that children generally have at different developmental stages. I use the list as a guide to assess children's growth. I compare children's skills before a program of class meetings with those after six months. As children mature, they are better able to reflect, consider multiple viewpoints, anticipate the outcome of various solutions, and even control the impulse to speak out of turn.

Class meetings—and the skills they require—take practice. Teachers need practice in creating a comfortable and secure atmosphere. It's usually best to start with Morning Meetings, or circle times, which focus on group sharing and lively group interactions such as games, singing, and personal sharing. Next comes work on developing cooperative skills and teamwork in academic or artistic enterprises, in small or large groups. Teachers and children build familiarity and trust gradually, through many group activities. Once the class has established some common ground, problem-solving meetings can deal with the tougher issues and result in deeper bonds.

There are a few things that do *not* belong in any class meetings:

✦ *Do not* allow children to blame or accuse others.

✦ *Do not* enlist other children to detect and identify wrongdoers.

✦ *Do not* target the whole class for the behavior of a few individuals.

These tactics build resentment and suspicion, not cooperation. To involve the class in finding a just solution is to enlist cooperative and collective enterprise. "What do we need to do right now to keep our classroom safe?" is a good question to initiate a meeting. "Who did it?" is not.

Here are a few procedural suggestions that can also help create a comfortable meeting atmosphere:

Meet once a week at a regular time

Students need experience with class meetings to develop skills and successes. Meeting once a week gives children time to digest and reflect and makes the procedure special. When students are comfortable and skilled with the process, meetings may be held "as needed."

Keep time

The maximum length for meetings is thirty minutes for third to fifth graders, forty-five minutes for sixth to eighth graders. There is a tendency to prolong a meeting when the discussion is going well or in order to finish up an issue. But long meetings are difficult for many children, who may begin to dislike them. It is better to come back to the issue next week, with a fresh and renewed interest.

Meet in a circle, not at desks

A circle promotes inclusion and face-to-face contact. I prefer to have older children sit in chairs for this meeting, rather than on the floor.

Set up a weekly agenda

Teachers and children may put issues on the agenda. Teachers safeguard the agenda and make sure issues are appropriate and carefully focused. Issues that involve only a few students may be better saved for peer conferences or conflict mediation; issues set up to blame or vent anger need to be rephrased into problem statements. "We hate art class" needs to be presented as a more specific question or concern. A better approach might be "We want to have more choices in art class and wonder what we can do to help make that happen." When the teacher works with the students to make agenda items workable, this, too, becomes part of the learning.

With older students, the agenda continues to reflect current school experiences and observed problems. However, I often draw on current events, movies, or social themes that translate the issues and offer application to a broader setting. We might first explore power dynamics in *The Outsiders* and then consider sorting in our own class, for example.

FIGURE 13.1

Problem-Solving Skills at Different Ages

In *Discovery Time for Cooperation and Conflict Resolution* by Sarah Pirtle (1998, 165–166) and *Conflict Resolution in the Middle School* by William J. Kreidler (1997, 376–377), the authors articulate the problem-solving skills that children acquire at different ages. Below is a summary of the general trends.

Kindergarten through Third Grade

At these ages, children generally can:

+ Describe problems or give information without using put-downs or blame

+ Give their own opinions in a group

+ Express their own views and thoughts (using the "I voice")

+ Listen while others share ideas or opinions

+ Maintain eye contact

+ Wait rather than interrupt

+ Say something affirming about the ideas or solutions of others

+ Accept more than one possible solution to a problem

+ Choose the most workable solution to the problem and stick to it

Fourth through Sixth Grade

At these ages, children generally can:

+ Develop more than one solution to a problem

+ Explore different points of view

+ Anticipate different outcomes of proposed solutions

+ Evaluate the advantages and disadvantages of solutions and give logical reasons

+ Use active listening to paraphrase and recall the ideas of others

- Listen and respond to others empathetically

- Agree to consequences and abide by them

Seventh and Eighth Grades

At these ages, children generally can:

- Begin to formulate and test their own values

- Focus intensely on sorting out right from wrong (in this sorting, boys tend to focus more on justice, whereas girls tend to focus more on caring)

- Lead others and develop good ideas for solving social problems

- Engage in more abstract thinking: considering possibilities rather than just realities, better at seeing things from another's point of view

- Think through the consequences of behavior and use that information to temper the desire for immediate gratification

- Consider exceptions to the rules

....

STEPS FOR PROBLEM-SOLVING MEETINGS

1. Introduce the problem and review the meeting rules
2. Gather information
3. Begin and focus discussion
4. Brainstorm solutions
5. Choose a solution
6. Define progress and consequences
7. Close the meeting

1. Introduce the problem and review the meeting rules

- "This is what I notice."

- "This is why it's a problem."

FRAMING AN INTRODUCTION around these two statements helps initiate a class meeting that is direct and yet open. I might begin, "I have noticed that there has been a lot of tattling and picking on one another lately. I hear complaints about name-calling and see that some people are feeling bad. I don't think this makes our classroom a good place to work. I want to talk about it in our meeting today. Does everyone agree to try to work on solving this problem, with no put-downs and by listening to each other?"

If a problem is generalized in the classroom, I try to provide clear and concrete specifics: "I hear people saying things about each other's hair and clothes or calling each other 'morons.'" If I am drawing on an incident that a few students provoked, but that many others sanctioned or joined in on, then I generalize the issue. For example, in a situation where a few people misused e-mail privileges, I framed the question around the ways we protect or invade each other's privacy.

In the introduction, I also want to explain, using my own "I voice," why I, as their teacher, think it is a problem. I may refer to the rules that guide our behavior in the room and to the ethics that build our community. "This is happening in our room right now, and it makes it hard for everyone to feel included or safe."

After the topic is explained, we review the ground rules of a problem-solving class meeting. I go around the circle. Everyone nods to show agreement with the rules. If I know that some students have a hard time with meetings, I emphasize that participating is a choice and a decision. "Are there people who feel they may have difficulty with these rules and would rather not participate today?" Sometimes a student leaves, but he/she usually returns the next week with much better behavior.

If the rules break down during the meeting, I give one reminder. If the rules still aren't working, I stop the meeting. I might say, "I see that it's hard for you to keep to your agreement right now to try to solve a problem; therefore, we need to stop. We will see if this problem is on the agenda for next week." Children are far more likely to come back to class meeting in a positive way if the meeting is stopped rather than allowed to deteriorate. The teacher also has time to think about whether the children were having difficulty with the subject or whether it was merely the pre-spring blues. Often the problem is with the subject.

In initial meetings, I may select problems from a list "brainstormed" by the class. I want to make sure that the content of the meeting matters—the problem discussed should be immediate, real, and solvable. I tackle easy-to-solve problems first to build success and confidence.

2. Gather information

+ "You heard me say what I notice. What do you notice?"

+ Describing and defining the problem

+ Asking why the behavior poses a problem for the class

DURING THIS EARLY STAGE in the problem-solving meeting, I'm on a fishing expedition. I want to understand what's going on in my group, to see what's underneath the problematic behaviors. I begin by asking a specific question, so that everyone has a chance to respond. It needs to be a question that leads to a description of the situation—a question that invites students to add their personal observations and feelings—without making (or asking children to make) moral judgments. I do not want to ask if it's wrong to pick on others, partly because the answer is so obvious and partly because children continue to do it despite everyone's agreement that it is wrong. If I begin with the wrong question, the discussion can only become accusatory or defensive, depending on whether you are a "picker" or a "pickee." Instead, I want to phrase an open question:

"We all probably pick on people sometimes or deliberately tattle. Sometimes, if I'm in a bad mood, I might begin to pick on someone. I remember tattling on my brother if I wanted to get him in trouble. I wonder if you could remember a time this week, for example, when you picked on someone or tattled? Gerry, will you begin, please? Do you tend to be a tattler or a picker?"

At this moment the class chuckles a bit, but they are involved. As I go around the circle, I find that most of the children quickly describe their place:

"I pick on people," one child admits.

"I get picked on," another adds.

"Both," a number reply. The nods of others in the group seem to confirm the personal testimonies. The honesty is striking.

"What makes you feel like picking on someone?" I ask next. Or, if a child seems uncomfortable, I'll ask, "What's your guess—why do you think some kids might want to pick on other kids?" When a child is reticent, I might say, "Would you like more time to think? I'll come back to you if you raise your hand when you are ready." A few children will hold back in the early meetings or have difficulty expressing their own feelings, but they may take part in finding solutions.

As you gather information, it is important to give everyone a chance to have a say. This is a time for only brief comments, not conversation. In the beginning, teachers will often need to redirect and reinforce expectations:

"See, Billy is always bothering me and he don't listen when I tell him to stop, so then I tell the teacher," says James.

"So, when you are bothered and the person doesn't stop, you feel like you have to tell the teacher." I rephrase the statement, eliminating Billy's name.

"I stop but…" begins Billy.

"Billy, let's wait on discussion. Molly, you're next."

To encourage information gathering:

+ Go around the circle.

+ Make questions specific.

+ Narrow or refocus a question if a child seems unsure.

+ Encourage short responses but not conversation.

At the end of the information gathering, the teacher sums up what s/he heard and models active listening.

"I heard many of you say that sometimes you pick on someone else and sometimes you feel picked on. A lot of you said that it's a way to be funny and a way to be cool, especially between boys and girls. I heard some people say that they like making people laugh, but I also heard someone say that they think it's funny to get people mad. I also heard that mostly you told a teacher when you ask others to stop and they didn't. So you weren't listening to each other. It sounds like it's hard to know when picking on people is just 'dumb' or when it gets 'mean.' And I still think that most people don't always feel good about it when it gets mean, although a few think it's not a problem, just 'comedy.' Did anyone hear anything else?"

I try to discern attitudes about the issues and to find the common themes. In this case, it seemed that much of the taunting was a way to get attention and make contact, particularly with the opposite sex. In only a few instances was there an undercurrent of actual hostility, and that seemed restricted to one or two children. The taunting and the tattling both resulted from insufficient social skills.

I next pose the question "Why is this behavior a problem?" At this point, students, particularly older ones, often disagree that the behavior is problematic. "Everyone says it; lighten up" was one excuse offered for calling others "retards" or "homos." About the issues of a faked love letter, Wilson asserted, "It was just a joke. Everyone else thought it was funny."

We must remember that students' intentions are often short-sighted; the need to belong and "have fun" can be so great at some points that their awareness of hurting others may disappear from the radar screen. Though it is tempting to disagree or directly refute their remarks, it is seldom productive. Instead, remember that this is a class meeting and not a back-and-forth between a few students and the teacher. "I wonder what other people think. Is it funny?" I might ask. As teachers we can also offer other perspectives, sometimes extending students' historical and social understandings. "Just a few years ago, it was legal to bar citizens from certain clubs because of gender, race, or religion" helped broaden a discussion of exclusionary classroom "clubs."

Gathering information with an open mind is key. With older students, we miss a lot of the things that are really going on. I find that kids are relieved to share as long as there isn't a tone of blame. Students will often reenact a scene or describe it with precise language and behavior, making no attempt to muddle or conceal information. ("I sometimes take stuff from someone's backpack without asking first" or "I don't say anything when Jeremy keeps calling Alexis an airhead because I'm afraid he'll just tease *me* then.") Their sense of why things occur may demonstrate perspectives teachers are unaware of and provide a very different slant.

But accurate or honest reporting by itself does not always lead to the best actions. Discussions often focus on why such familiar behaviors are a problem and why we might all sometimes make rating lists, join "clubs that exclude," deliberately hurt others, take things that aren't ours, or act without thinking about the consequences. This approach to gathering information validates the many urges and motives that are a real part of making choices. It builds self-awareness and understanding. It also helps us move toward alternatives and solutions.

3. Begin and focus the discussion

+ "How do we contribute to the problem?"

+ "What are other things that contribute to this problem?"

+ "What do we need to fix the problem?"

"IT SOUNDS LIKE people in this class like each other pretty well and want to be friendly. What do you think you would need in order to be more friendly and stop picking on people?" This is an unusual question to consider—what do I (or we) need in order to stop picking on people, or stop tattling, or whatever the issue might be. Other questions might be:

+ "What do you think might help with _____?"

+ "What do you think helps people with _____?"

+ "What can we do to make it easier to stop _____?"

Sometimes good leading questions focus on feelings. This encourages students to see a problem from the point of view of another, building empathy. "What does it feel like to be picked on?" "What does it feel like to tell someone to stop and they don't listen to you?" "I wonder what it feels like to get a fake letter?" I do not expect children to automatically know the answer. Questions give focus, point in a productive direction, and stimulate thoughtful discussion.

The discussion that followed (in a group of eleven-year-olds) focused on the nature of the joking in the group.

"No one should be joking about someone else's mother."

"Nobody should be calling you fat or ugly or stuff."

"Like if someone says your clothes look like you got 'em at the dog pound or something, you feel like you want to say something bad back, but you should be able to just not mind and not say nothin' back."

The first two comments reveal concerns with the language they used to joke—probably a crude imitation of the "ranking" they observed with older children, but lacking subtlety. The last comment goes a bit further and considers the ethics of retaliation. It contrasts what the person feels like doing ("say something bad back") with what a person should do ("not mind"). However, none of the statements were phrased to answer the "What do I need" question. When I rephrased the statements, there was some discomfort.

"You mean 'I, Joseph, need to stop making jokes about people's hair or ways of dressing'? Try saying it that way," I asked. Reluctantly, Joseph did.

"Sometimes we know we should do things differently, but we feel like doing them anyway. Why is that?" I asked. "Why do you feel a little like making these kinds of jokes?"

Again, it was a relief for the children to be allowed to talk about the reality of their joking. Many agreed that it made them feel smart, or cool, or powerful.

"You know, Ms. Charney, if you put somebody down good and everyone laughs, then you feel, well, important."

About tattling, there were numerous statements about children not listening to each other. "I tell her to stop but she don't listen to me. She only listens to the teacher."

"Can you think of some times when children do listen to each other?" I asked.

"At meeting."

"In groups with the teacher or sometimes when we do something like a project."

"I notice how well you listen during those times. Would you like to be able to listen even when the teacher isn't there? How would that make you feel?"

There was general acknowledgment that it would feel good. "Would you feel important, like Joseph was saying?" I asked. Most nodded. At that point, the group was ready to "brainstorm" solutions to the two problems, which I stated as the "bad jokes" and "kids not listening to kids."

"How do we start to have good jokes, and how do we get kids to listen to kids?" The meeting had taken forty minutes, and it was time to stop. I asked if they would agree to think about solutions and bring them to next week's class meeting. I went around the circle, receiving a "yes" from everyone. I closed the meeting by affirming the way I saw them use three meeting rules. "I really liked your interest in solving this problem. It felt good that you were able to share honest thoughts. I noticed good listening, and there were no put downs. Excellent meeting, class."

4. Brainstorm solutions

+ Brainstorming ideas

+ Discussing ideas

IN THE NEXT MEETING (or as part of the same meeting), I want children to brainstorm solutions. Real solutions have to come from discoveries about their needs. When we rush to solutions, or skip over the question of personal needs, we usually end up with "we should" solutions, which tell us what is supposed to happen but do not bring us any closer to acting differently.

"We should all be nice to each other," one child says. "We should ignore it when someone says something mean." But what will really happen? It's important to help children look for real solutions resulting from a true explanation of the problem. That often means prodding or questioning. "Give me an explanation of how you could be nice to people, even people you don't like a lot." Sometimes it means framing a question so that children confront the contradictions of *wants* and *shoulds*, as in:

- "You *should* ignore it, but you *want* to hurt back."

- "You *should* be quiet, but you *want* to talk."

- "You *should* be nice, but you *want* to ignore someone."

I find that when children are able to explore these contradictions honestly, they also begin to recognize possible solutions.

When the class is ready to seek solutions, the aim is to explore as many ideas as possible and suggest things without a critical response. To do good brainstorming, children need a sense of release and ease. I ask children to say whatever ideas pop into their heads and assure them that they will not be "married" to the ideas. I write each idea on a chart. I keep this phase short and lively, about ten minutes. If the brainstorming is successful, I move on to a serious consideration of the solutions. If not, I may decide we need more time to consider ideas, and either go back to more discussion or postpone it for a week.

In the example of picking on and tattling, the children's solutions involved creating taxonomies of jokes—what was OK to joke about and what wasn't. It got very complicated, and I feared it would be unwieldy, but thinking about what was funny or hurtful was very useful, and was endlessly controversial.

It is very tempting for teachers to offer solutions, but we must resist. As soon as we give in, the children stop working. The teacher becomes the solution finder. We convey that there is only one good solution, one deposited in the teacher's head for students to dig out. For children to learn to solve problems, it's important that we encourage their investment but keep our good advice to ourselves. If there is only one solution, and it is ours, the problem is not a subject for a class meeting. It is simply a teacher mandate and must be presented as such.

Older students need to be reminded of their class "hopes and dreams" (if these were used in making the classroom rules or in creating a Critical Contract) and of their part in making the rules really work. Solutions are, in a sense, a class "action plan" to achieve the goals and visions of community. I see the teacher's primary task as keeping the focus on the struggle to achieve idealistic goals. Some examples follow:

- In a class meeting on unfair games: "If we want to be able to have a choice of independent games, what can we do in order to make sure games are inclusive and fair for everyone?"

- In a class meeting on poor care of materials: "We need good materials to work on projects. How can we do a better job of putting things away properly?"

+ In a class meeting on exclusion: "I know that friendships are very important to everyone, and that some people are part of friendship groups and some people are not. But in school, our rules say that we try to take care of each other. How can we honor friendship and still make sure that no one is excluded and left out in school?"

As children get older, they are apt to develop more assigned roles. It is important to draw out the quiet and less confident in the group. Going around a circle rather than "yelling out your ideas" as a brainstorming format helps. I now routinely use that strategy in my class meetings with older students. I find it also helps to give thinking time. If many students "pass" or their best energies are already exhausted, I postpone solutions until another meeting.

Sometimes, with older children, I provide writing time. Assigning students to spend a period writing about the problem and their proposed solutions allows them time to process at different rates and to compose thoughts. One teacher I know has her students detach their solutions from the rest of their writing and hand them to a "designated reporter" who lists them on a chart without attribution. Or I have students write on note cards, collect and shuffle them, and distribute them to different students to read. These strategies often free students to make stronger proposals than they might in a simple discussion.

5. Choose a solution

I PRESENT THREE CRITERIA for any solution the class adopts. The solution must be:

+ Workable and realistic

+ Respectful of everyone

+ In accordance with school rules

The following steps may be used to decide on a solution:

*All ideas are written on a large chart
and read over by the teacher (or a student).*

Each idea is reconsidered briefly in terms of the three criteria. A quick strategy is for students to show thumbs up if it meets the criteria. When a thumb goes down, a reason is required. Ideas which don't meet the criteria are eliminated, with teacher input. If there is disagreement, the solution remains on the active list, which often boils down to no more than three or four suggestions. I often give students a few minutes to think about advantages and disadvantages of potential solutions before deciding which solution is best. I point out that no single solution is perfect, but that students should try to choose one. I ask them to think of at least two good reasons for supporting their choice (rather than reasons for negating the others).

After they've thought for a few minutes, I ask someone to tell what solution s/he picked and her/his reasons for choosing it. I stay with that solution and ask if anyone else thought of other advantages. I then move to disadvantages, modeling ways to disagree without insult. These include "I think" or "It seems to me" sentences: "I don't think it would work because…" instead of "That's stupid." "I agree with the part about…, but I don't agree about…"

It's best to avoid linking children's names with ideas to help establish some objectivity: it's not "George's idea" but "an idea." If I feel that the children are choosing on the merits of George, not the merits of his idea, I intervene.

Agreement about a final list may include a vote after discussion.

"I can live with this idea" is sometimes suggested as a basic endorsement, indicating agreement to try and make it work. If the solution is to be binding, it needs a consensus or a unanimous decision. "We need a solution that everyone feels comfortable accepting, even if it isn't your most preferred one." Seeking a unanimous decision gives weight to a minority opinion, since one lone voice can hold up the decision. Children generally take this seriously, but if I believe that dissension is merely a power struggle, I invoke "majority rule" or speak privately to the student.

In the meeting about tattling, the children decided on this solution: "You only tell the teacher if you told someone to stop three times and they didn't. But if someone says to stop, you gotta try to stop whatever you are doing wrong to them." (I thought that telling someone to stop three times before going to the teacher was two times too many. But it was the children's solution, and it was important that I let them try it.)

How we decide may be as important as what we decide, especially for older students. We are building the tools and commitments for a democratic and participatory community. In the process, we are also developing intellectual assets. Students apply critical thinking skills through active listening, oral expression, analysis of information, and evaluation of solutions. It's important to give students time to consider the different options and not to rush a decision because we feel pressure to get this done. We also want to make sure that students use the basic criteria for all solutions: Is it workable and realistic, respectful of all, and within school-wide rules?

I have observed remarkable changes as students realize something is really going to happen. I have seen students change their minds about solutions, even about their own proposals. I have seen a highly unpopular idea take on new meaning when considered further. I have seen a lone dissenter affect the ultimate decision with reasoned arguments.

Sometimes the solutions don't work or are short-lived. Sometimes they work far better than I ever imagined. But it is the smiles, the congratulations, the handshakes, and the sense of investment that close the meeting that work best of all. The process is often more important than the product.

6. Define progress and consequences

+ "How will we know if the solution is working?"

BEFORE THE MEETING ENDS, we consider how and when we will check in. I might ask, "How will we know whether we are taking care of each other's things?" It is always important to affirm effort and to remember that small changes are to be applauded.

In the tattling case, we agreed we would know our solution was working if:

+ There was less picking on each other and less tattling.

+ There was more friendly conversation and activity.

+ There were jokes, but not about bodies or family or clothing.

To judge our progress, we designed a self-rating checklist and a class-rating checklist to be filled out weekly. (See Figure 13.2.)

"What if people don't stop, and you tell them and then they're still picking on you?" someone asked.

"There should be a consequence," someone else suggested.

In a departure from my earlier thinking, I have come to believe that it is teachers who almost always need to take responsibility for consequences. If necessary, the teacher may restate the consequences that are already in place in the classroom. "If I continue to see name-calling, there will be time-outs in another classroom. I hope everyone is ready to work really hard on the suggestions."

In the weeks that followed our meeting about jokes, there was visible effort and improvement. The children seemed proud of their work on the problem and anxious for their solutions to work. The cooperative spirit of the meeting spilled over, and the tone of the room improved. I began to introduce other types of jokes and joke books into Morning Meeting and other parts of the curriculum. Children especially liked finding out about puns and doodles.

Individual and Class Self-Rating Checklists

Individual checklist

Name: _____ Date: _____

This week I picked on people:

        ☐ not at all   ☐ sometimes   ☐ a lot

This week I was picked on:

        ☐ not at all   ☐ sometimes   ☐ a lot

Class checklist

Class Tally for Week of _____

	Tally marks	*Class totals*
Was picked on		
not at all		
sometimes		
a lot		
Picked on others		
not at all		
sometimes		
a lot		

Conclusions:

7. Close the meeting

AT THE END OF THE MEETING, the teacher compliments the class. It is also important to give the students a chance to reflect on their process and to compliment the group. "How did it go?" some teachers ask. The group goes once more around the circle with a check-in to see if "everyone felt safe and heard." This reinforces the positive efforts of the children to follow the rules, to listen, to respond, and to show respect.

CHOOSING AND PRESENTING APPROPRIATE TOPICS

A WIDE VARIETY OF TOPICS can be explored in class meetings if the problems are presented well. It is critical to frame questions and define problems so that they seriously engage students. They should require students to think about the social or academic conflicts that concern them. Also, we must phrase our concerns so that they provoke insight and empathy rather than blame.

When faced with a recurring problem of stolen lunches, for example, I observed the classroom for a few days. I realized that students had become generally casual and careless about respecting others' property. They were picking up pens and books, taking paper out of binders, and extracting markers from personal cubicles. A stolen lunch seemed an extension of the same attitude, with more serious repercussions. I framed the question for class meeting around the general theme of consideration for others' belongings.

"I notice that many of us leave our things around the room and then we take whatever we happen to find, even if it isn't ours. Sometimes we also go into notebooks and backpacks when we need something. I know I picked up a pen that wasn't mine the other day. I'm afraid we are not taking care of ourselves or each other very well. What do you notice?"

Topics should be appropriate for the entire class and shouldn't target the behavior of a few students. However, an incident that originally involved a fraction of the class may be carefully framed to have wider interest and application. For example, a teacher observed that eight-year-old Hector was trying hard to find a place with the boys in the room. He was struggling for an "in" by doing favors or clowning for attention. Still, he was left out. In a class meeting, the teacher raised the topics of acceptance and exclusion. "I see a problem in this class," he said. "Some people seem to be accepted and some people seem not to be. What makes people feel accepted, and how do you show that you accept others?" he asked. The children were very specific. He then asked if classmates should be accepted even if sometimes they act like "jerks." This question grew into an animated discussion of ways we might all sometimes act "jerky" and things to do about it without leaving someone out.

In general, topics drawn from exposure to the media or to older siblings—drugs, scandals, or teenage pregnancies, for example—do not make for productive dialogues. Children need to work from their own experiences rather than from vicarious ones. They also need to work on problems that are appropriate to their skills and conceptual development, not ones that call for adult expertise.

But it may be possible to take these larger issues and redirect them into meaningful topics. For example, when a class began talking about parents and teenagers who smoke, I translated it into a discussion of "ways you take care of yourself and ways you might not." The students were no longer talking about what others did, but why they themselves ate candy or watched scary TV programs. By redirecting some questions, I have encouraged rich discussions about fears and what kinds of things children do when they feel worried or afraid.

Particularly with older children, discussions of current events and appropriate magazine and newspaper articles offer impersonal subject matter which can be connected to individuals' and classroom interests and can be wonderful practice for class meetings. These discussions help provide a context and common vocabulary for airing different points of view. For example, the issue of the right of free speech versus personal safety and offensive behavior came up in a conversation about John Rocker's suspension from baseball for making racially insensitive public remarks. The class talked about the responsibility of public figures, but also about our own tolerance for taunting and put-downs. Movies and literature can also spawn fruitful practice in the skills necessary for productive class meetings. Meaty explorations can come out of discussions of the choices made by fictional as well as real-life characters.

In a seventh and eighth grade discussion of the shootings at Columbine High School, students looked at ways their judgments intimidated one another. In a class meeting, students expressed a feeling that although they didn't feel physically bullied, the threat of being made fun of and considered "uncool" "made me afraid to just be myself." They decided to adopt a student-circulated pledge to cease all teasing for a day. Although this strategy was very hard to implement, it raised consciousness. Students seemed more aware of what they were saying, and "everyone says it, so it's okay" was no longer a valid excuse.

FIGURE 13.3

Some Possible Topics for Older Students

The following topics or incidents have inspired class meetings at sixth through eighth grade:

✦ Name-calling and threats yelled at sports events in school or beyond

✦ Pop music star T-shirts with provocative song lyrics worn to school

✦ A plan for "Secret Valentines" in school to include some, not all, classmates

✦ Overnights, birthday parties, and concerts that include some, not all, but which are planned or talked about widely in school

✦ E-mail passwords stolen and fake messages sent

✦ Fake love letters sent to a few girls in the class

✦ An "in-group" ganging up and distorting game rules for less-liked students

✦ The need to set standards for homework and "proud work completions"

✦ The circulation of rating lists for boys and girls that specify their level of "coolness"

....

A class vows to "de-clique"

A number of years ago, I accompanied my class of seventh and eighth graders on a field trip to a performing arts center. It was a beautiful day, the Alvin Ailey dancers were thrilling, and yet many of my students did not have a good time. "Are you having fun?" I asked. "Not really," many of them responded. When I observed the interactions within the group, I noticed that a small cluster had made themselves the center of attention, talking loudly, laughing deliberately, and standing apart. The other students seemed to mill around them, dumbstruck in their role as an audience. The class was separating into cliques that created "ins" and "outs," and it was not fun.

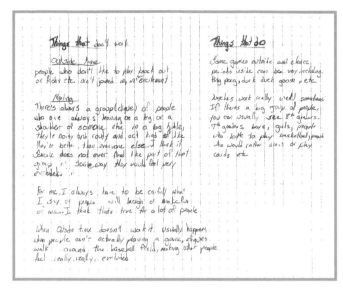

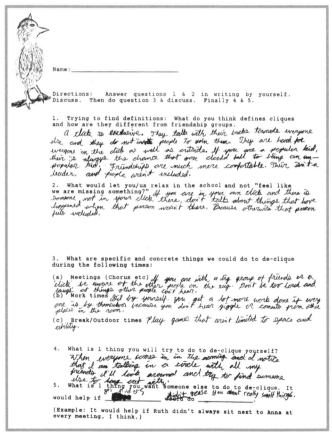

Two middle-school aged students' writings about cliques

TEACHING CHILDREN TO CARE

The next day, I shared with students what I had observed. I asked them what they had noticed. Our perceptions were remarkably alike. I pointed out that we had a number of field trips ahead, and I was worried that if they went in their cliques, it wouldn't be fun for most of the class. Did they want to "de-clique?" I asked.

We discussed the distinctions between friendships and cliques, concluding that cliques required a special currency, such as clothes, looks, or athletic status, while friendship groups were based on common interests and values and were more open to others.

After a meeting which included time for discussion, personal writing, and further perceptions, all except two of the students voted to "de-clique" and to work on ways to "mix it up more." Subsequent meetings and reflections produced a list of specific strategies affecting partner selections and work details.

"But you can't just do it because you have to," someone stated. "Yes. You really have to try to be with your partner," another agreed. Awareness, they noted, is not equivalent to accomplishment, but it is a start—even a stretch. Though far from perfect, the next trip, in which student suggestions were implemented, was much better.

When I shared this story with other teachers, someone asked, "What if they didn't want to de-clique? Would you still have taken more field trips?" I wondered. But even more importantly, I wondered: What if we didn't have our class meeting ritual? Then what would we have done? ❖

SUMMARY

Research shows that children who feel they have a stake in their schools
will work to make them better. This means giving students a voice
in how things are done and how problems are solved.

DAVID T. GORDON
"Rising to the Discipline Challenge"
Harvard Education Letter *(September/October 99)*

PROBLEM-SOLVING CLASS MEETINGS are a powerful way to enable students at all grade levels to take greater responsibility for their academic and social life. The meetings can be used for preventive problem solving (how to make next week go smoothly when a guest teacher takes over during the regular teacher's absence, for example) or reactive problem solving (for example, what to do about the teasing and fighting that went on during recess today).

Regardless of what type of problem they are being used to address, class meetings provide a structure and ritual for students to use to help each other through difficult times in their school life. Conducted well, the meetings allow different opinions to be heard and give students permission to say what they really think. Students learn to name their own feelings, respect other perspectives, and negotiate to reach a just solution.

In class meetings, it is the students, rather than the teacher, who choose the solutions to try. Often the solutions will work not because they are perfect, but because students are invested in them. Other times the solutions will fail. But out of those failures can come even greater learning, as students reflect on their mistakes and revise their solutions.

Works Cited

DEVELOPMENTAL STUDIES CENTER. 1996. *Ways We Want Our Class To Be: Class Meetings That Build Commitment to Kindness and Learning*. Oakland, CA: Developmental Studies Center.

GLASSER, WILLIAM. 1969. *Schools Without Failure*. New York: Harper & Row.

GORDON, DAVID T. 1999. "Rising to the Discipline Challenge." *Harvard Education Letter* (September/October): 1–4.

KREIDLER, WILLIAM J. 1997. *Conflict Resolution in the Middle School*. Cambridge, MA: Educators for Social Responsibility.

Mediation & Training Collaborative. 2001. Greenfield, MA: "Mediation Steps for Parents or Teachers," "Problems Solving Steps for Students," and "Student Mediation Steps." (handouts)

NELSEN, JANE, EdD. 1996. *Positive Discipline*. Revised edition. New York: Ballantine Books.

PIRTLE, SARAH. 1998. *Discovery Time for Cooperation and Conflict Resolution*. Nyack, NY: Children's Creative Response to Conflict.

CHAPTER 14
Teachers as Mirrors:
Using Social Conferences

Children communicate with us through their eyes, the quality of their voice,
their body postures, their gestures, their mannerisms, their smiles,
their jumping up and down, their listlessness. They show us, by the way
they do things as well as what they do, what is going on inside them.

When we have come to see children's behavior through the eyes of its meaning
to them, from the inside out, we shall be well on the way to understanding
them. Only by learning to see children as they are, and especially as
they see themselves, will we get our clues. It is not as simple as it sounds.

DOROTHY COHEN
Observing and Recording the Behavior of Young Children

CHILDREN CONTINUALLY SEEK ATTENTION and guidance from their teachers—
for protection and justice, direction and understanding. Sometimes they express
their concerns verbally, and sometimes they act them out. As teachers, we often
feel better prepared to explain fractions than fractious behavior. Yet the continual
signs and signals for help don't go away. We need appropriate strategies and techniques to help us respond, not as surrogate parents or ad hoc therapists but as
teachers.

I remember an exchange between two teachers in a workshop. Sharon, a third
grade teacher, described three boys "who would *not* line up after recess." Sharon
continued, "They simply wouldn't respond. I tried threats, incentives, taking away
recesses—you name it. What do I do?"

Chris, a guidance counselor, responded. "Did you ask them what they thought might help them line up on time? I always give kids one chance to be part of a plan. I say, 'What do you think…?' I remember so well my own school years and how difficult I could be, and no one ever asked what I thought. It would have made things so different. Just to be asked. Just once." This response, informed by Chris's firsthand experience, spoke eloquently of the power of inviting children into a conversation about their behavior.

"Teachers as Mirrors" is a technique to address specific social problems for individual students. It begins with the basic skill and habit of "noticing"—both "good" things and "bad"—and then moves on to a "social conference" which allows us to help children work on social problems in a nonjudgmental way.

THE IMPORTANCE OF NOTICING

GOOD TEACHING DEPENDS on being keenly aware of our individual students and their interactions. I call this skill "noticing." If we aren't aware of what is going on, we have no basis for making accurate appraisals or informed decisions.

Noticing children is ingrained in the practice of teaching. We watch how children assemble, we notice their moods and dispositions, we clock their pace and assess their attitudes. We skillfully interpret the quiet and take the pulse of the noise. When we use the technique "Teachers as Mirrors," we use this skill to "see" and then to reflect what we see without judgment or interpretation.

When a child is having a hard day, I might say, "I notice that you had a hard day today." Or when another sticks with a tough project, I'll say, "I noticed how long you worked to draw that map." When Mitchell, my baseball fan, shuffles into class late, I say, "It looks like you had a long night at the baseball game!" Our greetings or casual comments pay notice on a daily basis.

"Good morning, Derek. How's your puppy doing?"

"Good morning, Cath'. How was the birthday party?"

"Good morning, Maurice. I see you remembered your lunch today!"

When we reflect back to children what we notice, we communicate that we know them. Children need to feel that we, their teachers, know them. One way that we show what we know is by noticing. And we pay attention to *how* they do as well as to *what* they do. Leon's report, though still containing spelling errors and a few scrambled sentences, represents hours of diligence. We notice that, and are proud of his results. Margie sat in her place and raised her hand during meeting

today, without flopping or calling out. "Good job at meeting, Margie. I see you really tried today." When we reflect, we are careful to notice the kindnesses, the excitements, the discoveries, and the improvements along with the hard moments.

But there are times when it is important to try to understand what is causing the discomfort or disruption. We often do that by asking children the leading question "Why?"

"Why are you having so many fights in the playground?"

"Why can't you get along better in your group?"

"Why are you getting in trouble in the lunchroom?" I ask Stacy.

"I dunno," she answers. "I just do."

"Why," I asked Brian, "did you write only a paragraph, when I assigned a story?"

"I don't know," Brian replied, looking puzzled and confused.

The children most at odds with their classroom or classmates are frequently at odds with themselves, too. Sometimes, children do know and don't want to tell, fearing censure or exposure. But more often, when children say "I don't know," they mean it. They truly don't know.

We are not therapists. We are not trained to look for hidden or unconscious dynamics. It is not our job to help children with analysis or self-disclosure. We are, however, trained to "notice" children, to observe them as they really are in the context of school. Our capacity as child-watchers is the foundation for a powerful technique that helps children explore and cope with events and feelings in school. Our skill in noticing can initiate a social conference where student and teacher can work on solving problems.

THE SOCIAL CONFERENCE

A SOCIAL CONFERENCE BUILDS a responsive relationship upon two elements: behavioral boundaries and autonomy. The first draws on external discipline; the second on internal discipline. Both are acknowledged as part of the responsive exchange. Teachers set behavioral boundaries by providing structure and appropriate alternatives. They also provide opportunities for autonomous thinking and self-discipline by giving children a voice in their own problem solving and suggesting reasoned alternatives for their choices.

"I notice this," says the teacher, providing the structure that comes from information and description. "What do you notice?" s/he asks, giving the student a voice. The teacher does not give the student the unreasonable choice to continue to disrupt the group, but suggests several ways to contribute something positive. The teacher describes the problem in a way that helps frame workable alternatives. "When you disturb the group, you prevent others from learning. You may simply choose to stop, or you may decide on your own that it's a problem we need to work on together. What do you think?"

The main objective of the social conference is to solve an immediate problem. However, the outcomes are often broader. When teachers notice and urge children to notice, they teach the discipline of self-awareness and self-determination. Child psychologist Sheila Kelly, speaking to a group of parents, noted, "It's what children say to themselves about themselves that constitutes and builds self-esteem."

I borrow the term "conference" from the dynamic "writing process" approach. In a writing conference, we talk to children individually about their writing work. We start with the text, but we are concerned with teaching the writer, not the writing. Lucy Calkins, an advocate of writing process, also suggests, in *The Art of Teaching Writing*, that a significant variable in the development of competent writers is a connection with the teacher. The interest of the teacher in the life-subjects of the student builds confidence and voice (Calkins 1994).

In the same way, the interest of the teacher in the *social* life of the students also seeks to build confidence and voice. We often talk about social issues occurring in our classrooms, playgrounds, or hallways. We apply words to the actions, which helps children to hold them up to scrutiny. We also attempt to uncover connections between observed behavior and the thoughts, feelings, and attitudes of our children. Above all, we seek an authentic conversation in which both the teacher and the student play an active role.

There are several basic steps in solving problems through social conferences. The steps, explained below and summarized in Figure 14.1, are intended as flexible guidelines to be adjusted to differing needs and situations. Some conferences take five minutes; others spread out over several days. Some lead to immediate solutions, and others will have to be reviewed and repeated. Some conferences take only the first step, while others need all of them. It's always important to understand the developmental levels of children—how they think, what they know, and what they are prepared to accomplish.

1. Establishing what teachers and students notice

THIS STEP FOLLOWS a logical progression of beginning with a positive foundation, then building on it to acknowledge problem behaviors and children's perceptions in a nonjudgmental atmosphere. I break this step down into three parts:

+ The teacher noticing positive things

+ The teacher noticing things that don't work

+ The teacher asking what the student notices

Teacher noticing positive things

I begin a social conference by establishing positive things that I notice. When I let children know that I see their efforts, likes, interests, and goings-on, I provide a sense of belonging. I refer to observable and verifiable behaviors: the smiles and frowns, the concentrated efforts and frustrating attempts, the gestures and manners, the signs and sighs of comfort or distress. I notice the "what," not the "why," of behaviors:

"I notice that you really worked hard on making the outline for your map and added careful labeling."

FIGURE 14.1

Steps in a Social Conference

1. Establishing what the teacher and the student notice

The teacher and the student notice specific events, actions, feelings, or expressions. This step always includes:

✦ The teacher noticing positive things

✦ The teacher noticing things that don't work

✦ The teacher asking what the student notices

2. Naming the problem and the need to solve it

The teacher and student "receive" and acknowledge a problem— something that interferes with caring for oneself or others in school.

3. Understanding the problem

The teacher uses "Could it be...?" questions to help the student recognize and understand the possible cause of the problem.

4. Generating alternatives

The teacher and the student (if possible) suggest two or three strategies that might make a difference. These may include a way for the teacher to do something differently (e.g., give the student a reminder or signal). The student decides which strategy to try.

5. Establishing an agreement to try

The teacher and the student agree to try one of the strategies. The agreement may be in writing or may consist of a handshake, and it includes a time to evaluate progress together and a way to know if the strategy is working.

In general:

- Use a kind but businesslike manner.

- Speak to the student in private.

- Be prepared to propose some options and to accept options from the student (but don't depend on the student for direction).

- Be prepared to end the conference at any point if the student becomes defensive or resistant.

- Leave options open for teacher and student.

- Keep conferences as short as possible.

- Avoid lectures and sermons.

- Focus on solving immediate problems.

....

"I noticed that you practiced your spelling words with a partner."

"I noticed that you were helping others in your group with the assignment."

"I noticed that you asked new people to be partners this week."

"I notice that you really like to do art."

I recall one teacher commenting how good she felt when a colleague, on a particularly dreary morning, brought her a cup of coffee—milk, no sugar. Her tastes were recalled, her needs felt. A sense of belonging permeated the day. I think that we provide that "cup of coffee" for children through our noticing. Julie likes art, especially painting. Martin loves baseball and plays first base. Jackie has an older brother in the tech school who tells him a lot about cars. Michelle has a young sister who can be a pest. "How's your little sister doing?" I ask. "Any new tricks?" Michelle laughs and happily tells me another tale.

Of course, children are not always direct and forthcoming. Eight-year-old Willie began the school term by bringing in several computer disks each day. He never used the disks or talked about them, and he took them home at the end of each day. Finally, one day I told him that I had noticed he was bringing the computer disks to school. He showed me the disks, and we talked about his mom's new computer and how he would learn to use it one day when she had time. I asked him to let me know what he found out, especially about math programs and games we could use at school. After our short conversation, he didn't bring the disks back to school. Apparently, they had served their purpose.

Children wish to be noticed, whether they show it subtly or more directly. When we notice their disks, baseball cards, or new puppy, we establish a foundation for a relationship and a supportive connection. It's essential to establish that we care enough to notice before moving on to behavior that doesn't work for them or for the class.

Teacher noticing things that don't work

When teachers act like mirrors for behaviors that don't work, they also focus on specific, observable behaviors. They do not call names, make judgments, or interpret. I do not label what I see. I simply describe:

- ✦ "I notice that every time we have outdoor games, you have a stomachache."

- ✦ "I notice that when you get frustrated or angry, you swear, sometimes at yourself and sometimes at others."

- ✦ "I notice that you can't find your things a lot."

- ✦ "I notice that you cheat playing cards if you're not winning the game."

- ✦ "I notice that you won't sit next to certain people in our class."

- ✦ "I notice that you don't seem to want to share at circle times."

- ✦ "I notice that you ignore some people when they ask you to play."

- ✦ "I notice that you have a hard time sitting still and paying attention to your work."

- ✦ "I notice that some of the kids in our class avoid playing with you, and that you always want to be in charge of the games."

- ✦ "I notice that when I have to leave the room, you get silly. You leave your seat and run around. You start talking in a loud voice."

Eva is acting "off the wall" this week, probably because her parents are away and she is staying with Grandma. I am careful to say "I see you are having a hard time," rather than "Your parents are away, so you're having a hard time this week." By starting with what I notice (not an interpretation), I validate the clues that children give, and invite them to enter the conversation and notice as well. If Eva agrees that she has been having a hard time, or Martin agrees that he acts foolish when the teacher isn't looking, we have the beginnings of shared perceptions. When children notice, they are more likely to take responsibility for their behavior.

Establishing what the teacher notices sets up three things:

- A concrete, here-and-now focus. The teacher does not give opinions, make judgments, or offer interpretations.

- A straightforward and matter-of-fact tone. The teacher tries to name the "deeds" openly and accurately, without blame or severity.

- Fact-finding as a method of thinking. The teacher models an approach that requires information gathering before conclusions are drawn and solutions are considered.

Teacher asking what the student notices

After I share what I notice, I ask the child, "And what do you notice?" When we ask children to notice, we:

- Encourage them to examine their own behavior

- Name that behavior without finding fault, blaming, or judging

"Robbie and Mark, every time you play a game together this week, one of you quits or gets mad. It doesn't look like you are having much fun with your games. What do you notice?"

"Sean, I notice that you are upset about not getting your work done this week. I see that you get out your math book, but then it takes you a while to settle down to work. You get up a lot, hunt for pencils, talk with friends, search for pages. What do you notice?"

"Christie and Maggie, I hear you call each other names. I see whispering and tears. I see you make up quickly, but it must be hard to fight with your good friends. What do you notice?"

Maria, age eight, starts her new class in a quiet manner, and after several weeks becomes more withdrawn and detached. The year before, she was generally outgoing and chatty with teachers and peers. The teacher approaches her one morning, saying that she would like to have a "conference" with her, asking if this is a good time. Maria nods assent.

"I notice that you have been quiet in your new class. I see you by yourself a lot. In the morning when you come into school, you look at books by yourself or draw pictures. At choice time, I also notice you do things alone. What do you notice?"

"I'm just quiet."

"Last year, I used to see you talking to your friends. And you always said such a cheerful 'Good morning' to everyone. I saw lots of smiles."

"I'm feeling like a quiet person this year."

Maria has not contradicted the teacher's perceptions. She is quiet. She is by herself. If Maria had objected or denied being quiet, the teacher might have said, "Well, I notice that you are quiet and by yourself a lot. You notice that you join in with others and are having lots of nice conversations. Perhaps we should both notice things for the next few days. How shall we do that?" And she would make a plan with Maria.

But most often, children do notice and name either a general trait ("Yeah, I get restless at meeting") or a specific one ("I shove sometimes").

Children generally do notice and, if given permission, readily acknowledge and take interest in their own behavior. However, their perceptions do not always match our observations. At times, the perceptions are reasonably convergent. I notice that a child is slow to get to his work; he notices that he has trouble finding his book. I notice that another acts bossy with friends; she notices that she likes to tell her ideas.

At other times, there is a wider gulf. I notice that Amy didn't study for her test; Amy notices that she practiced every day. I notice that Seth teases; he notices that he tells jokes. In these cases, I may suggest more "fact-finding," possibly collecting our observations as a shared record of our attention. Usually, faulty perceptions need to be examined before we can begin to solve problems.

Lisa and Darlene

Lisa and Darlene are both upset with the results of their math test. Both feel they did poorly. The teacher knows that both have faulty perceptions, but of entirely different types. Darlene's faulty perception is that she is "dumb" because she practiced a lot and still got a "B," instead of an "A" like others in the class. Lisa, on the other hand, thinks she practiced, when what she did was to glance over the material for short spells, which didn't allow her to learn anything. Some of her "study" consisted of taking out her book and talking to her neighbor. Lisa complains that she didn't have enough time to finish and blames the teacher for rushing her. Conferences with the two students have totally different goals.

By comparing herself to others, Darlene loses sight of her own achievement. Her performance showed real progress, as well as considerable effort, which she is unable to appreciate. Because her goals are often unrealistic, she suffers bouts of disappointment and hopelessness. She shifts frequently from "That's easy and I know that!" to "I'm stupid."

The conversation with Darlene begins with a validation of her practice. "I noticed that you worked hard studying. I saw you practice with flash cards that you made yourself. That was a good idea."

"Yeah. But I still didn't get them all right."

"That's true. But you got a lot more right on this test than you did last week. I consider that significant progress. Do you know which ones you knew today that you missed last week?" (The teacher attempts to redirect Darlene to see her progress and not just to measure failures.) Although Darlene is quick to point out the ones she knew today, she is not satisfied.

"I also noticed that when you practiced, you flashed all the cards each time. Is that right?" the teacher continues. Darlene agrees. The teacher then suggests a different strategy so that Darlene can review the harder material more frequently. He shows her how to make three piles: sure facts, "iffy" facts, and trouble-facts. They talk about how to move a fact from one pile to the next and how to concentrate her efforts. "I bet you'll have most of them by next week."

"Maybe it's just hopeless," Darlene retorts with a smile, and goes back to sorting her cards. In this dialogue, the teacher does not confront Darlene about her attitude. Primarily, he wants to encourage and redirect her attention away from comparisons with others—to "see" that the pile of cards representing what she knew was much thicker than the pile representing what she didn't know.

Lisa has difficulty focusing on her work independently. She confuses the appearance of study with the practice of it. In order to help Lisa, the teacher needs to help her develop habits of independent study.

"I know you like math. I also notice that you aren't so pleased with how you did on your test today. Is that right?" Lisa nods. "I wonder if it has something to do with the way you practiced. I noticed that when you were studying your times tables, you were also talking to Cindy. It's hard to memorize facts and also do other things. What did you notice?"

"I did 'em at home, too."

"That's a good idea to practice at home. I wonder if you found a quiet corner at home or sat in front of a TV. Somehow I picture you with the TV or radio…sort of like what I see in school." Lisa nods and giggles. "I wonder if you could tell me where you would study right now if you had to? Show me, where's the best place in the classroom?" The teacher begins to engage Lisa in instructional role-play—finding a workspace, organizing her task, and using a study technique. He lets Lisa experiment with a study task by suggesting that she try to memorize ten examples that she missed.

Sometimes the best way to get children to "see" is to enact positive behaviors rather than to focus on mistakes. It might be hard for Lisa to recognize or "admit" her lack of focus, since it's probably not a clear image for her. But her response is enough to engage her support and cooperation. She and the teacher can then work together on solving the problem. ❖

Stephen

Sometimes children give such mixed messages that teachers, as well as children, are unable to notice what is really happening. Stephen complained that his reading group was "boring. It's too easy." His teacher, noting his frequent complaints and stammering over the page, and his surly manner toward a lot of things lately, continued with the reading group. But, in fact, Stephen had progressed in his reading, and the level of instruction was lower than necessary. Finally, in a conference, the teacher reflected, "I notice that you are unhappy with your reading group. You say that it's boring for you. Sometimes boring means it's too easy and sometimes boring means you don't like to do it—maybe because you're not so comfortable with reading. What do you notice?"

Stephen was adamant that the reading was easy and demonstrated his proficiency on a one-to-one basis. He was very pleased when he received more difficult reading material, although he continued to struggle in a new group. He had other anxieties about reading as well. Still, for the time being he felt "heard," and his general attitude about school improved. ❖

Kim

Sometimes, there is no noticing on the part of the child, as was the case with Kim, age seven.

Kim didn't want to come to school this morning, explained her mother at a social conference she initiated to talk about her daughter's resistance to school.

Asked during the conference why she didn't want to come to school, Kim responded with her usual "I dunno." Asked what she didn't like about school, she said she didn't know. Asked what she didn't like yesterday in school, she still said she didn't know. But all in all, "Yesterday was an okay day," Kim said. This morning, however, there were stomachaches, headaches, and tantrums.

Sevens often experience fears that are diffuse as well as intense. I could also tell that this child's slowness in coming to reading and writing reflected special worries and fears inside of her, and that she needed help setting realistic goals for herself.

I suggested to Kim that students often have two main worries about school: "can't-do's" and "don't-want-to-do's." She could be a detective and see if her bad feelings about school were "can't-do's" or "don't-want-to-do's." She agreed. I equipped her with a "detecting pad" and sent her off into the classroom to notice. For several weeks, she carried her pad and made her lists, jotting down things in her own spellings and partial phrases. Once, but only once, she showed me the list. Her "can'ts" included spelling and writing. Her "don't wants" included being quiet, having certain partners, and "I don't wont to hay mi dane [brain] not do stuf rit."

Once Kim had "discovered" and named her own fears, the tantrums disappeared, as did the lists. She would continue to express anxiety at times and have hard moments, but then we could refer back to "her brain" and agree that together we could "teach her brain to do stuff right." ❖

WHEN THE TEACHER NOTICES, s/he shows children the strength and value of attention. When the teacher urges them to notice, s/he begins teaching the discipline of self-awareness. When a child is able to say "I see. I am making faces… I am acting bossy…I am afraid that writing is too hard for me," the faces may stop, the boss may decide (by him/herself) that someone else would make a better captain, and the writing may not be so blocked. Acting as mirrors, teachers make it possible for children to look more steadily at themselves. It is a reflection that is clear but also loving.

2. Naming the problem and the need to solve it

SOME CONFERENCES MAY INCLUDE only the first step—establishing what teachers and students notice:

"Is that something you can change, or do you think you need some help?"

"I think I can do it myself," the child replies.

"Fine."

And the conference is over.

Or, there may need to be more stages in order to progress to problem solving. With Darlene and Lisa, the noticing led directly to alternatives. But more often, it's important to go slowly and help children uncover a connection between their current behavior and what they think is needed in order to make a change. Solutions are more realistic when they grow out of a child's awareness of a need—and they work better if they are not imposed upon the student.

First, we need to establish that the noticed behaviors pose a problem. I define problems as those things that interfere with students' ability to care for themselves or for others in school. These might include issues of self-respect, making and keeping friends, pride in schoolwork, friendliness toward others, and physical care of oneself and of the school environment.

Second, we must establish that it is a problem we want to try to solve together. In general, I use this type of statement: "When I see children looking (acting) angry (upset, frustrated, not doing their work, not getting along), I feel that there is a problem. Something is not working for students. I would like to figure out a way to help you feel good about your work (friends, place in the group). What do you think? Would you like to work on that problem with me?"

For example, I might say:

- To Jeffrey, age six, who has been struggling with his behavior at group meeting time: "When I see you have so much trouble being at circle time, making silly noises, bothering and poking, I think, 'Where are Jeffrey's good listening and sharing?' Then I think that meeting isn't working very well for you. And that's a problem for you and for us. What do you think?"

- To Kyle, age seven, who has been highly aggressive with peers: "When teachers notice someone grabbing, shoving, and swearing, they worry that the person won't have friends or won't have a good time with friends. That seems like a problem we should work on. What do you think?"

- To Emily, age twelve, who often seeks a teacher's or parent's assistance with friendship conflicts: "When I notice you need to come to me or your parents so often when you are mad or hurt or upset with friends, I worry that you don't feel you can speak up for yourself. That seems like a problem to me. What do you think?"

- To the entire class, after a dismal math lesson with a new problem to solve: "I noticed that many of you found this a hard math problem. I saw some people give up; I noticed some people got angry, and only a few tried different ways to find an answer. I know the problem was hard and new. If you all knew the solution beforehand, it wouldn't be a problem. I want you to find out that you can be problem solvers. When I see so many of you get frustrated and give up quickly, I worry that you don't know that you can be problem solvers. What do you think?"

Sometimes I will use the more general term "teachers," as in the example of "Kyle" above. Other times I speak with the "I voice." The general gives more distance and sometimes safety. "Teachers and parents often think that..." offers a more hypothetical approach, which puts the child more at ease. "What do children think..." also allows the child to respond in a safer, hypothetical manner. I rely more on the "I voice" when I feel children will respond to intimacy and the personal concern of the teacher without feeling threatened. Sometimes I switch midstream, if I think the child is becoming defensive or, alternatively, needs a more personal approach.

Keep these guidelines in mind when naming the problem and the need to solve it:

+ The problem is not the child but the behavior observed by both teacher and student. There is no reference to personality or character. The problem is associated with the deed, not the doer.

+ Be sure to express positive motive and intent. I express my desire for students to get along with others, have friends, enjoy and take pride in their work, feel good about their efforts.

+ Emphasize that the teacher and the student are a "problem-solving team." "Something isn't working. Let's see what we can figure out together." The teacher cannot solve the problem by her/himself. It must be a collaboration.

+ To truly collaborate, children must be permitted to do their own work. As with a writing process approach, it's not enough to tell children what to revise. They must decide, with the teacher's input, what rule is clear or not clear, what works or doesn't work. We want to encourage a concept of revision that views change as a way to extend and expand, rather than to make an ordeal of correction.

+ Set realistic goals. When children revise a piece of writing, they do not see every possible change or make every possible correction. Student (and adult) writers may get tired and pronounce it done while there is still more to do. Nevertheless, the writing revisions have improved our story, and we are pleased. Our social revisions improve our conduct. In helping children improve their social skills or conduct, we revise in stages, setting up drafts, asking one or two key questions, making one or two gratifying steps toward change.

I would like to add one caution. Sometimes when we ask a child if s/he wants to work with us on the problem, we get what Dreikurs calls "a recognition response" (Dreikurs 1982, 28). The child replies with only a slight gesture or nod of agreement—which is fine. We go ahead. Other times, a child is quite vocal: "No. I don't need help!" or "No. I don't think it's a problem." It doesn't work to then go ahead with the steps in the conference if the child doesn't want help or doesn't see a problem. I might offer to help if the child changes her/his mind, or, if I feel strongly, I might say, "I see that it's hard to discuss this right now. I'd like to help. Let me know a better time for us to meet."

3. Understanding the problem

EVEN IF CHILDREN CAN NAME the problem and the need to solve it, they can't always take the next step. Asked why they do something, they feel confused and uncertain. "I dunno. I just do" is a common reply. At this point, I try to help children by suggesting possible explanations based on an understanding of children's needs for acceptance and significance in the classroom.

The possible explanations are phrased as questions. We suggest reasonable hypotheses while maintaining the participation of the child in a search for understanding. I often use Dreikurs's "Could it be...?" questions to initiate the discussion (Dreikurs 1982, 28–31). I also may use a general hypothetical question, such as "Teachers think that when children have trouble listening, it may be because...Could that be the reason?" Or we can identify with the situation: "When I get angry with myself, I sometimes...Could that be what's happening here?" We want to guide children's understanding by suggesting a relationship between a particular way of acting and a possible purpose for the action.

Even when the connections are very clear between behavior and cause, we ask rather than assert. If I am sure that Marcy is "off the wall" this week because her mother is in the hospital, I don't say, "You must really be upset because your mother is in the hospital." Instead, I give the child the responsibility to name her own behavior, to name her motives. "When I am worried about someone special, I sometimes act funny and have trouble paying attention to my work. Could it be that you are worried about your mom?"

Marcy nods. Yes, she is worried about her mom. "She's in the hospital. She has to have an operation."

"It's scary to think about your mom's operation. And it's hard to do your schoolwork today. When you have scary feelings, what do you think might help you feel better?" Together we decide on some strategies. Marcy will make pictures for her mom. Marcy will come sit near me when she is worried. Marcy will sometimes get a hug. There is an understanding that it is okay when you are upset to get hugs, to draw pictures, and to have a special seating arrangement, even if it isn't okay to tear books or hit or run around the room. We are not denying the feelings or their importance, but simply looking for acceptable ways to express them in the classroom.

Maria

The teacher had suggested a conference after noticing that Maria was particularly quiet and was often by herself in the classroom.

"When teachers see one of their students quiet and alone, not sharing any time or thoughts with their friends or teachers, they are concerned. They think that maybe that student isn't feeling very good in school, and they want to help. What do you think, Maria? Do you think maybe we could figure out a way to make school feel better—not always so quiet and alone?"

Maria shrugged. "Maybe" she concedes.

"Sometimes when kids are very quiet, it's because they are afraid that they won't find a special friend in school this year. And sometimes it's because they feel unsure of some of the new routines or work. And sometimes when children are very quiet in the beginning of school, it's because they miss their old class. Could it be any of these things for you?"

Maria was quiet for a while, and then she said, her eyes clouding with tears, "I miss my teacher."

Maria missed last year's teacher, and it was too soon for her to have formed a bond with the new teacher. Teachers are still an important source of security for many "young" eights. The connecting link with the teacher continues to be critical for some children, even as they move toward more peer involvement. The teacher had imagined that the issue concerned peers, but that assumption was wrong. With some prompting, Maria had recognized and named the feelings inside herself.

"Ms. Clayton was a special teacher for you, wasn't she?"

"Yes."

"And you really liked seeing her every day and talking to her?"

"Yeah, and she helped me a lot with my writing."

"You like to write, don't you?"

"Yeah. I like writing stories and reading them to Ms. Clayton."

"Well, I have an idea. Have you ever written a letter to anyone?"

"I write to my grandma sometimes."

"Do you think you might write a letter to Ms. Clayton? Maybe telling her some things about your new class?"

"Maybe."

"You might even invite her to come to see you sometime—that is, when you both have time. You'd have to both figure out your schedules."

"Yeah. We could do that. I could start today."

"Why don't you get some paper, and let's see what you know about letter writing."

Several things were accomplished in this conference. Maria was able to name and share feelings and take a concrete action. She found a way to push forward rather than stepping back. She could affirm her need for a connection by using the skills that Ms. Clayton had carefully helped her acquire. She and the teacher quickly moved to the next step in a social conference by generating alternatives. The idea of the letters grew out of the conversation with Maria. Would she have been as receptive if the teacher had started by telling her she missed her teacher and therefore should write her a letter? ❖

EVEN AT OUR MOST DIPLOMATIC or subtle, we gain the confidence of children only when we invite them to participate in the conversations. This confidence grows not because teachers have brilliantly solved the mystery, but because the child was part of the process.

Derek, my bathroom writer

"I notice that every writing time, you have to go to the bathroom," I say to Derek. "What do you notice?"

"I guess so. I just have to go to the bathroom a lot."

"So, you also notice that writing has become a bathroom time for you? Do you also notice that by the time you get back, you have to hurry up, and often you've only gotten about a sentence written?"

"Yeah. There's not enough time."

"So your story hasn't gotten very far."

"Nah. I only have the first page."

"When I see kids go to the bathroom at a particular time like that every day, I think that they want to avoid something they don't like or find hard—like math or writing. So I wonder if maybe writing seems like a problem for you this year?"

Derek grins and loosens his vise-like grip on the pencil. "Sort of. It's sort of hard."

"There are several reasons that writing could be hard for someone. I wonder if any of these make sense for you? Could it be that writing is hard because you have trouble thinking of ideas and what you want to say? Or could it be that you know your main ideas, but you get confused about what you want to say next, or what words you will need to use? Sometimes writers start to worry about the spelling or the handwriting. Could it be that as you think about how to spell a word, you forget your good ideas?"

"I'm not so sure. Could you tell me the choices again?"

"Sure." (I decide to write them on a sheet of paper for Derek to look at as I say them.) Derek looks over the list for a minute and says, "I don't think it's Number 1. 'Cause I have a pretty good idea about the time this truck broke down and I helped my dad fix it."

"Yes. That seems right. You told me about your story. I thought you were pretty excited about telling that story."

"Sometimes I forget what I want to write next. I can't think of the words I want, like in this one (points to Number 3). So it's sorta both things."

"It helps that you have figured out what may be the problem with your writing. Do you think we could also think of some ways to help you plan or remember words you need? I have some ideas. Would you like to try out some strategies and see if any of them will help?"

Here we moved to the next step by generating alternatives or "strategies." I deliberately use the word "strategy" because children like it—it conjures up a tactic used in sports by a coach. Derek agrees to try out a "strategy." In this case, I will help with a strategy to access and organize ideas. We may try brainstorming lists of words. We may try some "mapping" exercises. I don't know what will release his best potential. To find acceptable alternatives, it will be important to experiment. But the rightness of the technique may be less significant than the attitude of searching for solutions—solutions that Derek tests and explores. ❖

4. Generating alternatives

THE MORE I CAN INVOLVE children in distinguishing an alternative strategy that works for them, the more they become problem solvers. They no longer think "I can't write" or "I hate writing," but rather "I have trouble with a first sentence" or "It's hard for me to choose a topic." These are problems that can be solved, not "global" aversions. The key is to narrow and redefine the issues.

"I hate school" becomes a search. "Let's see if we can discover one thing you like to do in school."

"I hate writing" turns into a joint survey of forms or functions. "What kinds of writing are most fun? Least fun? What part of writing is hard? Is it the thinking part or the copying over?"

The best strategies or alternatives grow out of specifics, not generalities. In order to complete an independent math assignment (or be a better speller or a nicer friend), what needs to happen?

- ✦ "What will you need to be able to concentrate more effectively?"

- ✦ "What do you think you will need to do to get along with each other?"

- ✦ "What will you need in order to be able to manage a quiet talking period?"

It often helps to list several alternatives rather than to focus on finding just one solution. And a thoughtful and experimental attitude makes the problem less personal. "What might kids do when they want to make friends?" "What are some ways students can get attention and not get in trouble?" In the spirit of brainstorming, both teacher and student present ideas. Then I ask the student to choose one idea to try and give reasons for why s/he thinks it will work. If it doesn't work, we can learn from the experience. When we return to the list for another try, a better selection can be made. We are revising.

In the end, it's important that students feel they are selecting an alternative that *they* believe will work, not one that just pleases the teacher. A strategy chosen by students because they believe it will solve the problem is more effective than a strategy provided by the teacher.

In general, alternatives seek to repair some loss of belonging or significance. They seek to find a more constructive avenue for children to meet their needs—their need for acceptance (from peers as well as from teachers), for working toward beautiful completions, and for recognition and membership in the school community. William Glasser, in *Schools without Failure*, also identified other needs which he felt must be met in children if they are to participate fully in school. These include the need to have power, to have freedom, and to have fun (Glasser 1969). Children need times in school that are relaxed and comfortable—they need to have fun! They are much more apt to invest in work that may not be fun if there are also wonderful art projects, plays to put on, rowdy games outdoors, or chances to tell jokes and laugh. Sometimes finding an alternative means helping a child find that fun.

The strength of this approach is in its openness and responsiveness. We try to see children as they really are, "from the inside out," listening and exploring with them to find what they need in order to feel better about their lives in school. We try one way, and if that doesn't work, we try another. The best hope of the social conference is to increase children's capacity to deal with disappointments, setbacks, and sorrows. A connection to a listening and responsive adult can provide faith and comfort—crucial to the struggle for growth.

5. Establishing an agreement to try

THE CONFERENCE CONCLUDES with an oral or written agreement to try one of the alternatives. The agreement may be reached after a few minutes or over several days. The agreement is to *try*—and it includes the teacher as well as the student. Both agree to try alternatives, to do something different so that the classroom will work better.

The following example illustrates a more volatile problem. It was actually one of the first times I learned to "mirror and reflect," when I realized the essential importance of an agreement to try. Although clumsy at the start, the approach helped me to teach a troubled student. I do not want to minimize the task of trying to help children who bear terrible scars and the open sores of poverty and neglect. I also do not want to minimize the importance of the teacher.

Charles

At eleven, Charles was a charming, good natured, and generous fifth grader at an urban school with limited special needs resources. He loved to help everyone and encourage others in their efforts. He was a natural athlete and team leader, giving tender assistance to the clumsy and inept players on his teams.

When it came to his own studies, however, Charles was anything but confident or patient. He bluffed, cheated, evaded, and faked. He did very little of his own work in school; he kept busy sharpening pencils, repairing the pencil sharpener, emptying trash, finding a friend's missing book, opening the window for the teacher. When pressed, he found endless excuses. He did his work, but left it at home. He did it, but left it at his grandma's. He would have done it, but the teacher didn't tell him the right page, so he did the wrong page...

When pressed further, made to stay in from recess to do the forgotten work, kept after school, or seated next to the teacher, the agreeable and likable manners disappeared. Charles became sullen, threatening, and destructive. Punishments had not altered the pattern. Additional help with his work was refused. He didn't need help, he claimed. Besides, the work was "babyish," "too easy," "dumb," and he hated this "stupid junk."

To his grandmother, his primary guardian, Charles was an "easy child who didn't like to be crossed." She worried about "that temper," but he was always helpful to her and good with the little ones. She had her hands full.

Charles got further and further behind in his schoolwork. He had been held back once and was functioning two years below grade expectation when he started fifth grade. His ultimate recourse when confronted was to skip school. Charles was on his way to becoming a dropout. After about two months of getting to know Charles, enjoying his humor, his cheerful nature, and his small gifts and avoiding any serious challenge, I assigned a book report. He sputtered and argued; finally I agreed that he could give it orally.

His oral book report was short and ingenious; however, with the exception of character names and chapter captions, it bore no resemblance to the book.

"You didn't read the book," I charged.

"It's a stupid book and you're a fuckin' jerk," he yelled and then stormed out of the room, ending up in the principal's office, where I went to redeem him. I felt furious and guilty at the same time—angry at this boy for denouncing me, humiliated by the provocation of his profanity, guilty for confronting him so publicly. In the principal's office, Charles stated that he'd rather be suspended than have to go back to my classroom. He wanted his old teacher back. I was a bad teacher. He wouldn't come to school if he had to be in my class.

Charles was effectively playing several parts. He was victim and he was rebel. It was a clever power struggle—"I did read the book/You didn't read the book." He was in command of the terms, issuing warnings and threats if he didn't get his way. I could yield or I could lose the student—a miserable choice for any teacher.

It was clear, even as he appeared angry and insolent, that Charles was miserable—his decisions weren't working and he needed help. I understood that. What I didn't know was whether I knew how to help him. But I made a decision to try. I started with an acknowledgement of my mistake. I explained that it was my mistake to challenge him about the book in front of the class. I realized that my mistake made him angry, although I didn't like being cursed at, even by people who are angry. I asked him if he thought it was still possible to work things out, even after my mistake. I liked him and would like to continue to be his teacher, I said. Would he be willing to try to work things out with me?

Surprised or perhaps mollified by my conciliatory tone, he agreed. I told him that I was going to write down some things that I noticed in the classroom and some things that I would like to see change. I told him he could do the same. If we could agree on some changes, he would come back to class. If we couldn't agree, maybe the principal would place him in a different class. He seemed pleased with that option. It was decided that we would share our lists right after school, and in the meantime, he remained in the office.

I presented Charles with a list of about eight things that I noticed that included both his positive and negative behavior:

✦ Always remembered to say hello to kids and teachers in the morning

✦ Took out books but didn't read them

✦ Did only one or two problems on a page of math

- Made mistakes but didn't fix them

- Helped others find things or open containers

- Got angry if a teacher tried to help him do his work

- Handed in only two papers but wanted to hang up one of the stories on the wall

- Told jokes and made other people smile and feel good

All these items were straightforward, true, and simply stated. "Just to make sure you can read my writing," I said, "I'll read them to you." I asked him to check any of the things he thought might be true. I explained that I wasn't angry at him for these things, but that I did observe all these behaviors. Did he notice anything different?

Interestingly, Charles checked them all, no questions, no defiance.

"Is there anything else that you notice?"

"I swear and I shouldn't."

"Yes."

The difference between "You didn't read the book" and "Here are some things I noticed" created distinct outcomes. The first approach was confrontational and accusatory and led to insult and rebellion. The second allowed Charles to remain in control and to name himself, which led to discussion. At the same time, I didn't feel as if I was yielding to the destructive environment created by this boy. I was able to be honest and direct. Giving Charles the choice to work on the problem was the key to his participation.

I do not recall the exact words or sequence of events that followed, but I can construct a rough script. I do know that it involved naming the problem and working together to propose possible solutions.

"When I see kids want to help others but not help themselves, I worry that they don't feel very good about themselves as learners. I think that's a problem, because then you can get stuck and not go on learning. I might be able to help you with that problem, if you want to work on it with me."

"I dunno. I don't really need help. If I want to do things, I do."

"Okay. But sometimes I find that kids have other reasons they don't do work. Like you said, one reason is that they don't want to do things. Could it also be that the work is not hard, but confusing? Maybe it's confusing because kids got behind or didn't keep up practice. Maybe it's confusing because they need some special ways to learn. Like, remember the way you showed Ronnie to tie the knot? You showed him a different way to do it so it would hold tight. It didn't work the first way. But it worked the second way. Then Ronnie could do it. You helped him. Maybe there are different ways to do reading or math also. What do you think?"

"Well…"

"Suppose I write these down for you and you think about it overnight. You may decide it's that you are confused and want to try some different ways with reading, writing, and math. I think that if you decide that you want to work on it, I can help you. I suspect that you can do hard things. What do you think?"

"Well, yeah, I do some hard things."

"Yes. You mind your little cousins every day and shop for your grandma. She says you always have the right change, too. That's hard for lots of kids."

"Yeah. It's not hard for me."

"Charles, you do need to work on your studies. Really work. If you don't think you want to work with me, maybe you want to think about another teacher."

Charles did come back the next day ready to return to his class and, he said, to "work on hard things." He did say that he thought he got confused when he missed some school and was left back. He was still defensive and afraid to be seen as behind or not able. When I showed him a book that he could read, but at a lower level, he dismissed it as "babyish." He also was reluctant to do math that looked different from what his peers were doing. He needed to learn in secret.

I was, for that year, able to find a tutor and, to explain Charles's absence from the class, I devised a "cover" that satisfied his image. He continued to do "fake" work or busywork for much of the time. The tutor, an enthusiastic and inventive intern, was slowly able to find ways to link him back to the classroom. Charles brought in models and directions he had read. He brought in stories he had written. He taught kids how to play Twenty-One, a card game that involved swift calculations. He used new cursive skills and a calligraphy pen from his tutor to make beautiful signs for our room. He would proudly demonstrate a new spelling proficiency.

Finally, he worked very hard preparing a book report during the spring about Willie Mays, his hero, but refused to read it aloud, saying that the book was "babyish." He slipped me the report in private. "Don't show nobody," he said.

"I found out a lot of interesting things about Willie Mays, so I notice that you really read the book this time," I said. "I bet we could shake hands on it and not even have a little fight." So we shook.

I felt that Charles had come a distance. Clearly, the gains were shaky, and there was much more to do. Would Charles continue to work with his sixth grade teacher? Would he get another tutor? Would he take on more of the classroom program? Was he ready? There is a huge number of variables when we are dealing with children, and many that we don't control. But a link between teacher and child, child and teacher, which is established through a social conference can make an essential change in a child's approach to school and learning. ❖

FIGURE 14.2

Social Conference Starters for Common Behavior Problems

Here are some common behavior problems for which teachers might hold social conferences. Listed for each behavior are some examples of what the teacher and the student might notice, along with some possible "Could it be…?" questions for opening the conversation.

Attention-seeking behavior

The teacher might notice that the child:

+ Shows off and brags a lot (even lies) about accomplishments or possessions

+ Is clingy, showing *everything* to the teacher

+ Asks unnecessary questions

+ Repeats silly, mischievous bids for approval and for the teacher's time

+ Makes inappropriate noises and performs childish antics

✦ "Kids don't pick me."

✦ "Teachers ignore me or don't explain things to me."

✦ "I like to tell jokes. It's funny when I…"

Possible "Could it be…?" questions:

✦ "Could it be that you wish people would pay more attention to you?"

✦ "Could it be that you think the only way people will notice you is if you bother them or act silly?"

✦ "Could it be that you think the only way the teacher will notice you is if you act very good and show all your good work?"

✦ "Could it be that you feel you need to impress other people to get attention?"

✦ "Could it be that you wish people knew certain things about you and noticed you more?"

Defiance

The teacher may notice that the child:

✦ Frequently objects in critical, negative ways to peers, schoolwork, and the teacher—for example, "Oh man, didn't we just do this last year?"

✦ Habitually argues about facts, methods, even what was said as long ago as a month

✦ Makes faces, passes knowing glances, or mumbles rudely when asked to do something

✦ Often turns in poor and incomplete work

✦ Often ignores minor rules, testing limits (keeps talking when the bell rings, walks out of the room at will, takes things from the teacher's closets, tells lies about handing in work, ridicules the efforts of others)

The student may notice that:

✦ The teacher isn't fair—"You don't like me as much as others. You pick on me. You don't give me a chance."

- Assignments aren't right—"Stuff is too easy," "Stuff is too hard," "You ask us to do baby work," or "We talk about boring stuff."

- Other students don't listen—"Kids don't listen to me when I say something, or when I have an idea."

Possible "Could it be...?" questions:

- "Could it be that you need to show me that you can be a boss, too?"

- "Could it be that you want to impress me or other kids by showing us that you can do what you want and don't have to follow our rules?"

- "Could it be that you feel angry because you think grown-ups don't understand something important about you?"

- "Could it be that you feel not so good about some of your work in school, so you worry that people won't think you're a strong or smart person?"

Being a bad sport

The teacher may notice that the student:

- Has outbursts of temper during games or recess

- Bullies and cheats his/her way through games

- Often quits playing and storms off in tears

The student may notice that:

- "Teams aren't fair."

- "The referee is lousy."

- "Kids don't play right and don't follow rules."

Possible "Could it be...?" questions:

- "Could it be that it's hard for you to lose?"

- "Could it be that it feels bad if you don't always do as well as you want to?"

- "Could it be that it's hard for you to follow the rules and accept the decisions of referees, partners, or the boss of a game, if the boss isn't you?"

- "Could it be that you have trouble taking care of yourself when the teacher isn't there to help you?"

- "Could it be that you care about the game so much that you get frustrated when others on your team don't play as hard as you?"

Tattling

The teacher may notice that the child:

- Tattles or shows concern daily about what others are up to—"He called me names," "She pushed me," "He took and didn't ask," or "He's making stupid sounds and we can't concentrate."

- Makes whining complaints

- Interrupts frequently to report trouble

The student may notice:

- "Kids aren't following the rules."

- "I tell them to stop but they don't listen."

- "You said...and they shouldn't..."

Possible "Could it be...?" questions:

- "Could it be that you want to show me you know the rules and know how to follow them?"

- "Could it be that you want to see those children get in trouble?"

- "Could it be that you feel that you need my help to solve conflicts?"

- "Could it be that you are a little jealous, and maybe angry, when you feel that you are not included in what others are doing?"

- "Could it be that you are worried that children aren't taking good care of our class rules?

Losing and forgetting

The teacher may notice that:

+ The student often forgets lunch money, the bus pass, books, homework, directions, instructions, or where s/he just put something

+ The student floats and wanders about the classroom

+ The student's desk and cubby are always messy, and the student leaves a trail of belongings wherever s/he goes

+ The student's parent often running in with forgotten trip money, a forgotten lunch, or homework assignments left behind

The student may notice that:

+ "I always have too much to do."

+ "You never give me enough time."

+ "My parents are always rushing me."

+ "I remember, but afterwards, and then it's too late."

Possible "Could it be...?" questions:

+ "Could it be that you have trouble organizing your things?"

+ "Could it be that you don't remember well when you just try to keep everything in your head? Maybe your head needs some help?"

+ "Could it be that you have a lot of things to think about right now?"

+ "Could it be that you get so involved in what you're doing now that you don't think about what you'll need later?"

Dawdling

The teacher may notice that the child:

+ Avoids work (especially during independent work times), loafing, talking, or fooling around instead of doing assignments; offers excuses for not doing the work

+ Needs a lot of reminders and direction

+ Often hangs out without doing much

+ Has trouble making choices

+ Goes to the bathroom a lot

+ Wanders around the room, is slow to get going, seems lethargic, and is easily distracted

+ Asks questions but doesn't seem to listen to answers or to apply them

The student may notice that:

+ "You didn't explain what to do."

+ "I can't concentrate in here when there are other people."

+ "I don't understand what to do."

+ "I'm not trying to fool around. It's other kids that come and talk to me."

Possible "Could it be...?" questions:

+ "Could it be that you find this work hard, so you don't like to do it?"

+ "Could it be that you like the subject, but you feel bad because you're stuck on something, and it's easier to avoid it than to figure out how to get unstuck?"

+ "Could it be that you have trouble concentrating when you have to work on your own?"

+ "Could it be that you feel not so interested, and you don't like to do things that don't seem interesting?"

+ "Could it be that you kind of like it when kids come to you, so you don't want to tell them to leave you alone so you can do your work?"

Restlessness and lack of control

The teacher may notice that the student:

+ Hates to sit still, is inattentive, grabs or knocks into things, and bumps into people

+ Interrupts to talk to the teacher, regardless of what the teacher is doing

+ Wanders from tasks and jumps from thought to thought

The student may notice that:

- ✦ "Meetings take too long."

- ✦ "The worst thing about school is when you have to sit and sit."

- ✦ "My hand just flies up."

- ✦ "My words pop out of my mouth."

- ✦ "There's so much waiting, and I hate to wait."

Possible "Could it be...?" questions:

- ✦ "Could it be that you have trouble being the 'boss' of your own body? You want to sit still, but your body wants to get up?"

- ✦ "Could it be that you have so much energy, your muscles just need to work hard?"

- ✦ "Could it be that you have trouble telling your mind to pay attention? Maybe you start thinking about your own work, but then you notice other things, other children, the teacher, and the moving clouds you see through the window?"

SUMMARY

IN A RECENT WORKSHOP, a teacher from Maine voiced a familiar worry: "Many of the kids now are coming in with such baggage from home. You find out that the child is upset because he tells you that his parents were fighting so hard, he couldn't sleep and had the pillow over his head and was very scared. As a result, he's very inattentive the next day. His behavior isn't appropriate, but it's not as a result of what's happening in the class. It's hard to see it, and it's even harder to find time to address all these things."

Recent reports indicate that one in six children in the United States lives in poverty (Children's Defense Fund 2001). Nearly a million children a year are confirmed—and many more are suspected—of being victims of child abuse or neglect. And estimates of the number of children who witness family violence are in the millions (Children's Defense Fund 2000).

Many of our children will bring awful baggage to school—baggage that will seriously impair or compromise their capacity to learn and to be with others. Another teacher in a neighboring school told me, "I know a four-year-old who has no language, is not deaf, and runs around all day hitting and biting and howling. What do we do with such a child?" I, too, am worried.

Important answers lie outside the domain of education. Some answers would come with the obliteration of poverty from our country of conspicuous surplus and wealth. Other answers would grow from systemic educational reforms that reshape the physical size of schools and classrooms and empower teachers to teach. In the meantime, class begins at eight.

The child who comes in sad may need a hug. The one who comes in discouraged may need a pat on the back. The hungry child may need a peanut butter sandwich. And the child who seems too quiet, or is never quiet, may need a conversation with the teacher. At times it takes only five minutes. We listen, we hear, we offer a gesture or word of comfort. At other times, it is a longer process of noticing and seeking solutions. It is not the solution that is the answer. It is the responsiveness that is the answer. It is one of our jobs, in Sara Ruddick's apt phrase from *Maternal Thinking*, "to make truth serve lovingly the person known" (Ruddick 1994).

Works Cited

CALKINS, LUCY McCORMICK. 1994. *The Art of Teaching Writing.* New Edition. Portsmouth, NH: Heinemann.

CHILDREN'S DEFENSE FUND. 2000. Washington, DC. "Child Abuse and Neglect Fact Sheet." (Spring).

CHILDREN'S DEFENSE FUND. 2001. Washington, DC. "Overall Child Poverty Rate Dropped in 2000. But Poverty Rose for Children in Full-Time Working Families." (Press release, September 25).

COHEN, DOROTHY. 1983. *Observing and Recording the Behavior of Young Children.* Third edition, revised. New York: Teachers College Press.

DREIKURS, RUDOLF, FLOY C. PEPPER, AND BERNICE BRONIA GRUNWALD. 1982. *Maintaining Sanity in the Classroom: Classroom Management Techniques.* Second edition. Philadelphia, PA: Taylor & Francis, Inc.

GLASSER, WILLIAM. 1969. *Schools Without Failure.* New York: Harper & Row.

RUDDICK, SARA. 1989. *Maternal Thinking: Toward a Politics of Peace.* Boston: Beacon Press.

CHAPTER 15
Individual Contracts

Douglas

I watch as Douglas drags his chair to the meeting circle and sits down. He is one of the first to respond to the teacher's signal, ready before the rest. But he doesn't stay ready. Moments later, he is bulldozing through the room, in and out of the coat rack, bumping and pushing, fingering and touching, his voice a steady stream of noises and commentary. Teacher reprimands and the defensive cries of his fellow first graders follow in his wake. Finally, after all other students are in their place, he again comes to rest, back in his Morning Meeting seat. His name is now an exasperated sigh on his teacher's lips. "I'll be good," he says suddenly, quietly, directing himself.

"Yeah, right," his neighbor Stephanie replies, almost to herself. And for the next thirty seconds, Douglas is still, hands folded in his lap, a model of focus and attention, before his attention shifts and he is back out of his seat. He is a constant tumble of energy; his distractions and disturbances create a constant feeling of irritation in his teachers, his classmates, and himself. ❖

THIS DOUGLAS TYPIFIES MANY CHILDREN that I see in classrooms in schools everywhere. I have at least two of my own, year after year. They are children who badly want to be good, to please, to earn the applause of their group, and yet can't pull it off. They are often children with the poorest internal control. In the school environment we want to create, maybe Douglas will learn "to be good" through the never-ending refrain of reminders, warnings, and time-outs. "Yeah, right," says our own Stephanie-voice, cynical, tired, and already stretched too thin. When I hear that voice, I know I need to try a different approach.

The thirty seconds that Douglas sat quietly and with attention in his chair provide a foundation for change, if we can just see it and affirm that potential with the student. The teacher might say to Douglas, "You sat beautifully for thirty seconds today. Now, let's see if you can make it a minute." Douglas is noticed and praised by his teacher and feels the warmth of appreciation, while being prodded to the next challenge.

An individual student contract is an option that can help when reminders and redirection have little impact on unwanted behavior. Such behavioral contracts, whether verbal or written, focus on a child's strengths and capacity for self-control rather than giving negative orders—orders telling the child what not to do. "People can't change under a negative connotation," says psychologist Sally Crawford. When we see children honestly for their better selves and better intentions, without denying that their actions may not always deliver, we can motivate them to change.

When we find something real that a child can do, we provide a positive vision for the child and a hope for change. An individual contract asserts the potential of a student and establishes a positive agreement to work together to accomplish specified expectations.

Individual contracts define and name both social and academic expectations in clear actions and words. They may provide greater structure if necessary (such as a designated seat in the classroom circle or a check-in time for assignments to be copied) or modified expectations (ten rather than twenty math questions completed). The behavioral priority is broken down into manageable chunks and a sequence of steps. Contracts initiate a process in which successful steps, however small, are noted and celebrated.

CONTRACTS IN TODAY'S CLASSROOMS

CLASSROOMS TODAY HAVE numerous children with diagnosed or undiagnosed conditions and children with significant family difficulties. We see many children with unstable lives who have already changed families or schools too many times, and they are only in the third grade. In some cases, guidance for parents, diagnostic referrals, and community social services are needed but are outside the control of the classroom teachers. Most of these children want to "be good" in school and yet aren't. They find school a challenge and make it a challenge for others.

Whatever their background, it is dangerous for children to develop "bad kid" identities and reputations as a way to view themselves or to be seen by their peers.

And it is even more damaging for children to feel that they overwhelm the adults in their lives and render them helpless: helpless in the face of chronic needs and misbehavior, and helpless even to keep the classroom a safe place to learn.

Individual contracts are not a panacea or a quick fix, but they do provide a framework for tackling persistent and difficult behavioral problems within the resources of the classroom. Over the years, I have simplified the process I use so that it takes only a few minutes to oversee each day.

ASSUMPTIONS UNDERLYING STUDENT CONTRACTS

EFFECTIVE CONTRACTS REQUIRE several assumptions. I start by assuming that each student shares my goals for school. I have faith that the majority of children want to "be good" and do well in their work. They want to be liked by teachers and classmates, to feel competent and skillful, and to fit in and have friends. I state these assumptions directly to the student. Even when children retort "I don't care," I assume that they do care—almost all the time. They just don't know how to do what is required.

Contracts also assume the teacher has an interest in understanding a child and has respect for the child's efforts. Teachers need to convey a sense of empathy, a sense that we may know where the misbehavior is coming from and that we recognize the potential for change. I remember Robbie, a child at ease and graceful outdoors, who moved with awkwardness and sporadic focus inside the classroom walls. For years, he measured his days in school according to the number of times he went to time-out. His "tens" (awesome days) were days of only one or two time-outs. I came to truly admire his determination to gain control over his ever-ready impulses and high-spirited energies. In order for me to help Robbie, it was important that I recognize his skills with truck motors as well as his struggles to motor himself around the room without incident. Robbie needed to believe that his teachers understood and respected his intentions and his abilities.

The third assumption is that before we hold students accountable for their behavior with a contract, expectations must be carefully introduced, modeled, and practiced during the first six weeks of school. While the structures of the first six weeks provide enough exposure and practice for most children to master the classroom rules and routines, the students who continue to disrupt and disturb, grab attention, or demand endless surveillance may need an individual contract. In the contracts we create with them, we need to provide extra or alternative instruction and practice to make sure they can manage the behaviors we name and expect.

A final assumption is that a firm and supportive relationship is a basic condition for change. By firm, I mean expressing and enforcing clear expectations and limits. By supportive, I mean providing the adaptations and consistent encouragement to meet those expectations. Individual student contracts engage the student and the primary adults (teachers and parents) in a cooperative relationship. They are intended to create a more predictable and steady interaction based on mutually acknowledged terms, terms that combine the needs of the classroom with the needs of the individual.

STEPS IN USING INDIVIDUAL CONTRACTS

CONTRACTS WORK BEST when the procedures involved are consistent, affirmative, and simple to use in the midst of a normal, busy classroom day. The following steps can be easily adapted to meet the needs of unique individuals and classrooms:

1. The teacher determines that a student needs an individual contract and drafts a plan.

2. The teacher meets with the parents and the student for discussion and input and to assure mutual understanding and agreement. The methods of evaluation, the markers for success, the celebration, and the consequences are all discussed and agreed upon.

3. The contract is signed by the student, the parents, the teacher, and any other teachers who may be asked to enforce the contract.

4. The contract is put into action. Other teachers who may be using the contract are informed.

5. The teacher uses brief check-ins each day, as needed, to reinforce the expectations of the contract and to evaluate whether the goal was met that day.

6. The student receives a concrete marker each day to show whether the expectation was met. The markers may be kept in a special notebook or placed in an envelope that is taken home *each day*.

7. The student reports on success to the parents.

8. When the student achieves the ultimate goal by earning the agreed-upon number of markers, *parents* provide the agreed-upon celebration or reward.

9. The contract is completed and is no longer needed, or a new goal for the contract is determined. The same goal may be chosen again, but with a new challenge and reward.

A contract for Lauren

Lauren is a fifth grader who is disruptive, sometimes explosively so, when she doesn't get her way, particularly in group activities. If she doesn't like the choice of a game, she refuses to participate, intimidating and distracting others by angry gestures or yelling. If she doesn't get called on or if she doesn't agree with someone, she calls out or bangs her chair legs on the floor.

"That's so dumb," she yells, arms crossed, feet banging, face squinched into sullen insult. Though Lauren's behavior manifests itself all through the day, her teacher chooses to work initially on Morning Meeting because it is consistently difficult for Lauren and seems to offer a good possibility for success.

Conversations with Lauren and her parents result in a contract spelling out the goal, naming some specific behavior strategies for her to use, and stating what concrete markers will record her success. "Lauren will participate in Morning Meeting even if she doesn't get to do what she wants. She will keep her disappointments and angry thoughts to herself. She may say to herself, 'Oh well, maybe tomorrow.' She may shrug her shoulders and think, 'tough luck.' She may count to ten and then say to herself, 'Okay. I'll try to have fun and let others have fun.' For every Morning Meeting that she meets her goal, she will stamp an index card with a 'victory sign' stamp."

Consequences are also spelled out for Lauren in her contract:

+ When Lauren calls out or makes a face, she will get one reminder. The teacher will say her name and use the time-out signal.

+ The next time, Lauren will leave the circle for the remainder of the group time.

+ If Lauren insults anyone with words or gestures, she will leave the circle.

+ If Lauren has to leave the circle twice in one week, she will go to the principal's office for a half hour, and her parents will be called. She will write a letter or make an active apology to the class for her insult.

Each morning the teacher checks in with Lauren. The check-in is brief. "What do you need to remember before we start our morning circle, Lauren?"

"If I don't get picked, I can shrug and say to myself, 'Maybe next time'?"

"Good plan."

And each afternoon, prior to dismissal, the teacher approaches Lauren at her desk. "How did it go today?"

"I remembered, 'cause they chose that stupid radio game, and I didn't even get called on for my idea, but I shrugged and didn't get mad and have to leave."

"I agree." The teacher hands Lauren a green index card and a victory-sign stamp as her success symbol. Lauren carefully stamps her card and puts it in an envelope to take home.

Another afternoon's check-in goes a bit differently: "How did it go? Do you get your V-sign?"

"Well, they weren't playing fair. They was just picking the boys. I got mad."

"You called names and yelled? No V-sign, right?"

"Right. I said some names."

"I hope tomorrow works better and you remember to shrug and not call names."

"I'll remember. I'll try, anyway."

Every afternoon, Lauren takes her index cards home in an envelope for her parents to see, so that they can monitor her progress. Her celebration will involve a chance to lead a recess game with the second graders during each month that she meets her goal of fifteen V-signs. Lauren loves leading activities and being the boss and can be quite patient with younger students. Also, the second grade teacher knows Lauren and will be able to help her do a good job. Lauren's parents will also recognize her progress, taking her to a store where she can pick out a poster of a favorite music star to add to her collection.

After Lauren consistently meets her goals for Morning Meeting behavior, the goals will be transferred to structured recess games and eventually to a cooperative learning project in social studies. ❖

Elements of Individual Student Contracts

THE TEACHER PLANS the elements of the contract with input from the student and the parents. The teacher can make a realistic plan for the classroom, and the student and parents help to personalize it through their ideas and support. All individual contracts consist of the following elements, tailored to the needs of the particular student, parents, teacher, and classroom:

- ✦ Behavioral goals

- ✦ A system of communication

- ✦ A way to evaluate success

- ✦ A celebration of achievement

- ✦ Clear consequences when boundaries are broken

Behavioral goals

HERE ARE SOME sample goal statements:

We want you to feel good about your work in school this year. In order to feel good, you need to be able to hand your math and writing work in on time.

We want you to feel good about your year and not get in trouble so much. To do that, you need to be able to listen and respond to directions from your teacher with attention and an agreeable voice.

We want you to feel good in school and be a friend to your classmates. In order to be a friend, you need to keep your hands on your own body.

Like those listed above, all goals need to be:

◆ Realistic

◆ Named clearly and translated into concrete and clear behaviors and actions

◆ Observable and measurable by both teachers and students

◆ Enforceable—teachers and students will be able to agree without argument whether a certain behavior or task occurred. It will be possible to use consequences when behavior doesn't occur.

Notice that the first part of the goal statement refers to big reasons and motivations to participate in school. With older students, the vocabulary becomes more sophisticated and intriguing. "My hope is that you become an organized and efficient worker" replaces "I want you to do good work in school." We try to provide images that affirm the child in school and counter a student's negativity or discouragement.

These statements are not grandiose or impossible. We are not hoping a child becomes the "best" or "always good." To touch children, statements must also be genuine. We must believe in the potential for all children to like their classrooms, to be kinder to one another, to find some level of control and skillful participation. When our children say "I'll be good," we cannot be like Douglas's neighbor, uttering our own cynical "Yeah, right!"

We also need to develop more specific goals. The second part of the process names and specifies concrete, measurable actions and behaviors. What does the student most need to do to participate and not to get in constant trouble? We need to target the most important behaviors and limit the goal to one behavior at a time, especially for younger students. Because we want to assure immediate success, we may want to provide clear time or quantity limits, gradually increasing the expectations after the limited goals are achieved.

For example, knowing a student cannot sit for an entire thirty-minute period, we ask that she sit for fifteen minutes. Knowing that a student may not complete homework every day, our goal is one good homework assignment turned in each week. With successful completion, children gain self-confidence and build endurance. When a single goal is reached, the next steps may be addressed.

346

FIGURE 15.1

Some Goals for Younger Children

Goals for younger children may focus on the following areas:

+ Being a good listener

+ Following directions

+ Being a good participant, even if it's not your favorite activity

+ Letting others have a turn

+ Using a quiet voice

+ Staying in your seat

+ Keeping your hands and feet to yourself

+ Noticing something nice that a classmate does to help you or someone else

+ Giving compliments

+ Using "I don't like it when _____" words, not fists, when angry

+ Using internal "brakes" when asked by teachers or classmates to stop talking, teasing, or touching

Titles, succinct phrases, metaphors, and captivating images can help to instill clarity and significance for children. Note that some words are deliberately capitalized or highlighted.

+ Be the "boss" of your own self by choosing to follow the rules for _____.

+ Complete a piece of "Proud Work" every week.

+ Follow directions even when the teacher is not looking.

+ Use your Respect Words and use your "brakes" for the mean words.

+ Use Respect Words and not threats.

+ Use your Good Concentration.

FIGURE 15.2

Some Goals for Older Children

With older students, responsibility for work, tone of voice, and conduct with other students are often issues. Goals may focus on the following areas:

✦ Getting to your work in a timely fashion

✦ Listening and not interrupting others

✦ Asking questions when you don't understand something

✦ Responding appropriately to directions without argument

✦ Using appropriate words, not fists, when angry

✦ Handing in work that shows care and effort, and handing it in on time

✦ Conversing about topics that are appropriate for school and using appropriate language

Stating specific, quantified measures is important with older children as well as with younger children:

✦ Redo one piece of math work each week to make it 85% correct.

✦ Revise and edit one piece of writing each week to correct spelling and punctuation.

✦ Share positive comments or ask interested questions each week.

✦ Stay seated and focused for three-fourths of a work period with one appropriate break, such as getting a pencil sharpened or getting a drink without disturbing anyone else.

✦ Select a piece of work or an action that demonstrates your "best work" each week and share it with a teacher and parent.

✦ Organize your notebook each week under "Work To Do" and "Work Done" headings.

✦ Write down homework assignments in your Assignment Book and show Ms. Charney the book before leaving school each day. Check in with Ms. Charney to show completed assignments before the start of school each day.

A system of communication

CONSISTENT ATTENTION TO THE GOAL and regular communication among teacher, student, and parents are essential to a successful behavioral contract. Planned communications usually include the following:

A notebook or envelope taken home and returned each day

The child's success or failure to meet the goal is noted each day. Ideally, parents will check in, talk to their child, and sign their name before the child returns the next day. If this is not reasonable or possible, another adult at school may check progress, or the classroom teacher may keep the notebook or records in school.

A regular morning reminder and check-in

This may involve a quick and friendly reminder about the goal or a review of the notebook. The check-in allows the teacher to focus the student on the particular goal. The teacher can affirm success with a reminder that yesterday the goal was met. "You were able to get your checkmark sticker yesterday. What worked?" Strategies are suggested or reviewed. "Annie, remind me, what are we working on today?" Or if the goal was not reached the day before, the teacher can briefly help the child problem-solve, practice, and model for the coming day. "Show me how you will 'stop and think' today before you get out of your seat."

A daily time for evaluation

I have found that most students benefit from a visual, concrete mark or object that denotes success on a daily basis. Daily monitoring of behavioral concerns is more effective, even with middle-school-age students, than weekly or long-term arrangements. The arrangements include an end-of-the-day check-in with teacher and student and a tangible mark or object that denotes success: a card, a marker, or other "chit" that goes home to parents.

A way to evaluate success

THE EVALUATION PROCESS depends on clear and measurable goals. Evaluation is always done with the student, not for the student. In most cases, it takes only a few minutes and does not involve a long discussion. Evaluation requires the following:

A time to observe the behavior

Expectations need to be concrete and enforceable for both younger and older students. With younger students, the goal may apply initially to limited periods. "Staying in your seat for math period" may be a first step. Once math is a successful period for the student, language arts or Morning Meeting may be added. For older students, the limitations may involve whether the expectations apply only with the primary teacher initially or with specials and other teachers, too. For example, Anna was wonderful with her primary teacher after some work, but surly and resistant with everyone else. As she progressed, her contract became more generalized and inclusive of other adults.

A daily check-in to evaluate success

This is brief and is conducted in a matter-of-fact tone. It is important that good days are not overly remarked upon and that bad days not lead to lectures or rancor. I tend to start with the question that asks students for self-evaluation. The following is an example of a discussion with Greg, who has a contract to help him work on being more organized:

"Do you think that you should get your check mark today for being on time to your classes?"

"Well, except that I had to go back and get my book for English."

"So…no?"

"No," he grins.

When students are asked to reflect on their behavior, even if they are wrong, they become more self-aware, which stimulates growth. Sometimes students are too critical and hesitant to see success; our positive response can encourage interpretations that are accurate and honest. Teacher interpretation needs to be concrete and based on observation. "I noticed that…" frames a response that calls the student to task and helps him/her see that judgments aren't arbitrary or global. It is important that students feel seen and that the evaluation includes both teacher and student observation and interpretation.

How teachers (and parents) respond to days when the goal is not reached is also critical. It is important to be matter-of-fact and express faith in tomorrow. The conversation remains honest but not punishing. What was hard about today? What do you want to remember to do tomorrow? How can I help? We do not expect the contract to achieve total compliance but to encourage effort and investment. It is important to acknowledge that not all days earn the plus signs, but that success is still possible.

A marker to indicate success

A goal accomplished for the day is signified by a tangible marker: a teacher's check mark, a smiley-face sticker, a poker chip to go in a jar, a Popsicle stick to add to the collection in the envelope, an index card that reads "Jamie shared today," etc. We need to have a bag of tricks from which to pull the right trick for each unique child. I tend to suggest possible markers and then allow the student to choose a comfortable one. The marker must be cheap, concrete, easy to keep track of, easy to save, and easy to take home.

I have also learned that a contract works best when the teacher evaluates and records each day's results, but the parents hold the cards, keep the tally, and award the final appreciation. I hand the student the index card with the sticker, the Popsicle stick with the red dot that means success, the notebook, or the wizard stamp, which the student gives to his/her parents. The parents keep the markers until a certain number has accumulated. Then they and their child celebrate the accomplishment of the goal.

When we can strengthen home-school ties, our ability to help our students greatly increases. If parents are not willing or able participants, it is possible to assign the task to another faculty member who has some connection with the student— a guidance counselor, a former and beloved teacher, an assistant teacher, the PE teacher who has a special bond with the student. This surrogate authority figure receives the markers and provides the immediate check-in and feedback. This person will also offer the treat or celebration when the goal is achieved.

There are some situations in which the teacher alone keeps the records and provides the celebration. However, the separation of roles, when possible, helps to engage others, and to provide a circle of support that becomes an encouraging community for the student.

A celebration of achievement

WHEN THE STUDENT ATTAINS A GOAL, we want to celebrate that success (no matter how small). I see the use of a reward in this context as a necessary bridge between external and internal control and motivation. My colleague Roxann Kriete points out that a celebration offers a "positive logical consequence." It is the result of a job well done. It is recognition for the special efforts that may be required for even the most common tasks.

There are two important decisions that determine the celebration:

- ✦ How many times must a student successfully meet the goal to get the celebration?

- ✦ What will the celebration be?

In both cases, it often helps to frame some choices for students and then to allow them some say in the decision. In setting the number of successful days needed, we want to provide a tension between what is going to stretch the student and what is realistic. If the number is too high, the child becomes discouraged. If it is too low, it becomes a joke. Depending on the student's age and needs, a weekly or biweekly program might be implemented. With older students, we generally set the expectations higher and extend the time period. It took Greg a month to earn the sixteen chits required for a celebration.

Rewards need to be of sensible proportion as well. Teachers may need to help parents and students select celebrations that are appropriate. Rewards may be material—a trip to an amusement park or a special small stuffed animal—or may involve special activities, such as a chance to play a game with a friend. Some celebrations, in fact, feature a responsibility, such as Johnny's wish to care for his baby cousin, or include a social event that highlights and extends learned skills. One student got to take a class pet home over a holiday weekend. Another earned an opportunity to teach a younger class a favorite game. Another got to take a friend to lunch. These rewards provide a chance for a student to feel pride, to receive the appreciative gestures of others, and to know some success.

While the impetus for the student to achieve the goal may be to earn the external reward, the process also provides an opportunity to build internal motivation. We need to be aware of the immaterial rewards along with the material "carrots." I often notice that the receipt of just the card or sticker at the end of the day is affirmation in itself. The smile or handshake, the moment of attention from the teacher, the positive embrace of the parent, and the acknowledgment of good intentions all bolster self-image and morale.

We may want to detail the natural benefits of improved social skills as well. If you are more apt to play fair and not cheat, you are invited to join more games. If you take an interest in what others say, you will be chosen more often as a partner.

Stickers

During a visit to a second grade class, I was struck by the large oaktag cards taped to each desk. "I am a Star" was written in the center of the placards. Some were speckled with glossy silver and purple stars; others were sparsely decorated. The teacher explained that when students followed the rules, they received a star, and when they achieved a specific number of stars, they got to take home the card and show it off to their parents. There were other commendations and class prizes from their teacher as well.

Accumulated commendations earned special trips and festivities. For students who misbehaved, there would be fewer stars and stickers, accrued demerits, trips to the principal, suspensions, and the loss of attendance on the special outings. The aim was to motivate appropriate conduct through the awards and privileges, as well as to apply negative consequences for misconduct.

"What do you do to earn a star?" I asked.

"You gotta be good," responded a student.

"What do you do to be good?" prompted the teacher.

"Like if another teacher comes in the room and wants to talk to our teacher, you don't get out of your seat or talk."

"And you don't make noise," added another.

Another student pointed to a list of rules posted on the wall. "If you follow the rules." He began to read, "Raise your hand. Don't run in the halls. Don't leave your seat."

Another student interrupted. "Hey, she can read. She's a teacher, you know!" He smiles and bows to his friends.

The student reading the rules is now blushing and confused. He begins to stammer, "You do your work on time, you could get a star." He puts his head down on his desk.

I wondered to myself, "Is kindness a rule?" I didn't note any exchange of stars or demerits at this point.

Teachers in this same school were concerned that their students showed a lack of incentive to do assignments (without tangible rewards) and little pride in their own output. School was a "low priority" for too many of their students. "We have fourth and fifth graders who are already planning what they will do *when*, not *if*, they drop out of school," one reported. As a group, these teachers felt that the school environment needed to become a more enjoyable social experience, and that children needed to develop intrinsic motivations to learn and behave. What was missing, the teachers reiterated, "is a sense of responsibility and pride."

I observed a group of boys playing a lively and safe game of football during recess. Suddenly, an aide walked over and said to the boys, "Be good 'cause the lady is watching."

We must decide whether we are teaching children to be good because someone is watching, or whether we are teaching goodness as a better way to get along with people. We must decide whether we intend to teach conduct that draws on inner as well as external sanctions. I do not think it works to equivocate. I do not think that a system built on stickers can be used to reinforce self-motivation.

Months later, the same group of teachers met to consider specific classroom strategies to promote their goals of responsibility and sociability. The question of stickers came up. "Our kids need stickers," one teacher explained, because teachers and children often contend with overwhelming odds. Stickers offer tangible, positive feedback that provides immediate and visible short-term results. Children are excited and eager. They sit up, take notice, and work. Teachers are reassured by their "interest" and better behavior.

What happens when the stickers become bribery to get the job done rather than a reward for a job well done? I've seen a student demand a prize for completing a single sheet of math problems! What happens when the children work for promised awards but show no investment in the work itself? Have we actually conditioned children to expect and value material gain rather than such intangibles as pride, competence, and self-respect? If we do that, then external gains and sanctions, like status with peers and money from selling drugs, have little competition from rewards like good grades or a low-paying but legal job following a high school degree.

I fear that the prevalence of "stickers" means we have lost faith either in the inner resources of our children or in our capacity to reach those resources as teachers. I sent one of my students off one summer with a reading contract. I worried that the instant school was over, she would stop reading—a realistic assumption. In order to be a bit more persuasive, I promised a payment. She would earn two dollars for each book she read. We went to the library and found three wonderful books. The contract was signed. On day one of the new school year she greeted me, saying, "I read my books!" She was beaming. "And I loved them." I didn't hear a word about money.

"I don't think a teacher should have to pay me," she confided to her mother. "It was fun!" I hadn't trusted that Lydia would be able to read for fun, and not money. I had underestimated her investment and capacity to assert herself. Lydia was a reluctant reader, but not a reluctant student. There are other children far more detached and disaffected than Lydia. Those are children we often feel need a motivational "carrot," an external incentive which may or may not involve an individual contract as described in this chapter. Even when we offer carrots, we must be careful not to lose sight of our basic goal, which is for the student to see the value and meaning of the work itself. The aim is not to accrue stickers, stars, or money. The aim is to solve a problem, or enjoy a good book, or feel pride in competency or accomplishment.

"Tell me," I ask a student when I award a pizza-lunch prize, "how you managed to earn this treat."

"'Cause I finished all my books on time," he answers.

"What does that show us?" I continue. I want to emphasize the inner competencies and resources necessary for him to succeed with his challenge. "You were able to choose books you wanted to read and read them," I might prompt. "You learned fifty new vocabulary words."

We don't have to abandon all the short-term carrots, as long as we keep in mind that the carrots do not take the place of the inner meanings. I use my pizza-lunch prizes or stickers to add a temporary element of gamesmanship and challenge and to take the edge off a fearful experience. For children who have encountered failure, stickers and prizes may help them overcome a strong avoidance.

As a last resort, I will get out the stickers. But as a first resort, I will say, "Give yourself a big handshake. You should be proud of your hard work. Are you? Is it good work?"

In short, the majority of children should not need any kind of "stickers" to become invested in their school life. Some will need them intermittently when struggling with a particularly hard task or going through a tough time. (Don't we sometimes give ourselves a reward for a thorny job well done?) To be sure, a few children may continue to rely on external reinforcements throughout their school career. We can keep helping—but we cannot count on—these children to develop the internal judgment and critical thinking skills that will allow them to navigate on their own. We may need to continue to use "stickers" to keep these children on track. ❖

Clear consequences when boundaries are broken

I FREQUENTLY INCLUDE CONSEQUENCES as part of an individual contract with younger children, and always do so with older students. When we establish a behavioral contract, we recognize the special efforts and practice it takes for some children to meet expectations. We also recognize that success will be intermittent.

Consequences make the boundaries and limits clear. They preserve the safety of the individual student and of the community. It is critical that children know what happens when they fail to help themselves and the negative behavior occurs. I try to spell it out clearly, step by step, in each contract. "When you forget to stay in your seat (or keep your hands to yourself, or control your insults), here is what will happen."

Setting up consequences provides a time to differentiate and clarify socially acceptable actions. It's okay if children who have trouble sitting still get up and walk around and take a needed break—as long as they don't disturb others. "It is not the getting up," I tell Marcie, "it is the loud noise you make and the way you bang your feet. It is getting up when someone else is talking. What's a good time to get up and take a break? What's a good way to get up and not bother anyone else?"

The same approach may work for other behaviors. "It's fine to talk in class, but when and with what tone?" Or for a student who tunes out and relies too heavily on individual directions, I might say, "It is fine to ask questions, but not when the information was just given and you weren't listening. So let's think about when to ask questions." I end up providing her with a pattern for questions that must contain some gist of the information already given: "I heard you say that our papers need to have correct punctuation, but I still don't understand how to use quotation marks."

With older students, I often need to suggest appropriate ways to "question authority" as opposed to the ways that are getting them in trouble. An insult or a nasty tone is not acceptable. A respectfully offered "I disagree with..." statement is acceptable.

With children who have poor impulse control and/or attentional deficits, special signals may be effective as a first step. As they start to wander or interrupt, a pre-determined reminder from the teacher—a secret hand signal, a funny word, a pull on the ear—may help them regulate themselves. This is often posed as the first step in the consequences and may help teach some children strategies to self-regulate.

For example, Jo began to pull on her own ear (the teacher's reminder to refocus) as a way to remind herself that she had strayed far from the original task.

The consequences tend to follow the usual classroom progression: warning, time-out, time-out in another classroom, office, and suspension. I strongly recommend that consequences (like all aspects of the contract) be individualized and tailored to meet the particular needs, motivations, and situation of the child and not be codified or turned into a formula. Some children lose control and hurt others because they are in the middle of a custody battle at home. Some can't stop themselves. A few intend to be bullies and assert their power. We need to do something about the behavior, whatever its source, but what we do must be contingent on who and why.

CONTINUING THE CONTRACT AFTER GOALS ARE ACHIEVED

FOR SOME STUDENTS, contracts turn out to be a way of life. One of my colleagues joked that when Joey graduated, he had more contracts than the Pentagon! It was only a mild exaggeration.

For children with poor internal controls, maturation brings new demands with each accomplishment. Will, at age thirteen, sat for the entire forty-five-minute literature class, attentive and involved, but the transition through the hallways inevitably meant some trouble: a teasing comment that was too strong, a shove that went too far. He needed a behavioral contract every year he was in school.

For others, the contract is unique and reflects one developmental issue or a needed change in attitude or performance. Vicki, at age eleven, entered sixth grade determined to be "cool" and to show that she wasn't the teacher's pet, as everyone said she was. So she tested her teachers at every turn with a full battery of sneering looks and begrudging motions. Despite the teacher's attempts to respond to the behavior with both humor and serious conversation, Vicki's attitude worsened. When her teacher found a note passed that included several insults, a contract was put in place.

Tina inaugurated her eighth grade year by wearing suggestive T-shirts, flaunting sexual talk, flirting in class with the boys, and affecting a bored indifference to her schoolwork. Attempts to talk to her were met with contempt, and attempts to ignore her were met with more flagrant displays. In a few weeks, after the contract was initiated, her behavior toned down, and after two months, the contract was discontinued.

It is important that teachers pass on information about contracts from grade to grade for children who rely on them for support. Even when students are eager to start the year fresh and plead not to be on a contract, we find that it is easier to begin the year with a contract and discontinue it later if it is unnecessary than to begin over again after a problem occurs. The former becomes a demonstration of success, the latter a statement of failure.

CONTRACTS SET UP BY "SPECIAL" TEACHERS

INDIVIDUAL CONTRACTS MAY ALSO be set up by gym, art, music, or computer teachers. Some students have a particularly hard time shifting to new adults or adjusting to different expectations. A behavioral contract set up by special teachers may also help to acknowledge and clarify shifting expectations and recognize the effort it takes to accomplish the changes.

The contract may also help children manage specific tasks and skills that are difficult or frightening in these arenas. The student who falls apart and makes scenes when expected to jog around the gym may be allowed to walk four days and choose one day to jog. The student who storms and stomps when asked to play a position she doesn't like in softball may be given ten seconds to "blow off steam" and then be expected to go into the game with a good attitude. She may earn a "bonus day" to make her own choice, or she may be allowed to help the coach set up positions for teams when she does reenter and exercise the self-control specified in the contract.

I observed an art teacher's arrangement with a student who loved art but hated clean-up. She was given points for beautiful care and clean-up of brushes (and her teacher set strict standards for a well-washed brush!), sponges, tables, and scraps. When she earned so many points, she was allowed to spend extra time in the art room. Though it took almost a month, this student earned her extra time and, in the process, improved her ability to complete a job.

SUMMARY

AN INDIVIDUAL CONTRACT can bring parents, teacher, and child together to work on improving a behavior problem. In crafting a unique contract with the involvement of the parents and the child, the teacher establishes goals for conduct that convey realistic expectations for improvement and helps the student achieve that improvement with different approaches and strategies. Offering a firm but matter-of-fact structure for expectations, a contract can dissipate the negativity that builds up after repeated reminders, nagging, and punishment.

Contracts state a goal and name a concrete marker that will be used daily to track progress. A special celebration is planned to recognize an agreed-upon number of markers, signaling that the goal is met. At the same time, teachers and parents can emphasize the internal motivations required and the immaterial rewards gained. At the conclusion of a contract, a new goal can be articulated, or a new contract addressing the same goal can be drawn up.

SECTION V
Clear Positives

Introduction

What the effective people did seem to share was a quality
I first thought of as moralism and later came to think of as moral
passion. There were no laissez-faire teachers; the good ones preached,
made demands and seemed to indicate that learning is a serious business.

JOSEPH FEATHERSTONE
Schools Where Children Learn

Parents [Teachers] must not only have ways of guiding
by prohibition and permission; they must also be able to represent
to the child a deep, an almost somatic conviction
that there is meaning to what they are doing.

ERIK ERIKSON
Childhood & Society

MY BEST TEACHING comes from my deepest convictions. I believe that we are all strongest as teachers when our convictions infuse our teaching—our arrangements with children, the lessons we teach, the topics we study, the priorities of our schedules, the ways we organize our furniture and materials. When we teach from a strong foundation of what we believe and value most, we insert what I call "Clear Positives" into the classroom.

Clear Positives are, first, a set of ideals or principles, phrased in positive language, that allow us to imagine and describe what it is we wish and hope to achieve. They are not necessarily complicated or many. Second, Clear Positives can provide a structure for making decisions. We have reasons for what and how we teach, reasons that need to be based on belief rather than on external pressures or curricular mandates.

The more we are able to translate our internal values into conscious and deliberate actions, the less susceptible we are to what is expedient or stylish—the short-term programs, flitting policies, and facile solutions. Teaching toward our ideals takes endurance and may involve years of consistent teaching. We need conscious and clear-sighted criteria to make the best decisions. Clear Positives and the decisions they inspire are open to examination, but they are strongly rooted in a few well-established ideals held with faith and belief. Our Clear Positives are made real for the children by what we teach—explicitly in our words, and even more strongly in the experiences we guide children toward within the classroom.

Today it feels odd, naïve, or overly ambitious to speak about our ideals in education. We live in a world scarred by attitudes of cynicism, resignation, and even blank despair. We have generations of young people defined by some as "spiritually empty." Critics point to the failure of the schools—faulty curricula, burned-out teachers, ignorant students. Teachers find their authority chiseled away, reduced by systemic mandates, state regencies, and mandatory high-stakes testing. From time to time, most of us ask ourselves, "Why am I teaching?"

It is essential that we have positive answers to that question. These most fundamental answers are what we need to overcome the mood of negation, to show our conviction that things do matter, that there is meaning to what we do in school.

My father was a person who could not properly fix anything that was broken— he could not change a lightbulb, hammer a nail straight into anything, or make a meal that didn't come directly from a cereal box. Yet I turned to him (as did many others) when the world needed fixing. Not that he actually fixed that either, but he breathed new life into us, a renewed sense of courage and hope. He listened with interest, he expounded with calm reason and informed opinions, he touched lightly with humor. He had an abiding belief in the goodness of life and of people, and an unquenchable human spirit. He made us feel good for asking. We turned to him when we needed fixing.

All children need some "fixing," and some need an inordinate amount to keep them exploring and "plugged in" to their world. We must find, nurture, and project our faith. It is our task to fuel the spirits of children as well as to direct their actions. By using Clear Positives, we hope to transmit our belief in life and in living.

The process of using Clear Positives provides models and expectations that are:

◆ Clear—These statements of our most fundamental values and beliefs provide direction for children and teachers; they may range from broad ideals to specific actions at specific times.

◆ Positive—The statements frame the world positively and appeal to the deeper interests of children and teachers; they do not proscribe or prohibit.

To use Clear Positives in the classroom, each teacher must begin at the beginning. Each individual must answer some basic questions: Why am I teaching? What is it that I truly want to teach?

Chapter 16 deals with finding those answers and forming them into a few basic ideals (which might also be called "values" or "principles"). These ideals can serve as a foundation for other teaching decisions and actions. Examples of applying Clear Positives to group activities are provided in Chapter 17.

The crayons

In some schools, children bring their own boxes of crayons and markers to school. In other schools, the crayons are part of the communal property of the classroom. I discovered in a teacher's workshop that the question of sharing materials raises many central issues. Do you have to share with everyone, or is it okay to share only with "special friends"? Here are some of the teachers' responses from the discussion that followed:

"If you make them share their markers with everyone, by the end of the day the markers are pretty much ruined. So I don't insist."

"Some kids don't take care of other kids' things. I guess we could apply a logical consequence here. If you're not careful with other people's things, you can't use them."

"I say if it's too precious to share, don't bring it to school."

"Sometimes kids use their property as currency. 'I'll let you hold this, then you have to pick me for your team. Okay?'"

"There is a real fine line between children sharing, being polite and friendly to other people, and their being able to respect their own space and have something that belongs to them. At what point do we stop telling children they have to let others use their things? We want to teach children to share, but don't we *also* want to teach them there's a part of themselves they have a right to?"

"What about the child who never remembers her own crayons and always wants to borrow? Or the child with whom no one shares— because no one likes her?"

This discussion illustrates the complexities of everyday life in the classroom. Sharing is one example of the constant struggle to balance the needs of community with the "rights" of the individual. On the one hand, sharing possessions or communal property helps create a friendly community and promotes generosity and a concern for the welfare of others. On the other hand, we also want to demonstrate respect for personal boundaries.

Whether we offer communal boxes of crayons or have private supplies, conflicts over sharing will occur. How we help children negotiate these conflicting needs is crucial. I believe that our message about sharing should be embedded in a larger message. The larger message is that cooperative living is necessary and desirable, and that interdependence is the norm rather than the exception.

Teachers can establish expectations and routines for sharing. For example, personal items such as souvenirs from a trip, remote-control cars, books, and new games can be brought to school to share with others. In most cases, the student remains in charge, a "teacher" of his/her property, using a few simple guidelines—how many in a sharing group, how long each person gets with the object, etc. But children don't internalize values by rigid enforcement.

In a first grade class, during what was supposed to be a quiet drawing period, a group of children waged a crayon battle. Usually the best of friends, they fussed no matter what agreement was reached in a moment of calm. Who had more crayons? Who hoarded the blue ones? Who had the box nearer to her/his side? Finally, the teacher divided the box into separate containers and insisted that they use only their own. It worked; the fighting stopped.

But after a short while, the teacher noticed that the single bins had mixed and all four were now in the center of the table as the children peacefully traded and shared. The expectation of peaceful sharing was accomplished with the reassurance of a safe boundary, the reassurance that each child *could* have his/her own bin of crayons. It was a time when collective life was secured by attention to the rights of the individual.

There are no perfect arrangements for the markers or crayons as we try to balance community and individual needs. What is most important is that we inspire children to struggle with us, to search for the best possible balance. ❖

I WOULD LIKE TO EMPHASIZE that using Clear Positives is not a process that is cut and dried, with clearly defined steps and neatly tailored categories. Teaching is more intuitive and infinitely more variable than it is mechanistic. But to teach with conviction, solve problems, and present a consistent approach to children's intentions and actions, we must know our roots. Ideally, each action and decision of every day in the classroom could be traced back to our ideals—our basic reasons for teaching.

Works Cited

ERIKSON, ERIK. 1963. *Childhood & Society*. New York: W.W. Norton.

FEATHERSTONE, JOSEPH. 1971. *Schools Where Children Learn*. New York: Liveright.

CHAPTER 16
Teaching by Clear Positives:
Revisiting Ideals

USING CLEAR POSITIVES ASSUMES that we have strong reasons for what we teach and how we teach it. Most people who become teachers have an initial vision of what they will add to the world through their teaching. This vision is often lost in the pressures, confusions, and constant demands that exist for every teacher in every type of school. But holding on to or remembering this primary vision, and translating it into a few ideals, is essential to teaching with joy and conviction.

Establishing and defining our ideals can help us assess our plans, goals, techniques, and strategies. Yet as we identify, define, and redefine our ideals, we don't want to concoct laundry lists of aims for student behavior. That would diminish and diffuse our focus. At the drop of an eraser, any self-respecting teacher can produce at least twenty worthwhile goals: We want our children to be self-motivated, independent, reliable, careful with their work, invested, kind, polite, inventive…on and on. I suggest instead that we begin by looking at a higher level, seeking the larger principles that individual behavioral goals support.

When I examine my own ideals, three have the most bearing on my teaching:

+ Schools need to teach alternatives to violence and to stress nonviolence as an essential characteristic of the community.

+ Children need to learn to think for themselves.

+ We need to stretch, not track, potentials.

My ideals are not prescriptive—other teachers might well have different ones. But I hope the discussion of my ideals will help readers reflect on their own. I hope it will help them assess their teaching in light of their ideals and use the notion of Clear Positives in their classrooms.

Teaching nonviolence

No school advocates the use of violence, but few would define non-violence as a core curriculum. I envision schools actively engaged in a curriculum of nonviolence. I do not see this commitment only as a disapproval of violent behavior or as extra units of social studies. Instead, I see it as a distinctive way of acting and thinking that permeates the entire school.

Part of a nonviolent curriculum is teaching children to take an interest in others' lives and in views unlike their own. This helps children to develop a fondness for diversity rather than a fear or hatred of it. Our daily routines can encourage this type of caring—Morning Meetings that focus on actively listening and responding, writing conferences where one student attends to the meaning of another, and the process of training children as peer writers.

We also teach nonviolence when we organize cooperative learning projects, class problem-solving discussions, and team play. When children work cooperatively toward a common end, they come to rely on and to value differences. "To construct cooperatively is to lay the foundations of a peaceful community," wrote Herbert Read in his preface to Sylvia Ashton-Warner's book *Teacher* (Ashton-Warner 1963, 11).

Some years ago, I visited Central Park East in New York City, one of the elementary schools started by Deborah Meier. It was the start of the day, and the sixth graders were working in small groups on numerous projects that included mapping countries in Africa, doing acid rain experiments, and making pottery. There was a feeling of easy occupation. In each small group, I saw children of color and white children, girls and boys together. In this city, a window on our country's racial and "have/have-not" tensions, here was a small society of young people creating maps and clay pots in utter collaboration and peace.

Children become conscious of differences spontaneously, naturally, and at an early age. Often it begins with recognition of physical differences within a group. The sixes notice that Jimmy stutters. They notice that Mark doesn't understand what their teacher says. They notice that Kimmy cries a lot. And they notice that Tara

limps when she runs. Children are excellent observers and predictable commentators. But acceptance of diversity has to be constructed.

We may need to help children make space in their game for a classmate who limps and remember to talk to another who is partially deaf. "When I play with her, she doesn't say anything, and she just follows me around," complains one child about a peer with a disability. So we encourage inclusion while also supplying tools to help children work with each other. Sometimes an ordinary scuffle deteriorates further, revealing racial or religious prejudices fueled by the prejudices in our society. This can be a critical moment for a focused display of indignation and righteous teacher wrath.

Barriers between groups of children are not always easy to dismantle, and they require deliberate and constructive teaching. There are now many anti-bias curricula for kindergarten through high school which teach appreciation for cultural diversity and foster attitudes that combat intolerance. A few examples of organizations that offer such curricula are Teaching Tolerance, a project of the Southern Poverty Law Center in Montgomery, Alabama; Educators for Social Responsibility in Cambridge, Massachusetts; and Brotherhood/Sister Sol in New York City.

I regularly do a simulation exercise that creates a group of outsiders and a group of insiders. Seventh and eighth graders assume a given role and quickly respond in character when they are excluded. For many, the resulting insight and growth make for a memorable moment, a highlight of their year.

Another approach teaches children to manage conflict. This is different from structuring situations to try to avoid conflicts or leaving children to find their own solutions. I strongly believe that conflict resolution should be integrated into the curriculum—a lesson should be stopped or postponed so that a conflict can be confronted and discussed. Children learn, largely by necessity, as we lead them in considering issues of justice and equity.

Exciting programs that teach children from third grade through high school to mediate their own conflicts have been started in many schools. Both teachers and students receive special training, and student mediators are called to mediate problems between peers and between teachers and peers. There are also students involved in governing councils and "fairness groups." (See Appendix B for more about conflict resolution in elementary schools.)

A group of sixth graders that I observed identified name-calling as the central problem of their class and one that they most wanted to solve. Their first solutions ranged from corporal punishment to "If someone calls names, they should have to stand up in front of the class and everybody call them bad names."

While many were nodding agreement, one lone girl asked, "Isn't that sorta the same thing, and maybe just as bad?" The dissonance effectively hushed the rash of ideas for penalties, but then there was silence. Most of the children still lacked the intellectual and moral development to move between two points of view, in this case the view of the name-caller and the view of the person called a name. They needed help from the teacher to stretch their potentials and explore workable plans.

Finally, I believe that we teach nonviolence by creating a model for children through the social arrangements of our school: the ways we treat each other; the priorities we give to social concerns and to a responsive, respectful environment; the opportunities for input into school government; the tone of the lunchroom, the playground, and the hallways; our willingness to open the doors of the classroom to include the problems outside it.

Children need to see us, the grown-ups, behave decently and with integrity. I say to one of my students, "I don't treat you like that. I don't make faces or put down your requests. I treat you with respect, even if I disagree with something you do. I expect the same." And if I have, in fact, treated this child with respect in spite of his boasts and aggravating snits, I claim his attention. He may also move a step closer to internalizing a basic respect for others.

In a world too full of violence, we need to teach nonviolence. Schools do not create or advocate violence, and our best efforts will not eradicate the violence within or without. But teachers and schools can help instill peaceful alternatives.

ENCOURAGING CHILDREN
TO THINK FOR THEMSELVES

I WANT CHILDREN TO LEARN to think for themselves, and schools to become places where children learn to take charge of themselves and their learning. Children can learn to derive meaning from a text. But more importantly, they can learn to derive meaning from their schooling, meaning which helps them direct their lives and make good choices.

We do this by passing on skills and knowledge, but even more, we do this by encouraging attitudes about looking, listening, and speaking with one's own voice. We can arrange for children to discover the answers rather than supplying them all ourselves. We can balance analysis with experience by providing hands-on activities, field trips into the community, and opportunities to be playful and inventive. We can help children learn to define choices and become decision makers in their own education.

I stress the ability to define choices and participate in decisions, but with caution. I remember working at our school's construction site as part of an untrained crew of teachers. We waited nervously at the first meeting, hoping to help in the remodeling of our new school building. I chose to work on clean-up. I realized how often

I had assigned such a job to a student, and how often I had become irritated when the student wandered, dabbled, and chit-chatted his/her way about the room. Yet here I found myself stumbling, aimless, and talkative. I began to realize that I had no idea what "clean" meant in a setting that was constantly producing debris and dust. What rubble didn't belong? What did? The whole was overwhelming, the parts almost imperceptible.

To be productive, to contribute, even to think about what needed to be done, I needed enough knowledge to focus. I finally got up the nerve to ask the person in charge what he meant by "clean." He started to give me a list. "No," I said, "show me." After he explained one part and was ready to move on to the next, I stopped him again, knowing that I would never retain more than one job at a time. Children also get lost in a landscape with too many possibilities, too little definition, and no place to start. Choices and decisions become random or disconnected. The confusion becomes painful, and there is often an anxious plea for order and direction. "Please, teacher, tell me what I do now." And too often, we respond by withdrawing the choices rather than teaching children how to make them.

Children are growing up in a world with frightful persuasions and terrifying problems. Rather than providing prescriptions for them, we need to give them choices. Decision making must be part of the expected curriculum. There are many kinds of purposeful choices students may make in a regular school day. Some are important but spaced irregularly: picking a topic for a social studies report, selecting a book to read, choosing a partner.

I think it's also important to schedule choices through a regular "choice" time. This is a period each day when students decide what they want (or need) to do, and then do it. They are expected to plan and then to carry out their plan. It is not a fringe benefit, an incentive to finish assigned work, or a Friday treat. It is part of each day's schedule. Choices may vary from day to day or be ongoing. They may be solitary pursuits or include small groups, and may involve serious or playful activities. But the choices need to be a child's own.

Children who are conditioned to expect easy or passive diversions may find it hard to make a plan of action or engage in it more than superficially. Some students are most idle and disruptive during choice periods. They cannot find diversion and engagement, so they bother others or wait for me to direct them. Others may flit from one activity to another or do the same activity over and over, repeatedly drawing the same picture, tracing the same maze, or playing the same games.

In order to break the pattern, we may need to flex the four walls of the classroom, as well as find ways to develop children's capacities for choice. I know that I sometimes don't see a child's true potentials. I know I need to be mindful in encouraging the choices that mobilize the most physically active students, the ones who spend hours shooting baskets. I need to provide opportunities for children to tinker and fix things, and for children to stare through a microscope. By offering choices, we begin the process of identifying varied strengths and interests.

My ideal is for children to act as decision makers in their own education. They can decide, in collaboration with teachers and parents, what they think is important to learn, and they can share responsibility for that learning. One approach, covered in Chapter 5, is the "Critical Contract." It begins with the question "What do you most want to work on this year in school?" There are other goals, of course, but this one is self-directed. If I want children to share responsibility for their learning, I must be prepared to help them locate their own objectives and not merely to mouth my own.

We can also help children define choices and make decisions on ethical and moral issues. A few decades ago, some schools used a program called "Values Clarification" to teach ethical thinking. Students were presented with contrived dilemmas and asked to imagine and discuss various solutions. The game "Scruples" has a similar popular appeal. Hypothetical, "what-if" games are absorbing, but most school days provide many *real* moral dilemmas for discussion.

Several pens are missing. The whispering voices have already indicted someone. "What should we do, class?"

Tony is missing his trip money. There is talk of stealing, and a scapegoat is emerging. "What do we do?"

No one wants to hold hands with Julie. Joshua is passing out secret stashes of candy in hopes of securing a friend. Andy cheats on a test. Only a few children dare to speak up during Morning Meeting. Some children can't get homework done at home, even if they want to, and need assistance from the class.

We need to seize these opportunities for discussion. Our classrooms can become places where children think about what they do, express popular or unpopular opinions, confront discrepancies and fallacies about things that matter. When we help children to think for themselves, we need to remember that they won't necessarily think the way we want them to think. Sometimes they suffer their own mistakes—and learn from them. Other times we must intervene. But at least they are thinking.

This type of thinking helps to build and sustain relationships—it helps create community as well as self-control. It is intimately connected to my first ideal— teaching nonviolence.

One teacher described a group of fifth graders as having "chewed up and spit out" lunchroom aides during the year. The principal warned that they were now on their third and last one. In a class meeting, the students asserted that the lunchroom aide could not "cope" with them. They detailed several problems precisely. But in the course of the discussion, they began to realize that they could "cope" with themselves in the lunchroom. They could monitor themselves instead of challenging their aides. Soon after, their behavior changed. "They aren't wearing halos yet," reported their teacher, "but we all see improvement."

In this case, the children didn't develop an exceptional scheme, but they got beyond blaming and excuse making. By naming the problem and giving it serious thought, they began the process of healing and change. Because they worked together, the bond between class and teacher grew stronger.

The process of discussing moral dilemmas also helps children use their capacities for critical thinking. They can better manage the natural rifts between students and between themselves and teachers, aides, parents, and principals. The school climate ultimately depends on these relationships. When we develop our skills as a community to solve our own problems, we forge and strengthen a unity of purpose that is too often fragile and elusive.

STRETCHING, NOT TRACKING, POTENTIALS

The development of a child's potential depends on the ability of the teacher to perceive the child's possibilities....

RUDOLF DREIKURS
Maintaining Sanity in the Classroom

OUR SCHOOLS ARE FULL OF WRITERS, painters, scientists, athletes, bread makers, fixers-of-things, and dreamers. This is what we seek to inspire as teachers. To inspire, we need to help our children *do* even what they don't do well.

We often set up what we call "ability groupings." We have our high and low reading groups, our fast and slow classes, our "gifted and talented," our "special needs." We sort and sift children into teams, glee clubs, and shops. It is not that our sorting is necessarily inaccurate, not that there aren't better and worse readers, singers, or ball players. It's that this screening process often depresses rather than elevates potential.

I recall a third grader once telling me with utter precision the skills (or lack of them) of every member of his class. He knew who could hit a fast ball, who was good at multiplication, who couldn't read, who could dance, who couldn't spell, who could fix zippers, and who was good at cutting things out. He knew who could write neat cursive and who got in trouble most. So did everyone else in the class. Clearly, there are wide differences in aptitudes and skills within any group, as any third grader will tell you in the most matter-of-fact way.

The question is whether these aptitudes are the best criteria to determine what we do and do not do. "We are all operating at about fifteen percent of our potential," wrote Dreikurs in *Maintaining Sanity in the Classroom* (Dreikurs 1982, 3). Psychologist Howard Gardner, in *Frames of Mind*, documents multiple kinds of intelligence, many of which are untapped in school (Gardner 1983).

When I observe in a kindergarten, I note the ease with which a single child will go to the easel, beat on the drum, race madly in a tag game, and solemnly recite a poem. As children get older, more advanced, and more mature, they often lose this global ambition for life. Their potential to enjoy a rich and varied life is limited. As children grow, there are external selection processes like ability groupings as well as an internal weeding—"I want to do what I do well. I like to do what I do well." We need to consider not just the external groupings, but also this internal weeding.

There seem to be key moments in the natural stages of growing up when the sense of self is especially vulnerable. The seven/eight-year-old stage in school may be one of them. Sevens, for example, are especially self-critical and worry that their work isn't perfect. They write and draw in the tiniest circumference, their upper body hunched over in a protective shield. And then they whip out an eraser to blot out the "awfulest" mistakes it would take a microscope to locate, "'cause it doesn't look right." Everything that can be erased *will* be erased to be done better. And by eight, the critical awareness extends to others. Children scrutinize and judge others' talents and skills, and rank themselves and others to form pecking orders. Suddenly the child who loved to draw or spend hours on a craft project stops. The reason? "I can't make houses look real," explained Darrell. "Drawing is dumb anyway."

Maggie returned from a pond field trip complaining that it was "too boring." Maggie, often the quick one in the class, wasn't quick at spotting salamanders, nor was she an intrepid searcher in mud banks and pond bracken. Mostly she watched, inactive. She was perhaps "needy" for the first time in a school activity and didn't know how to ask for help. Rather than allow her to withdraw and decide that she hated science, on the next trip her teacher prodded her in the art of turning over the rocks, poking her fingers into the ground, and cupping her hands to catch a frog. This time the trip was "okay."

Children—and adults—mistake ease of learning for the overall potential to learn. They confuse speed with facility. The product or end result is overrated, and the process is diminished. We are all so conditioned to pay attention to end products—the fluent reader, the superathlete, the finished cloth—that the stages of production seem almost invisible and beyond our patience. We need to show respect for the doing as well as the done, and for a slow and steady rate of acquisition. Children with learning problems, particularly, need to have the grit to struggle, to accept a slow and uneven gait of progress. The willingness to sustain effort and the courage to persist may be as important to achievement as any teaching methodology.

"I hate math!"

"I can't write!"

"I stink at soccer!"

These judgments, uttered emphatically by seven-, eleven-, and thirteen-year-olds, are all premature. Too often they represent only superficial exposure coupled with harsh competition and comparison. Too often they mask feelings of inadequacy and fear of failure. They become an excuse to avoid and withdraw from delightful and meaningful activities. As teachers, we need to struggle against these tendencies to narrow and constrict potential.

I rediscovered math as a teacher attending workshops and playing with manipulatives. I felt profound relief when I was able to manipulate fractions and understand ideas I had given up on long ago. I became a more lively math teacher because I was able to become an excited learner of math. I am not "good at math," not fast or particularly clever, but I am interested. I am not an accomplished runner or late-blooming tennis star, but I greatly enjoy jogging slowly in the early evening and playing intense tennis matches against "formidable" opponents! I believe it is more wonderful to play than to play well.

We can arrange our classrooms to stretch potentials and encourage participation. Here are some guidelines. We need to ensure:

+ **Availability**—Every aspect of our programs must be available to every child.

+ **Universal participation**—Every child participates. Block-building, sewing, and kickball are "have-to's." The expectation is that each student will do a careful observation of the cricket and that all classroom members will complete a story they want to publish.

+ **Support**—We must provide support systems and encouragement that sets realistic goals and emphasizes effort, progress, and fun.

+ **A responsive climate**—We must establish and protect a climate that cherishes diversity of input, mistakes, and peer teaching. Children teach each other, and cooperative learning is central to the classroom. The emphasis on cooperative (rather than competitive) learning does not blur differences in skill levels, but it provides for self-acceptance and acceptance of others as both learners and teachers.

It's also important to confront gender expectations as we stretch potentials. I remember watching my daughter's class play a soccer game. Every member of the class was on the team. Some had exceptional skills. Some could barely run the length of the field or kick a ball. A few lost track of the direction of the play. And the goalie, a strong but dyslexic boy, reversed his stance and sent the ball between his own posts. His team barely noticed. This motley crew was winning against a bigger and more selective team. They often did. There was a drive and spirit that sometimes seemed to compensate for a lack of skills, even in the competitive arena of sports.

As a mother of a soccer daughter, I watched with pride the beaming faces of the girls, their faces red with exertion, their chatter full of bodily complaints. But they held their positions and pushed their way down the field, standing their ground against boys often twice their size. Then they slumped down on the bench after the game, crying, "I was lousy but it was a great game."

A character in *Cat's Eye* by Margaret Atwood defines the world of girls:

I don't have to keep up with anyone, run as fast, aim as well, make loud explosive noises, decode messages, die on cue....All I have to do is sit on the floor and cut frying pans out of the Eaton's catalogue with embroidery scissors and say I've done it badly.

This mirrors what we too often hear from our girls. But given a push, girls develop the sheer exuberance of playing, whether they ever say they're good or not. It may be a long haul: there may be excuses, refusals to play in the games, a preference for standing and watching or chatting with buddies during recesses. Given a choice at age eleven, many girls today would still stay indoors and draw. It may be with reluctance that they slouch out for their first days of soccer practice. They will fuss about positions and detail a long list of bruises. But when their coach sends them out to play, they go.

I add one more example of ways teachers can stretch potentials. Jeff Phelps was a young intern in a classroom of eights and nines. He was a skilled craftsperson and often wore sweaters he had knitted or scarves he had woven. It was decided that he would teach the entire class to knit. The class, however, was at an age when girls and boys are reluctant to participate in tasks they consider not properly feminine or masculine. When Jeff announced his knitting project, there were many rounds of snarly looks and disgusted glances. Still, it was a "have-to," and Sean could tell his mom as he sat knitting in the kitchen, "The teacher makes us do it."

In a few weeks, everyone had completed a knitting bag big enough for two needles, and everyone knew a basic stitch. Soon they were busy with the "first draft" bookmark and were learning to chain-on by themselves. If they forgot, they could check the Knitting Tutor Chart to find a certified expert. The role of expert was new for Angie, who was used to getting, not giving, help. With remarkable patience and pride, she unknotted Donny's yarn, repaired his snarled stitches, and showed him how to coil the threads around his finger.

Soon, it was clear that it was not only the dexterous and nimble who took their knitting everywhere. I was surprised to see that Richie, who cried if he had to copy over lines of writing, would knit at every available moment. It became a room of knitters, complete with the clack of needles and the soft murmur of voices. For a final project, Jeff bound together twenty-five colored squares (which were only "kinda square") to form an afghan representing the work of twenty-five students. It was the centerpiece of the room, so that long after Jeff left the class, his knitters admired their handiwork and continued to turn out bookmarks, mini scarves, or just more and more squares.

When we see children extend and deepen their interests, test their patience and endurance, tackle what's new or different, we are stretching potentials. We are getting beyond the fifteen percent.

Years ago, the staff members of my school set a goal for themselves. The goal was to learn to do something new. My goal was to learn to speak in front of an audience. The first time, my talk was terrible—long, rambling, and tiresome. The second time it was better, and now I speak before parent assemblies and workshops with more poise, though still with apprehension and a dry mouth. It's not one of my favorite activities, but it does give me a sense of power. I believe this is true for children, too. We need to stretch, not track, their potentials.

SUMMARY

AS TEACHERS, WE NEED TO KNOW why we teach and why we do what we do in the classroom. I call these ideals or values Clear Positives—conscious and clear statements of belief that serve as foundations for our work as teachers. We need to begin our teaching by establishing these Clear Positives and using them as guidelines for our social arrangements and expectations for groups and individuals.

It's easy to lose sight of our ideals among the complex demands of every teaching day. If necessary, we need to go back and identify them again and again, recovering them from the piles of roll books, lesson plans, and report cards—the "stuff" that may shroud our earliest spirit and most compelling desire to teach. When we truly know these ideals, we can use them to guide the specifics of our classrooms. I know that we are all strongest as teachers when our ideals inform our teaching.

Works Cited

ASHTON-WARNER, SYLVIA. 1963. *Teacher*. New York: Simon & Schuster.

ATWOOD, MARGARET. 1989. *Cat's Eye*. New York: Doubleday.

DREIKURS, RUDOLF, FLOY C. PEPPER, AND BERNICE BRONIA GRUNWALD. 1982. *Maintaining Sanity in the Classroom: Classroom Management Techniques*. Second edition. Philadelphia, PA: Taylor & Francis, Inc.

GARDNER, HOWARD. 1983. *Frames of Mind: The Theory of Multiple Intelligences*. New York: Basic Books.

CHAPTER 17
Clear Positives in Action

CLEAR POSITIVES CAN BE A WAY to explain to students why we do what we do in our classroom. They may be introduced to the whole class or to small groups, and they may frame specific content or direct children's behavior. They can give purpose to the study of geography or explain the nature of rules. They can guide the outlook of individuals or groups, and they can create a sense of purpose or help to recover one that has been lost. They may be established during the first weeks of school or evolve midyear.

Using Clear Positives at this specific level can be challenging and frustrating but also very rewarding. When we use Clear Positives, we can communicate faith in our children's will and aptitude and belief in the value of a particular activity. To do that, we must find the fewest words to convey the proper message, and eradicate "don't's," "not's," and negative syntax. Clear Positives provide a sense of conviction and challenge but do not moralize or lecture. We define specific tasks we will help children accomplish and describe the attitudes we hope they will develop—for example, to show interest, to observe closely, to be careful or precise or more open-minded. In general, we frame the work in a larger context of positive achievement, and we specify actions that will help us get there.

A field trip

I was teaching a class of ten- and eleven-year-olds. We were studying the geography of our area in the Connecticut River Valley. I had planned an all-day trip with an outstanding local geologist as our guide. It was a beautiful day. Everything was set—except the children. As it turned out, they did not need a geologist. What they needed was a sheep dog to nip at their heels, herd them into a group, and keep them reasonably on track. They wandered, complained about sore feet, and were perpetually hungry. When our guide, pointing to the river, asked, "Why do you think a river bends instead of going straight?" I noticed that half the group wasn't even looking at the river, let alone wondering about its contours! Not only was I exhausted by the end of the trip, I was furious.

I spent much of the ride home contemplating tortures: I could make students write "I'll never wear new shoes on a trip again" 1,000 times; or "I promise never to use my whiny voice in school again" 10,000 times. Or I could never let them leave their desks. The prospects were endless! Luckily, for them and for me, by the time we got back to school, it was time to go home.

After a very long night's sleep, I returned the next day refreshed. I realized that my class had no clear expectations for managing a trip. They had rules for safety, and they knew to put their names on their lunches and stick with their partner (sort of). But they had no true purpose and only a vague understanding of mine. Except for a very few "natural" geologists, the students had no clear focus. Their attention was easily scattered, shifting from their stomachs to social conversations and back to their feet. And since they were not paying attention to anything consequential, they were, of course, bored!

I began again. I began by defining the purpose of these trips. I named it. It was a "field trip." A field trip, I explained, is a study that scientists and anthropologists—"Who knows what an anthropologist does?"—conduct in the field, rather than in the laboratory. "Why is it important," I asked, "to study things 'in the field' rather than at your desk or from a book or a video or a computer?"

"To see things up close."

"To see for yourself."

"To know what is really there."

From continuing discussion and questions, we concluded that a field worker gets up close to find out answers to particular questions. We agreed that the questions might be very general, such as asking what is in the field, or specific, such as "Why do rivers change their course?" We defined the job of the field worker: to gather information. "What skills do you need when you go into a field that are different from desk work?" We decided the skills of the field worker were many. Children talked about observation, collecting, asking questions. These evolved into our Clear Positives for field trips:

- We are doing field work, which is work that many kinds of scientists need to do.

- The job of the field worker is to ask an interesting question, something s/he really wants to find out.

- To find out what they want to know, field workers need to observe, listen carefully, take notes, and be interested in the field.

We never went on another field trip without Clear Positives. The "ticket" for admission to a trip became "an interesting question," something each student wanted to find out. "No question, no ticket, no trip."

I considered an "interesting question" anything that showed a desire to know one thing. Not all children started off curiously or with a true question. Some questions were mechanical. But curiosity is contagious, and they began to learn from each other's questions as well as from the exercise of thinking up their own. On a general level, it was the curiosity which I hoped they would develop. The question would give the curiosity focus. The two together would animate and enliven their work.

Most children were more focused and prepared for the second field trip. They at least pretended to attend and listen. But the "pretend listening" led to sharing questions, spotting things in their environment, catching the contagion of discovery. Midway, I heard Justin exclaim, "Hey, this is interesting," as he ran off to locate an ancient mud ball hidden in rock. As our guide complimented the students on their day's work, noting their attention and involvement, I was once again struck with how important it is to pay attention to—and teach—behavior. In this case, it was the behavior of interest.

One of my Clear Positives is that I want children to find their world interesting, even more interesting than the latest TV sequel. Many of the "interested field workers" became more-interested students—prodding, probing, looking, and listening. ❖

WHEN SOMETHING ISN'T WORKING IN A CLASSROOM, it is often a signal to reconsider the Clear Positives. Here are a number of examples of Clear Positives and their use in various classrooms and content areas. They all deal with using Clear Positives to develop group expectations for academics or for social skills and routines.

A READING GROUP

A GROUP OF NINE-YEAR-OLDS gathers, waiting to begin the first reading group of the year. The teacher asks, "Why do you think we need to have a reading group this year?"

"To learn new words?"

"To learn to read harder books?"

"To read things like mysteries."

"So you know if we read?"

The teacher acknowledges each of these responses and writes them on the board. She begins the discussion of the responses with "learning new words." "Words with many syllables," she adds, writing the word "literature" on a chart. The children take turns trying to decode the word, as the teacher exposes one syllable at a time. She tells them that they will learn ways to figure out some long words. She then informs them of a second task. They will also learn meanings for new words. That's called "vocabulary," she tells them, and adds that word (syllable by syllable) to the chart, giving time for the group to spell phonetically. "Does anyone know where to go to find out what a word means if you don't know for sure?" One student suggests a dictionary, and the children go off to locate one in the room. Upon examination, they agree it's pretty heavy and might have at least 50,000 words. Soon, the students understand that they will be learning new words and trying to discover what they really mean by using a dictionary. Another new word is written on the chart.

Then the teacher goes back to the original survey of what they expect to learn in reading group. She agrees that they will be reading more books. "Someone mentioned mysteries. Is that a kind of book you like?" she asks, eliciting other kinds of books. The group responds with titles rather than categories, and there is a flurry of excitement as they recall and compare favorites.

"You know you will learn new vocabulary, use a dictionary, and read more books, but there's still one more *special* thing I want this group to accomplish." The teacher carefully pauses, building a little suspense and anticipation.

"For our *literature* group," shifting the name from a reading group to literature, "I want Book Talk," she trumpets.

"Huh?"

"What's Book Talk?"

"Books don't talk!" someone adds wittily.

"I want this group to have conversations about books," says the teacher. She goes on to discuss what conversations are and what it means to talk about books.

She tells them about book clubs where people share "book talk." She weaves in a connection between the purpose of this group and a way that books carry over into the world. She wants to emphasize an interest in reading and a community of readers. She is concerned that although these children have reading skills, they do not read for pleasure.

"Every week, we will have conversations about the books we are reading together. We will talk about what we think is happening in the story, or what you have found out about a new character. By the end of the year, I hope you will like having book conversations enough that you will talk not only during our groups, but at lunch, or even on the way to the bathroom. Once, I remember telling some students to be quiet because they were disturbing the class, and they said, 'But we were just talking about books!' Boy, was I in trouble!" The group laughs, their eyes twinkling, imagining getting their teacher in such trouble!

DOING WHAT SCIENTISTS DO— ELLEN DORIS

ELLEN DORIS, a teacher at Greenfield Center School for many years, initiated all science groups, whether with fives or thirteens, at the start of each year with the question "What is it that scientists do?" Her masterful book *Doing What Scientists Do* gives detailed accounts of the different ways children reply to this question across the ages (Doris 1991). The answers of the youngest children are literal and specific:

"Scientists look at things."

"Scientists make pictures of tigers."

"Scientists find bones."

As children get older, they say that scientists discover, experiment, conduct research in laboratories, and search for medical cures or planetary life. Whatever the level of sophistication or prior knowledge, the next step is the same:

"Well, right now, you're going to do some science work, and here's where we're going to start. Scientists look at things."

She quickly establishes a connection between the work the children will do and the work that scientists do. The purpose of the group is to do the work of scientists. As young scientists, the children will learn to observe, question, experiment, record, and see inconsistencies and errors (much in the same way as they construct meaning as they grow).

"What would scientists do," she asks, "if one scientist thought that crickets have four ears and another thought that crickets don't have any ears?"

When some eight-year-old scientists complain that they are tired of observing the pond critters, they are reminded, "Do you know that there are some scientists who spend their whole life just studying one thing? They only study insects or even just one kind of bug. What could they be finding out, looking at one bug over and over?"

To name the students as scientists gives particular meaning and focus to their work. It helps to define the process of learning as the process of scientific method. For Ellen Doris, it is a way she can help children develop respect for a method of acquiring knowledge that she believes "empowers scientists to solve new problems and find out new answers to new questions." This simple Clear Positive expresses a central faith—that there is indeed an interesting world out there and that children have access to that world.

A BEGINNING THEME STUDY

JAY LORD'S SEVENTH–EIGHTH GRADE CLASS is preparing to study the rain forests as a year-long thematic project. They will be investigating many different areas, from weather and climate to cultures and world markets. They will do their own research, share readings, and build models. In the end, they may organize a student conference or raise money to contribute to an international children's campaign to save the rain forests. Intellectually, these children are ready for thinking on a global scale; socially, they need frequent reminders to hang up their own book bags. Their teacher sees a connection. In fact, he believes strongly that we must all find connections between what we profess and how we choose to live our lives. He wants to communicate that connection to his students. He starts their rain forest study with the following assignment:

"You cannot begin to take care of the rain forest until you begin to take care of your own classroom. I want each of you to think of a project that you would really care to do that would help improve or maintain our school."

This was a group of industrious and competent adolescents, who often left trails of discarded clothing, remnants of food supplies, and clutters of papers and books behind them. They were now thoughtful. A few had immediate ideas. Some wanted to improve the bathrooms; some wanted to add plants, provide better containers, hang pictures, keep the school tidy and pretty. Someone suggested a recycling project, someone else a mural. Another wondered if it would be possible to vacuum the rug.

The response was different from the usual blank nods given the usual clean-up lectures. There was a call to action, an enthusiastic commotion—the connection

had been made. Many went to work right away; others began to assess their space. It was suddenly "their space." They had a task that demanded a responsible interpretation. What would it mean to improve and maintain? The teacher also asked that students submit a proposal, explaining and defending their project to the class, telling how or why it would work. In one case, a proposal for a loft interfered with student storage space. There were intriguing debates, and a compromise was reached.

The effectiveness of this Clear Positive—that students would connect global philosophy with local or personal action—was its ability to merge action and reason.

A GROUP OF MOODY SEVENS

MY CLASS OF SEVENS, in second grade, was becoming quarrelsome and cranky. Getting in line for a drink of water, making room in the circle for everyone, sharing pattern blocks, playing a game all involved minor but persistent irritations. I heard frequent complaints and tattling. The mood of the room was unfriendly and uneasy. I knew the tendency of sevens to be moody and negative, and did not expect the exuberance of sixes or the effusiveness of eights, but I didn't like the tone of the class.

I was also troubled by my own tone, which was becoming increasingly cranky and impatient. After contemplating the schedule and the curriculum, I was reasonably sure that the pressures were not programmatic. The routine seemed secure, the transitions were working smoothly, the academic pace seemed challenging but not severe. It wasn't near Halloween and it hadn't been raining for a month. No. The social tone of the room needed to be improved. The group needed a "stretch."

I began by sharing with the class at our daily Morning Meeting what I was observing. I started with the positive things: the way I see children follow the routines, take care with their work, do a beautiful job with their science observations, come to meeting so efficiently.

"I see lots of good things happening in this class. There is *one* thing that is bothering me now—something I notice that doesn't feel very good to me. I see people shoving each other to get to the water fountain first; I see people saving places in line for their buddies and not being fair; I see people making faces when they circle up and fussing about hand-holding; I hear tattling; I see unhelpful helpers, telling each other in rude ways when something is wrong.

"Raise your hand if you see some of these things, too. I'm not blaming anyone. I think we all do it. I know I'm feeling cranky, too, and then I snap at people. You might remember a time this week when you thought your teacher was grumpy. Perhaps we all have gotten a bit too grumpy. I wonder if someone has an idea about what gets them grumpy?"

Seeing the nodding heads, I knew that everyone had a grumpy story. I went around the circle collecting grumpy tales, but making sure that the focus and tone of this discussion was personal—in the "I voice"—not blameful. The grumpy narratives were spirited and amusing, and they relieved tension in the group. The children identified with and reveled in each other's tales: rushing in the morning (anything short of an hour per sock is a rush!), waking up too early, having to eat the wrong cereal, not being able to find the paper you know you put just so. After everyone related at least one incident, hands were still waving madly. The subject was far from exhausted. I remembered Gesell's characterization of this age in *The Child from Five to Ten* as "inwardized," given to periods of worry, fear, and self-absorption (Gesell 1977). I would often greet one of my students, Lucy, with a "Good morning," and she would often respond, "What's good about it?"

In order to continue the discussion, it was not important to exhaust this theme of grumpiness but to focus on improving the tone of the classroom. I wanted to move on, saving further narratives for art or writing or other discussions.

"We all do get grumpy, I see. And when we're grumpy, we aren't always so polite or nice or friendly. I may be grouchy because my alarm didn't ring, and then I yell at my son to hurry up. And it wasn't his fault at all, was it? It sounds like you do that, too." They respond with lots of nods!

I then state my Clear Positives. "I want this to be a friendly classroom. We spend so much time together in this classroom. I want it to be a place that feels friendly. I want to feel that I like to be here. I want to feel that this is a good place to do my work. It's not easy to work in a place that is cranky and grumpy. How can we make *our* classroom a place where we like to work, and still know that sometimes we might feel grumpy?"

At this point, the children offered a number of ideas. Many had to do with *not* doing the things I had listed—not saving line spaces, not pushing to get water, not making faces.

I write the suggestions on a chart. "So we will agree to hold only our own places on line. We will wait patiently for the water, and Jimmy suggested that people shouldn't push to be first." I had automatically rephrased most of the "not-do's" into "to-do's," but I still wanted a more positive framework.

"We talked about a number of things not to do, a number of good plans to help with the grumpiness. What do we do if we want to act friendly?" It was easier to elicit antidotes to grumpy than examples of friendly. "When Kevin comes into the classroom and I ignore him, am I grumpy?" I role-play shuffling my papers.

"Am I friendly?"

"Why not?"

"Well, you are just working. You didn't look at Kevin or say anything."

"What could I say?" To emphasize the point further, I ask Kevin to pretend that he is just coming into school with his lunch box, and I act out sitting at my table and ignoring his entrance. The drama captures the children and helps each to identify with Kevin, creating an emotional reality.

"Show me," I demand. "What would you do that is friendly?" Different children now act out a friendly greeting. From the passive response, phrased as a negative— a "not-to-do"—we are now thinking about active ways to generate friendly responses. The discussion has moved a long distance. I want to continue with other ways to respond actively later, but I don't want to dilute the message or overwhelm the children now. I like their enthusiasm and want to make sure to preserve the mood. The meeting needs closure.

"I like the good ideas you already have about making our room feel more friendly. If we try hard to do that, I also think it will make our work site safer. We talk about a safe work site in blocks or outdoors. But we can make it safe for our feelings, too. And sometimes I know we will forget. But what happens when we forget? Will you yell at me or tell me in a mean voice that I am supposed to follow the rules? Suppose Julie says 'Good morning' to me and I don't hear her or forget to stop my work, what will you say?"

"I'll say it again."

"I'd say, 'Good grumpy morning.'" Everyone laughs and repeats a sing-song of "Good grumpy morning!"

"Let's see if tomorrow we can remember friendly greetings. Thank you for such a good meeting."

TRANSITION TIMES

NANCY WEBSTER had twenty-eight third graders. "This is an extremely volatile class. Any part of the day that can go smoothly is valuable," she observed. The class had a particularly hard time making transitions from one activity to another. It was a clear issue, as her class exhibited the outgoing behavior that often characterizes eight-year-olds.

"Voices become very loud, students are visiting and not getting ready for the next activity." She also noted, after observing closely, that children were using the five-minute transition times to finish work and then, at the last second, shoving papers back into their desks, wrinkling or tearing them, or burying them in a heap. The system of filing that she had carefully instituted to help them order and preserve their work was useless. It took more time to search for the missing sheets or redo the ruined ones, which created further disorientation.

The transition time also revealed another product of their vigorous social agendas. The children who scurried most during transitions were making up for scattered work time. Instead of working, many had been gabbing. When the signal to end the period was sounded, there was a sudden frantic spurt as the short transition time turned into the work period!

Nancy focused on Clear Positives for better transitions in her class. "These children are just beginning to see the importance of organization and thinking and planning for themselves. This is one time of the day [transition] when they can exercise their new-found and developing skills."

In this goal, Nancy identified an exciting and profoundly affirmative prospect—to help children learn to think and plan and organize for themselves. Suddenly, the task of transitions assumed a more-than-mechanical purpose. It is not simply a physical shift from one activity to another. Transitions also entail problem solving and critical cognitive skills, such as anticipation, category making, concentration, and self-control. The recognition of learning processes embedded in the routines (or procedures) of our classrooms helps us teach children the skills and attitudes they need.

Nancy's procedure for working on transitions with her class began with a discussion. Transition time was defined. Expectations were clarified. A goal was declared—Efficient Transitions. The things the class would need to accomplish in order to meet the goal were established:

1. Transitions will take place in five minutes.

2. Papers will be put in proper folders and put away.

3. Appropriate folders for the next activity will be taken out.

4. Any other materials will be readied.

5. Pencils will be sharpened.

6. Quiet talking can take place within a group (if everything else is completed).

7. Safe stretching next to the desk is a good idea.

The class demonstrated "Efficient Transitions." Their teacher circulated and reinforced positives. Quiet talking, safe stretching, even "efficient" pencil sharpening were modeled repeatedly by teacher and students. Over the next weeks, everyone paid careful attention to transitions. They would stop and discuss transitions—what worked and what problems they or she noticed. The group took on the challenge. They enjoyed seeing their transitions become peaceful and effective. Their teacher observed that instead of prodding one another to mischief, they influenced each other in a positive way. She wrote in her journal:

I am sure that if children know what is expected from them, if they see it as reasonable and attainable, they will not only work hard for it themselves, but will try to help other students to do the same. A student telling another student to hurry up or speak more quietly is usually more powerful than an adult telling the same thing.

Over the past few weeks, the students have become increasingly more adept at calm transitions. My movements around the class have become punctuated by more "I like what I see" and "I like the way you…" than questions about "What should you be doing?" I feel good about this because we now have more time, and I have a few seconds to exchange a word or wink or hug with the kids. We still struggle with some students all the time, but now the students are helping me in the struggle. It is something we are all working on together in a positive way.

Figure 17.1 presents some Clear Positives in forming group expectations for content and routines.

....

FIGURE 17.1

Guidelines for Using Clear Positives in Forming Group Expectations

+ Make clear your goals for content groups and classroom routines.

+ Recognize the learning process embedded in the routines.

+ Discuss goals and strategies for implementation with children.

+ Carefully model the behavior and attitudes you wish to teach.

+ Continue to observe and reinforce effort and success.

+ Use extra time to exchange words and give hugs.

+ Remember to work together in a positive way.

+ Realize that some children will continue to struggle, and recognize the steps—baby steps or giant ones—that mark growth.

....

TEACHING CHILDREN TO CARE

HOMEWORK EXCUSES

A NUMBER OF CHILDREN in the math group had not done their homework. Actually, one student had done it, but forgot he had done it until he started to do it all over again! It was only the second month of school, and already the excuses came more quickly than the computations—and probably took more time.

"I forgot."

"You didn't tell me that."

"I didn't understand."

"I was late and my mom was rushing and…"

"I had practice and got home too late."

"My dog ate it."

This is a math group of ten sixth grade students. They are usually motivated and excited about their math. They like a fast pace and enjoy challenging tasks. Everything goes fine until they are asked to appear a day later with work in hand. Somewhere between leaving their seats and the next morning is a black hole.

"What do I do?" I wondered. If I send some of them out of the group to finish their work, then they miss instruction time and won't understand the next section. Should they have to miss something else to get the homework done? Is homework a reasonable expectation at this age? Should we make more time during the day instead of expecting them to do the work after school? What will we do? Everything in their day is important.

Clear Positives, which recall a sense of purpose and give direct strategies, needed to be reformulated. Did these students understand the reason for homework, other than as a system for capricious adults to torment children? Did they possess effective study skills for getting independent work done at all? Closer observation suggested that the students had little notion of purpose, but more importantly, they lacked independent work skills.

Generally, the purpose of homework is to reinforce skills and help children internalize ideas through guided assignments. It is contingent on independent work habits as well as academic competencies. The goal of independent work, similar to that of transitions, involves learning to plan, organize, and think for yourself. In group lessons, the teacher provides that structure. When we ask children to work on their own, they must be able to supply the structure. I decided to try a paradoxical response with this group. I do not think it would work every time, but it helped illuminate the Clear Positives emphatically for the students.

I took away the homework. I told them that from all the lame excuses and poor work, I understood that they weren't ready for homework; therefore, no homework. There would still be assignments, of course, but they would need to do them with supervision. Homework, I began to explain, was a "step up," a sign that they had mastered "not the content, but the challenging task of independent work." I also imported the image of a driving license as a proof of basic driving techniques. I wanted them to be "road tested" in homework before any more work would be permitted outside of school. (My colleague Chip Wood uses the metaphor of "climbing the mountain" as a way for fifth and sixth graders to understand the increased expectations.)

I explained that independent work in school or as homework consists of three processes:

- Planning

- Organizing

- Thinking for yourself

We worked together to define each of these terms.

Planning

WE ASSOCIATED PLANNING with anticipation and thinking ahead. The students differentiated "thinking work" from "busywork," deciding that the first was harder for them. Planning also involves decisions about what is needed—materials, time, and space.

Organizing

ORGANIZING INVOLVED ORDERING THE PHYSICAL SPACE, and then ordering the steps in the task. Children first need to organize a physical work space. Sometimes it is physical organization that is a problem—how materials are shelved or stored (scattered or carefully replaced and contained), how the important notebook or book gets home for homework, and how it gets returned for school.

Second, there is the task of organizing one's own concentration and attention effectively, which may also be affected by the physical space—lighting or noise.

Third, the work process may need to be consciously ordered into steps. What do I do first? I have seen many a child flounder for want of a starting place, a way to home in or narrow down. There are many different strategies to fit a range of styles—highlighting, key words, lists, verbalizing, webbing, outlining, and more. Some children verbalize, saying things aloud to themselves or to a partner: "This is what I will do." Others sit still and quiet, and then there is a flurry of work. Some work in spurts, others in a stream. Some work and walk, others talk and work, others prefer a solitary cave. We need to help children find their optimal arrangements and self-generating strategies.

Thinking for yourself

THIS INCLUDES INTERPRETING DIRECTIONS, understanding questions, solving problems, and applying information in different ways. Children need to be able to read and grasp directions. They need to be able to differentiate the aspects of a task they already know from what they need to find out. Often they need to make a number of different kinds of judgments and decisions. For example, they need to know whether a question requires retrieving information or drawing an inference from what they already know.

Thinking for yourself does not mean that you work alone or without input from others. An important part is the ability to formulate questions. The questions may point you toward asking for certain kinds of help or toward directing your own inquiry. When we know where to go for information, when we know what information we need, we work with confidence. It's not answers that give confidence, it's the ability to ask useful questions, again and again. Children need to practice asking questions and locating multiple sources of information—teachers, parents, books, peers, themselves.

AFTER DEFINING THE WORDS "planning," "organizing," and "thinking," we made a list of the features of each one, using the students' own words. I suggested that each student assess his/her own performance for each type of task. (See Figure 17.2.) It was interesting to find, when the personal evaluations were done, how many students had difficulty with physical space—losing things, forgetting assignments or books—but felt confident about their thinking skills.

FIGURE 17.2

Sample Homework Skills
Self-Evaluation Sheet

Rate 1–5   1 = Most needs improvement   5 = Mastery

1. Planning

_____I anticipate what I have to do for homework.

_____I know my assignments.

_____I remember to bring my books and papers from school.

_____I remember to return books and assignment papers.

2. Organization

_____I organize my work space.

_____I organize my materials. (I know where they are; I take care of them.) I am able to organize the steps and parts of a problem. (I know what I need to do first, second, and third. I complete my work.)

_____I show good attention for a sustained work time.

3. Thinking for myself

_____I read and understand directions.

_____I am able to locate information.

_____I think about what I need to find out.

_____I know how to get help from other people.

_____I know how to use other references.

_____I can generate new ideas using what I know.

Signed: _____

NO HOMEWORK WOULD BE ASSIGNED until each student demonstrated proficiency with assignments in school. The issue was important enough for us to rearrange the schedule, to make time for what I called, with great originality, "study hall." Study hall was a forty-five-minute period when everyone brought one assignment to work on. Students would be supervised, but given assistance only if they asked. It started with each student arranging two storage units for her/himself: one to use in class and the other (a book bag or knapsack) for transporting work. Second, each student had to identify the assignment s/he was going to work on and produce a plan (see Figure 17.3) that included:

+ The assignment

+ The materials to do the work

+ Attention requirements—would students need to talk about their assignment or work on their own?

+ Space and amount of time needed

+ The possible use of headphones, short breaks, etc., to help completion

· ·

FIGURE 17.3

Sample Assignment Planning Sheet

Name: _____ Date: _____

Plan

My assignment is: _____

I will need the following materials:

_____   _____

_____   _____

I will need to:

☐ work alone   ☐ work with others (names: _____)

My work space will be:

☐ solo desk   ☐ group table   ☐ rug   ☐ other: _____

This assignment will take about _____ minutes.

If my attention wanders, I will _____ .
(use headphones, take a short break, etc.)

Questions

For myself: _____

_____

For my teacher: _____

_____

For classmates: _____

_____

Results

Rate 1–5   1 = Poor   5 = Excellent

_____ Attention (staying on task)

_____ Organization (choosing good work space; having correct materials; following directions)

_____ Thinking (solving problems; doing careful work; using good ideas)

Comments

I feel good about _____

I had problems with _____

••

DURING THE FOLLOWING WEEKS, I regularly asked, "Did your plan work? Was it helpful?" During this period, children became more aware of their own needs and abilities to organize themselves. My next step was to provide less supervision. I did not circulate about their "hall"; I did not redirect students who wandered; I did not monitor the noise level or offer words of encouragement. I read my own book, stepped out of the room, took care of other business. Some students saw this as an invitation to shift their attention, talk to friends, or stare out of the window. Others kept on with their work. Most saw a direct correlation between their efforts to stay on task and the amount of work completed. While some students would still need the encouragement and support of an external structure, most exerted the inner control needed to stay focused. These children were ready to become "certified homeworkers." They were graduated from study hall.

While I wanted children to feel the achievement of taking on new responsibility, I also wanted everyone to accept the process for developing skills. Study hall was not a punishment or a sign of teacher disfavor. I had to be sure that this "experiment" was seen as a learning exercise, not as a detention. Two keys were my tone and the use of a student self-evaluation.

My tone stressed my own mistake as a teacher, and my desire to help them learn critical skills before they got to high school. It was presented as a common endeavor.

The self-evaluation enabled children to pinpoint some of their own weaknesses—such as becoming distracted or not putting away materials properly—and to identify areas that needed improvement. It also reinforced the positive spirit, which transferred to their work and to one another. There were nice reminders and many cheerleaders. When Debby left her folder on the table as she scurried to another activity, a classmate reminded her. When one day, weeks and weeks after we had begun this campaign, all children in the entire class remembered their homework, a roaring cheer erupted. It was a genuine burst of joy for a job well done.

I do approach homework with one caution. I am not convinced that homework always serves elementary children well as a way to acquire independent study skills. There are children who tell us frankly that their home life is too tumultuous for schoolwork. Other children, weary of school, need the time for vigorous play or relaxation. I don't think a responsible educational approach is implemented through an arbitrary homework policy. We need to assess the readiness of students for homework and of their families to support them, and also consider the children's needs for recreation, play, and family time. At the same time, helping children to plan, organize, and think through independent assignments is a vital feature of the curriculum.

SUMMARY

CLEAR POSITIVES PROVIDE A SENSE of conviction and challenge, but they do not moralize or lecture. They are clear—on a general or specific level—and are always stated positively. We want them to clarify a sense of purpose and give children an understanding of the reasons for their work. We can define specific tasks we will help children accomplish and describe attitudes we hope they will develop. Using Clear Positives helps us communicate our faith in children's will and aptitude, and our faith in the value of their work.

Works Cited

DORIS, ELLEN. 1991. *Doing What Scientists Do*. Portsmouth, NH: Heinemann.

GESELL, ARNOLD, FRANCES L. ILG, AND LOUISE BATES AMES. 1977. *The Child from Five to Ten*. Revised edition. New York: Harper and Row.

CONCLUSION

....

Authentic Teaching

We were never the carriers of our own stories. We never
trusted our own voices. Reforms came, but we didn't make them.
They were invented by people far removed from schools—by "experts."
Such reforms bypassed the kind of school-by-school changes,
both small and structurally radical, that teachers and parents
might have been able to suggest—changes that, however slow,
could have made a powerful difference.

DEBORAH MEIER
"Good Schools Are Still Possible"
Conflicts and Constituencies *(Fall 1987)*

I CONCLUDE WITH THE IDEA OF AUTHENTIC TEACHING, which is central to every approach, technique, and guideline in this book. Change and reform, as Deborah Meier stated, need to reflect real issues identified by those who experience the daily activities and events of school life—parents, students, teachers, and principals. And real change, she went on, needs the specific and detailed insights and perspective that teachers can offer, concrete and practical changes rather than the broad, general, often vague changes that policy makers favor (Meier 1987).

This book is one teacher's telling, but it is really a collage of many teachers' stories. It is dedicated to the concrete change, the "detailed specificity" that comes from the perspectives and voices of real teachers teaching in real classrooms. It assumes that teachers are skilled and knowledgeable, and that they need to regain more control over their curriculum and their workplace. Teachers need to be able to decide what they want to teach, when, and for how long—freed from a manic pace and a cluttered day mandated by those far from the classroom. They need to be able to make critical decisions and give voice to the central concerns of their children.

Teachers currently have few choices. Budgets, schedules, standards, and curricula are imposed, often by state regents or invisible bureaucrats who never see or meet the teachers or children they are supposed to serve. Few teachers even have a tiny "slush fund" to go out and buy a ten-dollar paperback on King Arthur or Wilma Rudolph for that child who needs a special recognition.

But teachers have also let choices slip away by being afraid to advocate for their children or for themselves, uncertain of their own knowledge and rights. To use every bit of their power, teachers must acknowledge their authenticity—they must be empowered by confidence in their own perceptions and values. When we are able to infuse our teaching with the dynamic force of our perceptions and values, we teach with strength and resounding voices—we teach authentically.

Teaching is an extension and projection of a person, not just transplanted skills or acquired methods. Every day we reveal ourselves—our manners of organizing, habits of dealing with frustration, entrenched patterns of thought and interest. Just as we aim to teach the whole child by responding to affective as well as intellectual development, so we aim to teach from the whole teacher—the cognitive, social-emotional teacher. The inner resources of the teacher register deeply in the climate of the classroom and the consciousness of the students. Schools as they currently exist often stultify and stunt the passions and dedication of their teachers, battering them into indifference and silence.

If teaching is to be infused with conviction and joy, the best hopes and creative powers of teachers need to be nourished. In the last fifteen years, I have met with many teachers in workshops across the country. There are some who come only because it is required by their system or for the credits that affect income differentials and promotions. But so many others attend out of sincere interest in their work. They are a mix of all types of teachers, young and old, new and experienced, from public and private schools. I particularly recall a group of teachers in Maine, sitting in a warm, dusty classroom, two days after the end of their school term. They were full of humor and laughter, eager to learn a new way to do science or blocks only days after school let out in June. Whether their hands were covered with "oobleck" or they crouched on the floor erecting sturdy buildings, their stamina and exuberance for teaching were apparent and contagious.

How do we hold on to that exuberance? How do we keep it at the center of our teaching? It is certainly an essential resource for our children, and it can't be falsified.

I believe it will survive and prosper where there is permission and potential for authentic teaching and for authentic teachers to teach.

To teach authentically, we must accept the realities of teaching and of who we are—including our limitations, our frailties, our mistakes. One of the hardest things to get used to as a teacher is being observed by parents, visitors, and supervisors. It is hard because we reveal so much. I recall the first time I had a lesson video-taped so that I could study it to discover things about my children. Instead, I watched myself. I noticed the hard set to my jaw, the excessive use of my hands, and the way my hemline rode up over my knee. When we teach, we reveal far more than a lesson plan. We reveal aspects of our deepest selves. We reveal our vulnerabilities, whether we want to or not. One masterful teacher wrote in his journal, soon after an observation, "I have met the enemy and it is me!" He wanted to give his fifth grade students more responsibility. He needed to combat his natural inclination to direct and explain—he would have to learn to "bite his tongue."

As a child I would sometimes dream that I was naked in a crowded room. As a teacher, I dream that I am shorn of all power in a room crowded with children who run around despite my cries to be seated. As authentic teachers, we must accept that the practice of teaching is one which often leaves us semi-dressed. Just when everyone is watching (and often when no one is), everything goes wrong. Our best plans fail. Our best controls crumble like cookie dust. We cry; we yell; we suffer shame and we grieve. We want to cover up.

We take our responsibilities seriously. When the principal yells at my class, which is behaving in some outrageous fashion, my feelings are mixed. I feel pangs of shame for not handling them well enough; I feel anger that my children made me look bad in front of the world; and I feel resentful that the principal intruded upon—"violated"—my brood. I might stand up for my children and protect them from the misperceptions or intrusions of other adults, or I might scold them soundly, or both. Through it all, I must realize that sometimes children act badly, no matter what I do or say. That is not our "shame"; it is our job. Facing these realities, without guise or cover, is essential for authenticity to survive.

Authentic teaching requires individual courage as well as courage and trust from administrators. Teachers must have license and sanction to make mistakes and risky decisions. Parents may disagree with things we do. The children themselves repeatedly challenge us. And we always face scrutiny from supervisors. But the most intense scrutiny comes from within, because we are usually our harshest critics. Authenticity rests, finally, on our capacity to make mistakes and to admit error rather than needing to cover it up.

Accountability never seemed to me to be primarily an issue of public record, but rather a private matter. We can continue to be accountable to ourselves only when we feel safe to make mistakes and safe to make the mistakes known. I believe the single most important factor in the preservation of a good teacher is the courage to admit failure rather than to deny it in order to feel like a "good teacher."

Vulnerability seems to me a constant, only partially relieved by experience. Children will always be there to unravel us or our plans. Sylvia Ashton-Warner captures the fragile confidence of even experienced teachers in *Teacher*. "If only I had the confidence of being a good teacher. But I'm not even an appalling teacher. I don't even claim to be a teacher at all. I'm just a nitwit somehow let loose among children" (Ashton-Warner 1963, 198).

Because authentic teaching is founded on our acceptance of limitations and vulnerabilities, it allows for our unique strengths and passions as well. Authentic teaching permits individuality and personal style to emerge. We share our love of birds or history or photography with children. We reveal and share our personality— humor, playfulness, concentration, quietness, investigation. We share much more than skills. We share our passion for learning in our own unique ways.

Some teachers have a quiet and soft-spoken manner, while others are more emotive and dramatic. One teacher in our school is known for the force of her "glare," another for his booming voice. Some teachers thrive on organization and detailed planning; others are more spontaneous and flexible. Some of us tend to be more directive, others more nondirective. We may be more playful or more businesslike. We may love to sing with children or to invent puzzles.

I don't want to imply that our style must be one thing or the other—organized or disorganized. A style is composed of many shades and attributes. I happily copy and repeat what I learn from colleagues, but it is filtered through my voice and perceptions. The virtues of sound teaching—patience, attention, the capacity to structure, the flexibility to individualize—are conveyed through a multitude of styles. But affection and respect—for children and for ourselves—are conveyed only when we are willing to trust ourselves.

It is important to distinguish authentic teaching from self-promotion. When teachers become self-promoting, children become instruments to aggrandize the teacher. The teacher, consciously or not, seeks to gain from the children a sense of importance and love. Authenticity is not about getting children to love or obey us, or even to admire our talents. Authenticity is about knowing oneself well enough to allow others to know themselves.

We cannot teach authentically without the capacity to like children as they really are. My friend, a kindergarten teacher of fifteen years, collapsed into the nearest kitchen chair, saying, "I don't understand how some days I just can't stand it, and other days, I feel so good." To like being with children does not mean ignoring or dismissing the frustrations and failures. It does not mean denying those rainy days, pre- or post-Halloween days, or just hellish days for whatever reason, when classroom survival is a dubious proposal; it doesn't mean denying those times when our own worries and preoccupations—with family, the world, or self—have depleted our mental and physical resources. It doesn't mean denying times when we feel like a pincushion, poked by children, punctured by parental criticism, prodded by administrative fiats.

To like being and working with children, we must acknowledge the difficulties. It takes humor, patience, stamina, conviction. We can preserve our authenticity by confessing the irritations while maintaining our care. This care for children is both a burden and a gift of our spirit.

Authentic teaching requires and encourages personal authority. This authority is not so much an office as it is a way of acting. We stake a claim—in the classroom and in the larger context of schools and systems—to what is personally, intimately known and felt. Personal authority means that perceptions and values are not easily repudiated or pushed aside because others—even those with official authority—disagree. Disagreements may spark investigation and spirited discussions, but they can't force denial of our thoughts and principles. Authenticity involves accepting our personal authority—and the risks that go with it—so that we can be agents of the changes needed in our schools.

The majority of elementary teachers that I see in schools, conferences, and workshops are women. The majority of administrators are men. This fact, which mirrors a general social norm, contributes to a disenfranchised community, with teachers (mainly women) having little say over the most elementary resources of the work site. In order to achieve a stronger role, it is necessary to change the structures of school society for both men and women. I do not mean that women must become administrators in order for these changes to occur. I do mean, however, that administrators and policy makers must become more integrated with and more dependent on the classroom "experts" than they currently are. For that to happen, teachers must be willing to raise their voices, to say aloud to administrators as well as to students, "Listen to me, I have something to say."

We raise our voices when we find courage, not in certainty but in the authenticity that springs from belief in ourselves and our task. When we teach children through our own disciplined and caring actions in the world, we take an authentic stance. We use the most basic and fundamental principle of teaching: Our actions speak louder than our words. It is then that children say, "I see you, I see everything."

Works Cited

ASHTON-WARNER, SYLVIA. 1963. *Teacher.* New York: Simon & Schuster.

MEIER, DEBORAH. 1987. "Good Schools Are Still Possible." *Conflicts and Constituencies* (Fall).

Horse

Story by Ruth Sidney Charney

Illustrated by Apple Lord, then age nine

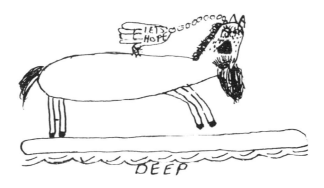

THIS STORY I'm about to tell you is mostly true, though since it happened more than a week ago, it may have come into some changes. I shall tell you what I heard.

Well, it happened that Horse was leading Fox, Dog, Rat, Sheep, Goat, and other gentle beasts from the old forest to the new. It had been a long winter, but the day was grand and Horse pranced along, his mane flying in the wind, as if he were a flag-bearer. At times, as the procession continued, the shorter-legged creatures would climb aboard his back and rest when they became weary.

Suddenly they came to a rushing river. Across the river there fell a log. The log was just long enough, narrow enough, and high enough to need careful feet to cross safely. Horse was first, and he stepped up. No sooner did he have all fours on the log than he was filled with dread. Suppose he slipped? Suppose he lost his balance and fell over? Suppose the log began to shake with his weight? Horse

backed off the log. He turned to Goat and ordered, "You are lighter. You go first."

Goat was nimble, a climber of steep cliffs. He was over the log in no time. Even Donkey did not pause or ponder. He swayed a bit, his hind quarters seeming to go on their crooked way apart from his fore quarters, but soon he, too, was across. And then there was only Horse. He considered swimming the river. The current looked swift; the waters were icy. There was no telling where he would end up or if he would end up. Now the others were waiting. Horse could not go forward or backward. Could he stop here and make this his new settlement? He knew there were better places ahead. Could he go back to the old place? There wasn't much food left. He would not—could not—go on. While he stood still in uncertainty and fear, the other animals were meeting.

"Horse has left us," cried Rabbit.

"Horse doesn't like us," said Sheep.

"Horse has found the best spot and wants to keep it for himself," said Turtle.

"Horse is scared stiff," said Beaver.

Horse scared??? The other animals couldn't imagine that! What is he scared of? It couldn't be that something they accomplished would trouble the fast and strong Horse.

"Perhaps a monster lurks in the depths of the river and only Horse knows," murmured Mouse. "He let us almost die," thought Mouse bitterly.

So for the next long time, all the animals stood still and watched Horse being scared. Finally, after a forever long time, Fox cried out, "Horse? Are you thinking?" And Horse said, "Yes."

"What—if I may ask—are you thinking about?" said Fox.

Horse answered, "The log."

Fox said, "The log? What about the log, Horse?"

Horse sighed. "Why must a log be round on all sides, Fox?"

Fox replied, "Round it is, Horse."

Horse said, "I was thinking it would be better to make logs flat."

Then Rat piped up. "Horse, are you coming or staying?"

Horse said in a soft voice, not at all usual for him, "I would come—if I could come—but I can't come."

And Beaver repeated, "He's scared stiff."

So the animals stood silent for awhile more and watched Horse being scared on the far shore. Then a creature who had not yet spoken said, "Let's help Horse cross the log."

The other beasts opened their eyes as wide as possible and grinned a most incredulous grin. "We cannot pull Horse. We cannot push Horse."

And the small but knowing creature said wisely, "We can keep him company."

So all the animals, big and small, sure and awkward of foot, returned across the log. They explained the plan to Horse. Then they all lined up. Donkey, seeing Horse tremble a bit, went over and said in a quiet tone so only Horse could hear, "Just pay attention, Horse, to what's most important."

"What's that, Donkey?" said Horse.

"To keep going," said Donkey.

And so it happened that there was a trail across the log and Horse was in the middle, Fox holding his tail from behind and Horse holding Goat's stub of a tail in front. Slow, and slower, and pause, and slow, they marched until each and every animal crossed the log. Safely.

And that is—from what I heard—how it came to be that the animals came to the new forests where they have been for some time now. Which goes to show that there is always some point, often along the most important journeys, where fear is great and the best care from others helps us make it. And, perhaps we must also remember to pay attention to what's most important. ❖

APPENDIX B
A Conflict Resolution Protocol for Elementary Classrooms

By Paula Denton and Roxann Kriete
Adapted from The First Six Weeks of School,
Northeast Foundation for Children, 2000

A BASIC BELIEF underlying *The Responsive Classroom*® approach to teaching is that how children learn to treat one another is as important as what they learn in reading, writing, and arithmetic. We believe that social skills such as cooperation, assertion, responsibility, empathy, and self-control are essential to children's academic and social success, and we emphasize the teaching of these skills, along with academics, throughout the school day.

There are many strategies we use to teach these social skills at the elementary level (K–6), one of which is teaching a protocol for conflict resolution. Many good conflict resolution procedures have been developed and articulated in recent years (some excellent resources are cited at the end of this appendix). Below we outline one that has worked well in our classrooms.

THE STEPS

WE USUALLY INTRODUCE a conflict resolution protocol around the fourth or fifth week of school, once children are familiar with basic rules and routines, and a sense of trust and community has been established in the classroom. As with most conflict resolution protocols, ours involves teaching children the following steps:

1. Calming down (walk away, count to ten, etc.)
2. Explanation of the upset
3. Discussion and resolution
4. Some kind of acknowledgment (handshake, for example)

THE "I STATEMENT"

BEFORE TEACHING THESE STEPS, however, we teach students to deliver emotion-laden information as "I statements," using the formula "When you _____, I feel _____ because _____, so what I would like is _____." When a child wants to meet with a classmate for conflict resolution, we require that s/he first compose an "I statement" before arranging a time and a place for the meeting.

We display the "I statement" formula and practice as a class.

First, we practice with positive, fun statements, such as "When you giggle, I feel happy, because it makes me giggle, too, so what I would like is for you to keep on giggling."

Next, we practice with statements containing more difficult emotions, working with examples removed from direct personal experience. For example, we might use a situation from a book we are reading: "In *Charlotte's Web*, when Wilbur heard he would get eaten, he felt scared, because he didn't want to die, so what he would like is to be allowed to keep living."

We also generate a list of words, from literature as well as from our own experience, to expand our vocabulary for describing feelings—words such as "scared," "sorry," "sad," "angry," "frustrated," "nervous," "irritated." We display this list prominently in the room. Children will often glance at it when composing "I statements."

THE MEETING

IN A CONFLICT RESOLUTION MEETING, the first child begins by making an "I statement," and the second child listens, then repeats back his/her understanding of what was said. Once the first child agrees that the second has heard correctly, the second child may make an "I statement." The routine continues in which one child makes an "I statement," then the other repeats back what s/he heard (a simple form of active listening), until both (or all) parties feel satisfied that an understanding has been reached and peace has been made.

In the early weeks, a teacher always attends conflict resolution meetings as a "fair witness" to ensure safety and protocol, but speaks as little as possible. As children become more adept with the process, the teacher asks if either one would like a teacher's presence. If not, we leave them alone. We know that this approach to conflict resolution has become a part of our classroom culture when a student comes to a teacher and says, "Can we meet? I have an 'I statement' for you."

The strategy in action

A solemn-looking Pearl approaches her fourth grade teacher. "I have an 'I statement' for Robby," she says.

"Okay. Let's hear it," responds her teacher.

Pearl takes a deep breath. "Robby, when you said, 'Pearly, Pearly, silly girly,' I felt mad, because you were making fun of me, so what I would like is...so what I would like is..." There is a pause while she looks up at the poster with our "I statement" formula and searches to define what she would like. "I would like for you to call me 'Pearl,' not 'Pearly, silly girly.'"

"Sounds good," says her teacher. "I will meet with you both after lunch."

After lunch:

"Robby, Pearl has asked to meet with you," the teacher informs him matter-of-factly. "Let's go to the problem-solving table." Robby looks apprehensive and grins sheepishly at his buddy Mike as he accompanies his teacher to the table where Pearl is already seated.

Robby takes a seat, shifting nervously and looking sideways at Pearl as he chews a fingernail. Pearl sits up straight, glances at the wall chart, and clears her throat. Even with rehearsal, to speak directly of upset is no easy feat. Out comes her "I statement," exactly as she had practiced. As soon as she finishes speaking, Robby's words start to tumble out. "Well, she was..."

His teacher interrupts. "Robby, you will have a chance for your own 'I statement.' Right now, it's time to tell Pearl what you heard her say."

"You don't want me to say 'Pearly, silly girly.'"

"Pearl, is that right?" asks their teacher.

"Yes."

"OK, Robby. Would you like to make an 'I statement' or end with a handshake?" His choices are clear and defined.

"I want to make an 'I statement,'" asserts Robby. "Umm…" He glances at the chart for a cue. "When you said my new backpack was ugly…I felt…annoyed because…I like my backpack, so I would like…for you not to say it's ugly."

Pearl needs no cue. "You don't want me to say it's ugly?"

"Yeah!" comes Robby's emphatic response.

"Okay. I'm sorry." There is silence while Robby digests this apology. (While often a child will apologize spontaneously during a conflict resolution meeting, we never require apologies as part of this process.)

"Robby," asks his teacher quietly, "are you ready to shake hands or do you have another 'I statement'?"

The session closes with Robby and Pearl shaking hands (the handshake brings closure to the meeting, symbolizing that both parties have been heard, and a mutual understanding has been reached). ❖

NOTICE THAT PEARL'S TEACHER listens to Pearl's "I statement" before setting up the meeting. It is important for the teacher to have a preview of the issue and to make sure that the student has a legitimate statement. It is also important for the student to have practice saying it aloud. Though it may seem a simple and formulaic process, it takes great courage for students to initiate it and carry it through, and, in the meeting itself, it helps to have the starting words ready. Notice, too, how many times Pearl and Robby both look to the chart for prompts. This happens not just in the beginning of the year but all year long. It's important to keep the chart clearly visible from the problem-solving spot.

Over and over again, we find that having a ritualized procedure for solving problems can help even the youngest elementary school children resolve conflicts peacefully with a minimum of adult intervention. The communication and social skills developed in the process empower students to assert their feelings and experiences while maintaining respect for the feelings and experiences of others.

Selected Resources for Teaching Conflict Resolution in Elementary Schools

KREIDLER, WILLIAM J. 1990. *Elementary Perspectives: Teaching Concepts of Peace and Conflict*. Cambridge, MA: Educators for Social Responsibility.

LEVIN, D. E. 1994. *Teaching Young Children in Violent Times: Building a Peaceable Classroom*. Cambridge, MA: Educators for Social Responsibility.

PORRO, B. 1996. *Talk It Out: Conflict Resolution in the Elementary Classroom*. Alexandria, VA: Association for Supervision and Curriculum Development.

PRUTZMAN, PRISCILLA., M. BURGER, GRETCHEN BODENHAMER, AND LEE STERN. 1988. *The Friendly Classroom for a Small Planet*. Philadelphia: New Society Publishers.

RESOLVING CONFLICT CREATIVELY PROGRAM (RCCP): A comprehensive school-based program in conflict resolution and intergroup relations that provides a model for preventing violence and creating caring and peaceable communities of learning. Contact Linda Lantieri, director, RCCP National Center, 40 Exchange Place, Suite 1111, New York, NY 10005, telephone (212) 509-0022, fax (212) 509-1095, e-mail llantieri@rccp.org.

APPENDIX C

Apology of Action: Teaching Children to Make Amends

By Mary Beth Forton

Reprinted from Responsive Classroom® *newsletter, Winter 1998*

IT'S MID-OCTOBER in Carol Davis's fourth grade class, and the children are drawing pictures of what they'll be for Halloween. Jonathan, Peter, and Lee, three friends, are working together at a table with a few others. Lee draws a beautiful picture of a pirate ship with seeming ease. Peter, sitting next to Lee, looks discouraged as he struggles to create something that resembles a vampire. After much erasing and sighing, Peter finally finishes and raises his picture triumphantly, "I did it!"

Lee takes a quick look and with a smile says, "Man, that's ugly." Peter takes this as a compliment until Lee asks, "What is it?"

For a moment, Peter seems confused, as all eyes turn toward him. He looks across the table at his friend Jonathan, who has just started wearing glasses. Peter lets out a quick, nervous laugh and announces, "It's Jonathan with his new glasses!"

Laughter erupts as Peter holds up the picture for everyone to see. Jonathan, tears welling up in his eyes, quickly stands up and walks away. ❖

Scenes like this one, in which children's feelings get hurt by their classmates, are not uncommon in elementary school classrooms. While acknowledging that it's impossible to prevent every one of these incidents from occurring, fourth grade teacher Carol Davis has found a way to help students learn to stand up for themselves when their feelings have been hurt, and to make amends when they have been the ones who have done the hurting.

Carol recalls a feeling she had several years ago that prompted her to try something new in her classroom. "I was tired of having kids leave school at the end of the day with hurt feelings, and I was tired of feeling responsible for fixing these feelings when I wasn't even the one who caused them."

A CONVERSATION

AT THIS SAME TIME, while attending a *Responsive Classroom* workshop, she had a conversation with consulting teacher Chip Wood about Rules and Logical Consequences. Chip mentioned that the rule "you break it, you fix it" could be applied to hurt feelings as well as broken objects: when a child hurts someone's feelings, he/she does something to help fix these feelings. Carol was excited by this notion of an "apology of action" and immediately began planning a way to implement it with her fourth graders.

BEYOND "I'M SORRY"

WHILE CAROL FEELS that saying "I'm sorry" is often appropriate and needed, she also feels that it's frequently inadequate. The process Carol uses for an apology of action not only gives the children who have done the hurting an opportunity to do something to make amends, but it also gives the children who have been hurt the opportunity to stand up for themselves and assert their needs.

When introducing the idea to her students, Carol begins by telling them that we all make mistakes and hurt people's feelings, sometimes intentionally and sometimes without even knowing it. What's important, she emphasizes, is that we learn to pay attention to how our actions affect others, and that we learn to take responsibility for these actions.

A CLASS DISCUSSION

CAROL STARTS with a class discussion in October. She asks her students, "How many of you have ever had your feelings hurt?" All hands go up. "What types of things have you done or seen others do that hurt people's feelings?" Eager to share examples, her class generates a long list:

+ Laughing when someone makes a mistake

+ Calling someone a name

+ Ignoring someone during conversation in the lunchroom

+ Telling someone he/she can't play at recess

+ Making faces and rolling your eyes when someone is talking

Carol then asks her students to talk about how they feel when these things are done to them, and whether an "I'm sorry" helps them to feel better. "Over and over, the children tell me that having those three words said to them doesn't do much to help them feel better." One child articulated it quite clearly when she said, "When someone says 'I'm sorry,' it doesn't take away the bad feeling inside."

"What would make you feel better when your feelings are hurt?" is the next question. "What if, for example, someone laughed when you made a mistake; what could that person then do to help you feel better?" She doesn't expect there to be any simple answers. Rather, what's important at this point is that the children begin to think about the question.

"You break it, you fix it"

CAROL EXPLAINS that in her classroom they'll be using the "you break it, you fix it" rule (which by now the children are very familiar with) when people's feelings get broken. "If you hurt someone's feelings, you'll have the chance to make it up to them by doing something for that person that helps to fix these feelings. We'll call this an apology of action."

In addition to learning to take responsibility for their actions, Carol wants her students to learn to stand up for themselves when they have been hurt. "Some children are afraid to speak up when someone does something that hurts them. This process encourages them to do so, which is especially important for the kids who are not as assertive," says Carol.

A procedure

HERE'S HOW IT WORKS. In the above scenario, Jonathan's feelings were hurt by Peter. After walking away from the table and taking some time to calm down,

Jonathan approaches Peter and says, "You hurt my feelings when you said that about your picture looking like me with my new glasses." Peter apologizes and says he was only kidding. "I want an apology of action," says Jonathan.

Sometimes children are able to ask for this on their own; at other times they need support from the teacher. Now Peter has until the end of the day to decide upon an appropriate action.

CHOOSING AN APPROPRIATE ACTION

THE MOST IMPORTANT GUIDELINE for choosing an apology of action is that it's related to the hurtful behavior. Take, for instance, the time when a child had been excluded from a game, and the proposed apology of action was to draw the child a nice picture. Through a brief discussion with Carol, the child responsible was able to see that this action was not related to the hurtful behavior, and instead decided to invite the classmate to play with her at recess on the following day.

In October, the class generates a list of possible actions which are left on the wall all year. Many of the students use this list as a starting point, something to refer to when they're having trouble coming up with an appropriate action.

FOLLOW-THROUGH

IN THE BEGINNING, Carol keeps track of the incidents so that she can make sure there is follow-through. "I jot down on Post-it notes who owes whom what so that I can hold my students accountable. I want to send them a clear message that this is important and that I will expect them to follow through with it." As the year goes on, her students become more independent, and it becomes the responsibility of the child who has been hurt to make sure there is follow-through. Still, Carol remains watchful to make sure the process is being used well. Are the children being respectful and reasonable in their requests for an apology of action? Is the giving being done in a real and generous way?

TAGGER'S CHOICE

TO PREVENT ARGUMENTS about whether or not someone's feelings were hurt, Carol uses a rule from tag games called "Tagger's Choice." This rules states that if the tagger says you've been tagged, then you have. Similarly, if someone says that you've hurt her/his feelings, then you have. Carol explains to her students, "Lots of times we hurt others' feelings and we don't even know it. Whether we intend to be hurtful or not, we still need to take responsibility for how our actions affect others."

IT'S THE END OF THE DAY, and Peter stops Jonathan in the hallway to tell him that he has decided to draw a picture of him and write an apology on the back. He has already talked with Lee, who has offered to help him make the drawing look "really cool." Peter waits for Jonathan's response. According to class rules, the person who has been hurt needs to give his/her okay to the plan. Jonathan's thumbs-up lets Peter know he likes the idea, and the two walk together to their lockers to get ready to go home.

This chart and others like it are created by the children and left on display all year. Students use it as a springboard for ideas when trying to think of an appropriate apology of action.

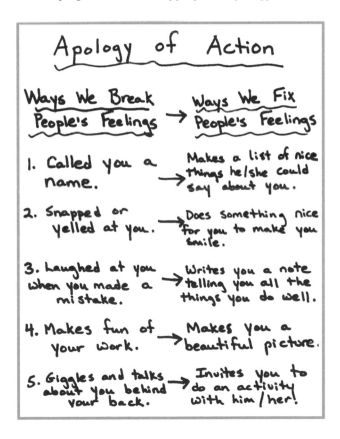

APPENDIX D
Steps to Self-Control

A sample school discipline policy statement
from Fitchburg Public Schools, K–8, Fitchburg, Massachusetts

1. Students will be given a reminder about inappropriate behavior.

2. If the reminder is not enough, the student will have a brief time-out or thinking time within view of the supervising adult, for the purpose of regaining self-control. After the time-out, the student will return to the lesson or activity. Discussion of the behavioral incident does not take place at the initiation of time-out. However, at a later time, a discussion of rules and expectations may occur at staff discretion.

   a. If the misbehavior is flagrant or repeated, students may go to time-out directly, without the reminder step. In such cases, the teacher should notify the parents.

   b. Teachers will use the strategy of time-out for small infractions consistently, rather than waiting for extreme behavioral incidents. Time-out is an opportunity to stop, regain self-control, and make a better plan, and all children may need it occasionally. Staff, students, and parents should understand that time-out is an intervention designed to help students regain self-control. It is not a punishment for losing self-control.

3. If, during time-out, a student continues to behave inappropriately or continues to be disruptive, the classroom teacher will have the student go to time-out in a "buddy teacher's" room. An adult will accompany the student to and from a time-out area in that room. The student will return to his/her own classroom to resume regular activity when appropriate. In most cases, if the buddy teacher step is needed, the classroom teacher will contact the parents to inform them that

425

the buddy teacher strategy was used and that the child may need to use it again from time to time.

4. If a student becomes disruptive in the buddy teacher's room or continues to misbehave upon return, the principal or a designee will escort the student to the office for a time-out there. The student will remain there until the principal or designee determines that the student is ready to reenter the classroom. The principal or designee will contact the parent at his/her discretion.

5. For safety reasons, teachers may skip the buddy teacher step and send directly for the principal or designee, who will escort the student to the office. The principal or designee will contact the parents at the administration's discretion.

6. Steps 1 through 5 are used for inappropriate behavior to help children regain their self-control in the shortest time possible. Teachers will help students improve their behavior through these and other means that are reasonable and respectful of student needs.

7. For most students, the steps to self-control described here will be successful. In other cases, further specific management plans may be developed with the knowledge and help of parents, teachers, specialists, and administrators. Other consequences, as established in the student/parent handbook, may also be applied. Parents and students are expected to be familiar with the consequences described there.

Appendix E
Common Behavior Challenges by Age

Age Five

Children may:

+ Have difficulty with body and mouth controls
+ Not be able to sit still for more than fifteen minutes
+ Have trouble keeping their hands to themselves
+ Raise their hands to speak but call out anyway
+ Get physical when they don't get their own way
+ Shout or use baby-talk
+ Have difficulty sharing
+ Take more than their share—of snack, blocks, etc.
+ Take things that don't belong to them because "I want it"
+ Always want to be first
+ Want their teacher's undivided attention
+ Have trouble taking turns
+ Need to be seen
+ Need their teacher to release them to do the next task
+ Need constant approval
+ Be afraid to try new things or make a mistake
+ Tattle to get approval or show that they know the rules

AGE FIVE AND A HALF

Children may:

- See the teacher as "a jerk"
- Shout "I hate you" at a buddy
- Have poor impulse and motor controls
- Move from tears to tantrums more easily
- Have a shorter attention span and be more wiggly, fidgety, and floppy
- Be more clumsy, falling down, falling out of a chair, and bumping into things
- Grab or push to get out the door first
- Have conflicts with friends and peers
- Shout "You're not my friend anymore"—a friend one moment, an enemy the next
- Always give in, or never want to give in
- Use few common rules in game situations, "inventing" rules as they go along
- Lose interest and quit if rules don't work in their favor

AGE SIX

Children may:

- Test limits, particularly when they think their teacher doesn't see them
- Be very speedy, valuing quantity over quality
- Avoid fixing or changing finished work
- Be sloppy in their haste to finish and do more
- Be very talkative, sassy, noisy, often needing self-talk to direct their thinking
- Use self-talk and chatter to begin drawing or writing
- Have conversations rather than taking care of tasks during transitions
- Worry and fuss about every little ailment
- Need lots of Band-Aids and comfort
- Get frequent stomachaches
- Be highly social, wanting to work together more, and experience more trouble working together

- Be bossy rather than cooperative in play
- Cheat in games
- Love "power games"—good guys versus bad guys—but may become mean in playing these games
- Make up frequent stories and lies, enjoying fantasy and storytelling, including their own
- Lie when confronted with a misdeed

Age seven

Children may:

- Be perfectionists and need to be released from a task
- Start over endlessly, erasing until paper has a hole in it
- Need to dot every "i" but never complete a task
- Cover their work because nothing is good enough
- Not be able to take any criticism
- Cling to routines, avoiding changes and fearing the unknown
- Worry about a bus accident when a trip is announced
- Get frequent tension headaches or stomachaches
- Be very competitive
- Hate to lose
- Want to do everything right and well
- Be self-absorbed and not pay attention when others have their turn
- Continue their fascination with themes of power and identification with superheroes
- Try to boss and bully

Ages eight and nine

Children may:

- Feel a strong sense of gender identification
- Avoid holding hands with students of the opposite sex

- Tease or exclude peers who continue activities with the opposite sex, or activities stereotypically associated with the opposite sex

- Have awareness without empathy—they may take care of each other's physical well-being or possessions, but be unclear about feelings and uncomfortable with differences (yet show a cognitive interest in cultural diversity and a belief in the Golden Rule)

- Comfort Joe when he hurts his arm and Diana when she loses her book, but be unaware that Jeff is being left out or that Shannon is being treated differently than others

- Call names and be cruel about appearances or mannerisms—"Four-eyes," "Fatty," etc.

- Compare themselves and others, making strong judgments about what they themselves and others are good at and not good at

- Want to avoid things that are hard or that they are not very good at

- Say, "I hate art (math, tag, etc.)!"—Translation: "I'm not so good at art"

- Choose the same activities more often

- Feel the importance of peers and friendships

- Begin cliques and clubs

- Be very concerned about "fairness," frequently complaining "That's not fair"—particularly concerned about whether their teacher is being fair and whether a game is fair

- Frequently use "He (she, it) isn't fair" as an alibi

- Show greater interest in telling secrets and gossip

- Form class hierarchies in which some children dominate or have too much influence

AGES TEN AND ELEVEN

Children may:

- Have friendship conflicts that are intense and bitter, ready to proclaim "My friend isn't fair to me," while just beginning to ask "Am I fair to my friend?"

- Show interest in working things out with friends, but still be limited in their ability to see another's point of view without help

- Identify class scapegoats and exclude children socially

- Stick with the same friends unless the teacher assigns them new partners

- Begin to feel peer pressure, often to side with a friend against another friend

- Use common interests as a positive factor in selecting friends or groupings, but harshly reject those with different interests, often defending prejudices, such as picking on people who are short, fat, quiet, etc.

- Strongly relate self-esteem to their achievement in school or athletics and their ability to attract attention

- Fear inferiority, which may lead to reluctance to expose their weaknesses and take risks

- Want to fulfill gender stereotypes—girls want to avoid physical activities, boys want to avoid crafts and handwork

- Be afraid to explore and solve problems

- Be afraid to offer ideas and opinions

- Need to feel more in charge of themselves, but still rely strongly on teacher authority to set realistic goals and workable limits

- Test limits and routines

- Challenge and criticize their teacher or school codes

- Worry that things are "babyish" and demand privileges or responsibilities they are not ready to handle

- Not be consistent or logical, handling small responsibilities poorly yet lobbying for big ones

AGES TWELVE AND THIRTEEN

Children may:

- Struggle for a sense of identity—"Who am I?" is the big question

- Begin the search for fidelity—a true, meaningful relationship with someone becomes the all-consuming quest

- Spend hours on the phone or in front of the mirror and define themselves by jackets, hairstyles, shoes, CDs, movies, sports teams, and what older students are doing—all of which may be a byproduct of the search for identity and fidelity

- Want adults to both notice them and leave them alone, wanting to be acknowledged as individuals yet often extremely embarrassed by adult recognition

- Show lots of contempt for adult authority and often look bored, aloof, and disengaged, an outward appearance driven by their perception that adults don't see them as capable young people

- Often be withdrawn and touchy, sensitive about everything from their schoolwork to their physical appearance

- Swing from days of depression to days of giddiness, shrieks, and shouts

- Be more sarcastic

- Be disorganized—keeping track of assignments, books, and papers is a low priority

RECOMMENDED RESOURCES

Books, articles, and videotapes

ASHTON-WARNER, SYLVIA. 1963. *Teacher.* New York: Simon & Schuster.

BERMAN, SHELDON. 1997. *Children's Social Consciousness and the Development of Social Responsibility.* Albany, NY: State University of New York.

CALKINS, LUCY McCORMICK. 1994. *The Art of Teaching Writing.* New edition. Portsmouth, NH: Heinemann.

CHARNEY, RUTH SIDNEY. 1997. *Habits of Goodness: Case Studies in the Social Curriculum.* Greenfield, MA: Northeast Foundation for Children.

COHEN, DOROTHY H., VIRGINIA STERN, AND NANCY BALABAN. 1996. *Observing and Recording the Behavior of Young Children.* Fourth edition. New York: Teachers College Press.

COHEN, JONATHAN, ed. 2001. *Caring Classrooms/Intelligent Schools: The Social Emotional Education of Young Children.* New York: Teachers College Press.

COMER, JAMES, AND CHIP WOOD. 2000. *The Importance of Child Development in Education: A Conversation with James Comer and Chip Wood.* (Video) Greenfield, MA: Northeast Foundation for Children and New Haven, CT: Yale Child Study Center School Development Program.

CRAWFORD, LINDA. 1990. *To Hold Us Together: Seven Conversations for Multi-cultural Understanding.* Minneapolis, MN: The Origins Program.

DELPIT, LISA. 1995. *Other People's Children: Cultural Conflict in the Classroom.* New York: New Press.

DENTON, PAULA, AND ROXANN KRIETE. 2000. *The First Six Weeks of School.* Greenfield, MA: Northeast Foundation for Children.

DEVELOPMENTAL STUDIES CENTER. 1996. *Ways We Want Our Class To Be: Class Meetings That Build Commitment to Kindness and Learning*. Oakland, CA: Developmental Studies Center.

DEWEY, JOHN. 1963. *Experience & Education*. First Collier Books Edition. London: Collier Books.

DORIS, ELLEN. 1991. *Doing What Scientists Do*. Portsmouth, NH: Heinemann.

DREIKURS, RUDOLF, FLOY C. PEPPER, AND BERNICE BRONIA GRUNWALD. 1982. *Maintaining Sanity in the Classroom: Classroom Management Techniques*. Second edition. Philadelphia, PA: Taylor & Francis, Inc.

ERIKSON, ERIK. 1963. *Childhood & Society*. New York: W.W. Norton.

FAY, JIM, AND DAVID FUNK. 1995. *Teaching with Love and Logic: Taking Control of the Classroom*. Golden, CO: Love and Logic Institute, Inc.

FEATHERSTONE, JOSEPH. 1971. *Schools Where Children Learn*. New York: Liveright.

GARDNER, HOWARD. 1993. *Frames of Mind: The Theory of Multiple Intelligences*. Second edition. New York: Basic Books.

GATHERCOAL, FORREST. 2001. *Judicious Discipline*. Fifth, revised edition. San Francisco: Caddo Gap Press.

GESELL, ARNOLD, FRANCES L. ILG, AND LOUISE BATES AMES. 1977. *The Child from Five to Ten*. Revised edition. New York: Harper and Row.

GILLIGAN, CAROL. 1993. *In a Different Voice: Psychological Theory and Women's Development*. Revised edition. Cambridge, MA: Harvard University Press.

GLASSER, WILLIAM. 1965. *Reality Therapy: A New Approach to Psychiatry*. New York: Harper & Row.

GLASSER, WILLIAM, MD. 1969. *Schools Without Failure*. New York: Harper & Row.

GOODMAN, JOAN. 2000. "When Being Nice Isn't Good." *Education Week* (September 20): 30, 34.

GOOTMAN, MARILYN E. 1997. *The Caring Teacher's Guide to Discipline: Helping Young Students Learn Self-Control, Responsibility, and Respect*. Second edition. Thousand Oaks, CA: Corwin Press, Inc.

GORDON, DAVID T. 1999. "Rising to the Discipline Challenge." *Harvard Education Letter* (September/October): 1-4.

GOSSEN, DIANE CHELSOM. 1996. *Restitution: Restructuring School Discipline.* Second, revised edition. Chapel Hill, NC: New View Publications.

GREENE, ROSS W., PHD. 2001. *The Explosive Child: A New Approach for Understanding and Parenting Easily Frustrated, Chronically Inflexible Children.* Second edition. New York: Harper Collins Publishers.

GRESHAM, FRANK, AND STEPHEN N. ELLIOTT. 1990. *Social Skills Rating System.* Circle Pines, MN: American Guidance Service.

KESSLER, RACHAEL. 2000. *The Soul of Education: Helping Students Find Connection, Compassion and Character at School.* Alexandria, VA: Association for Supervision and Curriculum Development.

KOHLBERG, LAWRENCE. 1987. *The Philosophy of Moral Development.* New York: Harper & Row.

KREIDLER, WILLIAM J. 1990. *Elementary Perspectives 1: Teaching Concepts of Peace and Conflict.* Cambridge, MA: Educators for Social Responsibility.

KREIDLER, WILLIAM J. 1997. *Conflict Resolution in the Middle School.* Cambridge, MA: Educators for Social Responsibility.

KRIETE, ROXANN. 2002. *The Morning Meeting Book.* Expanded edition. Greenfield, MA: Northeast Foundation for Children.

LAZARRE, JANE. 1996. *Beyond the Whiteness of Whiteness: Memoir of a White Mother of Black Sons.* Durham, NC: Duke University Press.

LEVIN, D. E. 1994. *Teaching Young Children in Violent Times: Building a Peaceable Classroom.* Cambridge, MA: Educators for Social Responsibility.

MACKENZIE, ROBERT. 1997. "Setting Limits in the Classroom." *American Educator* (Fall): 32–43.

MEIER, DEBORAH. 1987. "Good Schools Are Still Possible." *Conflicts and Constituencies* (Fall).

NELSEN, JANE, EDD. 1996. *Positive Discipline.* Revised edition. New York: Ballantine Books.

NODDINGS, NEL. 1984. *Caring: A Feminine Approach to Ethics & Moral Education.* Berkeley, CA: University of California Press.

NODDINGS, NEL. 1992. *The Challenge to Care in Schools: An Alternative Approach to Education.* New York: Teachers College Press.

Northeast Foundation for Children. 1997. *Off to a Good Start: Launching the School Year.* Greenfield, MA: Northeast Foundation for Children.

Orenstein, Peggy. 1995. *Schoolgirls: Young Women, Self-Esteem, and the Confidence Gap.* New York: Anchor/Doubleday.

Paley, Vivian Gussin. 1995. *Kwanzaa and Me: A Teacher's Story.* Cambridge, MA: Harvard University Press.

Piaget, Jean. 1965. *The Moral Judgement of the Child.* New York: The Free Press.

Pirtle, Sarah. 1998. *Discovery Time for Cooperation and Conflict Resolution.* Nyack, NY: Children's Creative Response to Conflict.

Porro, Barbara. 1996. *Talk It Out: Conflict Resolution in the Elementary Classroom.* Alexandria, VA: Association for Supervision and Curriculum Development.

Prutzman, Priscilla, M. Burger, Gretchen Bodenhamer, and Lee Stern. 1988. *The Friendly Classroom for a Small Planet.* Philadelphia: New Society Publishers.

Rimm, Sylvia B. 1997. "An Underachievement Epidemic." *Educational Leadership* (April): 15–18.

Ruddick, Sara. 1989. *Maternal Thinking: Toward a Politics of Peace.* Boston: Beacon Press.

Schimmel, David. 1997. "Traditional Rule-Making and the Subversion of Citizenship Education." *Social Education* (February): 70–74.

Stevenson, Chris. 2001. *Teaching Ten to Fourteen Year Olds.* Third edition. Boston: Allyn & Bacon.

Strachota, Bob. 1996. *On Their Side: Helping Children Take Charge of Their Learning.* Greenfield, MA: Northeast Foundation for Children.

Tatum, Beverly Daniel. 1999. *Why Are All the Black Kids Sitting Together in the Cafeteria? And Other Conversations About Race.* Revised edition. New York: Basic Books.

Tobin, L. 1991. *What Do You Do with a Child Like This? Inside the Lives of Troubled Children.* Duluth, MN: Whole Person Associates, Inc.

Ward, Janie Victoria, EdD. 2000. *The Skin We're In: Teaching Our Children to Be Socially Smart, Emotionally Strong, Spiritually Connected.* New York: The Free Press.

WATSON, MARILYN. 1998. "The Child Development Project: Building Character by Building Community." Action in Teacher Education: *The Journal of the Association of Teacher Educators* (Winter).

WOOD, CHIP. 1997. *Yardsticks: Children in the Classroom Ages 4–14.* Greenfield, MA: Northeast Foundation for Children.

WOOD, CHIP. 1999. *Time to Teach, Time to Learn: Changing the Pace of School.* Greenfield, MA: Northeast Foundation for Children.

WOODFIN, LIBBY. 1998. *Familiar Ground: Traditions that Build School Community.* Greenfield, MA: Northeast Foundation for Children.

Organizations

Brotherhood/SisterSol. 512 West 143rd Street, New York, NY 10031. 212-283-7044. Fax 212-283-3700. www.brotherhood-sistersol.org.

Offers a variety of programs in the New York City area, including workshops on youth issues for educators and an after-school program, summer study-abroad opportunities, internships, and camps for young people.

Educators for Social Responsibility. 23 Garden Street, Cambridge, MA 02138. 800-370-2515 or 617-492-1764. Fax 617-864-5164. www.esrnational.org.

Offers school programs, teacher professional development, and resources in social and emotional learning, conflict resolution, diversity education, and character development.

Northeast Foundation for Children. 39 Montague City Road, Greenfield, MA 01301. 800-360-6332. Fax 413-774-1129. www.responsiveclassroom.org.

Helps teachers implement the Responsive Classroom® *approach for bringing together social and academic learning throughout the school day. Offers workshops for teachers, on-site consulting, institutes for administrators, books for educators, and a quarterly newsletter.*

Origins. 3805 Grand Avenue South, Minneapolis, MN 55409. 612-822-3422 or 800-543-8715. Fax 612-822-3585. www.originsonline.org.

Offers Building Academic Communities Through the Arts workshops and the Responsive Classroom *workshops. A regional center for the* Responsive Classroom *approach.*

Reach Out to Schools: Social Competency Program. The Stone Center, Wellesley College, 106 Central Street, Wellesley, MA 02481-8203. 781-283-3277. Fax 781-283-3717. www.open-circle.org.

Helps schools implement the "Open Circle Curriculum" to foster the development of relationships that support safe, caring, and respectful learning communities of children and adults.

Teaching Tolerance. A project of the Southern Poverty Law Center. 400 Washington Avenue, Montgomery, AL 36104. 334-956-8200. Fax 334-956-8488. www.tolerance.org.

Offers a twice-yearly magazine, educational materials, and web resources to help K-12 teachers foster respect and understanding in the classroom and beyond.

ACKNOWLEDGMENTS

But I must do what I believe in or nothing at all. Life's so short.

Sylvia Ashton-Warner
Teacher

TEACHING CHILDREN TO CARE is a book about teachers doing what they "must." The ideas in it represent what I learned from many teachers' classroom practice and many educators' writings. I want to acknowledge the courage and inspiration of all these people, who dare to teach and to persist in their best hopes for children.

My special thanks go to Roxann Kriete, who truly co-authored and piloted the creation of this second edition of the book. Roxann provided crucial intellectual as well as editorial counsel through the revision process. What started as a simple updating—a snip here, an addition there—became much more encompassing. Chapters grew and grew, revolting and retracing themselves. It was hard, at times, to hold on to the original objectives while weaving together all the new experiences I had gained since the writing of the first edition. Roxann took what seemed an impossible task and not only made it possible, but transformed it into a richly rewarding experience. She encouraged and invigorated discussion, asked questions, probed for answers, argued points of view, and offered critical commentary. The results of our conversations and back-and-forth rewrites were always a better chapter. I am grateful for her penetrating analysis and her invaluable company.

I HAD WONDERFUL editorial and design support in creating this second edition of *Teaching Children to Care*. I was fortunate to have Alice Yang oversee the project, to gain from her attention to detail and design, her care for quality and integrity. I also appreciated her personal care for the photographic content, well-researched

439

references, and her general enthusiasm and confidence in the project. Al Woods was also there for many of the early phases of the editorial process, from the original organization and direction to final editing. Also thanks to him, the sports references are contemporary.

There were many others on the editorial and design team, all of whom contributed in invaluable ways. I want to thank:

Mary Beth Forton, NEFC editorial director, whose wise leadership allowed the editorial staff to do their best work.

Leslie and Jeff Woodward, designers, for their unflagging commitment to creating a book design that is both aesthetically pleasing and functional.

Judith Bellamy, whose careful proofreading was a trusty safety net against errors large and small.

Peter Wrenn, for his photographs, which capture the true motion and expression of classroom interaction.

I remain indebted to everyone who contributed to the first edition of this book, especially readers and editors Zina Steinberg, John Clayton, and Sharon Dunn. This new edition rests on the solid foundation created by the wisdom and skill of the original team.

It is impossible to measure all I owe to my fellow co-founders of Northeast Foundation for Children. Their inspiration, example, and mentorship have guided my own work for over twenty years. I am grateful to them for the opportunity to grow and learn together. I want to thank:

Jay Lord, for his effusive energy, affection, and capacity to invent; for his noticing and enabling the very best efforts and strengths of others and of our organization; and for his ceaseless support and encouragement of my work and me.

Marlynn Clayton, who makes classrooms beautiful, safe, and fun; who brings nurture and structure to adult learners as well as children; and who's not afraid to mean what she says and say what she means. I feel fortunate to have shared with her a rich history of teaching, giving workshops, and consulting.

Chip Wood, for his vision, his leadership, his trust in children and teachers, his sometimes booming voice, and his always yearning and learning self.

I am indebted to the many colleagues who have shared the daily rounds, contributing so much to my vision of what a good school can be. My thanks go to:

My first colleagues, for their guidance, modeling, and endless hours of conversation and relief. In particular, I want to acknowledge Zina Steinberg, Corinne Price, Naomi Gutheil, Juana Culhane, Ann Green, and Rose Thompson.

Anna Foot, for her many years of teaching adolescents (and me) to build community with their hands, feet, brains, and hearts—whether it's through solving math problems together, playing soccer, or helping each other make kick beanbags.

The other Greenfield Center School (GCS) teachers with whom I worked most closely over the years—Deb Porter, Jane Stephenson, Kitty Douglas, Ellen Doris, Paula Denton, Darius Marder, Tassia Thomas, Simon MacLean, Timmy Sheyda, Sue Schwartz, Terry Kayne, and Beth Watrous. Their art, their singing, their games, their history lessons, their bird units, their class plays, their jump rope curricula, and all their other constructive, joyful lessons contributed invaluably to the school.

A special thanks to all the children and families who shared their strong, insistent voices, their stories, and their lives in my classes at GCS. They challenged assumptions, tested requirements, forgave mistakes, and always came through above and beyond. I was a better teacher for all they gave me.

I am also grateful for the help of hundreds of dedicated, feisty teachers, administrators, parents, and students willing to make things happen in their own communities. Many of these people appear in this book, but there are others, not obviously cited, whose support has been crucial in the ongoing development of the practices and ideas recorded here.

I want to acknowledge my connection with the Drop-Out Prevention Team of Savin Rock Elementary School, a connection which began in 1988. Many of the practices described in *Teaching Children to Care* became defined and documented through my work with this group.

Another significant early partnership that infused and encouraged my work involved a dedicated cadre of teachers, administrators, and consultants who helped pilot the *Responsive Classroom* approach in many Washington, DC, schools and whose efforts led to so much learning. I particularly want to thank Maurice Sykes, Barbara Nophlin, Linda Harrison, Andrea Robinson, Kathleen Thomas, Pat Harris, Mary Duru, Stephanie Abney, Anne Jenkins, Joyce Love, Pat Joyner, Sandra Norried, Betsy Mirel, Barbara Freeman, Austene Fowler, and Virginia Thompson. These teachers and administrators gave evidence in their classrooms and schools that it was possible to defy the odds and create communities of great affection and learning.

The ongoing contributions of *Responsive Classroom* consulting teachers and workshop participants are priceless. I thank these educators for their willingness to share their insights, struggles, and personal examples, which refresh as well as infuse the pages here. In particular, I want to recognize:

Responsive Classroom consulting teachers Carol Davis, Susan Roser, Joan Riordan, Melissa Correa-Connolly, Paula Denton, Marcia Bradley, and consulting director Pam Porter—invaluable colleagues all! A special thank-you to Eileen Mariani, who first welcomed me to country living and kept up the wonderful intimacies of teaching and friendship.

The special "movers and shakers" of Fitchburg and the adventurous middle-school crew of B.F. Brown—principal Bernie DiPasquale and consultants Kathy Brady, Bonnie Baer-Simahk, and Jennifer Fichtel. Thanks to Lourdes Mercado and the many other teachers who shared their programs and stories, and allowed NEFC to take photos in their classrooms.

The staff at K.T. Murphy School and former principal Larry Nichols, who inspire and teach others through their own classroom practices, structured recesses, and adult community meetings and who welcomed us into their classrooms for photo shoots.

Greg Bagley and the many teachers in Island Falls, Maine, whose ideas resonate in the examples included here.

Nancy Forsberg and the talented and dedicated educators in Paterson, New Jersey, who continue to believe and make it happen.

The special teams from the Regional Multicultural Magnet School in New London, Connecticut—principal Dick Spindler-Virgin, physical education teacher Mark Farnsworth, and others on the staff who bravely continue to dialogue and dance.

I want to acknowledge all the teachers and administrators I meet at workshops and in schools who, despite an increasingly difficult job, continue to offer up their own hopes and powerful caring to make their classrooms or schools an example of possibility.

Finally, thank you, dear family, for holding my hand across the log.

INDEX

Academic choice 33, 49, 56, 374–375
Anger
    expressing 184, 248, 256
Apology of action 154, 419
Ashton-Warner, Sylvia 370, 406
Atwood, Margaret 379
Authenticity in teaching 34, 403
Bargaining
    defined 197
    individual behavior contract 201,
        339
    steps in 197
Bathroom routine 40
Behavior
    challenges by age 427
    common problems 331
    modeling 108
Behavioral contracts (See Individual
    student contracts)
Behavioral skill deficits 203
Berman, Sheldon 70, 74
Buddy teacher 213
Calkins, Lucy 308
Care
    giving and receiving 22

Choice (See also Academic choice)
    providing 244
Circling up 39
Class meetings
    appropriate topics 299
    establishing meeting rules 282
    purpose 279
    sample rules 282
    setting the tone 280
Classroom
    mapping 132
    organizing 33
Classroom management
    curriculum for 17
    purpose of 19
    stages of 35
Clear Positives
    defined 363
    process of using 364
    teaching by 369
Cohen, Dorothy 305
Commenting
    on what you see 19
    to redirect 33
    to reinforce 32
    to remind 32

Communicating
    expectations 31, 80
Community
    building 25
    creation of 19
Compliments
    Compliment Club 253
    giving 253
Conflicts
    class meetings for 277
    conflict resolution meeting 414
    resolving 79, 413
Consequences
    logical 143
    natural 147
Contracts (See Critical Contract and
    Individual student contracts)
Convictions (See Clear Positives)
Cooperation
    soliciting 197, 242, 244
Crawford, Linda 256
Crawford, Sally 167, 207, 340
Critical Contract 123
    guidelines for making 127
Curriculum of self-control 17
Denton, Paula 252, 413
Developmental stages of children 71
Developmental Studies Center 277
Dewey, John 19, 20, 21, 144, 166
Discipline
    defined 19
    language of 235
    teaching 19
Doris, Ellen 387
Dreikurs, Rudolf 17, 150, 200, 279,
    320, 321, 376–377
Elliott, Stephen N. 19
Ellis, Rick 254

Empathy 19, 151
Erikson, Erik 71, 72, 94, 363
Expectations
    communicating 31
    formulating 31
    modeling 112
Explosive child 189, 203
External controls 21
Featherstone, Joseph 363
First six weeks of school
    journal writing during 41
    purpose of 27
    stages of 35
    teaching expectations during 34
Forton, Mary Beth 417
Gardner, Howard 377
Gesell, Arnold 391
Gilligan, Carol 71, 75, 76
Glasser, William 257, 279, 325
Goals
    achieving 137
    criteria for 346
    evaluating 137
    focusing on the most important 125
    for older children 349
    for younger children 348
    formulating 129
    specific 130
    stating positively 130
Golden Rule 94, 265
Gordon, David T. 303
Greene, Ross 189, 192, 193, 204–206
Gresham, Frank 19
Group work 54, 61
Guided Discovery
    defined 49
    objectives of 49
    steps in 51

Homework skills 398

Hope

   generating 80

   sustaining 30

Hopes and dreams 77

   with older children 84

   with young children 80

"I statements" 252

Ideals (See Clear Positives)

Independent work 56

Individual student contracts

   celebrating achievement 352

   communication with parents 350, 352

   consequences 357

   elements of 345

   evaluating success 350

   for older children 349

   for younger children 348

   steps in using 342

Interruptions 90

Journal writing 41

Kelly, Sheila 167, 308

Knowing children 29, 68, 125

Kohlberg, Lawrence 68

Kriete, Roxann 45, 352, 413

Language

   empowering 235

   non-negotiables 241

   redirecting, reinforcing, reminding 32, 107

   saying what you mean 236

   stressing the deed 247

   using the "I voice" 249

Learning

   foundation of 27

   from mistakes 121, 144

   how students learn 71

   stages of 71

Listening skills 111

Logical consequences

   apology of action 154, 419

   defined 144

   guidelines for implementing 150

   losing a privilege 157

   time-out 161

   types of 153

Love

   attentive love defined 228

Mackenzie, Robert J. 143, 145

Meier, Deborah 370, 402

Misbehavior

   attention-seeking 331

   being a bad sport 333

   common problems by age 427

   dawdling 335

   defiance 332

   losing and forgetting 335

   restlessness and lack of control 336

   severe 203, 218, 221

   stressing the deed 247

   tattling 334

Modeling behavior 108

Morning Meeting

   components 45

   purpose 45

   sharing during 47

   taking time for 18

   with older children 48

Nelsen, Jane 22, 142, 151, 279

Nonviolence 370

Noticing 306

   positive behaviors 30, 309

   things that don't work 312

   what the student notices 313

Observing children (See Knowing children and Noticing)

Paradoxical groups 56
Parents
   goals for their child 123
   role in implementing logical
     consequences 202, 223
   role in individual student
     contracts 342–360
   role in supporting rules 94–95,
     100–102, 223
Participation
   encouraging 242
Piaget, Jean 71, 100
Positive accomplishments
   focusing on 30
   reinforcing 32
Potential
   stretching 376
Power
   and rules 71
   defined 19, 166
   struggles 193
Praise 251
"Pretzels" 257
Privileges
   losing group 159
   losing individual 158
Problem solving
   at different ages 286
   class meeting 279
   generating alternatives 310
   social conference 305
   steps in 287
   understanding the problem 310
Punishment 144–146
Quiet time 49
Recess
   taking away 146

Redirecting 33
Reentry
   conference 220
   plan sheet 215
Reinforcing 32
Reminding 32
   only twice 240
Reparation 153 (See also Apology of
   action)
Representing
   defined 134
   meetings 255
Responsive Classroom® approach 413,
   449
Rewards 147, 257, 352–356
Rimm, Sylvia 192, 210
Role-playing 112–117
   time-out 171
Routines
   establishing 38
Ruddick, Sara 29, 230, 338
Rules
   as positive guidelines 70
   authority of 269
   based on adult power 71
   based on ethical ideas 73
   based on social conventions 72
   being consistent 118
   collaborative 69
   combining 91
   compliance 71
   following through 119
   for safety and order 268
   Golden Rule 94, 265
   hopes and dreams 77
   in specials 102
   individual plans 117

making 76, 94

posting 94, 99

role-playing 112

sample of 89, 92, 99

teaching 107

team approach 211

Safety signal 38

Salinger, J. D. 245

Schimmel, David 107

School-wide discipline sample 425

Self-control 12

promoting 165

the goal of education 19

"Self-Portraits" project 61

Signals

classroom 38

Small groups 56

Social conference

naming the problem 317

purpose of 308

sample questions 331

steps in 309

Social habits

establishing 61

Special area teachers 102

Stages of classroom management

1: whole-class learning 37

2: paradoxical groups 56

3: Independence and
responsibility 65

summarized 66

Stevenson, Chris 73, 163

Stickers

as acknowledgment, not reward
353–356

Stop Step

in handling behavior problems 148

Time

setting priorities 18, 125

Time-out

checking in 180

defined 161, 165

duration of 169

for minor misbehavior 173

goal of 171

guidelines for 167

in another room 186

introducing 171

letting students choose time-out
place 195

location in the room 169

reentry conference 220

reentry plan sheet 215

release from 170

role playing 171

using a buddy teacher 213

when not effective 189

Tobin, L. 191

Transitions 392

Voices of authority

personal voice 269

voice of principle 265

voice of procedure 268

Ward, Janie Victoria 85

Weil, Simone 230

Wood, Chip 48, 69, 74, 396, 420

Work habits

establishing 37, 43

Work sharing meetings 255